T-Group Theory and Laboratory Method

Contributors

KENNETH D. BENNE, PH.D.
*Theodore W. Berenson Professor
of Human Relations
Boston University*

WARREN G. BENNIS, PH.D.
*Professor of Industrial
Management
Massachusetts Institute of
Technology*

ROBERT R. BLAKE, PH.D.
*Professor of Psychology
The University of Texas*

LELAND P. BRADFORD, PH.D.
*Director
National Training Laboratories,
NEA*

JEROME D. FRANK, M.D., PH.D.
*Professor of Psychiatry
Johns Hopkins University*

JACK R. GIBB, PH.D.
*Consulting Psychologist
Newark, Delaware*

MURRAY HORWITZ, PH.D.
*Professor of Psychology
New York University*

RONALD LIPPITT, PH.D.
*Professor of Sociology and
Psychology
Institute for Social Research
The University of Michigan*

MATTHEW B. MILES, ED.D.
*Associate Professor of Psychology
and Education
Teachers College, Columbia
University*

HERBERT A. SHEPARD, PH.D.
*Professor of Behavioral Science
Case Institute of Technology*

DOROTHY STOCK, PH.D.
*Associate Professor of Psychology
The University of Chicago*

ROY M. WHITMAN, B.S., M.D.
*Associate Professor of Psychiatry
University of Cincinnati College
of Medicine*

T-Group Theory
and Laboratory Method

Innovation in Re-education

Edited by

Leland P. Bradford, Ph.D.
Director, National Training Laboratories, NEA

Jack R. Gibb, Ph.D.
Consulting Psychologist, Newark, Delaware

Kenneth D. Benne, Ph.D.
Theodore W. Berenson Professor of Human Relations
Boston University

John Wiley & Sons, Inc., New York • London • Sydney

ISBN 0 471 09510 9

Library of Congress Catalog Card Number: 64-11499
Printed in the United States of America

To the many thousands of staff and participants
in laboratories throughout the world
who are the true begetters
of this innovation in education.

Preface

Increased understanding of personal and social change has a high priority on the agenda of contemporary behavioral science. New and improved methods for facilitating the humane management of change are increasingly required in democratic action. Creative social practitioners are seeking widely to bring the resources of the behavioral sciences and the needs of democratic action into a reciprocal working relationship.

Efforts in contemporary America to improve social practice in the spirit of science and democracy are numerous and varied. One such effort began in a training laboratory at Bethel, Maine, during the summer of 1947. This laboratory was designed to try out new methods for re-educating human behavior and social relationships. Joint experimentation with laboratory methods by a growing number of behavioral scientists and social practitioners has followed this beginning. Reported here are some aspects of these sixteen years of experimental effort.

The training events, in which the methods reported and explained in this book have been developed, are called "laboratories" for a good reason. The major method of learning employed is one in which participants are helped to diagnose and experiment with their own behavior and relationships in a specially designed environment. Participants are both experimenters and subjects in joint learning activities. Staff members or trainers serve as guides in the institutionalization of experimental and collaborative approaches to learning in the laboratory community. They also guide participants in the transfer of these approaches outside the laboratory.

This approach to re-education is rightly associated with the National Training Laboratory in Group Development, of the National Education Association, which held its first laboratory session at Bethel, Maine, in 1947. Since that time, the National Training Laboratories, the name used since 1951, has conducted many training laboratories at Bethel and elsewhere. Some of these laboratories have been conducted for occupationally heterogeneous, others for occupationally homogeneous, groups of participants. More recently, various university centers have also conducted training laboratories, and laboratories have been established in nations outside the United States and for various cross-cultural groups.

During this period of experimentation, several hundred students of human behavior—most of them regularly employed in the faculties of various universities—have served on laboratory staffs. Staff members have brought the resources of a number of disciplines into the development of laboratory training: individual and social psychology, sociology, cultural anthropology, and social philosophy and ethics. Other staff members have imported technologies of helping from various disciplines of social practice: psychiatry, counseling, education, administration, social work, clinical psychology, and organizational and community consultation. The laboratory approach to re-education is thus inherently multi-disciplinary and multi-professional. Always staff members have sought a confrontation between their disparate outlooks, both in cognitive and in value dimensions. Some significant community of orientation has been attained, but rather large differences in orientation persist as the various essays in this book make clear. Those associated with the laboratory approach to education regard these differences as healthy and as conducive to continued experimentation.

While this book attempts to describe the general development of laboratory training, its emphasis is upon the T (Training) Group. In a T Group, participants have the task of constructing a group which will meet the requirements of all of its members for growth. Members have the opportunity to learn about themselves, about interpersonal relations, about groups, and about larger social systems. Trainers help to establish processes of data collection, data analysis, and diagnosis of the changing here-and-now experiences of the group and its members. The major part of this book consists of efforts by various T-Group trainers to conceptualize processes of life and learning in the T Group.

Since the T Group and the laboratory constitute serious attempts to utilize the findings and methodologies of the behavioral sciences in inducing and reinforcing behavioral changes, behavioral scientists should find this account of interest. Research into its processes and programs has been a part of the training laboratory from the beginning, and at least some of this research has found its way back into changes in laboratory methods and designs. This fact should add to the interest of behavioral scientists in this report of experience and experimentation.

This report should also be of interest to the thousands of professional practitioners who have been experimenting in comparable ways with the use of small groups in various practice settings—psychotherapists, counselors, educators of young people and adults, social workers, nurses, religious workers, and organizational trainers and consultants.

Laboratory and T-Group methods have increasingly been incorporated into programs of management development and inservice education. Thus administrators and those who make policy decisions concerning such programs should find this book of interest and help.

It should be of particular interest to the thousands of men and women who have participated in T-Group and laboratory training over the years, in the United States and in other countries. In a very real sense they have helped to write this book.

The book is organized into three sections. The first section has been designed to describe and explain the laboratory setting in which the T Group has developed and to provide historical and philosophical perspectives from which the T Group as an educational medium and method can be understood.

The second section includes chapters by nine experienced T-Group trainers. Each has sought to conceptualize the development of the T Group and its learning goals and processes. Since their viewpoints differ, the essays taken together provide varied avenues into understanding the diverse aspects and possibilities of T-Group training. Gibb's introductory chapter to this section places these various theorizing efforts in a common perspective and provides a viewpoint from which readers can assess the present state of development of T-Group theory.

The third section compares and contrasts the T Group with other educational media which also employ group processes to support learning and re-education—group psychotherapy and the classroom. It also offers a comprehensive survey of researches conducted in laboratory settings and, more specifically, researches which bear upon the composition and development of T Groups and upon the processes and effects of T-Group experiences.

The debt of this book to the thousands of people who have participated in laboratory and T-Group training through the past sixteen years has already been acknowledged. Our further indebtedness to the several hundred persons who have been members of laboratory staffs over the years is also profound. The development of T-Group theory and practice has been a collaborative effort. This fact can be gladly acknowledged without detracting from the individual contributions which make up the bulk of this book.

The assistance which Dorothy Mial and Aieleen Waldie have provided in shaping the manuscript of this book for publication deserves special acknowledgment.   Mrs. Mial cut the original manuscript by twenty-five per cent and improved its quality in the process.   Mrs. Waldie edited each part of the manuscript, prepared the index, and guided the book through the process of publication.

LELAND P. BRADFORD
JACK R. GIBB
KENNETH D. BENNE

October 1963

Contents

1

Two Educational Innovations

Leland P. Bradford
Jack R. Gibb
Kenneth D. Benne

This book is the story of an innovation in education—the T (Training) Group. The T Group is an innovation in the technology of education. As a technology, work with T Groups has generated a variety of technical problems concerning stimulation, support, and stabilization of certain learning outcomes. Many methods have been developed and tested in efforts toward solutions. These problems and solutions will be emphasized in this account.

To the educators who work with T Groups, however, and to the thousands of men and women who have participated in them, the T Group is more than an educational technology. It has its roots in a system of values relative to mature, productive, and right relationships among people. It is grounded in assumptions about human nature, human learning, and human change. Part of its meaning stems from the commitment of its practitioners and participants to a set of educational goals—both personal and social. This story will attempt to clarify the deeper meaning of T-Group experience.

A T Group is a relatively unstructured group in which individuals participate as learners. The data for learning are not outside these individuals or remote from their immediate experience within the T Group. The data are the transactions among members, their own behavior in the group, as they struggle to create a productive and viable organization, a miniature society; and as they work to stimulate and support one another's learning within that society. Involving experiences are a necessary, but not the only, condition of learning. T-Group members must establish a process of inquiry in which data about their own behaviors are collected and analyzed simultaneously with the experience which generates the behaviors. Learnings thus achieved are tested and generalized for continuing use. Each individual may learn about his own motives, feelings, and strategies in dealing with other persons. He learns also of the reactions he produces in others as he interacts with them. From the confrontation of intentions and effects, he locates barriers to full and autonomous functioning in his relations with others. Out of these he develops new images of potentiality in himself and seeks help from others in converting potentialities into actualities.

Each individual may learn also about groups in the processes of helping to build one. He may develop skills of membership and skills for changing and improving his social environment as well as himself. The staff who work with T Groups do not see any necessary opposition between participation in groups and autonomous individual functioning, though they are well aware that opposition does occur in many associations of our lives and that group forces may be used to inhibit personal development. In the T Group, on the contrary, the objective is to mobilize group forces to support the growth of members as unique individuals simultaneously with their growth as collaborators. Influences among peers are paramount in this learning process. In the T Group, members develop their own skills in giving and receiving help. They learn to help the trainer (or teacher) as he assists in the development of individual and group learnings.

While there are many obvious similarities between the T Group and the therapy group—in part because any effective education has therapeutic overtones—the T Group differs in a number of important ways. It tends to utilize data about present behavior and its consequences rather than delving into genetic causes. It tends to deal with conscious and preconscious behavior rather than with unconscious motivation. The T Group makes the important assumption that persons participating are well rather than ill.

This book is mainly concerned with the T Group, but in order to understand the T Group it is necessary to give some degree of attention to another educational innovation—the training laboratory. T-Group learning was a central part of the larger curriculum of the first training laboratory held at Bethel, Maine, in the summer of 1947. And T Groups have been a central part of training laboratories during the subsequent years in which laboratories have multiplied both in America and abroad. The training laboratory is a temporary residential community shaped to the learning requirements of all of its members. This community provides formal and informal social process events which support and expand learnings within the T Groups. The term, "laboratory," was not idly chosen. A training laboratory is a community dedicated to the stimulation and support of experimental learning and change. New patterns of behavior are invented and tested in a climate supporting change and protected for the time from the full practical consequences of innovative action in ongoing associations. And help is provided in planning change efforts in associational life outside the laboratory. The first part of this book is a clarification of the orientations and methodologies of the training laboratory.[1]

The Dynamics of Educational Innovation

It may be well first to place laboratory training in the perspective of the culture out of which it developed. Every educational innovation represents a set of cultural conditions. First, the innovators perceive needs for learning inadequately met by existing practices. Second,

[1] The full story of educational innovations, in which the T Group occupies a key place, would include the story of the National Training Laboratories (NTL). This organization, a unit of the National Education Association, grew out of its immediate forerunner, the National Training Laboratory in Group Development which, co-sponsored by the National Education Association and the Research Center for Group Dynamics, first at the Massachusetts Institute of Technology and later at The University of Michigan, held the first summer training laboratories at Bethel, Maine. Later NTL became a year-round operation. NTL was for several years the sole organizer and developer of training laboratories. In the last eleven years, laboratories have been organized under other auspices as well. From the beginning, however, NTL has served a number of essential functions within the training laboratory movement. Its responsibilities have been to foster the development of training laboratories in many segments of society, at first in America and later in other countries as well, to select and develop persons competent to serve as laboratory trainers, to provide a professional home base for this growing network of trainers and, informally, to determine and maintain standards of professional quality in laboratory training. The development of this organization is an interesting story which cannot be fully told here. Its uniqueness lies in its determined effort to embody and maintain in the processes of its own organization and management the same values of collaboration and experimentation which are basic to the educational processes it seeks to make available to its clientele. The detailed story of this effort belongs to another book. But, since NTL has been so centrally identified with the history of training laboratories and T Groups, accounts of these educational innovations will give glimpses into the history of NTL as well.

underlying these needs are cherished values seen as threatened in the drift of historical events. These values assume a central role in shaping the new processes of education designed to give them renewed power. Third, new resources in knowledge and skill are seen as available, at least in embryo. Such conditions as these motivated the persons responsible for the "laboratory movement" in education.

Unmet Learning Needs in Contemporary Culture

Although most educational innovators have tended to turn to the practices of childhood or youth education to institutionalize their innovations, the founders of the training laboratory began with a venture in adult education. This is consistent with the laboratory emphasis upon finding ways to release and support continuing learning in *all* the relations and associations of life. The choice of adult education as a setting for introducing laboratory methods of learning into our society was further based on strategic considerations. The people now in control of our educational institutions are adults. If they can experience and validate new ways of learning for themselves, they should be inclined to support rather than to resist similar opportunities for children.

The founders of the first laboratory were concerned about unmet needs in the various organized associations of adult life, not just in formal education. They saw failure in meeting these needs as a dangerous condition in contemporary life.

. . . The development of the physical sciences and related technology thrusts upon all of us problems of individual and group relations of progressive complexity. The acceleration in number and complexity of such relational problems to be solved is increasingly disproportionate to our relatively slow advance in understanding and controlling the dynamics of individual and group behavior. . . . Such skill and understanding can be developed only through the focus of research effort upon current pressing problems of human relations and of training individuals and groups in solving these problems. And such research (and training) can succeed only through the cooperative effort of social scientists, educators, and action leaders.

Effective membership in modern society demands participation by all citizens in a large and increasing number of interacting groups. If group functioning is to be productive and intelligent, members and leaders need to understand the dynamics of effective group thinking and action and to . . . [become] masters of the skills of effective member and leader functioning. . . . Typically, training in group leadership neglects the correlative training of group members. Leadership training tends to take the form of passing on a limited number of empirical techniques for transmitting information or for group manipulation. Until we acquire experimentally grounded knowledge of the leader and member skills required for productive group thinking and action and of the methods which are effective for training group personnel in these skills, we fail to release and develop the intelligence and productivity latent in our organized life.[2]

Those who launched the laboratory movement, then, believed that individuals are being compelled to change by inexorable pressures from natural sciences and related technologies with little, if any, preparation for handling changes, with sensitivity and effectiveness, in themselves and their relationships. Yet creative and collaborative adaptations are essential in achieving and maintaining personal and collective integrity and health in contemporary culture. This condition defines the area of unmet learning needs that the training laboratory was hopefully designed to meet.

The founders of the first laboratory saw the group as the link between the individual person and the larger social structure. They saw the group, therefore, as a medium for serving two sets of interrelated functions: the re-education of the individual toward greater integrity, greater understanding of himself and of the social conditions of his life, greater behavioral effectiveness in planning and achieving changes both in himself and in his social environment; and the facilitation of changes in the larger social structures upon which individual lives depend.

Can people learn to use groups for individual rehabilitation *and* for reconstruction of the social environment? And can groups be developed which are simultaneously alive to the needs of their members for growth as persons and to the needs of the social environment for reconstruction and improvement? The founders of the laboratory answered "yes." The laboratory was designed as a place where people might learn experimentally to develop groups to serve both purposes, and, in the process, to become skilled in extending similar experimental efforts into nonlaboratory settings.

To the founders of the laboratory, the widespread disintegrity of *what?* personal and collective responses to changing conditions reflected a separation of three functions—action, research, and education. These functions must be integrated if social life generally is to become more supportive of continuing learnings. Decisions about social action are typically taken without the utilization of relevant findings and methodologies from social and behavioral research, while research efforts,

[2] Faculty of the Training Laboratory in Group Development. "A Laboratory in Educational Dynamics." *School and Society,* **66:**475–476, December 20, 1947.

though incidentally producing findings relevant to action choices, typically are undertaken without awareness of the knowledges needed by people who must take action. Where action leaders do employ competences in the social and behavioral sciences, they often make a limited and truncated use of them—often in the service of unexamined goals, values, and assumptions. And researchers, concerned with the violation of their own inherent values and goals, resist superficial, applied employment of their resources. How can researchers and action leaders be brought into a significant relationship that does not violate but actually enhances the integrity and autonomy of each? The central need, as the laboratory founders saw it, is a confrontation, a dialectical interplay, and growing collaboration among action interests, research interests, and educational interests.

Since these interests are embodied in roles and the roles in persons, any adequate training community must bring into relationship persons representative of each. The training laboratory was designed not to set up a situation in which researchers could teach educators or in which educators could teach action leaders, but one in which each would increasingly value the resources of the others. The immediate goal was deeper collaboration. A research goal was to learn more about ways in which this desired collaboration could be effected. The envisaged long-range goal was a growing methodology for effective collaboration between men and women of action, of research, and of education in a context of self-directed development and training. The parallel concomitant was the institutionalization of such a methodology in various segments of our organizational and community life.

How has the vision changed in seventeen years of expanding laboratory experience? One change is a deeper vision of the problems of *individuals* confronted by demands for change and adaptation which threaten their needs for autonomous growth as persons. Playing the "culture game" of achieving upward mobility in a society uncertain both of its future and of its roots produces individuals uncertain of their identity. The re-educative task has deeper therapeutic dimensions than the founders of the laboratory realized, though they were not unaware that their conception of personal change through group experience led them into the borderland between education and therapy as traditionally institutionalized. Clarification of the therapeutic dimension of the educational task has come about through three sorts of influences. The first is through experimentation with T Groups. In efforts to build a group of their own, participants were dealing with personal problems inadequately solved in the processes of their earlier socialization. Learnings about self became more prominent in the agenda of T Groups through self-selection of learning emphases by participants. The second influence has come through the involvement of more clinically oriented professionals (psychiatrists and psychologists) within the growing network of professional trainers. The third influence has been from studies of social and organizational life outside the laboratory movement—which have been focused since 1947 upon the vicissitudes of individuals in their questing for identity within a fragmented society. Closely related have been parallel developments in group therapy.

A second change has been a deepened awareness of the importance of formal, bureaucratic organization as a factor in achieving or failing to achieve the educational task. The eclipse of community in modern life has, in fact, stemmed from the depersonalization of human relationships as complex bureaucratic organization has extended into the provision of health, welfare, and educational services. The restoration of growth-sustaining community to human relationships thus means, in part, efforts to rehumanize relationships within bureaucratic structures. This means the invention of new or revised models of organizational behavior as well as models of group and interpersonal behavior.

This dimension of the re-educative task of laboratory training has also stemmed from three kinds of influences. One is the development of laboratories for organizational managers and supervisors which served to force problems of organizational behavior and its reconstruction upon the attention of trainers. Another influence has come from the incorporation of students of organizational behavior into laboratory training staffs. Many of these "scientific" students of organizational life are also engaged as consultants to organizations concerning the better handling of change. A third closely related influence has been the growth of studies of organizational life, outside the laboratory movement, which have highlighted the personal, interpersonal, and group dimensions of life within bureaucracies.

A further change in the vision of unmet learning needs is not so much a change in social diagnosis as a growing realization of the limitations of the training laboratory as the sole way to meet these needs. From the first, laboratory trainers had been aware that the utilization of laboratory learnings by participants ideally required preparatory efforts within their social environment in order to create receptivity for changes. It also ideally required supportive efforts after training during a period of stabilizing changes in the home settings. The limitations upon early experimentation with these concomitants to laboratory experience were practical rather than ideological. Recently, promising beginnings have been made in joining laboratory experience with related processes of consultation, research, and prelaboratory and postlaboratory training. These efforts should further illuminate learning needs and permit better evaluation of the place of laboratory training in meeting them.

Values Threatened or Underdeveloped in Contemporary Practice and Action

Significant educational innovations are directed toward meeting learning needs in a society, but innovators are quickened in their efforts by concern with the fate of cherished values perceived as threatened by the trend of historical events. Three sets of overlapping values were central in the concerns of the innovators of the training laboratory and the T Group: the values of science, of democracy, and of the helping relationship.

Concern for Science. Concern with the under-utilization of the social and behavioral sciences in practical affairs has already been underlined. More basic was the concern that the values implicit in science did not function potently in processes of problem solving in practical settings. Science as a human enterprise has an implicit morality. It is this morality which is widely neglected or rejected in processes of action-decision where efficiency, win-lose competition, and "tribal" defense and offense tend to dominate.

What is the morality of science? One element is an obligation to face all of the facts involved in a problem and its solution. Frequently, human facts are not faced by practical decision makers—facts about feelings, motivations, personal and collective potentialities for growth, contribution potentials of persons and subgroups—as they define and attempt to solve social problems. Not only do decision makers neglect to face the facts of other people's behavioral involvements, but they also frequently neglect to face and manage their own involvements as persons. Their difficulty arises partly from lack of knowledge and skill in making sense of behavioral facts, and also from resistances toward becoming aware of the human consequences of their actions. Ideally, behavioral scientists have faced both of these difficulties in their studies and can be of help to practical men in facing their own similar difficulties.

Another value of the scientific enterprise is objectivity toward the collection and treatment of data. Such objectivity is not a gift but an achievement. The achievement rests on the acceptance of methodological safeguards against distortion by biases and prejudices inherent in subjective needs. In human studies, this means awareness by the investigator of his own value-laden assumptions. This usually involves the rational consideration of differing views of other investigators who operate out of different assumptions. Can a similar morality of self-objectivity come to operate in decision makers in practical affairs? Such objectivity is frequently denied as impossible or resisted as fatal to decisiveness.

A third value is the obligation to collaborate with other investigators in the pursuit of truth. This obligation is evident in the requirement to publish the bases as well as the conclusions of investigations. This opens any investigation to testing and eventual incorporation into some rational consensus within the community of scientists. Can the moral obligation to collaborate in problem solving be instituted in practical affairs in the interest of consensual solutions to action problems? This obligation is unevenly institutionalized in contemporary policy making. In fact, a countermorality is widely prevalent. Lack of collaboration in decision making tends to deepen the fragmentation of an already dangerously fragmented society. The future of a science of human affairs is threatened by this fragmentation.

The innovators of the training laboratory felt that practical decision making would gain in validity only if the moralities and methodologies of the scientific enterprise were more deeply infused into the moralities and methodologies of contemporary action.

Concern for Democracy. Although verbally honored, democratic values as operational determiners of important processes of decision making in organizational and community life in our society are widely neglected. Frequently, they are rejected as impractical or as threatening to power relations in the status quo. The innovators of the training laboratory recognized very real difficulties in utilizing democratic processes. They believed that operational redefinition of democratic values to make them more relevant to conditions of contemporary life was demanded. Increasing size and complexity of units of interdependence bring increasingly complex problems for participative solutions by individuals and groups, and complexity requires expertness in its management. This factor combines with increasing remoteness from decision-making opportunities to remove the individual from responsible involvement in managing his own affairs. How can such involvement be restored and extended? The problem is partly educational in character.

Democracy is an ideology which above all others demands that its practitioners be masters of skills of human relationship adequate to help groups of people make intelligent decisions concerning the changing problems that confront them. . . . Without appropriate and experimentally tested skills and methods for building efficient cooperative relationships, democracy has no hands and feet.[3]

The innovators of the training laboratory believed that there is a close kinship between the values inherent in the scientific enterprise and the values of democracy. This kinship is not due solely to the historical Western mix of democracy and science. The values implicit in science and explicit in democracy are, to a large degree, coincident. The intellectual problem posed here was, on the one hand, to make more explicit the moral values inherent in the methodologies of science as a human enterprise and, on the other hand, to define democratic values in terms of a methodology for managing human conflicts and for making decisions. (The interpretation of science as possessing an inherent morality is resisted by some scientists who are fearful of the contamination of "pure" science by moral concerns. Their resistance shows a certain lack of self-objectivity, since the resistance itself betrays a valid moral concern—a concern that the autonomy and freedom of the scientist in choosing his problems for study and in publishing his results not be subordinated to extra-scientific demands. It is doubtful that denial of an inherent morality in science is the best way to counter robustly the countermoralities of many extra-scientific enterprises in contemporary life.)

The innovators of the training laboratory saw a large degree of coincidence between the democratic ethic and the scientific ethic. A reality orientation in facing difficulties and problems, an objectivity which extends to one's own assumptions, perspectives, and preferences as factors in problem solving, and a commitment to rational collaboration in problem definition and solution are obviously scientific in mood and temper, and they are also requirements of a democratic morality. The practical task was to design educational processes to help learners incorporate these values into their own processes of personal and collective decision making and problem solving.

Concern for the Values of the Helping Relationship. The innovators of the training laboratory put great emphasis upon the importance of the helping professions.

While an increase in tested human-relations skills and understandings is important to all members of a democratic society, it is of central importance

[3] *Ibid.,* p. 475.

for those whose job is to improve the learning, the maturity, and the productivity of others—educators, trainers, supervisors, social workers, and the like. . . . They are often blocked by typical resistance to the communication of problems and pertinent experience from level to level in a community or organization and from group to group. They are frustrated by the typically large areas of privacy that individuals have built. . . . Finally, they are blocked by a failure which they share with many others in our society—a failure to see that groups have their own immaturity and maturity as groups and that they require training as groups in improving their ways of thinking and producing.[4]

Values guide the efforts of a person to help other persons. Many of these are inherent in a commitment to the facilitation of learning and maturation in the client, whether the client is a person, a group, an organization, or a community.

The training laboratory and T Group were conceived as places where the helping relationship could be studied and improved. It was hoped that participants would be motivated to extend the helping relationship into their associational lives beyond the laboratory. Some of the perceived blocks in contemporary culture to the spread of the helping relationship into action and practice are cited above. Another block lay in the existing fragmentation among the helping professions themselves. These professions had emerged to help people caught in the conflicting demands for change and adaptation which mechanization and industrialization had thrust upon them. Typically, many helping professions, like social work and psychiatry, focused on helping people who had experienced "abnormal" difficulties in handling these conflicts. But in most helping professions efforts were being made to reorient work toward prevention and away from a primary emphasis on therapy. What orientation might enable the helping professions to find common ground in their specialized efforts to help clients? The innovators of laboratory training found such an orientation in the generalized conception of the change agent—an agent committed to help others in improving their abilities to cope with change and conflict.

An early report makes clear this commitment to finding a common ground in value and orientation for helpers in our society.

What is the common framework which helps the group worker, the public school supervisor, the personnel consultant in industry, the PTA president, the training officer in a government bureau, and others to see their special jobs as resources one to the other? The faculty believed, and laboratory experience confirmed the belief, that all of these helpers and trainers of other

4 *Ibid.*, p. 476.

people can find common ground in the role of the "change agent." All . . .
[helpers] . . . work to produce changes in the understandings, attitudes,
and skills of the persons and groups with whom they work. All . . .
[helpers] . . . must, for example, help persons to plan ways of solving
problems, to evaluate their plans as these are tried and tested, and so on.
These helps to persons and groups require certain basic human relationship
skills which can be identified, analyzed, and practiced.[5]

The training laboratory was thus designed to increase intelligent
commitment to three sets of values beleaguered and inadequately
utilized in contemporary society. These are the values associated with
the social and behavioral sciences, with democracy, and with the building of the helping relationship among people. It was these values,
seen in interrelationship, that the laboratory innovators believed were
best calculated to guide efforts to meet the unmet learning needs of a
changing, industrialized society. And these values have continued
to guide laboratory training during the seventeen years of its development.

Resources for Linking Values and Needs

Where did the founders of the training laboratory seek resources to
guide and inform their educational methodologies? They drew first
on the resources of the academic desciplines and professional fields
in which they had been trained and in which they were currently engaged in research and in teaching. Members of the training staff of
the first laboratory were trained in social psychology, adult education,
sociology, and the philosophy of education. In addition, the research
staff had members trained in clinical psychology and in cultural anthropology. The staff drew also upon various fields of social practice.

Resources from the Social and Behavioral Sciences

1. The innovators of the training laboratory found encouragement
in the shift in theorizing and research over a wide number of social
and behavioral sciences from an emphasis upon "static" description
and classification to an emphasis upon dynamics. The dynamic approach was seen as especially relevant in providing knowledge and

[5] Kenneth D. Benne. "Principles of Training Method." *The Group,* 10, 2:17,
January 1948.

concepts useful in diagnosing situations and in planning processes of change—processes with which laboratory training is centrally concerned. Much of the initial interest was in the developing field of group dynamics, with particular attention to the theoretical contributions of Kurt Lewin.

2. Theoretical and practical developments in action research methodology were of particular interest. Action research provided a model for utilizing scientific methodology in improving processes of practical problem solving. It also provided a model for inducing change by collaborative and scientific means.

Resources from Philosophy

Certain philosophic developments were also resources. Interest in democratic and scientific methodologies for increasing social intelligence pointed to the thinking of John Dewey and other American experimentalists as resources. Particularly useful were studies of the logic of practical judgment by R. Bruce Raup and others seeking an integration of democratic and scientific methods of policy and decision making. The kinship between this methodology and Lewin's theory of action research was noted.

Resources from Developments in Social Practice

1. The founders of the laboratory were aware of the several early attempts to use primary group processes as a means of re-education. They noted developments in group psychotherapy by S. R. Slavson, J. L. Moreno, and others, though they differentiated training from psychotherapy. They were influenced by the widening use of group discussion methods in adult education, and to some extent, by social group work.

2. Efforts, in workshops and work conferences, to design a total learning experience in which participation by members is a major vehicle of learning were influential in shaping the format of the training laboratory.

3. Programs of leadership training developed in various organizations were seen as directed toward the learning needs with which the laboratory was also concerned. Criticisms of many such programs for their lack of grounding in the social and behavioral sciences and in a democratic ethic have already been noted.

These, then, were the resources, many of them in the pioneering stage, that staffs of early training laboratories saw as important. Other important resources have been brought in by the widening circle of scientists and practitioners who have joined laboratory staffs over the years. Two areas of research in the behavioral sciences, as previously noted, have come to loom larger in laboratory thinking and planning. These are the developing fields of organizational and individual behavior and dynamics. These influences have been mediated by increasing representation from these fields in laboratory staffs and by the continuing education of other staff members in these fields. In addition, studies of conflict and conflict resolution and of the dynamics of intergroup relations have been influential.

As concerns methodology, the action research model of changing, prominent in early laboratory practice, has been supplemented by clinical models. While some integration of these two models has been effected, differential preferences still tend to divide laboratory trainers.

Laboratory staffs have continued to draw upon the developing resources of professions of social practice as well as those of the human sciences. Prominent influences have been exerted by methodologies of organizational and community consultation and by developments in group and individual counseling and psychotherapy.

The accumulating resources available to successive laboratory staffs are thus substantial. Training laboratories have been equally important agents in the accumulation of relevant resources. This book is one account of this accumulation of knowledge, skills, and wisdom, particularly in relation to T-Group training. These resources have been generated partly from experimentation with new training methods and their evaluation and partly from resources augmented by more carefully designed research as discussed in Chapter 15. The training laboratory was conceived initially as an experimental enterprise. Where training laboratories have been most successful, they have maintained an experimental and self-correcting posture toward the goals, methods, and assumptions of laboratory education.

This is a book about an educational innovation. Thus far our account has viewed this innovation from outside, attempting to place it within its larger cultural setting. The sense of educational need which motivated the innovators has been described from this viewpoint, and the value orientations which have guided the practitioners of laboratory education have been clarified. Finally, the laboratory movement has been identified by the resources upon which it has drawn and to which it has sought to contribute. The next task is to clarify laboratory education by a more internal look into its goals, methods, and assumptions.

2

The Laboratory Method

Kenneth D. Benne
Leland P. Bradford
Ronald Lippitt

The laboratory method of education incorporates concepts of several kinds, including concepts about goals and values. Underlying the method are also distinctive assumptions about how learning takes place. And, finally, training technologies, along with principles of practice for guiding their use, have developed over the years to give operational meaning to the broader commitments and assumptions. This chapter will explore these concepts which, taken together, give meaning to the educational innovation which we are calling laboratory method.

The Goals of Laboratory Method

The training laboratory offers opportunities to improve the quality of membership in various associations and of participation in diverse human affairs. The achievement of this general goal requires that learners understand their internal needs, values, perceptions, and resources. They must also become aware of the opportunities and expectations of the social (and material) environments in which they function. But awareness and understanding, however important and however difficult to achieve, particularly in the intimate areas of life, are not enough. Improving the quality of participation requires also the creative integration of "inner" needs and "outer" demands. An individual must grow in his ability to diagnose disintegrities in his inner life, in the environments that condition his actions, and in the patterning of behavior by which he seeks to join his two worlds. In addition, he must increase his abilities to respond, integratively and adaptively, to situations. Skills in creating appropriate responses must be conjoined with skills in diagnosing situations if robust growth is to be achieved. Moreover, if the individual is to reject an ethic of passive adjustment to outside forces he must learn ways of altering and changing the outer structures of his environment where these impede autonomy and integrity in both his own participation and that of others whose actions are interdependent with his own.

The laboratory is based on an assumption that understandings and skills of participation can be learned validly only through processes of participation in which the learner is involved. Training activities are thus social process events in which trainees are invited to participate. These events are designed, in the first instance, to help participants to discover and diagnose disintegrities in their patterns of participation. They are further designed to provide help from others in inventing and testing more integrative and less crippling patterns of response. Within this general aim, laboratory staff members have identified several specific areas of learning which are important to most participants in their efforts to achieve concurrent growth in personal autonomy and in social effectiveness.

1. One hoped-for outcome for the participant is increased awareness of and sensitivity to emotional reactions and expressions in himself and in others. Without such awareness (at latent as well as manifest levels), a human being's goals, values, and actions become incongruent with his reality as a total person. He fails to recognize, and so to achieve, the development of his full potential as an individual. Or he functions in partial blindness to the complex of human factors which every situation embodies.

2. Another desired objective is greater ability to perceive and to learn from the consequences of his actions through attention to feelings, his own and others'. Emphasis is placed on the development of sensitivity to cues furnished by the behavior of others and ability to utilize "feedback" in understanding his own behaviors.

3. The staff also attempts to stimulate the clarification and development of personal values and goals consonant with a democratic and scientific approach to problems of social and personal decision and action. Some of the more important learnings seem to result when individuals publicly confront previously unperceived discrepancies in their values, and when they receive nonjudgmental support in attempts to resolve these discrepancies.

4. Another objective is the development of concepts and theoretical insights which will serve as tools in linking personal values, goals, and intentions to actions consistent with these inner factors and with the requirements of the situation. Learners typically need better theory than their common sense notions about human behavior provide in order to perceive and diagnose interpersonal and group situations more accurately, to recognize the relationships between inner feelings and perceptions and outer events, and to choose between action alternatives. One important source of valid concepts is the findings and methodologies of the behavioral sciences. Laboratory designers struggle with the problem of presenting such resources in meaningful units which are both accurate and relevant to the backgrounds and needs of the trainees.

5. All laboratory programs foster the achievement of behavioral effectiveness in transactions with one's environments. A great waste in much human endeavor stems from the disconnection between intentions and diagnoses on the one hand and behavioral output on the other. The learning of concepts, the setting of goals, the clarification of values, and even the achievement of valid insight into self, are sometimes far ahead of the development of the performance skills necessary to expression in actual social transactions. For this reason laboratory programs normally focus on the development of behavioral skills to support better integrations of intentions and actions.

All five of these objectives focus in the individual learner. It is true, however, that in many social settings and organizational situations the individual is not the only or even the most appropriate unit for achieving action or change. A team of individuals who have achieved common goals and learned to coordinate their resources may be the significant action unit. In many laboratories, therefore, a central objective is the development of new social units or teams which will be able, creatively and adaptively, to apply the results of laboratory learning. Sometimes this is achieved when members of the same social system attend the same laboratory. Consultation and training focus upon the development of team relations, team diagnoses of problems in the larger social system in which members function, and team plans to deal with these problems. Sometimes it is achieved when a trainee recruits colleagues for later laboratories so that, over time, a team may be developed in the home situation. This does not mean that laboratory training neglects to provide opportunities for personal growth but rather that objectives of personal development and of team building are integrated within the laboratory design, as indeed they must be for optimum effect.

In other situations, the significant unit may be some natural unit already functioning, e.g., a supervisor and his immediate subordinates. Special laboratory programs, often called "family programs," have been initiated by some organizations for improving the inner relationships and the external effectiveness of such "natural" groups. Sometimes a total organization is taken as the target of improvement. In such cases, a variety of training and consulting activities is designed, all generally fitting concepts underlying a laboratory approach to learning and change.

In brief, a laboratory curriculum is designed to help some unit of human organization assess its needs for change and to support that unit in inventing and testing ways in which changes may be achieved. The focal unit may be a single individual or a team of individuals. In either case, the desired direction of learning and change is toward a more integrative and adaptive interconnection of values, concepts, feelings, perceptions, strategies, and skills.

The advancement of such integration requires that the learner, during any day of learning activity, shift in a more or less planned way among the roles of observer, diagnostician, evaluator, actor, and inquirer. In each role he deals with personal feelings of resistance, anxiety, threat, weakness, strength, euphoria, or satisfaction. Where inner and outer forces are discrepant and dissonant, the learner seeks to make changes in himself or in his environment which will establish greater congruence. A similar cycle of vision and revision, inner and outer, is involved when a group or team is seeking more adaptive and creative ways of dealing with the environment of the larger social system in which it operates.

6. Another objective grows out of recognition that continuing opportunities to apply new learnings will occur in back-home situations, though removed from the supportive environment of the laboratory. How to promote transfer of laboratory learnings is one of the most challenging questions before every laboratory staff. The curriculum of most laboratories provides help to learners in integrating new ways of behaving with typical ways of behaving in home settings.

7. A final objective underlying most laboratory education is "learning how to learn." Each learner is asked to become an analyst of his own processes of learning. This involves development of abilities to take initiative in seeking and using the resources of others to enhance his own learning. It involves, reciprocally, becoming an effective resource in giving help. This has deep implications for the kind of self the learner is seeking to become. It directs his efforts toward

achieving a self-identity which is active, reflective, realistically optimistic, and collaborative.

In working toward these seven educational objectives, a laboratory staff needs to be continuously aware that they are working with trainees toward *re-education*. Laboratory learners have already learned many values, concepts, and behaviors relevant to membership and to participation. Some of these past learnings are functional; some are dysfunctional. Some of them are already well articulated; others are held and used preconsciously and in an inarticulated fashion. For the learners, every day in a laboratory is full of episodes of relearning, of reorganization of previous learnings, of confrontations of old patterns with new possibilities, of recognition and understanding of own and others' motivations and feelings, and of conscious and unconscious explorations of the gains and losses potential in revising goals and modifying behavioral strategies. This means that the achievement of each learning objective ordinarily involves examination of the relationships between old and new experiences, between old and new learnings, and the arduous process of achieving some viable choice or synthesis between the old and the new.

Target Populations for Laboratory Training

The early training laboratories worked with heterogeneous groups of workers from various helping professions—education, social work, public health, psychiatry, nursing, religion, industrial relations, and clinical psychology. From this beginning, laboratories have been developed for quite different types of populations.

1. Laboratories have continued to work most broadly with the growing population of professional helpers who have educational and consultative responsibilities. These professional helpers function in a wide variety of community, educational, governmental, and industrial organizations. Varied as they are, they are seeking more effective helping relationships with their own client population and, in turn, receiving help from their clients in becoming more effective as helpers. They are also concerned with developing more effective team relationships with colleagues.

Program development has proceeded in three directions. One has been the development of homogeneous laboratories, such as the laboratory for professional workers in religion, cosponsored by the National Council of Churches and the National Training Laboratories. Another example is a laboratory for wives of presidents of industrial organizations in conjunction with the Young Presidents' Organization. Other examples are laboratories for school superintendents, classroom teachers, juvenile court judges, and youth workers.

A second approach has been that of recruiting workers from the same social context who have had little or no previous working relationship. This is seen in the Community Leadership Laboratory where several professional workers and volunteer leaders are recruited from the same community context with the objective of helping them to develop effective communication and to plan for future teamwork. A third approach is to recruit individuals from the same social context year after year so that there can be a cumulative input of trained individuals ready to collaborate in the pursuit of common change goals.

2. Another target population is the more or less professionalized supervisor, manager, or administrator, whose job is to work with and through people to get tasks done. This focus on managerial leadership is perhaps best illustrated by the several laboratories for middle management and top management which have become regular parts of the National Training Laboratories program. It has become clear that, even though the substantive work of the organization from which managers come may not be in the field of clinical or social practice, helping to get work done requires the utilization of knowledge from the behavioral sciences in the fields of leadership, individual and group decision making, building work units, and personal development of workers and managers.

3. A third type of target population is the total membership of an organization. The company laboratory, or an organizational program, such as The Annual American National Red Cross Executive Development School, is a relatively recent development of great promise. The staff accepts the challenge of collaborating with a total organization in the stimulation and maintenance of change or growth processes. In many instances, family groups, i.e., persons on two or three levels who customarily work with one another, become the unit for training, either in a formal program or in informal utilization of laboratory methods or in some combination of the two. In some instances, a laboratory population is drawn from several vertical levels in the organization. Trainees are grouped in such a way that no one is in the same laboratory group as anyone with whom he has direct authority relations at work. In still other instances, laboratory training is utilized to develop "change-agent teams" as a first step in a continuing program for organizational growth. In most such programs, strategically placed

persons participate in formal laboratories for persons from many organizations, and also in "in-company" training programs.

4. Work with laymen or with professions in cross-occupational laboratories has indicated that the laboratory may be designed to support participants in their quests for clarification of personal identity and in working on basic issues of personal development—activity-passivity, dependency-authority, conformity-autonomy, change versus stability. It seems clear that many persons are hungry for opportunities to explore their own problems of personal dynamics, of interpersonal and group relations, and of social action. The laboratory can be adapted to this need. In fact, in all laboratories, whether of a vocational nature or not, such issues are inevitably dealt with in some degree. Only when such a humanistic approach is taken will processes of organizational change and the growth needs of persons be adequately reconciled. Such an approach is the only approach fully consistent with a democratic ideology.

5. Another recent development is the application of the laboratory method in working with children and youth and with college students. Here the laboratory experience becomes a contribution to the socialization process and permits the exploration of intergeneration relations. A recent laboratory for high school youth revealed a strong desire to learn to work collaboratively on the improvement of relationships between teenagers and their parents, their teachers and their cross-sex peers, in order to achieve more effective use of learning opportunities inside and outside schools. Also, recent laboratories in higher education have brought together faculty and students to work on their problems of collaboration in building an educational environment.

6. Beginnings have been made in utilizing laboratory method with a new and important target population, the cross-cultural client group. The substantive aim here is the improvement of relationships between persons and groups coming from different cultural or national backgrounds. The focus is on the values, strategies, and skills basic to a creative process of conflict resolution and of collaboration across lines of cultural cleavage. Experience indicates that such a laboratory experience, short as it is, may do more to bring about realistic understanding of similarities and differences among groups than a year or more spent in formal campus or work situations.

Experience thus far indicates that the laboratory design for learning can make a significant contribution to many populations, ranging from children to cross-cultural groups concerned with international relations. Experience shows further that the basic ingredients of the learning process are the same, although some of the specific learning outcomes receive different emphasis. The laboratory method of education is based on the conviction that there are generic characteristics of learning experiences that are common for all clients.

Assumptions about Learning in Laboratory Method

A training laboratory is an institutionalized place for learning. One avenue toward understanding the laboratory method is to grasp the concepts about learning which guide its practitioners. Insofar as "learning how to learn" is a goal of laboratory training, these concepts become part of the content to be understood by participants as well as by practitioners.

One barrier to a clear understanding of learning in contemporary society stems from the dispersion of deliberate educational functions. Various institutions function, in whole or in part, to facilitate and direct learning. These may differ as to educational purposes. A health organization may be primarily concerned with behavioral change in the area of health habits. A school might put its emphasis on learning intellectual skills. A therapeutic institution may stress emotional relearning. Different professions of social practice have developed to assume responsibility for managing these different institutions. Practitioners from different professions operate with differing assumptions about how learning can best be facilitated. These assumptions are shaped in some large part by the purposes, limitations, and possibilities of the institutional complex, the agency, in which the practitioner operates.

Training programs, in turn, tend to be shaped by a vision of the limitations and opportunities which are seen as "real" in the institutions in which prospective professionals are to function. And visions of "reality" vary from institution to institution. A school is not a family, or a family a psychiatric clinic. Neither is a psychiatric clinic a training program in industry, nor a training program in industry a political campaign. It follows that "realistic" training for a teacher is not the same as that for a parent, or for a psychiatric worker, or for an industrial trainer, or for a political leader. Yet it is equally true that all these professions are engaged in influencing learning processes. All are responsible in some manner for advancing learning. The realistic shaping of particular technologies of social practice to particular institutional demands, combined with the segregation of various professionals in their training and to some large extent in their practice, have led to noncommunicating conceptualizations of learning in various segments of our society.

One may look on this variety of assumptions as a blemish or as an advantage. It is a blemish insofar as it delays and blocks the development of more valid conceptualizations than any single area of social practice can provide. It is an advantage insofar as each can contribute to a set of concepts and technologies which can serve simultaneously to provide a basis for communication and collaboration among practitioners of social practice and to furnish more objective criteria for remaking patterns of institutional practice.

One might well look to the basic disciplines of the behavioral sciences for the bases of more generally valid and applicable technologies for facilitating learning. But here again differing concepts of learning tend to characterize various special fields. Learning theory in experimental psychology has been developed with little regard to theories of socialization developing in sociological and anthropological researches. Yet each has much to say about how people learn. The personality theories which are basic to psychiatric and counseling practices often have little perceived relationship to the theories about learning which teachers are asked to acquire in educational psychology courses. And this is so for other disciplines which conceptualize human learning.

The laboratory approach to learning is a cross-professional and cross-disciplinary approach which attempts to draw relevant aspects from various approaches and to develop a more integrated model of social technology for facilitating learning. The development of training laboratories is thus one cultural response to the confusing dispersion of educational functions. The approach is not, for this reason, eclectic in the sense that it draws concepts indiscriminately and additively from various areas of social science and social practice. Its selection and integration of concepts are based on certain goal and value assumptions about the kinds and qualities of learning to be sought.

Many of the confusions among "outside" observers of laboratory practices as well as many of the conflicts among its "inside" practitioners seem to stem from the cross-disciplinary character of the laboratory approach. The observer may well wonder whether a training laboratory is a school or a therapeutic enterprise, whether it is an attempt to develop internalized assent to democratic values or to extend scientific attitudes into the diagnosis and handling of human predicaments, whether it is devoted to the better utilization of social science concepts and information in social practice or to the resocialization of inadequately socialized "organization" men and women. A laboratory may be all of these but none of these exclusively.

Inside practitioners differ in the weightings they give to the various elements which have been selectively integrated in a laboratory approach to learning. And conflicts occur among them as they try to collaborate in designing and conducting laboratory learning enterprises out of different orientations toward learning and its facilitation. Perhaps an attempt to suggest how "laboratory" concepts of learning have been drawn from various sources, professional and scientific, will help to dispel the confusion of the "outsiders" and clarify, but not eliminate, conflicts among the "insiders."

Formal Schooling and Related Learning Theory

It would be foolish to claim that any uniform set of concepts about learning underlies the complex processes of formal education in America today. Some of the current debates about schooling are grounded in conflicting notions about learning. Yet, through much of traditional schooling run concepts of a fixed cultural environment and of plastic learners who have not acquired the informations or skills required to negotiate this environment successfully. Learning, from this view, refers to the processes by which such learners acquire these informations and skills. The evidence that learning has taken place lies in testable changes in the behavior of the learner.

This traditional model also underlies learning theories developed by such psychological students of learning as Edward L. Thorndike, C. L. Hull, and E. R. Guthrie. It operates also in the work of B. F. Skinner, as exemplified in the development of teaching machines.

Laboratory method starts with a different over-all view of learning as a transaction between learner and environment in which neither learner nor environment is regarded as fixed and in which both undergo modification. But this does not mean that concepts of learning derived from the former model are unimportant in designing learning processes under laboratory conditions.

The concepts of "reinforcement" and "feedback"[1] are perhaps most useful in understanding laboratory learning. One learns about people as one learns about any other subject matter—by responding to a

---

[1] Feedback, as used here, signifies verbal and nonverbal responses from others to a unit of behavior provided as close in time to the behavior as possible, and capable of being perceived and utilized by the individual initiating the behavior. Feedback may serve a validating function with respect to the initial behavior. It may serve to steer and give direction to subsequent behavior. It may also serve to stimulate changes in the behavior, feeling, attitude, perception, and knowledge of the initiator.

stimulus. In the laboratory the stimulus is the behavior of other persons. "Correct" responses are reinforced positively and tend to be established in the learner's repertoire of responses. "Incorrect" responses are negatively reinforced and tend to disappear. The training laboratory provides a group of other people as agencies of positive and negative reinforcement.

The problem, of course, lies in the determination of which responses are "correct" and "appropriate." The laboratory group must work toward the formulation of standards against which "correctness" or "appropriateness" of member responses and group performances can be measured. Much individual learning about criteria of appropriateness occurs in this process. Much individual learning about self may also occur as a result of the multi-faceted responses from a variety of other group members.

In the working out of mutually satisfactory criteria of appropriateness, collaborative transactions between A and B (environment to A) and between B and A (environment to B) are required. In effect, stimulus and response must be mutually accommodated, a condition not ordinarily legitimized or emphasized in traditional learning theory. The correctness of the response to be learned tends rather to be predetermined by teacher, culture, or machine programmer. And this definition of correctness is held constant for the period of the learning experience. Nevertheless, mechanisms of negative and positive reinforcement are at work in laboratory learning as well as in learning in other settings. Stimulus and response do tend to interpenetrate in the laboratory setting where people function both as learners and as environment to one another and where standards of appropriateness of stimulation and response are worked out as actual stimuli and responses are mutually accommodated.

A closely related notion from learning theory is the powerful effect of instantaneous feedback concerning the effects of the learner's exploratory response. In learning about the effect of his behavior on other people, the learner needs to have some more or less immediate report of the effects of his response on the others.

Various factors account for the withholding or distortion of responses by persons with whom another person has tried to interact. The aim of those in charge of laboratory learning is to help the learning group to identify and manage these factors in such a way that withholding and distortion are reduced, and feedback becomes more instantaneous and authentic. Primarily, the building of a more effective feedback system into the learning group is a condition of valid learning. It serves also the mental health value of facing reality and the democratic value of authentic communication.

Psychiatry and Counseling—Personality Theory

There are at least as many schools of psychiatric and counseling practice as there are schools of learning theory in formal education. Yet some notions about effective ways of inducing behavioral change in psychiatric or counseling interviews are common. Some of these have been incorporated into laboratory methods. One distinctive emphasis stems from recognizing the learning that goes on in a counseling process as relearning.[2] Past learnings are dynamically active in the present learning situation. This is nowhere more evident than when the subject matter of learning is the behavior of self and others. Past learnings manifest themselves in the interview process in a number of ways. They tend to shape the stimuli which the behavior of another person presents to the learner in such a way as to serve his self-maintenance needs. Perceptions of the other's contemporary behavior and intention are thus distorted. Psychiatrists and counselors seek to help learners clarify the personal meaning of these distortions as an important avenue to learning about self.

Past learnings also function as resistances to change induction on the part of other people. Counselors and psychiatrists tend to encourage learners to recognize these resistances as important gateways to self-understanding. The emphases upon distortions of perception and resistances to influence are also incorporated into laboratory methods of learning, where understanding of self is a goal of learning and a necessary precursor to valid confrontation of social realities. The point here is that laboratory trainers encourage learners to reflect upon their resistances to influence as a way to understand the needs, feelings, and values which characterize the self.

Psychiatrists and counselors have also given focal attention to their relationships with those whose relearning they are trying to facilitate. It is in these relationships that distortions of perception and resistances to influence manifest themselves. A client may find himself distrust-

---

[2] It is true that emphasis upon the correction of past mislearnings as a goal of counseling varies among various schools of psychiatric practice. Psychoanalytic counselors would emphasize such correction more than counselors of a Rogerian or existentialist persuasion. Laboratory trainers also vary in the degree to which emphasis in training conversations is placed upon life history content and upon the here-and-now situation.

ing and hating the counselor "beyond reason." Working on the reasons for this difficulty may lead to insight into typical difficulties in relationship as well as to the establishment of a more reality-oriented relationship in the present situation. The relationship between learner and helper is seen as a major content in the process of relearning both in the counseling situation and in laboratory training.

The quality of this relationship also functions as a condition of the communication and revelation of self which processes of relearning require. If the learner does not trust the counselor, communication is inhibited and important data upon which relearning depends are not available. Those employing laboratory method are similarly concerned with the relationships between each learner and the others within the training environment. In laboratories, unlike many psychotherapeutic situations, much of the learning goes on in a group of learners, not in a dyadic relationship between "patient" and counselor or psychiatrist. Standards of mutual helpfulness and open communication of feelings must be built into the group by the group itself. And the relationships between learner and learner as well as between learner and trainer furnish powerful forces and significant content for the relearnings sought.

Socialization and Resocialization

Insofar as a training laboratory invites a participant to re-examine his value orientations and attitudes where these are contributing to ineffectiveness in handling human situations, the process is one of resocialization. The drama of human socialization moves ideally from a condition of dependence to a condition of autonomy and interdependence. The young child is, out of biological necessity, dependent upon the adults who surround and care for him. His first relationships with authority figures are with parental figures upon whom he is dependent for virtually all of his need-satisfactions and for his survival. The developmental process may be seen, in simplified terms, as a movement from a child of parents to a parent of children. One axis of a person's development is, therefore, his growth in ability to handle authority relations, initially as a subject and later as a bearer of authority as well.

Part of the dialectic of the process of winning independence from parental authority lies in using the extrafamilial peer group as a foil to parental authority, particularly in the period of adolescence. Actually, problems of peer relations present themselves earlier in working out competitions and collaborations with siblings in the family and with peers in agencies outside the family, such as in the school. Again, while sibling relationships in the family are prototypic of peer relations, peer relations come to permeate the developing person's life in work, citizenship, play, education, and religion.

The development of a person from the dependence of infancy toward the ideal autonomy and interdependence of maturity proceeds through the complex interplay of various peer and authority relationships. The autonomy of maturity is not independence from such relationships. It is rather marked by the abilities to function with reality orientation toward changing peer and authority relationships and to handle problems encountered in a way to maintain and enhance one's own integrity and growth, and that of others.

What have ideas about the drama of socialization to do with laboratory learning? First, there are critical phases in the movement of every human individual from dependence toward autonomy in interdependence. Any of these critical phases may not be well handled by the person or by other persons responsible for helping along his socialization. The person thus may carry areas of inadequately completed socialization into his adult years. His problems with autonomous functioning may center in the area of authority relations or in the area of peer relations or in both. Laboratory experience offers an opportunity to review and to begin remaking inadequate personal decisions. Group experiences in the laboratory require re-examination of personal strategies for dealing with others and tend to open up earlier decisions, particularly those made in adolescence—about identity, world-view, vocational choice, and personal adequacy. The laboratory seeks also to provide the emotional support of a membership group to sustain participants in reconsidering those earlier decisions.

The second line of answer comes from the fact that socialization is no longer complete with the end of adolescence in our society. Continuing and accelerating change makes the management of identity crisis and of personal and civic reorientation a continuing demand upon adults. Somehow, each person must learn how to deal consciously with his own problems of resocialization and to make deliberate use of specialized resources developed to help meet these problems. The laboratory experience provides an opportunity for each participant to receive help in improving his ways of handling these recurring problems with greater objectivity and rationality. In the same process, each participant gains experience in giving similar help to others.

Small-Group Theory and Group Psychotherapy

Students of early socialization of children emphasize the acquisition of group memberships as the fundamental way in which a child develops his value orientations, his basic attitudes toward himself and others—authority figures and peers—and his basic style of handling himself in human situations. Resocialization also involves the development of membership in a group. If the group is to stimulate relearning, it must contrast, in its standards, with those significant associations which have shaped and continue to shape the learner outside the laboratory. This suggests why laboratory method puts great emphasis upon participation by learners in building new groups in which membership becomes important to them because they are groups which they have built. The clash which leads to change in the learner may be seen as a clash between contradictory demands of the standards of the laboratory learning group and the demands of other memberships. These latter demands may come from current outside memberships or from reference groups within the learner's internal society. Laboratory trainers encourage learners to confront the conflicts which laboratory experience precipitates. They seek also to provide both emotional and intellectual support toward keeping the conflicts alive as learners search for integrative resolutions and to discourage premature rejection of the conflict in the interest of personal comfort.

Since the groups which develop in the laboratory are learning groups —groups supportive of learning by each member—the clash normally is between the standards of a deeply involving learning group and the standards of groups devoted to purposes other than member learning. The participant may contrast sharply the "irreality" of his learning group with the "reality" of work groups in the world outside. He may admit that he and others can face and share their feelings about one another constructively in the laboratory but insist that such sharing would be fatally disruptive outside. If the clash of standards can be faced by a learner, he acquires firsthand knowledge of the conditions which have made learning possible in the laboratory. One hope of transfer of laboratory learnings is that the learner will acquire a new reference group through membership in the laboratory. Commitment to the conditions which make his and others' learnings possible may thus come to operate in other associations.

The debt of laboratory training to psychotherapy has already been acknowledged. The distinctions between the two are found both in their clients and in the concepts of trainers and therapists concerning their roles in the re-educative process. It is the latter distinctions which we are concerned with here.

But the distinction between the clients of the group psychotherapist and those of the laboratory trainer should be noted in passing. (See Chapter 16, by Jerome D. Frank, for a fuller development of these distinctions.) The former clients are "patients," insofar as they accept the role, disturbed by subnormal or abnormal functioning in significant relationships. The goal of group psychotherapy is to help the patient come up to—or back to—normal functioning. The individuals who come to a training laboratory are, ideally at least, functioning normally in their significant relationships. As trainees, their aim is to improve their functioning above its present generally adequate level and thus to improve the functioning of the groups and organizations of which they are members. This distinction may seem slight. But it affects markedly the definition of the roles of both trainer and trainee.

The client of the laboratory trainer is not the individual trainee. His client is a group. This relationship is most clear when the group is a "natural" working unit. It is less clear with a group of strangers without previous or continuing identity. Yet, even in this case, where the trainer may be most tempted to function as psychotherapist, his fundamental relationship is that of consultant to a group which is seeking to become an effective learning environment for all of its members. He must understand the personal dynamics of individuals in diagnosing their difficulties in relation to the developing organization of the group. But his central task is to work with the group so that it may function more adequately in supporting common learning as well as individual learnings.

Intersystem Theory—Organizational and Community Consultation

The formal organization of the laboratory is akin to a bureaucratic organization, made up of interlocking groupings of participants and staff. Initial concerns center around the role of the trainer and the training staff. The staff has planned the laboratory, and the participants who come find them in charge of its skeletal organization. Thus it is quite natural that participants should see staff as "line" leaders of the laboratory organization. When staff members abdicate their "line" responsibilities, confusion results. Responses to staff members as authority figures may persist for quite a time, along with other responses to them as "head shrinkers" (psychotherapists), or as "researchers," i.e., experimenters who are using participants as guinea pigs without openly sharing their research aims and hypotheses. As the relationship between participants and staff as client and consultant gets sorted out and accepted, the projective materials revealed in the process become important learning content concerning attitudes and opinions relative to organizational authority and leadership, the relationship between person and organization, and the place of helping relationships in processes of social control. As these materials are analyzed, learnings transferable to other organizational settings may take place. The main point here is that laboratory trainers draw significantly upon ideas from organizational theory, especially those concerning the consultant or staff role in organizational life.

As already suggested, "system theory" also plays an important part in the designing of laboratory learning. It is through analyzing the encounters, conflicts, and confusions between systems at many levels of human organization that motivation to learn about human behavior and, hopefully, actual learning, in a context of use and application, are accomplished. The clashes between personal systems, between group systems, between group systems of participants and of staff are all utilized for learning.

Since laboratories normally occur in residential settings, participants function not only in the "bureaucratic" structure of formalized learning situations but also in informal association. In this respect, the laboratory is more like a community than a formal organization. If the laboratory is to facilitate rather than to block learnings, ideas from the practice of community organization and from intersystem theory should inform its design.

In one sense, the aim of community organization in the laboratory is to prevent individuals or cliques from being engulfed by organized group activity. Roommates are members of different laboratory groups. A library is often set aside where individuals can read or think without being thought anti-social. There is no required participation in mass recreation. A variety of recreational activities are legitimized and facilitated. Persons and cliques are defended against being required by social pressure to report to anyone the findings of their meditations or conversations in the informal group life of the laboratory. Outside associations may thus be used by persons to defend themselves against possibly unhealthful social pressures to overexpose themselves in training situations.

Yet channels are provided to tap the informal community structure

for learning purposes. One of these is through short interviews between paired members of a T Group outside group meeting hours.
Individuals have an opportunity to sort out what they are thinking
and feeling and to get advice from one another about which questions
they may choose to bring into the training group. Individual consultation opportunities are provided under conditions of confidentiality.
Sometimes "political" channels are provided for participants to communicate their discontents with laboratory arrangements to the staff.

One way of using for learning purposes the strong subgroup loyalties which develop toward the T Groups is to arrange for them to
encounter one another in a context either of competition or of collaboration. Data are collected on the behavior which results, and
"laws" of intersystem dynamics in competition and in collaboration
are developed and tested.

In a successful laboratory, community-wide standards that it is good
to learn about self and others through the observation and analysis
of behavior develop. These standards tend to bring what happens in
the informal associations of the laboratory into support of the learning
goals of its formal associations. The danger, of course, is that individuals may be hurt and mislearnings may occur through amateur
psychologizing in these informal situations. The protections are twofold. One is to distinguish between responsible and irresponsible
feedback of behavioral data early in the formal curriculum. The other
protection is to legitimize cliquings which serve as socially reinforced
resistance against overexposure.

Action Research and Scientific Methodology

Surprisingly, research is not typically seen in our society as a process
of learning. The orientations and assumptions of researchers, as distinguished from their findings, are seldom studied for possible transfer
to other learning situations, whether in schools, organizations, or families. The scientist sometimes sees little relationship between his research methodology and the processes of learning in his own classroom or family.

Proponents of laboratory method regard research as a process for
reaching valid learning results. It is a process of learning which seeks
to push back the frontiers of knowledge and intelligent control of
events. It is finally a process of learning in which the learner (researcher) assumes initiative in defining what needs to be learned and
in devising ways in which relevant learnings can be found and tested.

In the laboratory, members are encouraged to undertake processes of self-directed inquiry which utilizes others as partners and resources. This means that learning situations are set up to facilitate each individual's clarification of problems about himself and about his relations with other people. Answers are not given because they are not known. Resources are offered in the form of conceptual tools for thinking about the problem and as part of the feedback and "verification" process. Consensual validation is employed, but processes of testing consensus reached and the quality of thinking and communication that go into forming a consensus are continually criticized and tested by the group. Help is given to facilitate the collection of all relevant data, to challenge hasty overgeneralization from the data collected, and to suggest alternative hypotheses.

In other learning situations, the inquiry invited is a group inquiry. Alternative ways of handling a more or less controlled problematic situation are evaluated on the basis of data collected about their effects. Such "skill practice sessions" may be used to test two kinds of learning tools. One is a concept or set of concepts useful in understanding human behavior. Another kind is an inquiry tool—a methodology for gathering data—observation, for example, or designing a field experiment. Frequently, research designs are adapted into training designs in which participants are asked to become both subjects and experimenters in a process of problem solution. As a result, individuals may increase their ability to continue to learn by utilizing principles of inquiry in the process of learning from everyday experiences. A third kind of tool is an action-model tool. A means-end action pattern can help individuals and groups to take concrete steps toward learning and change.

Such notions about the creation of learning situations and their management are drawn both from the canons of scientific method and from the philosophy of science. The form they take in the laboratory may be thought of as action research. Action research is an application of scientific methodology in the clarification and solution of practical problems. It is also a process of planned personal and social change. In either view, it is a process of learning in which attention is given to the quality of collaboration in planning action and in the evaluation of results.

Democratic Practice—Democratic Theory

We have seen that concepts function both in establishing conditions for learning and in furnishing content and inquiry tools for learning. This is true also of democratic ideas as they operate in laboratories.

But democratic ideas operate as value-commitments, as well as "descriptive" concepts, in certain crucial choices that are made about the goals, content, and procedure of any given laboratory enterprise. This is equally true of the values implicit in the spirit and methodology of science discussed earlier. But this latter commitment does not jar academic men as commitment to democratic values sometimes does. The two sets of values are of a different order—scientific methods being related to the building and testing of knowledge and democratic methods to the management and control of individual and collective behavior. Those who have developed the laboratory method are more impressed by the kinship of the two sets of values as approaches to learning than by their differences.

Democracy stresses the potential ability of people collaboratively to define and solve the problems they encounter in trying to live and work together. It posits that common problems cannot be well solved without the participation of those affected by the solution. This view of democracy assumes a procedure of consensual validation as the final arbiter of the rightness of any collective judgment or arrangement. This does not mean that any psychological "consensus" at any given time is necessarily right. The democratic principle of "consensus" assumes that group agreements can be wrong and incorporates important safeguards against the "tyranny" and "mistakenness" of the majority or indeed of the entire group. Public and ready access to information relevant to a decision is one of these safeguards. The responsibility of each member to discuss and interpret the relevant information out of his own particular framework of values and to try to influence others toward a favorable view of his interpretation constitutes another safeguard. The freedom of each to participate equally in processes of decision that affect him is often interpreted in legal terms alone. But the spirit of democracy extends to the reduction of barriers to free participation inherent in economic, social, and psychological conditions as well. Finally, the spirit of experimentation pervades democratic ideology. Persons or parties to whom representative power is granted are subject to a continuing evaluation of their exercise of power, and the right of those who granted the authority to reallocate power and to operate experimentally with new leadership and new policies and procedures is a still further safeguard against the elevation of any temporary consensus into an irrevocable fetter upon future choices.

The important thing here is to see that consensual validation and the safeguards against false consensus, which are near to the heart of democracy as a method of social control, are also assumptions about the rights and responsibilities of people to learn and about the ways of facilitating learning. People must learn to meet new and unprecedented problems which require collective decision. People must learn to gather and furnish information necessary for valid decisions. People must learn to participate with others in the interpretation of the evidence and in the creation of forms and arrangements consistent with the evidence. This means facing and dealing constructively with value conflicts and power conflicts in any pluralistic group, organization, or community. People must learn to test commitments to established ways of doing and interpreting things and to work experimentally toward new ways more consistent with new evidence and newly articulated goals and values. None of these learnings comes naturally. Our society is a complex mixture of some associations in which democratic assumptions prevail and in which related skills are learned without deliberate tutelage and other associations in which other assumptions about men and their management are institutionalized. The laboratory supports the confrontation of these contradictions.

It is important to emphasize that democratic methodology is seen here as closely akin to scientific methodology. Both depend ultimately upon consensual validation of results achieved. Both build safeguards against "false" consensus into their ways of operating. Both are experimental in approach. Both are committed to incorporating a maximum induction from relevant individual experiences and from alternative modes of interpretation into learning results sought. Both insist on public processes of validation.

Where does the difference lie? Democratic methodology extends to the creation and testing of patterns of social control. Scientific methodology focuses upon the validation of knowledge. This means that democratic methodology must involve the validation of relevant moral and other values as well as the validation of knowledge relevant to a policy decision. The laboratory method invites people to learn in areas where previous value commitments may impede learning. Practitioners of laboratory method must, therefore, help people to open up their value commitments as well as their cognitive equipment to public examination and personal reconstruction. In this sense, the commitment of laboratory method to democratic methodology is more inclusive than its commitment to scientific methodology. However, its proponents believe that value commitments need to be based on valid knowledge. The aim of laboratory method is, therefore, to establish learning conditions which incorporate the use of scientific knowledge and methodology. A central aim of laboratory learning is, therefore, to extend the use of democratic-scientific methodologies into the management of human affairs in various institutional settings.

The Laboratory Process of Training and Learning

A closer examination of the dynamics of laboratory training and learning in actual operation is now in order.

Learning Opportunities for Laboratory Participants

OPPORTUNITIES TO TEST AND DISCOVER DISSATISFACTIONS. Usually individuals bring to a formal learning experience some dissatisfaction with their present situation or behavior. They bring at the same time some hesitations about fully committing themselves to a process of change designed to reduce this dissatisfaction. Fears of failure, anxieties about acceptance, and uncertainties about unanticipated consequences of change may create ambivalence about venturing into a deeply involving learning situation.

The initial motivational problem confronting the laboratory for learning, therefore, has two dimensions. One is to provide a situation in which the individual [3] can test the reality and depth of his conscious dissatisfactions. The individual may find realistic causes for his dissatisfactions. Or, he may discover that his perceived needs to change are unjustified. The second dimension is to provide situations in which the individual may face up to dissatisfactions not previously recognized—dissatisfactions growing out of a confrontation of incongruities between values, goals, resources, and behavior.

Dissatisfactions may remain diffuse and undefined unless they can be tested to determine whether they are symptomatic of deeper causes. Diffused and undefined dissatisfactions usually lead to large expenditures of emotional energy but to little focused effort. Without an opportunity to test dissatisfactions and the assumptions underlying them, the individual cannot make an accurate diagnosis of his learning needs.

Equally, when pain is not felt, there is little dissatisfaction. The provision of situations in which people may discover pain is also an avenue to learning.

[3] Groups in laboratories as well as individuals experience the motivational ambivalences discussed here. For clarity of expression, this account is written from the standpoint of the individual.

OPPORTUNITIES TO TEST CONGRUENCE BETWEEN GOALS AND ACTION. If learning is to lead toward growth, laboratories must provide opportunities in which congruences between goals and actions may be seen, accepted, and tested. Such testing is most effectively accomplished when the individual can take action, can feel free to discuss and consider the complexities of his goals with others, and can, with help from others, study the effectiveness with which his actions are related to his goals.

OPPORTUNITIES FOR COLLABORATION IN SETTING DIRECTIONS FOR CHANGE. Locating incongruences between goals and actions leads to frustration unless directions for change can be determined and accepted. Such directions usually cannot be determined and imposed by an outside person. The individual requires supportive assistance in sorting out his value and motivational conflicts, and in determining the directions of change which he sees as possible and desirable. Active collaboration between learner and trainer and between learners is crucial.

OPPORTUNITIES TO DETERMINE PATHWAYS TO CHANGE. The process in which the individual searches for appropriate pathways to behavioral change is even more complex than the above discussion implies. The pathways must be perceived by the individual as possible in terms of his abilities and anxieties. But his concerns about leaving a known pattern of behavior, inadequate as it may be, for the unknowns of change, must be met with support without saddling him with new dependencies. This requires opportunity to experiment with various pathways, to bring into the open the anxieties which block desirable movement, and to obtain help in alleviating anxieties when they impede forward movement.

OPPORTUNITIES TO ASSESS EFFECTIVENESS OF NEW BEHAVIOR. To try out new behavior in a group is like trying out a new pair of glasses to test what seeing and walking are like under new conditions. The learner needs help, through the reactions of others as well as through his own internal responses, in assessing the effectiveness of any newly developed behavior. The laboratory faces the necessity of providing continuous opportunities for experimentation and assessment.

OPPORTUNITIES TO PRACTICE, INTERNALIZE, AND APPLY NEW BEHAVIOR. Until the individual has opportunity to become comfortable with any new behavior, regressive movements to old behavior may occur. Practice opportunities help to maintain new patterns of behavior and new levels of performance within a previously established pattern.

The laboratory provides such opportunities and also creates situations in which the learner may expand and extend his learning through a better understanding of the principles underlying some particular behavioral change. A further step toward application to other aspects of life requires opportunity to diagnose barriers that must be overcome both in himself and in his situation, to plan further diagnosis with others in the outside situation, and, if possible, to try out the first planned steps under the partially protected conditions of the laboratory.

Barriers to Learning and Change

Barriers to learning and change, particularly when modifications in the behavior of an individual toward others are involved, are complex. When these are not recognized by those planning learning situations and by learners, results are relatively slight or perhaps quite different from those expected.

SEEKING EASY, EARLY ANSWERS. The traditional educational pattern, in which solutions are presented before problems are recognized and in which the teacher assumes responsibility for learning, reinforces desires to be given easy answers to complex problems—answers supplied by others without pain or effort for the learner. Many trainees thus come to laboratories with no expectation that they will be involved in diagnosing what needs to be learned and in finding solutions to problems revealed. The laboratory for learning must therefore be prepared to cope with shock and initial resistance.

CONFLICTS BETWEEN THE FAMILIAR AND THE UNFAMILIAR. The conflict in the trainee between holding to familiar patterns of behavior and trying out unfamiliar, but hopefully more satisfactory, patterns is particularly potent when the change challenges self-concepts or others' perception of him. Ways for supporting trainees in understanding this basis of their resistance to involvement are necessary if behavioral changes are to occur.

RESISTANCE TO BREAKDOWN OF COMPARTMENTALIZATIONS WITHIN THE INDIVIDUAL. Role behaviors, on the job and at home, may be perceived as totally determined by the situation and not at all by the individual personality. In this view, role behavior is seen as inviolate to re-examination and change. But if incongruities cannot be accepted as discrepancies within the person requiring self-examination, growth possibilities are limited. The individual has less knowledge or control of himself than he might have and is, to that extent, less of a whole person than he need be. The requirement in a laboratory is to develop situations which will induce the individual to examine his compartmentalizations and to endeavor to integrate his behavior, values, needs, knowledge, and feelings. "When in Rome do as the Romans do," seems to guide some individuals in meeting conflict. They learn to meet the expectations of others in the learning situation but with little or no commitment that they will continue to behave in this way. The alternative is to help trainees achieve a deeper involvement in the associational life of the laboratory.

RELUCTANCE TO EXPOSE THOUGHTS AND BEHAVIOR TO OTHERS. Without bringing forth his feelings and thoughts, the individual may not recognize needed changes in his behavior. Reactions from others which could be helpful in his growth cannot be forthcoming. Yet, in a competitive or hostile atmosphere, exposure of self can lead toward rejection, loss of reputation, or ridicule. Laboratory conditions must encourage collaboration and trust among members and thus reduce the threats inherent in self-exposure.

DEFENSIVE REACTIONS RESULTING FROM LACK OF INDIVIDUAL SECURITY. Learning and change require the admission that learning and change may be desirable. If the individual defends his present patterns against all changes, little learning will take place. The laboratory must work toward building an atmosphere that reduces personal defensiveness so that learnings and changes may occur.

LACK OF SKILL IN ASSESSING BEHAVIOR. If the individual has had no experience in testing out his own behavior through eliciting and evaluating the reactions of others to it, or if he has no model enabling him to try out new behaviors, he will find difficulty in participating in a learning situation having these requirements. The laboratory must provide experiences in trying out new behaviors and assessing them with the aid of others.

LACK OF CONCEPTUAL STRUCTURES TO PLAN THE DIRECTION OF CHANGE. Frequently, "common sense" conceptions of human behavior, such as, "It's just human nature," or, "Human nature never changes," serve to bolster resistances to learning and to discourage systematic approaches to change. The laboratory must include opportunities to internalize usable conceptual frameworks in determining the direction of change.

HESITATION TO ACCEPT OR TO GIVE HELPFUL REACTIONS. In any laboratory, a considerable amount of support comes from peers. If trainees have had no previous experience which legitimizes such help as part of a learning process, or if an atmosphere of mutual trust has not been developed, peer learning influences will not be offered, or they may even be deleterious, if indiscriminately released. A laboratory must encourage a pattern of interchange of support from individual to individual. Interpersonal feedback, however, if it precedes the emergence of such interpersonal relations, may actually increase distrust. Laboratory trainers generally discourage too early personal feedback.

LACK OF CONNECTION SEEN BETWEEN LABORATORY AND POTENTIAL UTILIZATION. The contrast between experience in the laboratory and life in other associations may be seen by trainees as so great that they find difficulty in relating behavioral gains made in the laboratory with the maintenance of such gains in their home situations. The laboratory design, consequently, must include assistance in planning the application of laboratory learnings.

Optimal Conditions of Training and Learning

A more or less systematic conception of training-learning processes in the laboratory has been implied in this exploration of participant reactions to entering and joining creatively in the life of the laboratory community. This conception has yet to be made explicit. The viewpoint necessarily shifts at this point from the standpoint of the learner to that of the trainer. The presentation is made in terms of conditions required for optimum training and learning in the laboratory setting.

THE GENERATING OF BEHAVIORAL OUTPUT FOR ANALYSIS AND LEARNING. If the major content for laboratory learning comprises the actions and interactions of members, situations must be created in the laboratory to bring forth such actions and interactions for open study. This behavioral output must take place under conditions conducive to testing patterns that may need improvement or change. Because the trainer cannot possibly know the specific areas of perception and action in which each individual may feel inadequate, he cannot establish fully directed experiences early, lest these conceal rather than reveal priority learning needs. If patterns of perception, valuation, and behavior are to be exposed for assessment and possible change, a range of learning situations needs to be provided. These will vary in the degree of prestructuring by trainers, but in all cases they will provide opportunities for free interaction among members of the learning group.

In the T Group, for example, the structure is minimal. Members of the group are usually told that they can learn much about their own behavior and that of others, and about group behavior, from continuous observation and analysis of experiences in the group. The trainer refuses to act as a discussion leader, but proposes to help group members to find ways of utilizing their experiences for learning.

Essentially, a kind of social vacuum is produced. Leadership, agenda, procedures, expectations, usually pre-established by some authority, are blurred or missing. As tension produced by the vacuum mounts, members endeavor to supply the missing elements and their behavior output also mounts. Because the group has not developed ways of making decisions, suggestions for action are generally not accepted by the group. In fact, because of the tensions produced by the ambiguous situation, individuals have difficulty in even hearing the contributions of others, let alone acting on them. Individuals, as the group endeavors to form some viable structure and organization, face situations and dilemmas they have not faced before, and so begin a process of testing, trying out, and testing again. The accompanying figure represents the beginning T Group as a way of generating a rich behavioral output for subsequent analysis and learning.

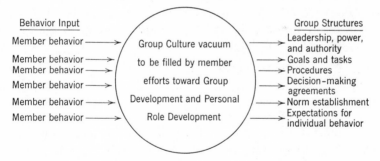

A VACUUM TO PRODUCE EXPERIENCES FOR LEARNING

Other more structured parts of the laboratory program do not elicit such a dramatic output of behavior as the T Group. But they too provide opportunity for individuals to act and interact and to assess their actions and interactions.

A CLIMATE OF PERMISSIVENESS AND INQUIRY. Creating learning experiences, through exposure of behavior in areas where learning is desired, requires a climate of permissiveness to behave without threat

of punishment and a climate which supports joint inquiry into behaviors and their consequences. Until trust between members and
between trainer and members in the group is developed, individuals
will inhibit actions and behave defensively toward efforts to encourage
them to talk about their behavior, feelings, perceptions, or thoughts.

Trust encourages candor and willingness to collect and study data
about the present and changing behavior of members. The training
staff, therefore, works to develop such a climate both through their
own efforts to model inquiring responses to incidents that occur—to
inhibit moralizing about member behavior, to resist pressures of the
group to silence "troublesome" members rather than listen to them,
to be open themselves to feedback from others—and through encouraging other members to enlarge the boundaries of trust and to establish
processes of inquiry within the group.

COLLABORATIVE RELATIONSHIPS FOR LEARNING. In a laboratory where
learning is sought concerning intrapersonal and interpersonal, as well
as intragroup and intergroup behaviors, the major learning impact for
each individual must come from other group members. As the individual contributes to group action through expressing thoughts, feelings, and perceptions, he receives reactions from the rest of the group
which may help him to assess and improve his behavior and perceptions. Thus, relations among peers are of paramount importance in
the learning of all members.

The role of the trainer is largely to work toward the development
of collaborative relations among members. As a special member of
the group he also shares his reactions with the group. And he may
expect reactions to his behaviors to be fed back to him.

MODELS FOR DATA COLLECTION AND STUDY. For effective learning to
take place, adequate models are needed for data collection and analysis. These may be suggested by the trainer or invented by the group.
Data-collection methods range widely. They include the use of: scales
and instruments to gather data about member perceptions of various
phases of group process; process observers; subgroups to diagnose
causes of certain problems; dyadic interviews among members to
compare and report reactions to specific group incidents; individual
reflection; and the replaying of tape recordings of a group meeting.
In all instances the data collected are the property of the group, and
use of the data is planned by the group.

The functions of the trainer in data collection are to collect data
himself and to encourage the group to develop and use data-collection
devices. He also encourages as wide and deep analysis of the data

as is possible within the limits of the group's current ability to tolerate and gain from such analysis. The laboratory trainer encourages the group to develop a feedback system through which it is legitimate and acceptable for various individuals' reactions to the here-and-now behavior of themselves and others to be fed back to the group.

MAPS FOR UNDERSTANDING AND ORGANIZING EXPERIENCES. Present experiences must be related to patterns which the individual has accumulated from past experiences, if learning is to occur. Effective learning requires examination and reassessment by participants of value systems, conceptual frameworks, prejudices and stereotypes, and ways of judging and deciding which they have developed before their entry into the laboratory.

The laboratory provides opportunities and encouragement for such reassessments; however, the staff is obligated also to present tested and usable "theories." Theoretical materials presented are of three general sorts.

1. Cognitive concepts for understanding human behavior at various levels of organization: the person, the "interperson," the group, and larger social systems.
2. Principles underlying various value positions, including the values of democracy.
3. Models for diagnosing and acting in human situations, particularly models useful to the agent of change.

EXPERIMENTATION WITH NEW BEHAVIORS. Learning becomes integrated into the total pattern of the behavior of an individual most effectively when he has opportunity to experiment in a clearly defined way with new ways of behaving. Unless he can try out new behaviors in a situation where he is not "playing for keeps" and where he can discard a new behavior if it does not work, he will be hesitant to behave differently when "the chips are down" back home. The training laboratory provides opportunities for individual and group experimentation with new behaviors both in the T Group and in more structured opportunities provided in many laboratory designs.

GENERALIZING AND PLANNING APPLICATIONS. Experiences need to be generalized if they are to be applied to other situations. Application of learning to other situations, where forces may be directed against learning, must be carefully considered and planned. Consultative help in diagnosing situational forces which will support or resist application attempts is provided. The responsibility for such diagnosis and planning rests with the participant, but the help of other partici-

pants and of staff members is ordinarily made available. The participant is asked particularly to use the self-knowledge he has acquired in
the laboratory to assess his place in his home situation both in creating
problems and in solving them.

In this chapter, the laboratory method of education has been examined from several vantage points. In the next chapter the processes
of designing a particular training experience utilizing this method will
be explored in detail.

3

Designing the Laboratory

Kenneth D. Benne
Leland P. Bradford
Ronald Lippitt

The design of a laboratory program grows out of the confrontation and interplay between general factors (principles and orientations) and particular factors (the concrete, empirical realities of staff, participants, time, and physical facilities and resources). Thus each laboratory design becomes almost a unique invention. The aim is to achieve organic rather than additive interrelations among the experiential parts of the laboratory program. This chapter attempts to clarify the processes of deliberation, participation, and decision which enter into the forging and testing of a laboratory design.

Challenges Faced by a Staff in Designing a Laboratory Program

The general principles and orientations of laboratory method operate in staff planning in several ways. They define the kind of educational enterprise the staff is seeking to create. They function in selecting, shaping, and pretesting particular training activities and continuities. And they supply criteria for evaluating particular training events and the design as a whole.

Five curriculum elements, or "experience continuities," can be derived from the general requirements of laboratory method. It will be useful to identify these briefly before discussing in greater detail the particular challenges which a laboratory staff must handle as they shape a laboratory design.

Experience Continuities Essential to a Laboratory Experience

THE HERE-AND-NOW FOCUS.   Immediate experiences of participants furnish the basic ingredients for laboratory learning.   The struggles of groups to achieve satisfactory organization and forward movement, the strivings by members to find a place in the formation and functioning of their groups, the efforts of members to integrate discrepant demands stemming from multiple memberships, within and without the laboratory—all of these experiences yield vivid and personal content for learning.   Such learning can be accomplished best if participants are assisted in collecting data about their efforts—personal and collective—and in analyzing these data collaboratively.   A major focus in every laboratory program is on releasing significant here-and-now experiences for analysis, conceptualization, practice, and generalization.

THE THERE-AND-THEN FOCUS.   At appropriate times, attention needs also to be directed to situations away from the laboratory, more particularly to those situations in which participants have lived and will live again after the laboratory is ended.   If learnings and behavioral gains begun in the training program are to weather transplanting from the laboratory island to mainlands of life and work, participant attention needs to be focused on the relations between here-and-now and there-and-then.   This ordinarily involves the diagnosis of forces at home which are resistant to or supportive of better ways of functioning.   It includes assistance in developing realistic commitments to continue such diagnosis in collaboration with associates at home.

FOCUS ON SOCIAL AND VALUE PERSPECTIVES.   In the associational life of the laboratory the participant is challenged to reassess the adequacy of his value orientations and social perspectives as well as his motivations, knowledges, and skills.   This may deeply threaten self-concepts. The participant ordinarily needs support in focusing reconstructive attention upon discrepancies among the differing values he lives by in various parts of his life or between his interpersonal values and the values implicit in his orientation to larger social issues and problems.

FOCUS ON THE USE OF TOOLS AND SKILLS OF INQUIRY.   Learning and growth can be materially advanced as the individual improves his skills in inquiry—in data collection, data analysis, diagnosis, experimentation, and evaluation. As these inquiry skills are developed, the individual becomes less dependent upon authority figures to teach him what he needs to learn and better able to use peer resources in clarifying and solving problems in his life. Skills of inquiry may also help him to be more competent in assessing forces which affect change in situations away from the laboratory and in enlisting others in joint assessment and modification of these forces.

FOCUS ON SELF AS AN AGENT OF CHANGE. Unless the individual perceives his need for continued learning and growth and accepts personal responsibility for initiating steps toward learning, unless he has reduced internal barriers and blocks to his learning, and unless he has learned to receive help from others and to give help to others in processes of changing, little continuing learning or change will take place in himself or in the social systems of which he is a part outside the laboratory. The training laboratory assists the participant to see himself, actually and potentially, as an agent of change.

Conditions in Developing Productive Staff-Learner Relationships

Relationships between staff members and learners in a laboratory are more complex than those normally found in educational programs. Because the input for learning comes mainly from the interactions of group members rather than from knowledge selected and assigned by the trainer, the staff member does not have the authority customary in teacher-student relationships. His primary function is to help learners form groups for learning purposes and to learn from the experiences they develop. Conditions which encourage the exploration and development of changing and flexible relations between trainer and learners must be part of a training design.

In an effective laboratory the staff member utilizes a variety of roles in facilitating learning. He functions alternately as participant, encourager, or reality tester, and as observer and interpreter of group and individual behavior. He may find it desirable to serve from time to time as consultant and as counselor. He usually finds it necessary to supply concepts and knowledge needed to analyze experiential situations.

These various functions may at times be in conflict in his own mind as well as in the minds of participants. The laboratory design must provide opportunity for the trainer to work through problems emerging in his relationships with learners. Staff designing should also include time for each staff member to consider, singly and with other staff members, the variety of functions he may be required to fulfill, the impact of his personal needs, personality characteristics, and trainer style, and ways by which he may better assist the group to develop a collaborative relationship with him and to cope effectively with his behavior.

Achieving Full Utilization and Growth of Staff

A training laboratory is most effective when staff members have planned the laboratory program together and have learned to work as a team. Building a team for more productive working together and for aiding in one another's professional growth occurs only if four more specific opportunities are planned.

OPPORTUNITY TO INTEGRATE DIFFERENT STAFF RESOURCES. Staff members come from different institutions and different job assignments. They operate with somewhat different constructs about human behavior and change. They not infrequently represent different disciplines within the behavioral sciences. And each brings a different profile of abilities. Staff members differ also in prestige and status in the community of trainers. Some of these differences are easy to discuss openly. Others present greater difficulty. Certain standards must therefore be built into processes of staff planning—for open expression of feelings, needs, and points of view; for avoidance of majority pressures to subdue a minority member or subgroup; for taking group time for analysis of staff processes as well as for work on staff tasks.

OPPORTUNITY TO EXPERIMENT WITH INNOVATIONS IN TRAINING. Each laboratory faces the task of developing a balance between utilizing tested learning experiences and encouraging training innovations so that the staff will contribute to the developing store of training technologies. Innovation is also important in enabling the staff to try out new training ideas in which they are interested. The appropriate balance between expected service to participants and opportunities for staff experimentation and professional development is difficult for a staff to determine and hold to, but it is an important problem to be worked through by each staff.

OPPORTUNITY FOR STAFF MEMBERS TO MEET DURING THE LABORATORY SESSION. Prelaboratory planning can never foretell completely the training problems which will emerge. Planning for a laboratory program means planning ways in which the laboratory may remain flexible and sensitive to the emerging learning needs of staff members and participants. To insure this flexibility, the laboratory plan should include ways of probing participant reactions and frequent meetings in which staff members can deal with unanticipated training problems, as well as continue their work on staff relationships and on problems of their own personal and professional growth.

INTEGRATION OF TRAINING AND RESEARCH INTERESTS AND PROGRAMS. Research should be a part of every training laboratory. Data should be systematically collected concerning the progress of the laboratory program, the integration of its parts, and the emergence of unanticipated learning needs in order that discussions about changes in the program can be adequately informed. In addition, long-range research into the processes and methods of laboratory training is necessary if laboratory training is to continue to improve.

Research data collected by research staff can frequently be fed into the learning processes of the laboratory to supplement the data participants and trainers are themselves collecting. The integration of research and training programs in a laboratory does not ordinarily come easily or naturally. Data collection and experimentation are sometimes seen, both by participants and by training staff, as an intrusion into learning activities. Laboratory planning should therefore include time and opportunity to work through relationships between research and training staff. Participants must also have opportunity to understand and accept their role in the research process. This is usually most easily accomplished if some promise of research feedback can be made.

Adapting Training to a Particular Population of Participants

Participants in one laboratory differ from participants in another laboratory. First, their needs for learning differ. Learning needs cannot, of course, be fully anticipated in advance of training, but data collected from participants before the laboratory are useful to a staff in getting a feeling for initially perceived learning needs of the particular population with whom they are to work. Expectations concerning what the laboratory will be like also vary from one participant group to another. While shock to unrealistic expectations is a part of every laboratory experience, it is well for staff members to know and respect the initial expectations of participants, even as they seek to reshape them realistically. Participants also differ widely in degree of sophistication in the content and language of the behavioral sciences and the helping professions. It is useful for staff members to know the sophistication level of the particular population as they make decisions about program content and emphasis.

Adapting Training Plans to Available Physical Limitations and Resources

One of the more obvious limitations to which a training staff must adjust its plans is the time available. Lack of adequate time makes more acute the difficulties of integrating staff differences which center in different valuations of various training experiences. Yet the same shortness of time forces a confrontation of differences in training ideology among staff members. If the resulting conflicts can be handled creatively, innovations in training technology and staff growth can result.

The residential facilities for a given laboratory must be chosen ahead of staff planning with the general requirements of laboratory training in mind. And basic library materials, supplies, and equipment are, of necessity, assembled before a specific laboratory design has been worked out in detail. A laboratory staff must always plan within the limits of available facilities. Not infrequently, the very lack of ideal facilities and equipment, if staff morale is high, can stimulate innovations in training methodology and designs.

How do these various determinants enter into the deliberations of a laboratory staff? And how can they be reconciled in shaping an organic and integrated educational plan? The following case record is an account of how one staff answered these questions. It is presented as a fairly representative picture of laboratory staff planning.

Staff Planning of a Training Laboratory: A Case Record

Four days before the beginning of the training laboratory, the staff came together to design the program. The participant body—nearly a hundred persons drawn from a variety of occupations and from many parts of the country—were to arrive the following Sunday. The staff was composed of fifteen persons. Eight were experienced trainers drawn from the fields of social and clinical psychology, sociology, education, and psychiatry. Two were training interns who had just finished an intensive six-week training program and were to serve as assistant trainers. One staff member, a psychiatrist, was designated as laboratory counselor. His functions included help to participants with personal problems which might arise as well as consultation with staff members about puzzling behavioral events in their laboratory groups. The four other members of the staff were a research team.

The staff coordinator, selected beforehand by the director of NTL, had met earlier with other staff coordinators to formulate some general policies to guide all NTL laboratories during the year. He opened the meeting of the total staff, suggesting that the staff talk about how they wished to utilize the four planning days. He reminded the group that they faced the task of developing a training design and of working out any problems which might develop in the accommodation and integration of research and training. But first, he reviewed the general agreements (of which the group had been informed by letter) arrived at by staff coordinators.

For example, a decision had been made that certain research projects would be repeated in each of the laboratory sessions in order that sufficient data could be collected and also to take advantage of comparisons between somewhat different populations. The research staff would review these projects with the training staff a little later.

He reminded them, further, of an agreement that all laboratory sessions would give attention to the problems of participants in attempting to apply laboratory learnings to their situations back home. The staff was perfectly free to design those learning situations pertaining to application that in their judgment would be most effective.

Finally, he stressed his hope that the staff could be creative and innovative in producing an interesting and effective design—and a sound one. To help, he reminded them of the wealth of material produced in former laboratories which was on hand for them to review.

There was then some general discussion focusing mainly on clarifying exactly what was expected and testing whether these expectations would limit staff planning. The research team then reviewed briefly the continuing projects on which they were working and set a time when they would meet again with the training staff.

At this point, the coordinator suggested that the staff might not want to get into the details of designing until they had had time to work on staff relationships and to share ideas and suggestions for new training approaches. He wondered, therefore, if they did not want to utilize at least the first day of planning time in talking generally about ideas for the program and in working on their relationships within the staff.

Perhaps they might want to have a short T Group of their own to help form an effective staff group in which conflicts could be used in creating new ideas.

Building the Staff Team and Assessing Staff Resources

The staff agreed that they would talk in a leisurely way about training, about individual hopes concerning the direction this laboratory would take, about innovations individuals were anxious to have considered, about ways in which the staff members could learn from one another, and finally about ways in which they could share feelings about difficulties among themselves, if and as such difficulties developed.

The first planning day did develop in this way. Issues among staff members began to emerge. Some staff members believed that the program should give primary emphasis to individual learnings about self and about self in relation to others. Others hoped that more emphasis might be placed on group behavior, on the role functions of group members, and on the consequences of individual member behavior. Two staff members urged that participants be given an opportunity to learn more about intergroup relations and about organizational and community behavior.

The staff agreed that all of these areas of learning were important. The issue was the emphasis that should be chosen, given the time limitation of two weeks. As they talked further, some staff members began to take issue concerning the basic purpose and direction laboratory training in general should take. Some members believed that the basic purpose of a laboratory in human behavior was almost solely to increase the internal satisfaction and wholeness of each individual by enabling him to understand and accept himself more completely. This required intensive work in T Groups on basic personal problems of authority, intimacy, relationships between sexes, and feelings of inadequacy, among others. As the person became more integrated as an individual, they argued, he could better perform role functions in the social systems in which he had membership. Other members thought that this approach verged on group therapy. The proponents argued that the line between therapy and learning is very indistinct and that a program of therapy for normals is needed.

Other staff members, while agreeing that effective learning and change in the area of personal behavior had therapeutic overtones, were concerned lest it be assumed that effective therapy could be accomplished in two weeks. One member pointed out that the issue was misunderstood if therapy was thought of only in connection with psychotic or highly neurotic cases. Normal people could enter more easily into a process of understanding difficulties in relationships and could utilize help more readily.

Another staff member felt it extremely important that any assistance from feedback from peers or even from the trainer should be related clearly and rather directly to role functioning of the individual in his various social organizations outside the laboratory. Trainers should try to see that this connection is made.

This led another member to remind the group that individuals coming to a laboratory were not indiscriminately chosen. In many instances they were being sent by an organization to improve their ability to function more effectively as leaders and members in the organization and to help the organization to find ways to improve its functioning. He felt that, while an increasing understanding of self is very important in improving role functioning, this emphasis should be balanced with emphasis on understanding the role and developing skills for functioning in the role, whether that of leader, member, or change agent.

Still another staff member pointed out that even if the purpose of the laboratory were solely to increase the adequacy of self, a learning group would need to be created. This would require attention to group processes, standards, and climate. Unless a group climate of trust could be built by the group, feedback of reactions to personal behavior could result in damage to individuals as well as in destruction of the group. He felt that gaining skills in group membership could be integrated with increasing understanding of self. Other comments indicated that, while differences among trainers would remain, all were concerned to create an effective program of training, and sufficient agreement could be found as they worked together toward this end.

The discussion moved on to a closely related issue: the time that should be devoted to T Groups as opposed to other learning activities such as skill-practice exercises, theory sessions, participative cases, simulation exercises, and application groups. Again there was a wide range of opinion. All agreed that the T Group was central. But some felt that experience in T Groups was generally all that was needed with some interspersed theory sessions, while others thought that learnings from the T Group could be better expanded and supported in other laboratory activities rather than by more work in the T Group itself. Still others felt there was content that should be taught and that this could be done better in groupings separate from the T Group. These differences were discussed at sufficient length to indicate that some agreement could probably be reached as the staff came to face the details of designing.

Before the group went to work on other issues, someone suggested that they examine data that were available about the participants who were coming to this laboratory. The others agreed. Accordingly, they took time out to read individually the participant application forms and accompanying letters. They saw that teams of two to six persons were coming from five different organizations. This raised the question as to whether a team should be placed in one T Group or split up among the groups. Based on successful experience with family programs in organizations, some felt that it would be better to keep each team intact. Others pointed out that no team was large enough to form a T Group by itself. A team within a T Group might create cleavages. While no decision was reached, the staff coordinator felt that the ultimate decision would probably be to split up team members but to plan time in other parts of the program when staff could help teams work out problems in relationships and plan for continued work in their home organizations.

One staff member pointed out that there were a number of participants who had no role anchorage in an organization larger than a family. These were wives of participants and staff members. There was some discussion as to whether these housewives, unable to relate learnings to an organizational setting, would feel out of place. Others pointed out, however, that these women did have a role anchorage in the family and that a family is an important and complex social organization.

This brought up the question of families accompanying participants to the laboratory. What efforts, if any, should be made to integrate families into the program, or to provide training programs for wives, teen-agers, or children? The staff coordinator reminded the staff of the day camp for younger children which the laboratory organization provided and suggested that they might discuss other possibilities for family programs later.

The latter part of the first evening was spent in talking directly about their own relationships. There was considerable openness as each shared with others his fears and hopes about the kinds of relationships that might develop in the staff. The interns were particularly concerned with discussing their status in the staff team. The staff agreed that they should meet periodically throughout the laboratory session, at lunch every weekday, and occasionally in late afternoon periods.

Detailed Designing of the Laboratory Program

On the morning of the second planning day the staff began to work on the details of the training design. The staff coordinator drew on the blackboard spaces for each period of the day in each of the thirteen training days.

DATA COLLECTION FOR LEARNING. As they turned their attention to the opening session scheduled for late Sunday afternoon, discussion came to focus on a data-collection device which might be useful for participant learning. One staff member had used it in another laboratory program. The device contained fourteen seven-point scales, each describing an aspect of member behavior in a group. By checking these scales, each participant, before he entered into any group experience in the laboratory, described his view of himself as a group member. He was also asked to choose the three or four scales along which he would most like to change and to indicate the direction and extent of change desired. Later, he checked the scales again and then received back his original coded effort. This enabled each participant to compare changes in his original perception of himself with later perceptions. Participants from the same T Group talked over their changes either with a subgroup of three or four members or with the entire group so that each could check his self-perceptions against the perceptions of others who had come to know him well.

The staff member suggesting the device said that most persons found perceptions of their own behavior changing quite radically after training. In many instances, in the second administration they chose entirely different areas of behavior in which they most desired to change, the change being from items dealing with ability to influence others, to items dealing with their own awareness of self and others and with ability to express feelings. A comparison of the two self-ratings could lead to considerable insight. In addition, as members reported changes and insights gained, other group members were able to feed back very useful observations. In fact, said the staff member, the T-Group session in which this activity was carried out was seen by many participants as one of the most meaningful. He proposed that the staff consider using it at the beginning and near the end of the present program.

The staff decided to use the set of scales, with the first administration during the opening session and the second during the opening of one of the T-Group sessions late in the second week. At this point, a staff member suggested that if this test was so valuable in the T Group, would not a similar scale dealing with perceptions of role functioning in the work organizations of the members also be valuable? Might it not provide insights important in planning application of laboratory learnings to the job situation?

Some felt that two tests might appear to be too much research to the participants. Others wondered whether one scale would contaminate the other. The suggestion also raised the question as to how much time should be spent on organizational behavior and on back-home application.

It became clear, after further discussion, that the decision would probably permit some emphasis on organizational behavior and some attention to application of learnings to there-and-then situations. The staff tentatively decided to give both scales, each requiring about a half hour's time, on the opening Sunday afternoon.

NUMBER AND DISTRIBUTION OF T-GROUP SESSIONS. The staff members quickly decided to hold the first meeting of the T Group on Sunday night. All agreed that there should be an intensification of T-Group time early in the laboratory session in order to create a considerable amount of behavioral data for subsequent analysis. This concentration of T-Group experience was also necessary to create a climate of trust and nondefensiveness as quickly as possible. Some staff thought that this heavy concentration of time in T Groups should continue throughout the period with at least two T-Group sessions every day. But most others felt that the T Groups needed the support of some skill training and practice both in observation and in the utilization of observational data. This point of view ultimately became accepted, and the discussion centered around the types of skill practice that would be most helpful.

SKILL-PRACTICE SESSIONS. One staff member went to the blackboard and sketched a design for a practice session in group observation. In this exercise, participants were organized into groups of six members each, with two of the six members serving as observers. The remaining four would be asked to carry through a group decision-making task. Afterward the two observers would feed back their observations for discussion. In a two-hour period all six members would receive experiences both as observers and as participants.

At first, the design contemplated forming groups of six with mem-

bers from different T Groups. Individuals might feel freer to participate in the small-group experiences, it was thought, if observation
were not by other members of their own T Group. Another staff member disagreed. As many experiences as possible should be related to
the T Group. Would the experience not work as well, he asked, if
each T Group were divided into two groups of six for the skill practice? Each half of the T Group could then report its experiences to
the other half.

Another staff member wondered whether the split T Group did not
create an artificial situation. If the skill practice would work in a
divided T Group, might it not work just as well in the total group?
Why not have one total T Group observe another T Group? T-Group
members could actually see similarities and differences between their
group and another T Group at a crucial time in the life of all T Groups.
This, he maintained, might lend perspective on the internal processes
of their own T Group. In addition, observations might arouse competitive feelings between the two groups and thus generate additional
problems for each T Group to work through and learn from. Finally,
what occurred in each group would provide common data for all to
discuss. And group members would gain experience in observing
and feeding back data to another group.

The staff finally came to the tentative decision to hold the intergroup observation exercise after each T Group had lived through two
sessions.

PAIRED INTERVIEWS. The staff considered at this point two earlier
suggestions related to work in the T Groups. One member had
brought up the question of again using a training device on feedback,
originally growing out of a research project. The method called for
pairing T-Group members, selected at random each day, to interview
each other for fifteen minutes before the T-Group session. During
the first few days interview questions would have to do with difficulties each person saw the group encountering and what each individual thought he might do to help. Later, suggested questions might be
changed.

The staff member thought that these interviews helped learning in
the T Group. Interview pairs frequently brought their conversations
into the T-Group discussions and this tended to produce a stimulating
beginning. Reticent and isolated individuals often found it easier to
start talking with one other person than with the entire group. In addition, the other person often helped open the way for the timid individual to participate more actively in the group.

Other staff members came in to agree as to the value of the method or to cast doubts upon it. Some were concerned that it drained off problems better handled, in terms of learning for all members, in the T Group. Others worried that anxious members received temporary support from the reassurance of one other member, rather than more enduring help in the T Group. But most staff members came to think that the interviews did help individuals to identify problems and to bring them into the group. As the group developed, this outside support would probably not be needed.

The final decision was to schedule the interviews the first week and to decide toward the end of the week whether they should be continued.

TAPE LISTENING. One tape recorder was available for use in each T Group for the entire session. Participants were to be reassured that the taping was strictly for training purposes. They would be encouraged to play back tapes of sessions to refresh themselves about crucial incidents, to check their individual perceptions of T-Group events, and to enable each individual to listen alone, or with a few others, to a session that had been particularly important to him.

Some groups spend considerable time late at night listening to tapes of their groups, while others spend little or no time. One staff member said that participants often had no awareness of the value of listening to tapes. He preferred, therefore, that one evening session early in the first week be spent in each T Group's listening to the tape of one or more previous sessions.

The staff discussed whether or not to schedule such a session; whether, if one were held, the sections of tape to listen to should be selected by staff or by a committee of participants; and whether predetermined sections of various tapes should be chosen or one tape played through with opportunity to stop the tape at any point for discussion. Some staff members thought that spending an entire session on tape listening might be robbing time from work on T-Group problems. Others thought that a listening session might help a group to gain new insight into its problems and perhaps move (or shock) some individuals into a process of personal learning and change.

Having participants select sections of tapes would avoid listening to long periods of interaction where no important data were produced and enable the group to concentrate on crucial episodes. It would also involve participants more actively in planning for their own learning. One staff member, however, recalled experiences where a subgroup of participants used their authority to select sections of tapes as a way of controlling the group and, in fact, prevented other members from listening to incidents which were important to them. He suggested that placing this responsibility in the hands of the participants this early in the program gave them training responsibilities they were not necessarily prepared to handle and failed to utilize the professional abilities of the trainers. No agreement on this issue could be reached.

Out of the discussion came the decision to utilize Tuesday evening's session for tape listening but to let each T-Group trainer decide how best to plan the meeting.

THEORY SESSIONS. Blocks of time were gradually being filled in the schedule, with T-Group meetings scheduled for each morning and for some of the evenings of the first week. As planning started in the evening session of the second day, one staff member said that he thought it was time to discuss what cognitive material should be fed into the learning of participants and how this was to be done.

The resulting discussion dealt with differences among staff members as to whether much cognitive input was required at all, whether trainer comments on group events, along with peer feedback, did not provide a sufficient framework for learning from these events. Some thought, in fact, that formal cognitive input tended to make immediate learning experiences artificial and to encourage verbal pseudo-resolutions of the dilemmas faced by the group. The discussion also dealt with differences of opinion as to what cognitive information it was most important to present. Individual staff needs and interests in giving favorite lectures and in being rewarded by the approval of participants became obvious in the comments of some members. This was pointed out and discussed. Feelings of inadequacy which some staff members felt in giving lectures or handling large-group meetings were also discussed. Past experiments with the input of cognitive material but with little total staff or participant satisfaction were cited. Most staff members came to agree on the need for cognitive input. They continued to disagree about the content, the frequency, and the methods.

A suggestion was made to hold daily town meetings in which participant interests in further knowledge could be tapped on the spot and supplied promptly by various staff members. Another suggestion that cognitive material be fed into each T Group during the hour following a T-Group session was also discussed. This was finally discarded because some staff members were concerned with the shift in role required and the further difficulties presented in terms of handling authority relations with the trainer.

The staff turned next to what content within the behavioral sciences would have most relevance in explaining and generalizing other laboratory experiences and most lasting value to participants both in their continued individual growth and in their functionings as leaders and members beyond the laboratory. The need to do everything possible to enable participants to discuss feelings as well as ideas and facts, was accepted by all staff members. It was agreed there should be one or two sessions on emotional reactions in interpersonal and group settings. Assistance in understanding the complexities of group behavior and in taking effective membership was also seen as necessary by most staff members. Three sessions dealing with problems of membership in groups and with the dynamics of group behavior were finally scheduled.

A third category of cognitive input finally agreed upon dealt with problems of learning through interaction with others and of giving and receiving help in learning. The staff decided that this was best tied in with skill-practice sessions.

Discussion about "theory" of organizational behavior resulted in the decision to give whatever was necessary to make meaningful any training exercise focused on problems of diagnosing organizational difficulties, in the event the staff decided that such an exercise was to be included in the schedule.

APPLICATION OF LEARNINGS TO OTHER SITUATIONS. With the issues about "theory" presentations at least partly settled and with a subcommittee appointed to work the next day in outlining the general content and order of theory sessions, the staff turned, during the morning session of its third planning day, to the question of how much emphasis should be given to training for application of learnings to situations apart from the laboratory.

One staff member said that he had watched staffs delay consideration of problems of application until they were well into the planning of the second week's program. This happened because it seemed logical to think about transferring learnings when the program approached its end and participants were thinking about returning home. But, as a result, training for application was hurried and not always well handled. In addition, because no emphasis had been placed on application until this point, participants had to wrench their thinking from problems which concerned them in the here-and-now to those which they would have to face in the future. Would it lead to better learning, he asked, if participants were helped to hold transfer problems in mind throughout the laboratory? Actually, he added, the scales to be used on the opening afternoon had this for one of their purposes.

The discussion which followed indicated that no one disagreed with the desirability of planning about transfer of learnings early in the program so long as it did not interrupt interest in here-and-now learning, but some members thought it might disrupt the flow of laboratory experiences and contaminate here-and-now data with there-and-then information. The T Groups, one member pointed out, needed intense involvement in present activities if they were to build an effective learning group. Anything which interfered could serve as flight from "real" learning.

There was obviously some ambivalence in the group. The staff coordinator reminded them of the policy-level agreement to include some emphasis on training for application in each laboratory. The problem, he said, was how much time to spend on such training and where to place it. The staff member who had urged early as well as later attention to transfer problems said he had thought of utilizing only one afternoon and one evening session of the program during the first week. He further thought he saw ways of gearing such sessions into the experiences of T Groups.

Staff members invited him to outline his plan. He suggested that a program might start with a short lecture on the problems of "being different back home" after a training experience, and of initiating changes. The lecture would stress the importance of diagnosis of the home situation and of the individual's own motivations, abilities, and power. Each participant could then be asked to spend an hour in writing a case description of one area of improvement he thought, at this time, he would like to encourage his organization to deal with, and to formulate questions he might ask members of his T Group to discuss in helping him to think realistically about what he could do.

After this period of individual reflection and writing, each individual would meet with two other individuals from his T Group. Each of the three would have nearly an hour in which to explore his present thinking about his situation at home and to get reactions from the other two, based primarily on their experiences with him during the first few days of the laboratory.

The staff discussed this proposal at considerable length. Some felt that the tie-in with T-Group data would make thoughts about application more realistic. Furthermore, it might stimulate processes of feedback in the T Groups and thus add to the impact on the T Group of the morning paired interviews.

Other staff members were concerned that feedback to individuals on a planned basis was premature at this stage. They believed it might result in judgmental feedback and advice giving if carried on when the trainer would not be present to moderate or point out judgmental responses.

Another staff member said that participants were being asked to give and receive help, tasks requiring great skill, with little understanding of the skills involved and no practice in using them. He suggested as an alternative a specific exercise in giving help. This involved four-man groups. One person would present his problem. Two individuals would have been briefed to help him, one by raising questions and probing to help the presenter redefine his problem or see aspects of it he had not considered before, the other by giving action recommendations as to how the presenter should solve his problem. An observer, the fourth member in the group, would take notes on reactions to the two styles of helping and, at the end of the exercise, initiate a discussion in the group about ways of giving help.

The staff members liked this plan, which could be contained in a single afternoon session. In replanning the exercise it was agreed that participants would still be encouraged first to write up a problem they faced back home and to list their questions or concerns. The participants who were not presenters in the first week would have an opportunity for consultation during the second week. Thus, the first week's exercise would not stand in isolation from later efforts to learn about application.

LEARNING ABOUT LARGER SOCIAL SYSTEMS. It had been apparent from the first that two staff members wanted the program to include some emphasis on organizational or community behavior. One of these now spoke of the importance to individuals of learning to face the problems of conflict among groups and learning the results of win-lose postures. He reviewed with the staff, most of whom had previously utilized intergroup competitive experiences in training, the values that could result from such experience. A T Group which loses in competition with another T Group, for example, generally passes through a process of "scapegoating" outside groups and/or specific members of their own group in rationalizing their failure, and then, with help, moves on to re-examine their own internal process and organization. This ordinarily leads to a period of reorganization and growth. A group which wins experiences a period of smugness and self-congratulations and then, with skillful assistance from the trainer, also moves on to examination of itself and to further growth. Thus, in addition to what participants learn about intergroup relations and conflict, an effective intergroup experience has beneficial impacts on the T Group and on subsequent learnings.

The other staff member interested in larger social systems said that while he found the intergroup competition experience excellent for learning purposes, he had also obtained valuable results from an exercise stressing cooperation between groups. After all, while the intergroup exercise revealed some of the regressive results from win-lose competition, it did not indicate the positive values in cooperative problem solving. If time permitted, he believed that an intergroup competitive exercise followed by an intergroup cooperative exercise provided opportunities for learnings of both kinds. If time were not available for both, he would recommend the exercise on cooperation.

Three other staff members had had experience with both exercises. One preferred the competition exercise and two the other. Various members were concerned over the loss of T-Group time if both exercises were used. A few trainers were also concerned over distracting members from emerging T-Group problems. Most others felt that such outside experiences enhanced learning by coming just when the group needed some way of testing its organizational structure.

One member here suggested another way in which new group experience could be provided to enhance learnings. This involved entering a new group with a different member composition. The different composition, with only two or three from each T Group included, would provide new interaction experiences. It might also enable individuals to try out different behavioral approaches which had been suggested by T-Group experiences but which they had had difficulty in trying out in the T Group. For additional learnings, the new groups might be composed experimentally with individuals of similar personality or behavioral characteristics grouped together.

Two other staff members had had experience with such groups formed during the middle of a laboratory period and lasting for a few days, along with T-Group sessions. They reported that participants, while they often did not like the first session of a new group because it was too reminiscent of the opening session of their T Group, found many values in it and many experiences to bring back to the T Group.

After considerable discussion it was decided not to hold an intergroup competition and to postpone the cooperation exercise until the second week. The staff group did decide to have N (New) Groups during the last two days of the first week. A subcommittee was appointed to consider the basis of the composition of these groups.

TRAINING-RESEARCH INTEGRATION. The research staff met with the training staff late in the third day of planning to discuss the time requirements of the research designs and to work out any difficulties this might entail.

Three major research projects were planned. Two were continuations of projects from previous sessions. In one, attempts were being made to measure attitudinal and behavioral changes in certain dimensions both during and after the laboratory. Another dealt with the consequences of different group compositions. This project had been modified from research done elsewhere as a result of staff decisions to hold N Groups, and the research staff was particularly concerned that the dimensions of group composition required by the research would not violate participant learnings. Agreement was made that the training staff committee on N-Group composition would work with the research team in determining the mix of N Groups. The third research project was concerned with decision making in groups and required having a research observer in all sessions of four T Groups. The training staff felt that the research staff was not making undue demands or introducing intrusions into learning. All three projects required a relatively small amount of the participants' time to fill out questionnaires, check scales, or be interviewed. The training staff felt that if the research team could explain their interest in research at the opening session and then report hypotheses they were testing and any data available near the end of the program, all three projects would be acceptable to participants as well as to training staff. Details about the time of tests were worked out by the two staffs.

GENERAL SESSION ON VALUES. One staff member had often mentioned his belief that time should be spent in dealing explicitly with problems of values and value reconstruction. He was concerned that training in self-awareness, in group understanding, and in membership skills was not completely helpful if the individuals were not also helped to examine the values basic to or incongruent with their own behavior. He proposed that the Friday evening session be devoted to this problem. He suggested a general session which would include a brief lecture to raise value issues relevant to laboratory training, small groups of six in the audience to indicate concrete value problems and issues they were concerned with and to challenge the staff as to the values underlying the laboratory, and, finally, a panel of audience-group and staff representatives to discuss the issues raised.

Staff members liked the idea generally but raised questions as to whether values could be taught in this way or whether it would not be better to deal with value issues by making them explicit when they arose in the T Group. Others saw the general session not as teaching values but rather as bringing the subject into focus. Individuals thus sensitized might be better able to deal with such issues when they occurred naturally. It was on this latter view that the staff decided to hold the general session.

WEEK-END REST AND RECREATION. As the staff moved toward completing the first week's schedule, it seemed desirable, particularly because of the inclusion of the N Groups, to hold a T-Group session Saturday morning, preceded by a general session which would enable the T Groups to look back on the directions of group growth. This raised the question of participant and staff fatigue and the need to get away from the training center. No free afternoons or evenings had been scheduled during the first week.

The staff reviewed the schedule to see what might be eliminated. They also talked about perceived versus real fatigue. The experience of many had been that participants deeply involved in laboratory training would work in informal groups during the first week even if training sessions were not scheduled. Most staff members reported that free time the second week would be better utilized. It was decided to hold T-Group sessions Saturday morning and again on Sunday evening (rather than spending Monday morning readjusting after week-end trips), and also to schedule a free afternoon and evening the second week.

Planning the first week's design had taken most of the second and third days of the planning session, leaving the final day for subcommittee work, special-decision situations, preparation of lectures and materials for the skill exercise, and a final review of the first week's design.

THE LABORATORY COMMUNITY. A considerable number of families were accompanying both staff members and participants, and the problems of involvement of families as well as of providing recreational opportunities for staff and participants during free time were complex. During previous years many approaches had been developed to handle such problems. A community room had been organized where individuals could come during the evening after training sessions. One member of the administrative staff had been assigned the role of coordinator of community affairs. A successful day camp had been developed for children from four to twelve years of age. But the problem of what training activities, if any, should be planned for wives and older children remained to be solved. The coordinator of community affairs met with the staff when these problems were considered.

Past experience indicated that some involvement of wives in the laboratory program was necessary. Otherwise, because they were unfamiliar with the intensity of the training program, their husbands' engrossment could create conflicts. At the same time, most wives, except for the few enrolled as participants, would not want to attend intensive training sessions. Nor did budget permit the employment of a full-time experienced trainer for such a program.

Balancing the need against the difficulties, the staff decided to have one staff member work with the community coordinator in arranging a series of informational meetings every other day in which various staff members would spend an hour explaining some aspect of training. Wives would also be invited to attend all theory sessions of the regular laboratory. In addition, one intern deeply interested in family problems volunteered to hold a discussion group, open to wives three afternoons each week, on family problems related to confusions in the role of wife.

The community coordinator was a skilled group worker and was willing to find time in her busy schedule for a series of meetings with the teen-age group. It was agreed that these would deal, with the help

Training Laboratory Schedule—First Week

	SUNDAY	MONDAY	TUESDAY	WEDNESDAY	THURSDAY	FRIDAY	SATURDAY
8:45 9:00		PAIRED				INTERVIEWS	
9:00 10:00		T GROUP					General Session
10:00 10:30							Coffee
10:30 11:00							
11:00 11:30		COFFEE TIME					T Group
11:30 12:30		THEORY SESSIONS					
12:30 2:00		LUNCH					
2:00 4:00	Opening Session Data Collection	Skill Exercise	T Group	Skill Practice On Giving And Receiving Help	N Group	N Group	FREE
4:00 8:00		FREE TIME & DINNER					
8:00 9:30	T Group	T Group	T Group Tape Listening	Film	N Group	General Session On Values	FREE

of the staff and participants from foreign countries, with problems of teen-age adjustment to parents, peers, and siblings in America as compared with other countries.

The staff spent the final part of the fourth planning day in reviewing the design, their decision-making process, and the relationships they had established during the four days. Staff members were able now to talk openly about interpersonal and group problems that needed to be worked through more effectively. They talked also about use of staff time during the coming two weeks. They decided that staff lunches could be devoted both to immediate decisions and to talk in clinic fashion about the problems trainers had encountered in different T Groups. They felt the laboratory counselor could be of great assistance in helping them to check the effectiveness of their own interventions in handling puzzling events. In addition, they could alert the counselor to individuals who they felt might be helped by talks with him.

They scheduled a few formal staff meetings during the week to assess reactions of participants, to make any necessary changes in the program, and to make final decisions about the design for the second week.

Planning the Schedule for the Second Week

On Saturday afternoon the staff evaluated the work of the first week and concentrated upon completing the design for the second week. Most decisions had been anticipated in planning for the first week. The major remaining decision dealt with the application of learnings to other situations.

It was finally decided that the second administration of the data-collection device dealing with organizational improvement would be made on Wednesday to open a three-session program on application. Each member would then have an opportunity to note changes in his own perception of his back-home problem chosen for consultation, to reflect upon the problem as he now saw it, and to prepare to describe it to three other members of his T Group in order to obtain as much help from them as possible. During the next two sessions each member in the small group of four would have an hour to seek help from the others. At the same time, they would use these application sessions in further examining their consultation skills.

Experience with the paired interviews indicated that some values had been obtained but that they were now less needed. Accordingly,

Training Laboratory Schedule—Second Week

	SUNDAY	MONDAY	TUESDAY	WEDNESDAY	THURSDAY	FRIDAY
9:00 11:00		T G R O U P				
11:00 11:30		C O F F E E T I M E				
11:30 12:30		T H E O R Y S E S S I O N S				Closing Session
12:30 2:00		L U N C H				
2:00 4:00		Intergroup Cooperation Exercise	Free Afternoon	Application Groups	Application Groups	
4:00 4:30					Research Feedback Session	
4:30 8:00		F R E E T I M E & D I N N E R				
8:00 9:30	T Group	Intergroup Cooperation Exercise	Application Session	T Group	Free Evening	

they were dropped from the design. As previously planned, one open afternoon and one free evening session were provided.

A committee was selected to plan the details of the intergroup cooperation exercise and to brief the rest of the staff on their part in the exercise at a special staff meeting late Sunday evening.

It was decided to continue the luncheon sessions of the staff.

Postlaboratory Evaluation

At the end of the session, after participants had left, the staff held a final evaluation meeting. Their description and evaluation of innovations undertaken were recorded, to be made available to future staffs. The staff also reviewed its ways of working together and recorded recommendations about the organization of staff planning and self-training activities in future laboratories.

The Training Program as Seen by a Participant: A Case Report

A training laboratory design may, and usually does, look quite different to the staff members who design it and the participants who experience it. This does not mean that the differing perceptions are necessarily in conflict, though they may be. In part, the differences stem from the role differences of participants and staff. It may help to round out the human meaning of a training laboratory to see the design we have watched taking shape in staff planning through the eyes of one participant. It would be hard to say how typical this participant is. Certainly the reactions and the learnings of another participant in the same program would be different, as should be expected in laboratory education.

Let us meet Mr. Hill, who is an assistant manager of a production department of the Williams Manufacturing Company. Mr. Hill is in his early forties. He came to this particular laboratory for a number of reasons. Several other managers in the company had attended previous sessions and, as far as Mr. Hill could observe, now were able to work more effectively with others. The top management favored attendance by managerial persons if they themselves wanted to attend. Finally, in two recent experiences with subordinates, Mr. Hill had been uncertain about the adequacy of his own behavior.

When he arrived at the training center, located some distance from a large city, Mr. Hill found he was one of a hundred participants. While some of the others worked in industry, he noted that the roster also listed government officials, school executives, college teachers, hospital administrators, psychiatric social workers, ministers, and officials of national and local organizations. There were a couple of officers from the Armed Services, and two participants from other countries.

When Mr. Hill had established himself in his room, he studied the schedule. It certainly seemed different. There were no course numbers and, despite past conversations with previous participants, words such as "T Group," "skill exercise," or "paired interview" did not really give him much understanding of what was to happen to him. The only familiar label he saw was "Theory Sessions." He assumed this meant the familiar lecture.

Mr. Hill began to find out what the program was like on Sunday. He found the two sets of scales he was asked to complete during the opening session both irritating and interesting. He felt some sense of intrusion into his private affairs, but he found that the thoughts about himself—which were stimulated by the questions—were intriguing. On Sunday night he entered the first meeting of the T Group. He thought he was prepared for its unstructured nature, but he was unprepared for the wide range of feelings he experienced. He was surprised at how tense and anxious he was as he took his place around the table with twelve others—all strangers. He found that he became bewildered in the apparently aimless shifting of conversation, frustrated because the group could not get organized, deeply angry at one member who tried to run the show, sympathetic and warm toward another person who said just exactly what he himself was thinking and who smiled directly at him. He found himself in violent disagreement with a man directly across the table from him. Later, as he thought about it, he was rather surprised at his vehemence because the point at issue was really insignificant.

It was quite an evening. Mr. Hill was not certain that he liked it. The staff was pretty negligent to allow arguments and conflicting efforts to dominate the group to go on unchecked. Was it not their job to facilitate learning? Mr. Hill found that he was pretty much stirred up. Yet, surprisingly, he found himself looking forward to the next morning's meeting of the group.

The T Group which Mr. Hill joined was to meet from two to four hours a day and to keep constant its membership of twelve participants and a trainer. The staff member, or trainer, did nothing to dispel confusion or to organize the group. He merely expressed the belief that participants could learn about individual and group behavior as they directed their own behavior toward building a group, and also toward observing and analyzing what happened in the process. He would try to be helpful in the process of converting their experiences into learning, but he would not take responsibility for determining what the group decided on as its focus for discussions.

Monday

At 8:45 Monday morning, Mr. Hill sat down in the lounge of the training center with Mr. Fulton to have a fifteen-minute conversation or "paired interview," as the schedule called it. As Mr. Hill understood it, he was to have a similar conversation each morning with a different member of the T Group. Mr. Hill and Mr. Fulton, a social worker, had been asked to discuss the questions:

"What happened in our group at its last meeting?" "What can I do to help?" Mr. Hill and Mr. Fulton quickly agreed that the night before had been quite a mess. But Mr. Hill was surprised that, beyond this point, Mr. Fulton saw things quite differently. Mr. Hill had felt the group made a mistake in not latching onto a suggestion made by one member that they discuss the responsibilities of leadership. This was something they all had in common. It would have gotten the group started. Mr. Fulton was not so certain. A sizeable number did not want to discuss the topic, and to have insisted to the point of a vote would have divided the group. Furthermore, would not such a topic have been a nice, easy escape from the tougher problem of forming a group and finding out what they all really wanted to accomplish? Mr. Hill had not thought of it this way, and he was silent for a moment while he did think about it.

Neither Mr. Hill nor Mr. Fulton had a really good proposal that would solve the group's problem or that either thought would be accepted. However, Mr. Hill privately resolved to listen a little more and not to jump to conclusions as to what should be done. Both Mr. Hill and Mr. Fulton wondered what the other two-person conversations would come up with.

The second session of the T Group began with somewhat less tension and anxiety. People knew one another a little better. But issues brought up were still surface issues. Open interpersonal conflicts had not yet developed. However, as group members pushed for some kind of organization and some topic to discuss—almost any organization and any topic—no suggestion found general agreement. There were times when some members blamed the trainer, one another, and the group in general, for their inability to agree on what they wanted to do. The trainer suggested that it might be more profitable to look at what was happening and at the blocks to achieving organization rather than to push for organization as such. He wondered how clear they were about their purposes. If this suggestion was heard, it was not responded to.

While this session was still frustrating to those who were uncomfortable in the fluid, ambiguous situation, some group movement had taken place. Subgroups emerged, cleavages appeared, issues were further clarified, and knowledge of one another increased with more interaction. While the consensus still was that the group had to get organized, some members began to admit that they no longer felt so compulsive about organization. They were learning from the struggles the group was going through. If the group became too nicely organized with leader and set agenda, would they not stop learning?

After coffee—when small clusters from the same or various T Groups kept on talking about events in the groups—everyone attended a lecture on "What To Observe in a Group." The lecture dealt with the need to look at both the content and the process of group discussion, the need for a group to work on its task and on its maintenance and development, the need to examine and improve its communication processes and its decision-making procedures, to help improve the role behaviors of its members, and to handle the emotional, self-oriented, and often disruptive behavior of individuals in the group. Toward the end of the lecture each individual was asked to use these aspects of group behavior as scales and to indicate where he felt his T Group was on the scale. He was then to discuss his perceptions with another member of his group. Mr. Hill felt he received some new understandings from the lecture. He suddenly saw new ways of looking at his T Group. Events that had been confused now seemed clearer. He thought ruefully of some of his own behavior in the T Group and resolved to try to be more discerning.

Mr. Hill was to find that the Theory Sessions seemed, oddly enough, to deal with the problem of greatest consequence to his T Group at the moment. Members of other T Groups he talked with seemed to have similar reactions. Evidently the struggles his group was going through were pretty basic to all groups.

The afternoon session had been labeled a "skill exercise," but Mr. Hill found that it would be carried on with his own T-Group members. He found that his T Group and another one were going to exchange observations. T Group 3, to which Mr. Hill belonged, was going to observe T Group 4 for half an hour. Members of T Group 3 were to make notes along such dimensions as adequacy of communication, how well people listened to one another, what was not being said that needed to be said, participation patterns, and expressions of emotion. Mr. Hill realized that these dimensions paralleled the morning Theory Session. He had wondered whether he could observe all of the things the speaker had mentioned. This would be a good opportunity to find out.

T-Group-3 members were cautioned to report their observations in nonjudgmental terms and to refrain from telling T Group 4 how they felt the group should proceed.

T Group 4 began its session with members of T Group 3 sitting around it in a larger circle. It was obvious to Mr. Hill that members of T Group 4 felt ill at ease. He did not blame them. He was glad his group would be observed last.

As Mr. Hill made notes, he wondered whether his group made as many mistakes as he thought he saw T Group 4 making. On the other hand, some of the discussion sounded very good and he wondered whether his group could do as well. Mr. Hill also began to see events in the movement of T Group 4 that normally escaped his attention while he was participating.

After a half hour, T Group 4 widened their circle to admit T-Group-3 members—who began to report some of their observations. They tended to be critical and vied with one another to see how many observations they could report. T-Group-4 members began to question the accuracy of the observations. Mr. Hill noticed that T-Group-4 members seemed pretty defensive, and at one point a fairly hot argument took place between members of the two groups. Mr. Hill realized that his group had violated the caution given to them earlier; they were advising T Group 4 as to how to proceed.

When the discussion was finished, T Group 3 took its place around the table, and T-Group-4 members became the observers. Mr. Hill felt that his group started with less hesitation than the other group, and that they were doing rather well. The usual conflict about what the group should do and how it should do it broke out, but Mr. Hill felt it was more thoughtfully handled than in previous sessions.

However, in reporting their observations, T Group 4 seemed intent on being extremely critical. Mr. Hill resented this. Then it occurred to him that they were expressing their resentment at previous criticism by T Group 3; they were getting even. Mr. Hill meditated on how easy it had been to create a competitive conflict situation despite good intentions, and how difficult it was to give help without creating hostility.

Mr. Hill now listened with less resentment. He began to see more clearly some problems in his own group. He realized for the first time that while they were bemoaning the lack of accomplishment, some important and fascinating problems were unfolding—problems of conflict, of poor communication, of inadequate participation—and that the group was either unaware of them, or studiously indifferent to them. A totally different direction for the group to take dawned on Mr. Hill. He was helped to this awareness by comments of one trainer, who brought out into the open the conflict that had developed naturally between the two groups and how this had blocked listening in both groups. The trainer indicated that perhaps this illustrated how difficult it was to be helpful to others but also how important it was to understand better why this is so.

T Group 3, on the surface, seemed to receive the observations of T Group 4 with some resistance. However, Mr. Hill had a hunch that he was not the only one who had received a shock. His hunch became a reality that night. While there were still those who fought hard for a rigid, controlling organization and who seemed bent on talking about things outside the group, an increasing number were recognizing that they had difficult problems within their own group and were ready to dig into them.

Mr. Hill found the laboratory skill exercises relevant. He liked the contrast as well as the help given to his T Group. The skill exercise was more structured and the learning goals were a little clearer and more pointed, if less penetrating. But it dealt with similar problems of individual and group behavior. (In the second skill exercise on Wednesday, Mr. Hill had the opportunity to present a back-home problem and to receive help from two persons who used contrasting ways of helping. An observer then fed in his observations, and the four-man group discussed them. Mr. Hill discovered a new angle on his back-home behavior and new ideas about counseling other people.)

The afternoon session on Monday ended at three-thirty, and Mr. Hill joined two other members of his T Group in nine holes of golf. Mr. Hill thought it would be a relief to forget for a while all that had happened; but, to his surprise, he found that all three talked about the T Group as they walked between shots.

During lunch and dinner, conversation seemed to come back continuously to events in the T Group, as members reviewed events in their own group or exchanged notes with members of other groups. After the evening T-Group session, most of Mr. Hill's T Group sat together in the community room, and T-Group talk continued over beer. Even when he returned to his room, Mr. Hill sat up another half hour comparing notes with his roommate, who was a member of another group. Mr. Hill decided that the training laboratory was going to be a fascinating experience.

Thursday

By Thursday Mr. Hill felt like an old veteran in T Groups. He had learned quite a bit about the difficulties of trying to be helpful to others as a result of the Wednesday afternoon exercise on giving and receiving help. T Group 3 had gone through a variety of struggles and vicissitudes. Members had come to know one another fairly well —better, some of them thought, than they knew many people with whom they had worked for years. They had patched up leadership struggles and cleavages so that there was harmony—at least on the surface. There was cohesion in the group, and members congratulated one another that theirs was the best group in the laboratory.

Late Thursday morning Mr. Hill learned that he was to become a member of an N (New) Group that would have substantially different membership from the T Group and a different trainer. The N Group would meet for only three sessions and would not take the place of the T Group, which would continue to meet. Mr. Hill did not think he would like the N Group. He had just become more relaxed and happy about his T Group and he did not relish starting in a new group all over again. He did resolve, however, to behave somewhat differently.

Mr. Hill still was not very happy with his N Group after the first session. Although the group had settled on their task more quickly, and although the trainer was more active than his T-Group trainer had been, Mr. Hill saw many events take place that he recalled happening in the T Group. Maybe, he thought, he was just able to see more.

By the end of the evening N-Group session, Mr. Hill felt better about the N Group. It had moved faster than the T Group. Mr. Hill saw distinct evidence of much more effective membership action than he thought he recalled in his T Group. In addition, he was seeing an entirely different set of individuals, with different idiosyncrasies and contributions. He found these differences and the rather direct reactions people gave to him highly rewarding.

On Friday morning Mr. Hill attended the first T-Group session since his first two N-Group meetings. In one sense it was like coming home. Members welcomed one another warmly. Mr. Hill was interested to see that there had been a variety of experiences. Some were very well pleased with their N Group. Others were not so happy. Mr. Hill noticed, also, that the input of experiences from the various N Groups seemed to help the T Group. Issues which had been kept under wraps were opened up. A realignment of the power structure of the group began to take place. New resources were discovered. Mr. Hill looked forward to the last session of his N Group and particularly to the further impact it might have on the T Group.

Saturday morning was spent by the group in looking back over its history. A group had formed from a collection of individuals, and an organization had emerged from the group itself, rather than from outside forces. But it had been an exhausting week.

Mr. Hill wanted to get away for two days. His home was too far away for a visit. Also, he had not visited this part of the country before. His two golfing companions felt the same way, and so they planned a leisurely one-and-one-half-day trip.

While there was no hectic conversation, they did think through together what had happened to each of them, and many of the experiences of the past week fell into place for Mr. Hill. Particularly, he enjoyed and profited from their rather long discussion of the general session on values held on Friday night.

Sunday night's T Group was a time for rejoining the group. Members reported their week-end experiences. Some had returned home. One or two had joined office colleagues on a work task. Both those who had gone home and those who had joined their office staff reported how different familiar situations seemed. Some said it was as if a bandage had been removed from their eyes.

Monday

The theory session Monday morning contrasted two basically different approaches to organization and management. One, based on assumptions that people were inherently lazy and needed to be controlled and motivated by external rewards and punishments, was essentially autocratic. The other, based on assumptions that people did want to be involved, were naturally active and inquiring, and did seek satisfaction in work and accomplishment, was essentially a participative organization—more like the organization in the T Group. This theory session led to intense discussion, as individuals reviewed their traditional concepts of organization. Even with the experience of the past week, there was much doubt that the concepts, basic to the several types of organization, could actually work. Monday afternoon and evening provided an opportunity to try them out.

T Groups 3 and 4, previously "antagonists" and still with some remnants of negative feeling, now were paired together. Together they were to form the Tennyson Greeting Card Company. A greeting card in this case was a sheet of paper containing two two-line rhyming stanzas dealing with the same subject. Spelling, punctuation, and capitalization had to be correct. Also, the cards produced had to meet these market specifications: 40 per cent New Year's cards, 40 per cent Mother's Day cards, and 20 per cent brother-in-law birthday cards.

Four functions had to be planned for: production of the stanzas, quality control, inventory control to maintain appropriate percentage according to topic, and coordination of these various functions. The pair of T Groups was to form a company to accomplish these functions. The group had two hours during Monday afternoon to organize and, if they desired, to conduct a practice session. Monday evening would provide time for actual production.

Mr. Hill noticed that at the beginning of the afternoon period there seemed to be some constraint between members of the two groups resulting from their past competitive experience. Someone mentioned that the constraint and tension seemed to be eased. A member of Mr.

Hill's group started the work with the reminder that they had only two hours to figure out their whole organization. Another member countered this statement by reminding them that their compulsion about time had got them into trouble when they had been observed by the other T Group. He had learned, he said, the value of talking first about their feelings, expectations, and ideas for an organization that would be both productive and satisfying to those working in it.

Several basic premises developed. First, maximum effort would be made to develop jobs satisfying to everyone. Second, to the greatest extent possible, control should be built into each job as the responsibility of everyone. Third, as far as possible, everyone should choose his own job. Fourth, there should be as few managerial jobs as possible.

After these principles were accepted, it was easy to develop an organization. An estimate was made of the minimum number of persons necessary to improve and correct the original stanzas. It was decided that each writer would try to build into his own job the responsibility for inventory control. Those who wanted to write chose their jobs first. Others assigned themselves jobs in the control and correction sections. Only one person was needed to keep the inventory of approved stanzas. One person was needed as a messenger between the two groups and one person as a general trouble shooter. Almost everyone had the job he preferred.

The afternoon ended with a questionnaire to be filled out relating to satisfaction with the organization and the job held. The results would be compared later with production figures.

The evening started with everyone ready to work. Sharply at eight o'clock, the order for 50 per cent New Year's cards and 50 per cent Mother's Day cards was received and the production line started. At 8:15 an order for different kinds of cards was received, and again at 8:30. At 8:45 the total production stopped.

Production figures were later compared with production expectations made at various times during the afternoon, and with measures of satisfaction with the job and the organization. T Groups 3 and 4 later learned that another pair of groups had organized in a more traditional way. Supervisory and controlling jobs were assigned first. Those left over became the writers. Neither morale nor production in this section was more than half as high as they were in T Groups 3 and 4.

Thursday

Thursday was devoted to problems of returning home and of improving work situations. Much of the discussion in the T Group dealt with problems of relating in a new way to persons back home.

In the afternoon, in groups of four, individuals were to continue to have an opportunity to present a real problem of relationship and to secure the help of the others. Mr. Hill had spent much of Wednesday night thinking about the problem he wished to present. He faced a problem of competition among a number of immediate subordinates. He had given much thought from time to time during the last few days to the factors at work in the situation, and to what he would do to help change the attitudes of his subordinates.

Thursday afternoon he presented his problem to the other three in his small group. He expected that they would feel he had done a thoughtful job of analyzing the situation, and he wondered what they would think of his plan for action. As they asked penetrating questions, it began to dawn on Mr. Hill that his diagnosis had been in terms of what his subordinates were doing incorrectly. It had not included assessment of his own role. Furthermore, his planning had been in terms of how he could change them, rather than how he and they could work together to improve the situation and the effectiveness of one another. Mr. Hill felt chastened, but helped.

Thursday night, the last night of the laboratory, Mr. Hill spent some time thinking back over the experience. He believed that the T Group was the heart of the program. Its unstructured nature and its continuity made possible much learning about group behavior and group development, about the values, limitations, requirements, and skills of group membership, and about relationships between groups. It also provided opportunities for each individual to learn about his own behavior through interaction with others and with help from others. It made it possible to practice task functions under intense emotional conditions.

At the same time, skill exercises and participative cases, usually utilizing the T-Group formation, had given opportunity to deal more thoroughly with certain aspects of individual and group behavior and to test out the growth of the T Group. And theory sessions had helped to clarify experiences and to generalize from them. Mr. Hill also reflected on how much time the trainers had spent in personal consultations and in unscheduled conversations. He thought, too, of the careful articulation of the parts of the laboratory and the way in which this enabled experiences to flow smoothly and to increase in impact as time went on.

Summary

This chapter has underlined how important it is for a staff to work through its team relationships. It has also suggested important requirements of laboratory design: (1) Design must support an integrative learning experience for each participant. This calls for developing creative interrelationships among a number of aspects of learning often treated as antitheses in educational programs—common and individual learning, emotions and ideas, involved action and objective analysis, practical experience and research knowledge, learning with the help of peers and learning from an expert teacher. (2) An adequate design is seen as a set of structures to induce and guide participant experience, analysis, and evaluation, with increasing initiative from participants in directing and evaluating their own learnings. (3) Finally, an adequate design achieves a balance between the use of tested methodologies and activities and the introduction of new training inventions which will advance staff learning and contribute to the professional knowledge of a growing community of laboratory trainers.

4

History of the T Group

in the Laboratory Setting

Kenneth D. Benne

One may look at the history of the T Group by placing its development in either of two principal contexts. The narrower context, and the focus of this chapter, is the training laboratory as it has grown in America, principally under the sponsorship and stimulation of the National Training Laboratories. It was in the setting of the training laboratory that the training group was born, christened, and confirmed. The broader context, briefly sketched in the first chapter, is the widespread, conscious use of primary group processes for purposes of reeducating people which has increasingly characterized social practice in America during the past generation.

Closely related to this augmented emphasis upon primary group processes has been the increasing attention paid to "small-group" structures and processes in psychological and sociological research. Certainly this wider ferment has affected the development of the T Group within laboratories. Those who launched the first training laboratory and those who have come to work in training laboratories over the years as staff members or participants have brought influences from various fields of study and practice to bear upon the technology and theory of group training in the laboratories, just as they have taken influences back into their various areas. In brief, the training labora-

Note: The author acknowledges with gratitude the help of the following persons in criticizing the first draft of this chapter: Richard Beckhard, Max Birnbaum, Robert Blake, Leland Bradford, Murray Horwitz, Ronald Lippitt, Barry Oshry, and John Weir.

tory and the training group, while maintaining distinctive qualities, have not been closed systems as they have developed over the years.[1]

Prelaboratory Beginnings

The genesis of the principles underlying the T Group may be traced to a workshop held on the campus of the State Teachers College in New Britain, Connecticut, during the summer of 1946. This training-research enterprise was jointly sponsored by the Connecticut Inter-racial Commission, the Connecticut Department of Education, and the Research Center for Group Dynamics, then located at the Massa-chusetts Institute of Technology. The aim of the "action sponsors" was to develop more effective local leaders in facilitating understanding of and compliance with the Fair Employment Practices Act under which the Interracial Commission had been recently created. Most participants came from the professions of teaching and social work, with a sprinkling of businessmen and other interested citizens. The aim of the research sponsor, the Research Center for Group Dynamics, was to test several hypotheses about the effects of conference experience and the conditions of differential effects among participants in terms of transfer of behavioral changes to back-home situations.

The training leaders were Kenneth D. Benne, then at Columbia University, Leland P. Bradford, of the National Education Association, and Ronald Lippitt, of the Research Center for Group Dynamics. The researchers were Kurt Lewin, of the Research Center, Ronald Lippitt, and three research observers, then graduate students in social psychology—Morton Deutsch, Murray Horwitz, and Melvin Seeman.

The three small groups of ten members each, in which the participants spent much of their formal training time, were not T Groups in the current usage of this term. They focused on the analysis of back-home problems brought in by the members, either as individuals or as teams. The major teaching-learning method employed was group discussion, supplemented by role playing both to diagnose behavioral aspects of the problems presented and to practice alternative ap-

[1] For a contrast and comparison of the developing uses of small-group processes for re-education in adult education, social group work, and group psychotherapy, see Harry Lerner and Herbert C. Kelman (Eds.), "Group Methods in Psychotherapy, Social Work, and Adult Education." *Journal of Social Issues*, VIII: 2: 1952. For a brief history of the staking out of the "small-group field" as an area for psychological and social research, see Edward Shils, "The Study of the Primary Group," Chapter 3 in Daniel Lerner and Harold Lasswell (Eds.), *The Policy Sciences*, Palo Alto: Stanford University Press, 1952.

proaches to the solution of these problems. The plan for the formal curriculum made no provision for the analysis of here-and-now behavioral events as a source of learning.[2]

A research observer was attached to each of the three groups. This observer focused on coding behavioral interactions in the groups and in recording behavioral sequences according to a previously developed and tested schedule of observation. No reporting of behavioral observations to the group had been planned as part of the training design.

Early in the conference, Kurt Lewin arranged for evening meetings of training staff members with research observers to pool and record on tape their process observations of each group. Analysis and interpretation of leader, member, and group behaviors observed were also to be undertaken and recorded.

The evening meeting was planned originally to include only staff members. Some participants, who were living on campus, asked if they might attend, and after some staff discussion the meeting was opened to participants on a voluntary basis. The staff had no prevision of the effects on the participants of the description and analysis of their own behaviors. Nor had they any clear notion of how they might handle participant and staff reactions to this experience.

Actually, the open discussion of their own behavior and its observed consequences had an electric effect both on the participants and on the training leaders. What had been a conversation between research observers and group leaders in earlier meetings was inexorably widened to include participants who had been part of the events being discussed. A research observer might report:

At 10:00 A.M. Mrs. X attacked the group leader. Mr. Y came to the defense of the leader, and he and Mrs. X became involved in a heated exchange. Some other members were drawn into taking sides. Other members seemed frightened and tried to make peace. But they were ignored by the combatants. At 10:10 A.M., the leader came in to redirect attention back to the problem, which had been forgotten in the exchange. Mrs. X and Mr. Y continued to contradict each other in the discussion which followed.

Immediately Mrs. X denied and Mr. Y defended the accuracy of the observation. Other members reinforced or qualified the data furnished by the observer. In brief, participants began to join observers and training leaders in trying to analyze and interpret behavioral events.

[2] See Ronald Lippitt. *Training in Community Relations.* New York: Harper & Bros., 1949, for a detailed description of the training program and of the research design and results.

Before many evenings had passed, all participants, the commuters as well as the residents, were attending these sessions. Many continued for as long as three hours. Participants reported that they were deriving important understandings of their own behavior and of the behavior of their groups.

To the training staff it seemed that a potentially powerful medium and process of re-education had been, somewhat inadvertently, hit upon. Group members, if they were confronted more or less objectively with data concerning their own behavior and its effects, and if they came to participate nondefensively in thinking about these data, might achieve highly meaningful learnings about themselves, about the responses of others to them, and about group behavior and group development in general. At this time, no thought was given to the exclusion of other content, whether in the form of cases suggested by staff, situations reported by members from outside the group, or of role-played incidents. Initially, the notion was to supplement this there-and-then content with the collection and analysis of here-and-now data concerning the members' own behaviors.

The Early Laboratories in Bethel and the T Group (1947–1948)

The training staff of the New Britain workshop involved other institutions in planning a summer session of three weeks' duration at Gould Academy in Bethel, Maine, for 1947. Joint sponsors were the National Education Association and the Research Center for Group Dynamics of the Massachusetts Institute of Technology. Cooperating institutions were Teachers College at Columbia University, Cornell University, Springfield College, and the University of California. The basic research was supported by a grant from the Office of Naval Research.

One of the features of this session was a small continuing group, called the Basic Skills Training (BST) Group, in which an anecdotal observer made observational data available for discussion and analysis by the group. One function of the training leader was to help the group in analyzing and evaluating these data, as supplemented with data from the participants and from the training leader.

The others who joined with Benne, Bradford, and Lippitt in planning the training design for the 1947 session were Robert Polson, of Cornell University, Paul Sheats, of the University of California at Los Angeles, Alvin Zander, of Springfield College, and John R. P. French, Jr., of the Research Center, who served as research director. (Kurt

Lewin, who was much interested in the project, died in early 1947.) It was this group who planned the program of the BST Group, the immediate progenitor of the T Group, as it has evolved in subsequent laboratory experiences.

The initial conception of the BST Group is clarified by descriptions of it that were published at the time.

A Place for Learning Change-Agent Skills and Concepts

What is the common framework which helps the group worker, the public school supervisor, the personnel consultant in industry, the PTA president, the training officer in a government bureau . . . to see their special jobs as resources one to the other? The faculty believed, and laboratory experience confirmed the belief, that all of these helpers and trainers of other people can find common ground in the role of the change agent. All . . . [helpers] work to produce changes in the understandings, attitudes, and skills of the persons and groups with whom they work. All . . . [helpers] must, for example, help persons to diagnose their problems, to plan ways of solving these, to evaluate their plans as these are tried and tested. . . . These helps to persons and groups require certain basic human relationship skills which can be identified, analyzed, and practiced. . . .

What were the skills which were identified, discussed, and practiced by the five BST Groups? The main skill areas are presented here.

Skill Area I: Assessment by the change agent of his personal motivations and his relationship to the "changee."

Skill Area II: Helping "changees" become aware of a need for change and for the diagnostic process.

Skill Area III: Diagnosis by change agent and changee, in collaboration, of their situation in terms of behavior, understanding, and feelings to be modified.

Skill Area IV: Deciding upon the problem, involving others in the decision, planning action, and practicing the plans.

Skill Area V: Carrying out the plan, successfully and productively.

Skill Area VI: Evaluation as assessment of joint progress—methods of working and thinking and human relations.

Skill Area VII: Continuing, spreading, and maintaining accomplished changes.[3]

A Place for Learning To Understand and To Help with Group Growth and Development

The first step was . . . to sensitize the delegates . . . to the realization that groups very probably show a growth process as do individuals, that a collection of mature adults will not necessarily make a mature group, that many committee and staff meeting failures result from expecting mature production from adolescent or infantile groups. A tentative list . . . gave such symptoms of group growth or strength as:

[3] Kenneth D. Benne. "Principles of Training Method." *The Group,* 10: 2: 17–18, January 1948.

a. Excellence of intercommunication among group members (common understanding, semantic sensitivity, permissiveness to discuss freely and not defensively, among others).

b. Group objectivity toward its own functioning (degree to which the group . . . [can] make and accept evaluations and analysis of its own functioning).

c. Acceptance of group responsibilities as members (willingness to accept and share leadership functions and membership responsibilities, as well as sensitivity to and encouragement of the potential contribution of each member).

d. Group cohesion or ego strength (sufficient to permit assimilation of new ideas and new members, to use conflict instead of being destroyed by it, to hold to long-term goals, and to profit both from failure and from success situations).

e. Group ability to inform itself and to think straight (ability to use resources both within and without the group and to detect and correct fallacies in group thinking).

f. Ability of group to detect and control rhythms of group metabolism (fatigue, tension, tempo, pace, emotional atmosphere).

g. Ability of group to recognize, control, and employ significant sociometric factors in its own growth.

h. Ability of group to integrate member ideologies, needs, and goals with common group traditions, ideology, and goals.

i. Ability of the group to create new functions and groups as needed and to terminate its existence when appropriate.

After fairly brief discussion of these dimensions of group growth, decisions were reached in most basic skill-training groups to test them against the behavior and development of the group itself. . . . In a typical basic skill-training group the observer . . . would report his observations to the group. These would stimulate discussion and help the group probe more deeply into its own processes.   As the basic skill-training groups progressed, they faced many crises, had temporary failure experiences as a result of group immaturity, were competitive and aggressive as individuals toward one another.   Both the observer and the leader endeavored to keep a spotlight trained on these symptoms of group immaturity or malfunctioning. . . . In this laboratory process of analysis and diagnosis of dynamic group functioning, the delegates grew in their ability to recognize stages in group growth. . . . The various basic skill-training groups analyzed not only the group process but also the various member abilities present and the member roles to be filled.[4]

The Several Functions of the BST Group

The BST Group, thus, was designed as a medium for several kinds of learnings.   In the first place, one of its functions was to help mem-

[4] Leland P. Bradford. "Human Relations Training." *The Group,* **10**: 2: 7–8, January 1948.

bers internalize some more or less systematic sets of concepts. One was a schema of deliberate or planned change and the skills required by the agent of such change. Another set had to do with indices and criteria of group development which in turn presupposed knowledge of and sensitivity to a rather complex set of group variables.

A second expectation was that the group would provide practice in diagnostic and action skills of the change agent and of the group member and leader. Skill practice, through role playing, thus played a fairly heavy part in the methodology of BST Groups in 1947 and 1948.

A third expectation was that the behavioral content would run the gamut of "human organization" from the interpersonal level and the group level to the intergroup level (both in formal organizations and in "communities"). There resulted a competition between discussing here-and-now happenings, which of necessity focused on the personal, interpersonal, and group levels, and discussing outside case materials. This sometimes resulted in the rejection of any serious consideration of the observer's report of behavioral data. More often, it led eventually to rejection of outside problems as less involving and fascinating.

A fourth expectation was that the BST Group would help its members to plan the application of laboratory learnings to back-home situations and to plan for continuing growth for themselves and their associates. A fifth expectation was that members would gain a more objective and accurate view of themselves in their relations to other persons in the group and to the developing group as a whole.

A sixth expectation was that participants would develop a clearer understanding of democratic values. These values were to be operationalized in terms of principles of methodology for functioning as a leader or member of a group and as an initiator and facilitator of change. As discussed in Chapter 1, the originators of the laboratory were convinced that the ethical commitments implicit in the scientific enterprise are consistent with the ethical commitments explicit in democratic patterns of social management and control, when these latter are formulated methodologically.[5] They believed that the BST-Group experience would reinforce the democratic values held by par-

[5] See *Report of the Second Laboratory Session*, 1948. National Training Laboratory in Group Development Bulletin 3, Washington, D.C., National Education Association and Research Center for Group Dynamics, The University of Michigan, pp. 114–115. See also Kenneth D. Benne. "Democratic Ethics in Social Engineering." *Progressive Education*, 26: 7: May 1949, for a fuller translation of democratic values into norms for the guidance of processes of planned change.

ticipants. An evaluation device was invented to measure changes in this dimension of learning. How training is conducted to facilitate value reorientation by group members was a much controverted point at that time and remains so to this day.

A seventh expectation was that members of the BST Group would not only acquire skills and understandings to help them function more adequately as change agents and as group members but that they would also acquire trainer skills and understandings required for communicating these to others. This is clearly indicated in the report of the second laboratory session (1948): "Practice of skills of group leadership, *of training in human relations,* and of inducing social change, was given major emphasis." [6]

This expectation proved embarrassing to the laboratory training staff after the first session. Some participants went home feeling that they were qualified to conduct human relations training. Where their previous education did not warrant this claim, a few participants carried out inadequate training projects in the name of "laboratory training." It was seen by the end of 1948 that both a background in one or another of the behavioral sciences and training beyond a three-week laboratory session were required to produce adequate competence in human relations training. It was not until 1955 that a special advanced program for the development of trainers was instituted at Bethel.

The training staff of 1948 became convinced that the training group was overloaded in terms of learning objectives. New groupings within the laboratory were seen as necessary to support at least some of the six sets of objectives. This posed the question as to which should be assigned to the BST Group or its equivalent, and which would be better reached through the use of other groupings and other training methodologies.

Two Periods in T-Group Evolution

As I have studied the records of laboratories conducted after 1948, particularly those under NTL auspices, the history of the T Group and of its place in laboratory designs seems to fall into two periods. The first period, roughly from 1949 through 1955, is marked by a variety of experimental attempts to create training formats and technologies to serve learning objectives seen as extraneous to those peculiarly within the province of the T Group. This led at times to virtual segre-

[6] *Ibid.,* p. 12 (italics added).

gation of T-Group activities. Separate groupings were formed for skill practice, for application of laboratory learnings, and for the study of change, among other activities. Sometimes, separate staff units for handling T-Group activities and non-T-Group activities were recruited. This experimentation was greatly aided by two large grants from the Carnegie Corporation of New York for the development of NTL's program.

The second period, roughly from 1956 to the present, is marked by efforts to reintegrate T-Group experiences into the designs of laboratories. Experimentation with new designs and with new uses of T Groups continues. This second period is harder to deal with historically than the first. It is difficult, particularly for one actively participating in laboratory and T-Group developments, to get perspective on these more recent events. Another part of the difficulty comes from the proliferation in numbers and kinds of laboratories. It is during this time that numerous occupational laboratories developed, while the more traditional cross-occupational laboratories continued. Regional and other laboratory programs also developed under auspices other than NTL. I have not had time to study the records of regional laboratories with the same care I have given to laboratories under NTL auspices. Many "errors" of omission may inadvertently have entered into my account. Yet my hypothesis concerning the direction of evolution in T-Group utilization during the past seven years seems generally correct. Of necessity, it takes me into a treatment of various parts of laboratory designs which have both conditioned and been conditioned by staff provision for collateral groupings and activities supportive of T-Group experiences.

The Separation of "Extraneous" Training Functions from the T Group (1949–1955)

In the several seminars during the winter of 1948 and the spring of 1949, core staff members of NTL came to agree that overloading the BST Group meant that the central function of examining and analyzing ongoing behavioral events in the developing group was impeded by other assigned functions.[7] Many of these other training functions

[7] The seminars were seen as opportunities for building theory concerning processes of training and change. The hope was that this theory building would serve as a guide for experimentation in training, and for empirical research into training processes. In some degree, the seminars were thought of as opportunities for in-

called for more didactic interventions by the trainer which clashed with his collaborative role of helper to the group in developing and testing learnings in the ongoing life of the group. The problem of reducing overload in the BST Group, looked at from the trainer's standpoint, was thus to reduce the dissonance between disparate trainer roles.

From the standpoint of member motivations, some of the "legitimized" content of BST-Group discussions tended to augment rather than to reduce the early resistances of members to examine and jointly analyze their own behavior in the group and the behavior of the group. There is a threat for any member in hearing others talk openly about his behavior and its effects upon them. He develops resistance to showing emotion and to sharing feelings about what is happening to him and about the perceived agents of these happenings. Effective learning requires the reduction of such resistances. If talking about the results of social research or about outside experiences is legitimized, resistance to sharing and analyzing feelings and perceptions about here-and-now events as a way to learning is augmented. Or, when a group has become deeply involved in seeking to understand its immediate experiences, introduction of outside material may be resisted and resented as an intrusion, whatever value such material might have as a tool for analyzing experience. The

service self-education for the staff. They were also designed to serve the function of long-range planning and policy formation for NTL.

The focal concerns may be gathered from a listing of a few of the issues dealt with. (1) How can we develop sufficient community in a laboratory staff with respect to goals, rationale, and methods of training to support a wide variety of individual variation and experimentation and yet insure contributions to the study and implementation of the democratic-scientific methodologies for which NTL basically stands? (2) How can we design a flexibility of conditions in a laboratory to permit complementary experiences in two types of problem solving? One is off-target problem solving addressed to problems inherent in the situation and the population with after-the-fact analysis and interpretation—this calls for a "clinical" approach to training. Another is consciously experimental problem solving, with predesigned hypotheses and plans for data collection—this calls for an "action research" approach to training. (3) How assist participants as persons to utilize their group experiences for individual exploration in sensitivity, yielding a recognition and acceptance of self at a new level, and to the formulation of individual goals for change and an opportunity to experiment with changes? (4) How adequate is our "action research" model of learning and change? The adequacy needs to be tested against its relation to the "clinical" approach suggested in (2) above. It needs also to be tested in terms of its adequacy in helping learners to reconstruct and redirect their basic moral imperatives in areas of crucial personal and collective choice and decision.

problem of "simplifying" T-Group experience, motivationally speaking, was how to avoid legitimizing there-and-then content and activities which interfered with experiential analysis.

There is a third approach to taking the "noise" out of the learning processes of the early BST Group. "Problem solving" in the T Group requires facing difficulties in actual group functioning—of a member, among members, between members and trainer, and in the operation of the group as a whole. It requires further the pooling of relevant data about the nature of the difficulty so that it can be defined in terms of alternative ways of dealing with it. But problem solving requires finally some way of testing alternative ways of dealing with the situation in future experience. No full cycle of problem solving is possible if some sort of testing of hypotheses is impossible in the laboratory of the group. Problems from the outside experiences of members cannot be solved realistically by and within the T Group. Nor can larger organizational or community problems be solved there. If BST-Group members were to internalize more effective processes of solving human problems, they would have to focus on difficulties that grew out of the group's developing experience that could be tested realistically in its ongoing experience. Thus a criterion for pruning inappropriate learning objectives was found.

The Dynamics of Change in Laboratory Designs

The story of stripping extraneous functions from the BST Group, however, was not so consciously purposeful as the telling of it suggests. The discovery of the limitations and strengths of the T Group as a medium of re-education actually took place through a series of experiments—a process which continues today—and not by *a priori* definition of the nature of the T Group. The training experiments undertaken were related in some cases to ideas or technologies which one or more staff members wanted to try out and evaluate in a laboratory setting. In other cases they grew primarily out of attempts to resolve conflicts due to staff differences in educational orientation and in training ideology.

The place of staff conflict in generating new training forms and new emphases is well illustrated by experience in the Bethel laboratories in 1949 and 1950. The conflicts were generated partly by the necessity of accommodating the ideas and skills of new disciplines and professions—deliberately brought in—and partly by the struggles of newcomers to the laboratory to alter traditional patterns in order to establish their equality with the old-timers. (Of course, the definition of the "old-timers," sometimes called the "inner circle," has varied from year to year. A staff member who came in 1951 and continued to attend summer laboratory sessions might appear like one of the inner circle in 1953. However, the extensive work in staff seminars by the core staff of NTL during 1948 and 1949 did lend realistic meaning to the category of the inner circle to the many newcomers in the 1949 staff.)

The training staff of 1948 had been fairly continuous with that of 1947. The principal additions to the major staff of 1948 had been Herbert Thelen, Gordon Hearn, and Siegman Blamberg. (Bingham Dai also joined the staff that year but functioned mainly as an individual counselor and an observer.) There were some creative modifications and clarifications in training methodology, but the training design of 1947 had remained intact through 1948. In 1949 a deliberate effort had been made to invite more clinically oriented staff members in order to work more on the issue of "action-research" and "clinical" models of training. The first staff had represented principally the discipline of social psychology, with others from education and sociology. Seven of the ten new major staff members were from psychiatry and clinical psychology.[8] These represented both Freudian and Rogerian outlooks. Conflicts between Freudian and Rogerian views of the processes of behavioral change were combined with conflicts between clinically oriented newcomers and Lewinian old-timers in the processes of staff planning. In the more or less democratic processes of staff planning, the old-timers were outnumbered. Bradford, Benne, and Lippitt were all deposed in 1949 from direct leadership of what had been the BST Group in the past. (They were assigned tasks of training and research coordination and supervision.) The group was rechristened the T Group. There were, of course, variations in the operation of different T Groups in 1949. But the general trend was clear. The improvement of change-agent concepts and skills as a training objective tended to disappear from the T Groups. Emphasis upon organizational and community structures in the back-home situations of members was also greatly reduced. The focus of trainer and member attention became the interpersonal events occurring between trainer and members or between members and, in varying degree, group events in the developing experiences

[8] Hereafter, for stylistic reasons, the names of staff members are generally not included. To include all names would impede the narrative flow. Exceptions to the rule of not citing names are made only when such citation is useful in explaining the motivation of some particular innovation.

of the T Group. The language of interpretation used in clarifying events became more psychoanalytic or Rogerian and less sociological and Lewinian.

Deliberate skill training was minimized in the training groups of 1949. Some attention to change problems and problems of operating as a change agent within organizational and community structures persisted, but outside the T Groups—in the seminars on methods, in short-term afternoon special interest groupings, and in some of the evening sessions. No training format providing equivalent time for these learnings was present in the laboratory design of 1949.

With all of the resistances of old-timers to the change of focus in the over-all laboratory design, the more clinical orientation in the T Group was not rejected by them. Its use of here-and-now material to increase understanding of interpersonal events in a group setting and to increase member competence in handling and managing such events was accepted as a valid and feasible objective. Of course, this objective had been present, along with other partly interfering objectives, in the original BST Groups. There was concern among old-timers, however, that the groups might pass over the borderline between training groups and therapy groups. This concern did not stem primarily from any rejection of group therapy or from lack of recognition of the therapeutic dimension present in all significant re-education in understanding and handling human relationships.

The concern stemmed rather from two other sources. The first was the feeling of a violation of the contract between the staff and the "normals," who had come to the laboratory for an educational experience in human relations, not for psychotherapy. The second was a fear that in the relatively few hours available little progress could be made in helping participants to clarify or solve problems at any deep therapeutic level.

Apart from these misgivings, the stripping of objectives which had tended to draw the T Group away from learning through analyzing its own developing experiences was accepted as desirable. The problem of laboratory planning came at first to be seen as one of inventing a design in which the objectives of conceptual learning, action skill training, and planning for back-home change efforts could be served along with those more limited objectives which the T Group now seemed best fitted to serve.

This differentiation is reflected in the 1950 laboratory design and in the staff composition. In addition to morning T Groups, the 1950 design incorporated afternoon A (Action) Groups. The T Groups were made as occupationally heterogeneous as possible; the A Groups included, insofar as possible, participants from the same occupation. The A-Group staff had a "sociological" orientation; the T-Group staff were more clinically oriented. The plan was to concentrate the attention of T-Group members upon the clarification and understanding of interpersonal and small-group phenomena,[9] while A-Group members focused upon problems and methodologies of change in larger social systems. Supporting readings and lectures were provided to furnish conceptual tools for the understanding of social change and action. Outside cases had to be used to furnish material for empirical analysis.

The problem in most A Groups was that they tended to become a second T Group. The involving focus on interpersonal dynamics tended to spill over into the afternoon groups. Since most trainers persisted in trying to carry out their educational plan for the A Groups, their behavior tended to be seen as authoritarian by the more counterdependent members who had become released through their T-Group experiences to examine, attack, and modify here-and-now structures. Such attacks led to polarizations of the group membership. The group was thus confronted with deep maintenance problems which had to be handled in some way before the training plan could be carried out.

This account does not mean that the staff failed to learn from their partly disappointing experimentation with the A Groups. (In fact, it would also be false to conclude that all participants learned little from their A-Group experiences. But we are more concerned here with learnings by the staff.) In the first place, learnings seemed to be greater in those A Groups where the trainers had had BST experience. This suggested that trainers for laboratory experiences more structured by design than the T Group need to be aware of the dynamics of group formation and of member adaptation and to be able to relate constructively to these dynamics, as manifested, in

---

[9] Innovation by honoring individual interests of staff members in educational experimentation is also illustrated in the 1950 design. Two of the eight T Groups, led by Alvin Zander and Irving Knickerbocker, went through a staff-planned sequence of activities designed to clarify various aspects of group and interpersonal life—goal setting, decision making, conflict resolution, leadership, membership. Subgroups of the T Group carried out, by role playing or reality practice, the handling of predesigned human situations. Analysis of what happened in these situations, aided by observations from observers, led to conceptualization and generalization concerning behavioral processes and events in small-group settings. These experimental "T Groups" became the prototype of the skill-practice groups which came to characterize the "afternoon programs" of Bethel laboratories between 1951 and 1955.

facilitating the more structured learning experience. Traditional "telling" approaches will not be successful in a laboratory community where collaborative and participative methods of helping and learning are honored. Second, it seemed that the learning experiences would need to be carefully designed and structured in advance, not to inhibit, but rather to support and facilitate free action, analysis, and evaluation by learners. It meant also that trainers would need to share their advance planning openly with the learners in order to gain intelligent acceptance of the design. Finally, some of the participative cases in organizational and community change, developed for use in the A Groups, laid the background for further experimentation with other ways of training for social action and change.

Training in Membership and Leadership Skills

What developed in the afternoon programs of laboratories from 1951 to 1955 illustrates the principle of differentiation (and to some extent segregation) of the alternative training formats already mentioned. In 1951 skill groups were formed—groups slightly smaller than the T Groups with membership crossing T-Group lines and manned by a separate afternoon staff. The skill group staff designed a series of skill exercises in which members were asked to practice various interpersonal, membership, leadership, and change-agent (consultant) skills. Some members enacted situations presented by role playing while others observed. Analysis of the developing situation led to generalizations about the relations between the variables involved—the effects of goal clarity or lack of clarity upon group organization, the effects of acceptance or rejection upon member behavior, the process of giving help to another, as examples, together with the implications of these generalizations for appropriate member or leader behavior in managing these variables. Sometimes suggestions concerning alternative ways of handling the situation were tried out and the results of the two trials compared.

In general, skill-practice sessions had little direct relation to the concurrently developing experiences of the T Groups. They were geared more or less closely to conceptual content presented in theory sessions or to other laboratory objectives. Tensions developed between morning and afternoon staffs, augmented by the higher value ascribed by most participants and frequently by staff as well to the T-Group experience. By extension, a higher status was ascribed to T-Group trainers in the laboratory society. Ways of integrating morning and afternoon staffs in the laboratory community became a clearly indicated need. Operationally, this meant ways of reintegrating the T-Group and skill-practice experiences of participants as well. The story of laboratory designs from 1956 to the present is, in some part, a story of developing more integral relationships between training in group membership and leadership and in change-agent skills and the developing experiences of members in T Groups.

This account should not be read to imply that no lasting values accrued from this period of laboratory experimentation with differentiated sessions for the practice of membership, leadership, and change-agent skills. On the contrary, a new training technology addressed to problems of effective skill training in human relationships, including the identification of more or less isolable and trainable skills, was an important product of this experience.[10] It was the development of this technology which has helped to make possible the later integration into laboratory designs of skill exercises designed to facilitate and enhance both T-Group and other learnings. And this technology has found important uses in educational settings outside training laboratories as well.

Training in group membership and leadership skills was only one of the learning objectives which overloaded the original BST Groups. A brief look at the process of differentiation and segregation of training formats to serve these objectives will help to document further the early pattern of evolution of the training laboratories, including the use of T Groups.

Learning the Skills and Knowledge of the Change Agent

The fate of the study and practice of the change-agent role in laboratories has been a complex and interesting one. In one sense, behavioral change is the objective of all laboratory training. And all laboratories attempt to create some awareness of the conditions and processes of behavioral change. This awareness is necessary if continuing change and learning by participants is to follow the termination of the laboratory. In this sense, all laboratory participants are invited to learn to think and discuss and act as change agents.

[10] See *NTL Skill Exercise Book*, Washington, D.C.: National Education Association, 1958, for a collection of some of the skill exercises developed in NTL laboratories during this period. See also *Explorations in Human Relations Training*, Washington, D.C.: National Education Association, 1953, pp. 36–44, for a description of the plan, rationale, and methodology for two typical skill exercises.

But it is possible to focus in a laboratory primarily upon change processes at the levels of personal, interpersonal, and small-group behavior. The earlier BST Groups attempted to focus also upon change in a wider spectrum of human organizations—including community and institutional systems. As has been seen, the early evolution of the T Group from the BST Group involved dropping this latter emphasis. Yet the effective application by participants of diagnostic and action skills with respect to the behavior of self and group in work, family, and civic life outside the laboratory usually requires some understanding and control of change processes in the larger social systems in which their lives go on. Teachers in most school systems, for example, will need to produce some changes in their school systems beyond their classrooms if they are to develop improved relationships with their classroom groups. Supervisors in most industries will be limited in the changes they can effect in their working relationships with colleagues and subordinates if they cannot build support and permissiveness for such changes in the *surrounding* organization in which they work. And so it goes for most participants. The logic of effective transfer of T-Group learnings to life outside the laboratory requires some help to participants in developing diagnostic and action skills relevant to the diagnosis and facilitation of changes in larger social systems.

In the early years of the Bethel laboratory it was hoped that processes of formation and re-formation of the laboratory community could be analyzed to yield learnings about community, comparable in depth and intensity to the learnings about self and small group which take place in the T Group. Partly to facilitate this process, and partly as evidence of staff commitment to democratic values, a Delegate Council was formed during each of the laboratory sessions from 1948 through 1951 to share with the staff in major decisions about needed changes in the structure and practices of the laboratory community. (A town meeting of delegates and staff had served this function in 1947.) Interesting and important data about the internal relations of T Groups and about problems of representation were revealed in the selection of their representatives to the Council and in their treatment of them after selection. Interesting and important data about the competition between T Groups were revealed in the relationships between representatives in Council meetings. But these data could not, it appeared at that time, be systematically collected or analyzed for the learnings about community operation implicit in them. The image of the Council as part of "government," not training, precluded the assumption of training responsibility by any of the staff who sat as members of the Council. (No plan of providing trainers or consultants for the Council was devised.)

The discontinuation of the Council after 1951 did not come solely from disappointment about its training value. It was felt that its added value of opening up channels of communication and influence from participants to staff was not being well served through its representative structure. Both members and staff of T Groups tended to regard consideration in T-Group time of Council business as an intrusion upon T-Group life. A system of informal community groupings of participants (C Groups) without staff membership, was instituted in 1951 in the hope that it would provide a better mechanism for channeling participant dissatisfactions to the staff. These groupings, of course, did not bring the community dimension of laboratory life into focus for training purposes.

In 1952 and 1953, sociologists were added to the staff to gather data on processes of community formation in the laboratory and on the emergence of a laboratory culture. It was hoped that feedback of these data would induce "real-life" learnings about community dynamics. While some interesting observations were made, no yield of data which could be used by participants and staff for self-training in community dynamics and participation resulted. The general report was that the jelling of community norms and laboratory culture took place so rapidly that the usual methods of participant observation did not yield any convincing evidence concerning the process. Norms could be identified only after their establishment, but the process which led to their community-wide establishment remained a mystery. The staff who were still concerned with participants' learning about community dynamics turned to simulated participative cases as a way of training when the study of natural processes proved abortive.

In 1952 and 1953, two training interests of at least some of the staff members were combined in a series of evening sessions. The aim was to provide an opportunity for participants to learn both from the content and from the methodology of these sessions. A description of the 1952 program illustrates how attention to the two training objectives was combined.[11]

The evening general sessions program consisted of a series of eight meetings, each dealing with a major aspect of social action. Each meeting was designed to illustrate some of the social inventions that can be used in solving action problems, as well as some of the underlying principles involved in effective social action.

[11] From "General Sessions Training Materials." *1952 Delegate Take-Home Packet*, Bethel, Maine.

The meetings dealt with the following aspects of the subject:

Initiating Social Action
Collecting Information for Social Action
Planning: Strategy, Tactics, and Ethics
Decision Making
Problems of Representatives and Representation
Evaluation in Social Action

The first meeting of the series gave an overview of the problem and set the stage for the meetings to follow. Two meetings were devoted to the subject of decision making in social action.

In addition to the content objectives, each meeting was designed to illustrate some methods of planning, preparing, staging, and evaluating large-group meetings. Each planning committee developed a design which they felt was applicable to the content being presented. A number of different data-collection devices were used. Various staging methods were employed for the different sessions, with the purpose of illustrating a number of different kinds of meeting techniques and presentation methods.

After each meeting an informal bull session was held at which the methodology of the meeting was discussed and analyzed. The meeting methods were discussed in terms of applicability to other situations, applicability to the specific content of the meeting, and effectiveness of actual use of the technique.

A "large meeting" was defined as a meeting in which a platform-audience relationship is established and utilized. The dynamics of interaction are different from the dynamics of the small-group meetings. The aim of this curriculum was to study processes of planning, conducting, and evaluating large meetings, both as a "research" program for interested staff and a training program for participants. Various forms of platform presentation and various methods for inducing and channeling audience participation, along with principles of design by which methods are selected and fitted to the audience and to the objectives of the meeting, suggest the methodological "subject matter." [12]

It was in 1954 that mass role playing by the entire laboratory population of a community in the process of reaching a decision on a controverted issue was first attempted. This was an enlargement of the role playing of community cases which had taken place in some A Groups in 1950. Various clusters of participants were briefed as com-

[12] For a report of staff theorizing which supported this work with "large-meeting" methodology, see Leland P. Bradford and Stephen M. Corey. *Leadership and Participation in Large Meetings.* NTL Bulletin No. 4, Washington, D.C.: National Education Association and the Research Center for Group Dynamics, The University of Michigan, 1951.

munity groups with a stake in the issue to be decided. Various forms of influence of group on group were invented and carried out by these clusters consistent with their briefed roles in the simulated community, prior to a decision by some authorized board. Data were collected, by observation mainly, on intergroup sociometry and on influence. These data were analyzed by participants and staff from the standpoint of a change agent concerned with community change, and generalizations about community structure and dynamics were formulated. Before their discontinuation in 1958, several versions of such participative cases in community decision making were developed at Bethel and in the regional laboratories. As occupational laboratories developed, particularly those for industrial and business managers at Arden House, similar participative cases were developed to explore decision making and change situations in formal organizations.

These cases of community or organizational action were not without important training values; but criticisms developed within laboratory staffs over the years. The major criticisms focused on the lack of relationship between the skills employed in the mass role playing and the skills and understandings concerning deliberate and collaborative changing which came to be practiced by members in their T Groups. Manipulations of members of one group by members of another, through withholding information and concealing interests and intentions, were practiced frequently in the mass role playing. In the T Groups, the same people had accepted a standard of openness in communication of facts and feelings, of leveling with one another. Conflicts among groups in the mass role playing were frequently handled by increasing pressure and counterpressure. In the T Groups, members were learning to convert conflicts into problems to be solved collaboratively by all parties to the conflict. These inconsistencies in methods of influence invented and employed by the same persons under differing conditions might have been used to yield important learning values. But there was no good opportunity for members systematically to confront these inconsistencies, since membership in the "community groups" was not coincident with membership in the T Groups. The criticism grew in the first instance, therefore, out of concern with the lack of integrity between learnings induced in various parts of the laboratory. But it was augmented also by concern about the transfer of learnings about change acquired in T Groups to processes of change in larger organizations, akin to the civic and work settings in which the participants functioned in their home situations. If there was only limited transfer of learnings by participants from the T Group to another part of the laboratory, what was the prospect for effective transfer of T-Group learnings from the laboratory to the home settings of the participants? Here, as in the case of skill-practice sessions, segregated from T-Group sessions, staff criticism pointed toward the invention of ways for better integrating T-Group learnings with learnings about influence, decision making, and change in larger social systems.

Training for Back-Home Application of Laboratory Learnings

This consideration leads to another related objective of laboratory training originally assigned to the BST Group—help to participants in planning for the transfer of laboratory learnings to their home settings. As the T Groups sloughed off this responsibility, alternative formats for training in back-home application had to be developed.

Actually, other groupings designed to supplement BST emphasis on back-home application were provided in the 1947 and 1948 laboratory designs. Participant groupings were formed around similar occupations or around similar work settings. Groups of teachers, industrial managers, or ministers (or, alternatively, hospital workers, or community workers, or church workers) met through a number of meetings—usually in the latter half of a laboratory session. These groups sought to explore problems of applying laboratory learnings to typical problems they identified as important.

Some of these occupational (or institutional) groups found significant common problems to work on and were able to build realistic bridges between laboratory experiences and back-home settings. The bridges were conceptual, perceptual, and motivational, or, in some cases, a combination of the three. But many of these groups failed to achieve any significant learning results. Part of the difficulty seemed to be a lack of fit between the back-home problems identified. Similarity in profession or in institutional work settings gave no guarantee of a similarity of problems as perceived by members themselves. The successful groups seemed to have been able to hit upon a common problem for analysis.

In 1949, an assessment and referral unit was formed. Data were collected from participants at successive periods in the laboratory concerning the back-home problems on which they wished help. A roster of staff and participant resources, organized by problem areas, was prepared. The unit sought to bring together persons with some identified problem and resource persons with knowledge of and experience with the kind of problem presented.

This consultation program probably resulted in a larger percentage of application groups which were able to locate a common problem. Frequently, the more genotypically stated problem attracted participants from various professions and work settings. Representative of such problem areas were: ways in which subordinates might increase their influence upward in a hierarchical organization; ways of improving staff meetings through institutionalizing self-observation and self-analysis; and ways of meeting ethical conflicts in initiating change in a group or organization.

Two other difficulties were still present. One centered in the lack of experience and sophistication in processes of giving and receiving help. Much of the experience of participants in using expert resources had been fashioned according to the "engineering" rather than the "clinical" mode, to use Gouldner's distinction.[13] The "engineer" accepts the client's definition of the problem and makes available "facts and figures" considered pertinent. The "clinical helper" works with the client as he seeks to clarify his problem and to invent ways of dealing with it. The participants were unfamiliar with the adaptation of client-centered methods in helping with difficulties in organizational or community structures. This seemed to call for attention to consultant skills in establishing and maintaining an effective helping relationship. It also called for access to conceptual tools for diagnosing and strategizing change problems and change processes in larger social systems.

It should be recalled that the scheme of change-agent skills around which the curriculum of the original BST Groups was formed was an attempt to meet these very training needs. The stripping of responsibility for these learnings from the evolving T Group had left a training void which somehow had to be filled if participants were to give and receive help in consultations on back-home problems.

The skill-practice groups in the 1951 laboratory design did deal in part with problems of consultation. But after 1952, the skill-practice curriculum tended to focus primarily in an exploration of problems in fulfilling leader and member roles in small groups. This shift in emphasis seems to have occurred for two principal reasons. One was an attempt to cut the training objectives of skill groups in a short laboratory session down to realistic size. The other was to bring the skill-practice sessions into closer relationship with the developing experience of the T Group which had come to focus rather exclusively upon interpersonal and small-group phenomena and events. Whatever the

[13] Alvin W. Gouldner. "Explorations in Applied Social Science." *Social Problems*, 3: 3: 173–181, January 1956.

validity of these arguments, the effect was to leave, in Bethel at least, any conscious focus on learning the skills and processes of giving and receiving help on problems of organizational or community improvement a neglected dimension of laboratory training for several years.

The second area of difficulty in the early consultation groups had to do with the limited time-span of their life as groups. Groups need time to develop to the point where the trust level is high enough to permit free sharing of feelings and reactions. A consultation group needs such a climate to do its task well. Ad hoc groups, however common the back-home problems of its members, will need to expend energy on processes of group formation, especially in a laboratory, where sensitivity to the need for achieving "community" has been heightened.

Closely related is the lack of firsthand knowledge of one another in a new group. Help to a member who is trying to assess himself in the role of change agent must be guided by some fairly intimate knowledge of his typical membership patterns and their effects on others. New, short-term groups do not provide this resource, especially when their legitimate focus of attention is on a problem external to the laboratory. The most economic answer to this difficulty seems to lie in using the T Group as the medium of consultation on back-home problems. And this is a direction which many recent laboratories have been following.

The Communication of Conceptual Content—Cognitive and Ideological

The three areas of conceptualization which the 1947 laboratory staff thought essential to effective functioning and development of the BST Group were: (1) concepts about the processes of behavioral change and of the functioning of the change agent in such processes; (2) concepts about group development and member and leader functioning; and (3) concepts about democracy, operationally defined as principles of method for collaboration among people in processes of growth (change, re-education, or problem solving).

While general sessions were used partially for presentation and discussion of these focal concepts, these meetings for the most part were designed to provide additional conceptual inputs into the experience and thinking of participants. During 1947 and 1948, these additional inputs were of three kinds. First, research data, collected from the participants themselves, along with the rationale for the research projects, were presented by staff members and discussed by participants. The training objectives of these sessions, over and above the reduction of crippling intergroup hostilities between participants and the research team, were two in number. One aim was to acquaint participants, most of whom were practitioners rather than social scientists, with the ways in which social researchers go about the study of a human problem. The second aim was to confront the participants with somewhat systematized data about themselves and their behavior, collected by members of the research team. The general session was thus used for feedback purposes, with individual members protected from public exposure, to aid the opening up of group and interpersonal problems for a more realistic assessment and analysis by the groups.

Second, general sessions were used to acquaint members with inquiry tools for the exploration and handling of group and member problems. Methods such as role playing, group observation, and feedback of observations or other behavioral data were experienced in general sessions and analyzed—along with whatever problem provided the content vehicle of discussion.

Third, general sessions were used to focus attention on current social issues and to provide models for public diagnosis and for collaborative planning to meet them. Examples of issues used were citizen responsibilities for the sane use of nuclear energy; intergeneration problems— conflicts between youth and adults; ethical problems of the change agent; the meaning of democracy as opposed to alternative modes of social control. Sometimes issues were introduced by staff or by staff-participant committees. Sometimes they arose out of controverted events in the laboratory community itself. Thus the meaning of what was being learned in other parts of the laboratory was tested against issues demanding decision in contemporary society.

In some measure, general sessions to communicate results and rationale for researches have persisted in laboratories with a research program. However, it is probably fair to say that the use of such conceptual input has decreased rather than increased over the years. General sessions to acquaint participants with methods of inquiry and problem exploration have persisted, in some measure, although these are more often tied to specific briefing for a particular laboratory activity—for example, giving and receiving help prior to joint consultation on back-home problems—rather than as a general method for exploring and clarifying larger social problems.

The attempt to involve participants in deliberation upon controverted, ideologically laden social issues tended to disappear from laboratories at Bethel after 1954, although such attempts have continued to characterize some regional laboratories, e.g., the Boston University laboratory, and some laboratories designed for special populations, notably the laboratories for college youth and for community leaders.[14]

Theory sessions presenting findings from personality and small-group research appeared in the 1949 laboratory session. Other general theory sessions that year focused on concepts about organizational change, ethical problems of the change agent, and the transfer of laboratory learnings to the home settings of participants, though these had little direct relevance to the developing experiences of participants in the T Groups.

In 1950, some sessions focused on problems of membership and leadership in a small group and on research and theory concerning selected aspects of small-group behavior. A second set of readings and presentations on the sociology of larger social systems and on the processes and strategies of social action and social change were provided as supports to the A-Group program.

Participant as well as staff evaluations of "theory sessions" in 1949 and 1950 revealed dissatisfactions with the adequacy of integration between concepts presented and the experience-based parts of the laboratory. In 1951, a concerted attempt was made to bring about greater integrity between the T Group and at least some of the theory presentations.

[14] The factors accounting for the lapse of this kind of conceptual input in many laboratories are no doubt many and various. (1) As the T Group becomes the central medium of training in some laboratory designs, the consideration of larger social issues in the curriculum may come to be seen as irrelevant. It is not that larger social issues do not enter into T-Group deliberations. A T Group with white and non-white members, for example, is bound to face the racial issue sooner or later. But the parameters set will ordinarily be intrapersonal or interpersonal. The problems involved in changing interracial relations in an organization or a community will not easily come into focus in such a design. (2) As some laboratories become more occupationally oriented, the relevance of issues of potential or actual concern to the participant as citizen is more difficult to establish and maintain. The measure of relevance tends to be applicability to the work situation and organization rather than to the life of citizenship. The definition of relevance may be widened more easily by most participants and staff members to include problems of family life than to include civic problems. (3) Many of the social-behavioral scientists who staff laboratories seem to avoid any frontal approach to ideologically tinged issues—in the formal curriculum at least. Some of the problems here may lie in difficulties in reconciling conflicts between the "scientist" and "reformer" roles. Another problem lies in the lack of well-developed technologies for helping participants to learn productively through a confrontation of discrepant ideologies. Ways of dealing rationally with conflicts related to massively articulated and socially reinforced systems of value have not been well developed.

Evolution within the T Group

The preceding account has indicated the refocusing of T-Group objectives between 1949 and 1955. In general, it was expected that here-and-now episodes and events within the developing experience of the group and its members would be analyzed to yield learnings about self, about interpersonal relations, and about the functioning and development of the group as a social system. The mix of learnings effected depended in some degree upon the valuation which the trainer placed upon each of these three levels of learning. In some degree, the mix depended also upon the orientations and individual learning goals brought by members to the group or developed there.

But methodology and social organization also distinguish one T Group from another. Actually, documentation of changes in the internal organization and operation of T Groups is difficult. Records of T-Group sessions have been only sporadically kept. Various seminars of T-Group trainers were attempted between 1951 and 1955, but it was hard to get objective reporting and analysis of what happened in various T Groups into these sessions. Clinic sessions between trainer and training associate (or between co-trainers) were usually considered more valuable. But neither seminars nor clinics kept any systematic records of their deliberations. A few generalizations, however, about trends in two features of T-Group operation can be made with some confidence, since they do not depend entirely upon detailed records of internal episodes for documentation.

THE FEEDBACK PROCESS. One enduring feature of T-Group methodology is its establishment of ways of providing feedback to the group concerning its behavior and development. It was the largely fortuitous feedback from researchers to participants at the New Britain Workshop in 1946 which launched the T Group. A primary feedback source, a member of the research team, was built deliberately into the BST Groups in 1947 in Bethel. In 1948, a training associate was added to each BST Group. The expectation was that he would be an initiator in feeding back behavioral observations. Orientation and training for all participants in methods of observing groups and in the processes of feeding back observational data to a group were provided in general sessions. A more or less common pattern in the BST Groups was to establish a rotating schedule of participants who acted as feedback observers from day to day in collaboration with the training associate.

Increasing dissatisfaction with the formalization of feedback sessions was felt by training staffs. Delaying feedback to a stated time period in a group session, usually near the end, militated against immediate and spontaneous feedback. The movement in 1951, and later, was toward legitimizing feedback by any member of the group to the group or to another member as near as possible to the time when the event which precipitated the feedback occurred. The trainers sought to role-model feedback of this sort in the group and supported members in establishing a standard which legitimized it for all members of the group. "Organic" arrangements in which feedback is undertaken by all members as part of a continuing action research into emerging problems of member, interpersonal, and group functioning have come more and more to prevail during the period of laboratory reintegration following 1955.

THE ROLE OF THE TRAINER IN THE GROUP. In the Lewinian tradition, the trainer conceived the group operation as a process of cooperative inquiry, after the model of action research. His role was to aid the group in getting as much relevant and well-validated data as possible into their discussions. This trainer was "member-like" in the amount and timing of his interventions and in the openness with which he expressed the feelings and values underlying his actions. He saw himself over time becoming a colleague within the group, although always a special member because of his simultaneous membership in the staff group and the responsibilities which this entailed.

In the clinical traditions, out of which many trainers came to the laboratory from 1949 on, particularly the psychoanalytic tradition, the trainer focused on exploring sources of distortion in data presented. He viewed himself as a "projection screen" in the group. He established himself as an ambiguous authority figure and tended to avoid revealing his real character and feelings, since this would reduce the ambiguity and, as a result, reduce the projections of members upon him. It was in these projections that member tendencies toward distortion were revealed. The group also revealed its tendencies to distort in projecting an image of happenings and events in keeping with its modal needs and assumptions. As distortions manifested themselves, they could be interpreted and analyzed by the trainer with help from the group and a higher degree of reality orientation attained. In this process, members learned deeply about themselves and about the group in emotional dimensions. A trainer could not become, in any full sense, a member of the group. Frequently trainers avoided fraternization with members outside the T Group. Sometimes the clinically oriented trainer resisted assuming leadership in other training activities where the role relationships between trainer and participants were necessarily different.

While these statements probably suggest a sharper dichotomy between trainers than their actual behavior in groups would reveal, it would be foolish to deny that these differing orientations do make a difference in the organization and functioning of the group. In 1955, in NTL and other laboratories, different T Groups did no doubt operate with modally differing relationships between group members and trainer and with corresponding differences, not alone in the content of learning, but in the processes by which learning was sought and attained. This does not deny that common directions and methodologies were also present.

The Reintegration of the T Group into the Laboratory Design (1956–   )

The initial pattern of evolution of the T Group out of its beginnings in the BST Group, as we have seen, was one of differentiation of new training formats and technologies to serve some of the learning objectives originally assigned to the BST Group.

Viewed historically, the virtual segregation of training activities was by no means a loss. It was the inadequate separation of T-Group experiences from A-Group experiences in the 1950 design that led to contamination of A Groups with "T-Group-like" phenomena. These phenomena, the staff believed, could not be constructively utilized for learning within the A Groups *as planned*. This experience led to the fairly complete segregation of skill-group staff and activities from T-Group staff and activities during the 1951 session. In this segregation, new variations of laboratory method were developed to become part of the accumulating technology of human relations training.

However, the commitment to integrative learning which is central to the value systems of most laboratory trainers was dissonant with any extended segregation of training activities and staffs within the laboratory design. As a matter of fact, forces toward reintegration were present in staff planning throughout the period of differentiation and partial segregation.

Tendencies toward reintegration of the T Group into the total laboratory design have become dominant in laboratories under NTL sponsorship since 1956 and apparently in laboratories under other auspices as well. Three alternative patterns can be noted in this movement toward reintegration. Any actual design may incorporate features from each type, but the "pattern constructs" may be useful in analyzing the proliferating uses of T Groups.

One pattern of reintegration is to make the T Group the center of a laboratory experience. This normally involves accepting as the principal learning objective the clarification and resolution of intrapersonal and interpersonal problems, along with a varying degree of emphasis upon learning about small-group phenomena. Every effort is made to select ideas and theories for presentation on the basis of the need of T-Group members for concepts at a given time and to present these as nearly as possible to the time they are most needed. Skill practice is utilized to sharpen inquiry tools which are useful in optimizing T-Group learning. Usually, such skill practice is conducted in special sessions of T Groups. Skills of observing behavior, of listening, of reporting observations constructively to others (feedback) are illustrative of such tools of inquiry. Integration is achieved by minimizing learning objectives seen as inconsistent with the learning objectives that T-Group processes are seen as peculiarly fitted to facilitate.

A second pattern of reintegration is premised on the continuing validity of the full range of learning objectives established early in the laboratory movement. The T Group is designed to stimulate and facilitate learnings by each participant about self and about his own patterns and problems of membership; but the learnings which the T-Group medium may be used to facilitate are by no means limited to these, however important and varied. The focused inquiry into its own building and maintenance problems by the group, with the resultant learnings about self and group, is necessary to build the T Group as a medium of re-education. But it is not accepted that the T Group can sustain inquiries only into problems generated within its own processes of development. The T-Group formation is used for giving and receiving help to members on problems of change in their back-home situations. It serves also as a medium for practice of change-agent skills and for clarification and application of concepts about change. And it is used in the generation and analysis of processes of organizational (and community) conflict and collaboration.

A third pattern of integration utilizes different groupings of participants with differing technologies of training in the service of various learning objectives. Staff members are in continuous communication in order to establish and maintain relationships among the parts of the laboratory experience. As the laboratory proceeds in time, participants are brought together in integrating sessions designed to help them relate the parts of their over-all laboratory experience. Integration of learnings becomes a central concern for participants in work on problems of application of laboratory learnings in their home situations.

The Dynamics of Reintegration

Two dynamic factors were noted earlier as important in the differentiation of the T Group out of the early BST Group. One of these was the interest of staff members in experimenting with some new training format and/or technology. The other was the more or less creative resolution of conflicts among members of training staffs who differ in educational background and training philosophy. These two forces have continued to play an important part in laboratory innovations, though now they tend to be directed to the invention of more integrated patterns of laboratory design.

Three other factors have become influential in the development of recent innovations. One is the development of more occupationally homogeneous laboratories, first under NTL auspices and later under other auspices as well. NTL has developed laboratories for various occupational groups, as follows (beginning dates indicated in parentheses): American Red Cross workers (1955); industrial managers (1956); Protestant religious workers (1956); Puerto Rican government workers (1956); staff leaders from various national voluntary organizations (1957); public school teachers and administrators (1959); college students and faculty members (1960); and leaders in community development (1960). In addition, one or more series of "in-company" laboratories have been conducted by the Protestant Episcopal Church of the U.S.A., by the Methodist Church, by the Esso-Humble Oil Company, by the Aluminum Company of Canada, and by other industrial organizations and government agencies.

The challenge of adapting training technologies to the requirements of a specific occupational population was bound to stimulate innovations. "Role" and "organizational" behavior were inevitably stressed more as curriculum content in meeting the expectations of participants for learnings which would help them to make more sense of their work settings and to function more adequately in these situations. The earlier emphasis upon "self" and "group" and "change agent," in general human relations laboratories, while by no means abandoned, had to come to terms with these new expectations.

A second factor in recent innovations is the development of regional laboratories, most of them as part of the program of various university centers. The Western Training Laboratory began its career in connection with University of California Extension in 1952. Others followed in rather rapid succession—Boston University Laboratory in the Improvement of Human Relations (1954), Pacific Northwest Laboratory (1954), Intermountain Laboratory—Utah (1955), and the Southwest Human Relations Training Laboratory—Texas (1955). Since many of the staff members of these laboratories have been members of the staff network of NTL as well, a complex exchange of information has been maintained over the years. Pressures toward innovation in the regional laboratories (and related university centers) stemmed in part from the relatively free hand which the founders had in selecting from the accumulated traditions of NTL and other sources of basic and applied behavioral science, and in developing inventions of their own. Adaptations to local university and regional conditions, including local research interests and findings, has further stimulated innovation. Competitive feelings toward the "parent" organization, NTL, no doubt has played a part in stimulating experimental efforts. The reverse sort of stimulation may have quickened innovative efforts in NTL as well.

A third factor which has encouraged experimentation is the development, in NTL and in some regional laboratories, of "alumni programs." The experimental thrust of these programs is illustrated by the programs for Staff and Action Leaders at Bethel during the summers of 1957 and 1958. These programs were designed for alumni from various basic laboratory programs who were primarily concerned to improve their change-agent skills as consultants or administrators, not primarily as human relations trainers. This program stimulated experimentation with curricular materials, methods, and designs for learning change agentry. Some of these innovations have found their way back into basic laboratory designs.

As training laboratories under NTL auspices grew in number and variety, an acute need for professionally qualified trainers developed. The development of additional laboratories under auspices other than NTL's served to augment this need. The need is the more acute since human relations training is for most trainers a part-time occupation, the vast majority being regularly employed in university teaching and research and, to a lesser extent, in various kinds of clinical and social practice.

An immediate need is thus to enlarge the pool of professional trainers out of which NTL and other laboratories can be staffed. A more long-range need is to establish standards of professional quality for trainers in commercial and other nonacademic agencies which have increasingly entered the field of laboratory training. This calls for the articulation of criteria both for selecting potential trainers and for defining the qualifications to be developed through training and experience.

In the first ten years of its operations, NTL depended primarily upon an apprenticeship system in expanding its network of qualified trainers. Abandonment of the early plan to train trainers in the basic laboratory program was based in part on a growing conviction that qualified trainers required a doctoral degree (or its equivalent) in one or another of the disciplines of basic or applied behavioral science prior to laboratory experience. The persons whom NTL drew into its informal apprenticeship system over the years for the most part met this standard. Most of these newcomers had received their graduate education in one of the academic disciplines—psychology, sociology, or anthropology. By far the larger number were psychologists. Psychiatry and education were the applied disciplines from which most of the minority of professionally trained apprentices were drawn. The apprenticeship system was not well defined. Some of the apprentices had attended a basic laboratory; others had not. Many served in one or more laboratory staffs as training associates before assuming full responsibilities as a laboratory staff member. Others served first as skill-practice trainers during the period of segregation of skill-practice and T-Group training. Systematic orientation of new staff members to the traditions and rationale of laboratory training was seldom attempted. Only sketchy printed materials for such orientation existed before 1956.

The first alumni program for training trainers was organized at Bethel in the summer of 1955, the actual occasion being a training responsibility which NTL had undertaken with the support of the Foreign Operations Administration of the U.S. Government and the European Productivity Agency. The responsibility was to train a team of twenty-six social scientists and educators from seven Western European nations as human relations trainers. The larger aim was to develop qualified persons who could conduct laboratory training in their respective nations, particularly in the industries of these countries. (NTL had previously provided personnel to introduce laboratories for industrial managers in a number of Western European countries and had earlier arranged training for teams of persons from Austria and The Netherlands.)

Members of the European team attended a first laboratory at Bethel as participants. After an intervening period of seminars on the utilization of the behavioral sciences in industry, conducted by the Boston

University Human Relations Center in North Andover, Massachusetts, the team returned to Bethel for an advanced alumni program, designed to further their development as human relations trainers. This program required a more careful articulation of concepts about the aims, assumptions, and methodologies of laboratory training than any which had been developed during the apprenticeship period of trainer development. It required the provision of experiences for advanced trainees in observing T-Group and other training activities from the standpoint of a trainer. It required a systematization of clinics between the experienced trainer and the trainees observing his sessions. It also required the invention of skill-practice exercises in trainer diagnosis and intervention.

In brief, the development of alumni programs for developing trainers pressed laboratory staffs to codify and articulate their thinking about the goals and processes of laboratory training. Codification and articulation have required the serious confrontation by laboratory staffs of their differences. In this continuing confrontation, issues with respect to laboratory training are being clarified and sharpened. Common ground has also been discovered or rediscovered to support and stimulate processes of reintegration. It is hard to estimate the strength of various forces which have powered the trend toward reintegration of laboratory designs. But the forces released by serious efforts to develop programs for training a new generation of laboratory trainers have certainly been prominent within the whole complex of forces operating upon laboratory training during recent years.

Alumni programs for developing trainers continued until 1959 at Bethel. Other comparable programs have been organized and conducted in other NTL laboratories and in some regional laboratories as well.

Beginning in 1960, NTL has conducted a more comprehensive intern program addressed to the pressing need to professionalize the field of human relations training. This program is designed primarily to help in the development as trainers of university-based persons who can subsequently undertake a variety of training and consultation tasks under NTL and other auspices. With this aim in mind, interns selected have earned, or nearly earned, their doctorate in one of the basic or applied behavioral sciences. Typically, they have demonstrated aptitude for developing and handling "helping" relationships with other persons or with groups or organizations. Their initial program occupies a complete summer. It typically includes participation in one basic laboratory program, serving as an observer in a second, and joining the staff, ordinarily as an active associate, in a third. The first two phases of the experience are interspersed with seminars on the aims, assumptions, and methodologies of laboratory training. Practice experiences in designing and conducting training sessions are usually provided. During the year following their summer program, interns are admitted to the staff of one or more NTL laboratories, ordinarily under the supervision of more experienced staff members.

NTL has also assumed some responsibility for the development of trainers, not based in universities, whose job includes responsibilities for training programs for a particular nonacademic organization or agency operating in industry, organized labor, health, government, welfare, or religion. The trainer development programs conducted at NTL or other laboratories, as well as the program for staff and action leaders already mentioned, have, in some degree, served the interests of this population. But new programs, comparable in selectivity and in scope with the intern program but specifically tailored to the problems of organizational trainers, are now in the process of development.

The alumni programs discussed up to this point have been vocational in orientation. Other alumni programs have developed, particularly in NTL and in the Western Training Laboratory, which have more of the character of continuing general or liberal education. Alumni return primarily to deepen and broaden processes of exploration begun in a basic laboratory experience. Such programs may help to solve a problem which laboratory training has faced from its beginning—the shortness of time which a basic laboratory provides for a re-educative experience. Laboratory staffs are confronted with two temptations. One is to cram the basic experience too full in an attempt to help participants explore under laboratory conditions all of the dimensions of a re-educative experience whose effects can be built upon in life outside the laboratory. The other temptation is to select radically from the possible elements of a re-educative experience—in this different way jeopardizing the continuity of the experience.

If the expectation can be developed in many, if not all, participants that their first laboratory participation is the first in a series of two or three such experiences, both of these staff temptations may be reduced. Moreover, the time between training experiences may come to be perceived, by participants and staff, as an opportunity for testing learnings from the latest laboratory experience and for preparing to learn more fully in the next.

The Presentation of Conceptual Content

The trend in basic laboratory training, it has been argued in general terms, has been toward the reintegration of T-Group experience into the larger design of a laboratory. The period of reintegration has been identified, somewhat arbitrarily, as beginning in 1956. As early as 1951, dissatisfactions with the lack of fit between "theory sessions" and T-Group experiences led to the institutionalization of a "third hour" immediately following a T-Group session of two hours. The plan was for each trainer and associate trainer to use this third hour to discuss concepts which seemed most useful in clarifying the difficulties faced at the time by the group. T-Group members and trainers were, in effect, asked each day to shift to role relationships more appropriate to a teaching seminar. This arrangement proved unsatisfactory in most T Groups and was abandoned after one year's trial. Both group members and trainers seemed to find difficulty in achieving the necessary shift in roles and role relationships. The communication and discussion of concepts were distorted in the image of the difficulties in relationship developed or revealed in T-Group experience and still clamoring for clarification. In many cases, the "third hour" became largely an extension of time for "normal" T-Group operation.

There was less difficulty in the skill-practice or S Groups of 1951, when the trainer presented concepts as part of the briefing for a practice session or, more inductively, as part of the summary of the analysis of a skill-practice experience. This is not surprising since the role relationship between the trainer and the members of the S Group was defined more didactically from the beginning.

A series of general "theory sessions" was restored after 1951, but efforts were made to gear content more closely to the modal needs of T-Group members at the time of presentation. As long as a sharp differentiation between morning and afternoon programs persisted in the design, some pulling and hauling between the needs of each characterized staff planning.

A third demand upon the theory sessions was for some internal consistency in the sequence of concepts presented from day to day. One attempted solution to this problem, tried in 1956, 1957, and 1958, was to assign the sequence of the first week's theory sessions—usually on individual and group dynamics—to one staff member. It is not entirely clear why the use of a single lecturer for a block of conceptual presentations in his field was abandoned at Bethel after 1958 and why it has not been widely adopted in laboratories outside Bethel. One factor is probably that the plan ran against the wishes of various staff members to present theory sessions in content areas where they possess some special competence. In part, this reflects a realistic appraisal of the differences in special competences among members of a staff. But it also involves at times the desire to share in the prestige which is ascribed to a public presentation. The use of special lecturers to develop sequences of theory sessions, abandoned in cross-occupational laboratories, has persisted in occupational laboratories where a person with a strong background in relevant research and experience is brought in as a special resource.

As the use of the T-Group medium for a variety of training functions has made headway in laboratories, the competition among parts of the staff for a share of general theory session time has been reduced. The following sequence for theory presentations has become fairly common in laboratories integrated according to type pattern number two, in which the T-Group medium is used for the full range of objectives. (1) A series of presentations on individual and small-group dynamics is given in the early days of the laboratory, where T Groups are meeting several times daily. (2) Presentations on organizational (or community) and role dynamics are made during the middle period of the laboratory, where T Groups are engaged during part of their time in developing and analyzing various organizational (or community) experiences. (3) Ideas about change, change agentry, and application are made available during the final period of the laboratory.

Considerable differences continue to exist among staff members in their evaluation of the effects of conceptual presentations upon the learning of laboratory members. No staff member, so far as I know, would deny the necessity or value of concepts used or developed relevantly to clinical interpretation of T-Group episodes and events. But some staff members, who emphasize experience-based learning and the therapeutic or semitherapeutic character of T-Group experience, are inclined to doubt the value of general theory sessions as an uneconomic use of learning time, and as leading to intellectualization by participants and thus to avoidance of facing and dealing with significant emotional problems. General theory sessions have thus tended to disappear, or have been greatly reduced in number, in many laboratories integrated in type pattern number one, where the T Group is central.

Other trainers, who employ more of an action research model (as contrasted with a clinical model) of training, emphasize participants' needs for valid concepts to be used as tools in diagnosing problems and in testing and evaluating solutions. These trainers are likely to stress also the continuing dedication of the laboratory to the building of bridges between the needs of social practice and the resources of social science research. Most of these trainers would admit that T Groups can use a discussion of concepts from the behavioral sciences as a flight from facing difficult emotional problems, but, they insist, discussions of outside, "practical" affairs can be used in the same way. This problem, they would say, is a general training problem of helping groups and group members face and deal with difficult and painful realities in their lives.

The constructive resolution of staff differences concerning the value of theory presentations probably calls for two lines of staff effort. One is for staff members to confront their differences with respect to the values and objectives which they consider to be centrally important in laboratory education. The second line of resolution is to institute further researches, along the lines begun by three staff members at Bethel in 1957, concerning the effects and effectiveness of various methods and formats for the communication of social science concepts to laboratory participants.[15] It is interesting to note that early experimentation with large-meeting methods has had relatively little effect upon the methods employed in theory sessions at the laboratory. The joining of these two lines of investigation in future research on the communication of concepts may help to resolve some of the issues which now tend to divide laboratory staffs.

It has been noted that the "conceptual" input in early laboratories at Bethel was "ideological" as well as "descriptive." The tendency has been to move away from "ideological" inputs, in terms of the communication and testing of value generalizations and of the involvement of participants in diagnosing social issues in which massive value orientations are in conflict. In general, both processes require confrontation of discrepant but compartmentalized value orientations. Staff and participant support is needed in helping a participant work toward some meaningful reconciliation of these discrepancies. Such normative inquiry does occur in the course of T-Group experience. Whether it needs encouragement in other parts of a laboratory design is a moot question.

Two sets of issues seem to divide current laboratory staffs at this point. One set of issues has to do with the nature of the person who is participating in training and, by extension, with the processes in which

[15] Charles Seashore, Ronald Lippitt, and Jack R. Gibb. *Study of Communication of Theory in a Human Relations Laboratory*. Ann Arbor, Michigan: Foundation for the Study of Human Behavior, 1962.

the person may be most fruitfully involved in rethinking and remaking his value orientations toward himself, toward others, and toward life.

According to one view, the person is seen primarily in existential terms. The "real" person is a private individual stripped of his roles and statuses. "Role" and "status" tend to be opposed to "individuality." The task of clarifying identity and commitment is seen as an individual attainment. Significant normative reorientation will occur only as the person is helped in setting aside the roles and statuses in which he is enmeshed outside the laboratory, and in facing himself as an individual. The proper focus of training attention, on this view, insofar as the goal of training involves normative reorientation for the individual participant, is upon life values internal to the person. These life values are revealed most authentically in the language of feelings and behavior as these are manifested in here-and-now "gut level" encounters in the laboratory situation. Consideration of ideological issues interferes with this process of value recommitment.[16]

According to a second view, the person is a composition of roles as well as a biologic individual, however unique and distinctive his personal patterning of these roles and his private value orientations toward the patterning may be. Personal confrontation of discrepant values, in any complete sense, is a confrontation of the person to himself in the whole range of his roles—as family member, as lover, as husband or wife, as man or woman, as citizen, as member of an occupational group, as worker in an organization. This involves reconsideration of publicly professed ideologies as well as inner value systems. To limit re-educative attention to the person as he involves himself in the here-and-now events of a laboratory situation is a healthy and necessary propaedeutic to confrontation of himself in other public relationships—with all the discrepancies and conflicts in value orientation which these various "selves" often embody. The full confrontation of himself as a person comes as he accepts the discrepancies and conflicts in his various roles as his problem to resolve with the help of others. Resolution cannot occur in isolation from the demands, requirements, and ideologies of the various roles which life in his culture embodies It occurs rather in creative interadaptation of roles to roles, of roles to

[16] Among laboratory trainers, I find this point of view most clearly expressed and most consistently carried through into a rounded training orientation by Irving Weschler, Fred Massarik, and Robert Tannenbaum, in "The Self in Process: A Sensitivity Training Emphasis," in Irving Weschler and Edgar Schein (Eds.), *Issues in Human Relations Training*, Washington, D.C.: NTL Selected Readings Series, No. 5, 1962. Their conception of the T Group will be examined later in this chapter.

self, and of self to roles. It is in facing deeply the problems of "back-home application of laboratory learnings and experiences," not in the T Group, that the realistic problems of value reorientation may come most sharply into focus for the laboratory participant.[17]

Both points of view accept clarification and reorientation of central life values as a primary aim of laboratory training. Proponents of both points of view would question another tendency in some streams of laboratory practice. This is a tendency to focus attention primarily on problems of the participant in functioning within his occupational and work role to the virtual exclusion of attention to personal problems in nonvocational relationships or in relations to self. This tendency is most prevalent in occupational laboratories and least prevalent in general human relations laboratories. Perhaps it is most prevalent in "family" training conducted with a working unit of an organization. The tendency may be due not so much to the convictions of the train-ers caught up in it as to the demands for results that will "pay off" more immediately. Attention to civic issues, for example, may be seen as irrelevant or even mischievous.

It is the trend toward greater integration within laboratory designs which has brought issues concerning re-education in value orientations and ideologies to the fore once again in staff discussions. Future dis-cussions in this area are bound to become more "philosophical" than before.

Training in the Skills of Group Membership and Leadership

It was in the 1956 summer laboratory session at Bethel that the de-segregation of skill-practice groups and T Groups was first accom-plished after their separation in 1951. In that laboratory, half T Groups were used as the medium for skill practice of group member-ship and leadership skills. The trainer and associate trainer met to decide after the morning session what area of skill practice was most needed by members of the T Group. Each trainer then worked with half the T Group in the area identified. The result was a much closer relationship between what was learned in the skill-practice session and the problems being grappled with in the T Group. Since that

[17] This second point of view is developed more fully in Kenneth D. Benne. *Education in the Quest for Identity and Community.* The Boyd H. Bode Memo-rial Lectures, 1961. Columbus, Ohio: The College of Education, The Ohio State University, 1962.

time the trend has been toward the inclusion of skill-practice exercises within the total T Group.

One variation in skill-practice sessions deserves notice here. This is a shift from role playing, which involves more or less elaborate briefing of situations and members, to the use of games in which members play "themselves" within the context of the rules of the game. The use of games was pioneered in the Esso laboratories (1958–1959) and has found extensive use subsequently in NTL and other laboratories for industrial managers. More recently, games have been used for skill training in cross-occupational laboratories as well.

One advantage of the game for skill practice is that in its use members reveal their own behavior more directly for analysis than they may do in role playing. Hence, the behavior produced for learning is "more real." However, the situation of the game may be taken as "less real" than a constructed case like those in which participants live and work. One practice may yield more insight into "self" in general; the other, more insight into "self" in situations of a given type. Probably some combination of the two kinds of skill practice will continue, pending further evaluation research into the differential learning effects of the two.

Study of the Dynamics of Larger Social Systems

An important breakthrough in the area of training in the dynamics of larger social systems developed at the Southwest Human Relations Training Laboratory in Texas in 1957.[18] The staff built a training design upon the design of earlier experimentation by Muzafer and Carolyn Sherif in inducing intergroup conflict in the field setting of a boys' camp and studying its effects.[19] A number of variations on this training design have developed over the years. In essential form, the experience pits two or more T Groups, after they have established a group history and identity, in a win-lose competition. Each group produces a specified product. One of these products is judged better than the other by some judging mechanism. Data are collected from all groups concerning both the "goodness" or "badness" of the group products and of their own and other groups during the course of the

[18] Robert R. Blake and Jane Srygley Mouton. "Reactions to Intergroup Competition under Win-Lose Conditions." *Management Science*, 7, 420–435, 1961.

[19] Muzafer Sherif and Carolyn Sherif. *Groups in Harmony and Tension.* New York: Harper & Bros., 1953.

competition, before and following the judgment. These data illuminate many of the effects of conflict upon the internal functioning of each group and upon the relationships among groups. Analysis of the data by each group and by the assembly of the groups involved yields important learnings about intergroup relations.

A collaborative organizational exercise was introduced into the NTL Management Work Conference at Arden House in 1960. Two T Groups which had formerly engaged in competition were asked to form a collaborative organization for producing greeting cards. This experience had been preceded by theory presentations on various types of organizational theory. The groups built an organization, tried it out in production, and analyzed the results. Various assumptions about organizational control, about the relations of management and workers, among others, were given an empirical test under laboratory conditions. Since that time both intergroup competitions and collaborations have been used in many cross-occupational as well as occupational laboratories.

These designs show how the T-Group medium may be used to produce learnings about the dynamics of larger social systems. They represent an important step in facilitating the second type pattern of laboratory integration.

One design of the third type pattern for achieving integration of learnings about self and interpersonal relations with learnings about organizational behavior and change is well illustrated by recent training laboratories conducted in the Aluminum Company of Canada.[20] A first week includes heavy emphasis on T Groups with supporting theory sessions and with skill-practice sessions conducted in T Groups. A methodology of organizational diagnosis is taught concurrently through the discussion and analysis of cases. During the second week, T-Group activity is diminished, and the emphasis on case discussion and analysis increased. During the third week, participants' back-home problems of change and application of laboratory learnings are analyzed in T-Group formations. The trainer continues to work with his T Group during this final laboratory period. Case discussions focus on problems of organizational change, paralleling the planning for change that is occurring in the T Groups. A staff, skilled both in laboratory training and in case discussion, facilitates the integration of laboratory learnings about self, group, and organization at various

---

[20] For a discussion of this laboratory variant—its design and rationale—see James V. Clark, *Education for the Use of Behavioral Science*, U.C.L.A. Institute of Industrial Relations, 1962, Chapter 6. Additional information may be obtained from Mr. Alec Winn, Montreal Headquarters, Aluminum Company of Canada.

stages of laboratory development, but especially during the final week in which bridging between the cultural island of the laboratory and the cultural mainland of life and work becomes a focal concern.

The Learning of Change-Agent Skills and Planning for Back-Home Application

The alumni program for Staff and Action Leaders (SAL) conducted at Bethel during the summers of 1957 and 1958 has been mentioned. A training program was built around concepts of planned change and of the functioning of the change agent, both as outside consultant and inside supervisor and administrator.[21]

Members of the SAL group worked to build a group in which they could give and receive help to one another on back-home problems. "T-Group-like" processes emerged and were facilitated and used for personal learning. The SAL group also discussed ideas about institutional change and the change agent and practiced consultation skills through a sequence of role-played episodes. As the group took shape, members alternately became clients and consultants to one another in diagnosing and strategizing change problems in which the client-member was involved at home. (Work, family, and civic problems were explored.) Consultation practice beyond the SAL group itself was also provided through work by SAL members with clients in the basic laboratory and in the Bethel community.[22]

The development of this alumni program contributed to subsequent designs of basic laboratories in the following ways: (1) It identified change-agent skills which could be learned in a laboratory setting and developed materials and formats for conducting such training. (2) It demonstrated that change-agent skills could be practiced through meaningful integration of skill training with substantive work on the back-home problems. (3) It utilized the medium of a developing T Group for skill practice of change-agent skills, for intensive diagnosis and planning directed to back-home problems of participants, and for dealing with problems in the normative reorientation of members.

[21] The building of this curriculum was greatly facilitated by the analysis of planned changes prepared by R. Lippitt, J. Watson, and B. Westley. *The Dynamics of Planned Change.* New York: Harcourt, Brace & Co., 1958. This work was continuous with the analysis of change-agent skills around which the original BST Groups had been built.

[22] Similar alumni programs have been conducted at the Green Lake Laboratory for religious workers in 1959 and 1961 and at the Boston University Laboratory in 1962.

In 1957, a similar sequence was introduced into the afternoon program of T Groups in the NTL laboratory for staff members from various national organizations at Buck Hill Falls, Pennsylvania. And, in 1958, a similar design was used at the Management Work Conference at Arden House. Since that time, variations have become a part of a number of cross-occupational as well as occupational laboratories.

Another form of integration of the second type pattern, as in the Aluminum Company of Canada program, focuses heavily upon T-Group work during the early part of the laboratory with supporting theory and skill-practice sessions. After the T Groups have taken shape as re-educative media, some part of their time is spent in studying change, practicing change-agent skills, and helping one another on back-home problems.

An integration of the third type pattern has also been tried in a number of laboratories. In 1960, at a three-week laboratory for school leaders in Bethel, separate application groups were formed after a first week of intensive concentration on learnings about self and small groups in T-Group settings. During the following two weeks, members of these application groups worked intensively on giving help to one another on some actual back-home situations. These groups alternated between a concentration on back-home problems and a focus upon the processes and relationships involved in acting as change agents and clients. Over time, members increasingly used application groups for testing insights into their own behavior acquired in their T Group. The reverse process also took place. Trainers encouraged these processes of participant integration of experiences in the two parts of the laboratory program.

Each of these designs represents an attempt to bring various laboratory training objectives into a relationship of mutual support.

The Fortunes of the T Group in the Reintegration of Laboratories: Theme and Variations

The central theme in T-Group operation has become clarified in the seventeen years of its evolution. It is now seen basically as a group devoted to the mutual facilitation of learning by all of its members. A major content of the learning sought is the developing experience of the group and its members in here-and-now behavioral events. Each member is encouraged to function as observer-participant, as diagnostician-actor, as planner-executor-evaluator, as theorist-practitioner, as expresser of feeling and critic of expression, and as helper-client.

In much of life as it is lived, these hyphenated functions of participation are separated, both among persons and within persons. They tend to be allocated to different persons or groups of persons within the larger society—theorists theorize and practitioners practice, planners plan and executives execute, helpers give help and clients receive help. Differential allocation of functions occurs also in particular groups and organizations—in families and factories, in schools and hospitals. The segregation of these functions penetrates into personalities as well. Intentions are separated from responses, valuations from emotions and feelings, thinking from patterns of overt action.

Segregation of the human functions involved in full participation leads to disintegrity and fragmentation of response. Personal action and response tend to lose health and wholeness. Collective action loses the quality of a "community" of effort which supports in the same process personal growth and social progress.

T-Group experience confronts members with areas of disintegrity and fragmentation in their own patterns of response, personal and collective. It presses each member to understand, with the help of others, the bases of his disintegrities in thought, feeling, valuation, perception, and action and to invent patterns of response that are more integral in quality and in effect. It presses each member equally to help others in their somewhat unique quests for understanding and growth.

Some such theme, I believe, runs through all current variations in T-Group operation and rationale. Yet the developing experience of a T Group is so complex that it can be interpreted with validity in many ways. Variations occur in part because of different emphases in the learning sought. They occur also because of different "theories" of learning and participation used by different trainers. The problems which any T Group throw up experientially for clarification and solution will also vary with the mix of its membership along various dimensions—personality styles, occupational background, cultural background, age, and sex.

The principal challenge which recent patterns of laboratory re-integration have brought to the T Group is a reconsideration of the range of its uses. No laboratory trainer today denies the importance of the T Group for achieving learnings about self, interpersonal relations, and small-group functioning through a focus upon here-and-now intragroup episodes and events. That the T Group can be used to facilitate learning also through analysis of the outside involvements of its members is no longer a theory but a demonstrated fact. Some of these outside involvements can be generated within the laboratory setting, involving T Groups and T-Group members in transactions with other groups in the laboratory environment. The analysis of these transactions in the T Group can yield added learnings about self and group and about the dynamics of larger social systems as well. Examination of extralaboratory involvements of members may also be brought into the ambit of T-Group concern. In brief, the T Group has been found to be a more robust and resilient medium for a wide range of re-educative effects than would have been considered possible during the period of its relative segregation within laboratory designs. (Extralaboratory uses of T-Group processes have further demonstrated the adaptability of the T-Group medium in achieving a wide range of learning objectives.) But issues are still encountered as to the "best" use of T Groups in laboratory settings. Recent developments have brought the focus of attention in such issues upon evaluation of the importance of various learning objectives. They can no longer be settled by arguments concerning technical feasibility alone.

Idiosyncratic variations upon the basic theme of the T Group are thus many and various. Recently, two "technologies" of T-Group operation have emerged and have been practiced, standardized, and studied sufficiently to warrant characterization as "distinctive types" within the larger picture of T-Group development, inside and outside NTL. One of these is the use of the T Group to provide "therapy for normals." This variant type has been pioneered by the Graduate School of Business Administration at the University of California in Los Angeles and, to some extent, within the Western Training Laboratory. The second is the instrumented T Group, invented at the Southwest Human Relations Laboratory in Texas and developed further in Esso-Humble Oil Company training programs.

A description of these "typical" variations may be useful in two ways in closing this historical account. First, they illustrate concretely the operation of an important factor in current and prospective innovations in the practice of laboratory training—a factor previously noted. This is the emergence of regional laboratories and university centers devoted to experimentation with processes of training and change. Second, since the two types diverge somewhat sharply from each other in learning outcomes sought, they permit the clear posing of alternative axes in human relations education around which future developments in this field of social practice will probably swing and to which further integrative efforts may be addressed.

Variation I: Therapy for Normals

In an admirably clear and candid account of this approach to T-Group training, three of its practitioners—Irving Weschler, Fred Massarik, and Robert Tannenbaum—have identified the learning outcomes that it is designed to help participants to effect.

The network of social relationships which vitally influences our lives is replete with contradictory demands and inconsistencies.   These not only take their toll of the clinically recognized psychotic, but they also affect the lives of most of us who seem to be "getting along" tolerably well with the world and the people around us. . . .
Our recent approach to sensitivity training represents one means for facilitating the personal growth of persons who, while "normal" by most accepted cultural standards, may indeed be affected in subtle and complex ways by these very standards. For us . . . sensitivity training is no longer primarily a technique for the improvement of group functioning, the development of interpersonal skills, the intellectual discussion of human relations problems, or the more surface discussion of neurotic manifestations. . . . Rather, sensitivity training is now pointed in the direction of the total enhancement of the individual.
Our version of sensitivity training increasingly concerns itself with the strengthening of the individual in his desires to experience people and events more fully, to know himself more intimately and accurately, to find a more significant meaning for his life, and to initiate or sustain a process of individual growth toward ever-increasing personal adequacy.
We are beginning to deal with life values which come to be deeply reflected in the total pattern of a person's attitudes and behavior. We are involved, for instance, with his tendency to control or be controlled by others, with his management of anger, with his ability to express and receive love or affection, with his feelings of loneliness, with his search for personal identity, with his testing of his own adequacy, and with other similar concerns.   Any one of these "themes" is typically of somewhat greater personal significance to one person than to another, yet each is likely to have real meaning to all, as they go through a training experience together.[23]

The authors make it clear that the selection of these learning outcomes for emphasis has emerged in a process of development in their own experiences with training. They have tried other emphases and have chosen the one they now espouse.

[23] Irving Weschler, Fred Massarik, and Robert Tannenbaum, *op. cit.*, pp. 34–35. See also Irving Weschler, and Jerome Reisel, *Inside a Sensitivity Group.* Los Angeles: Institute of Industrial Relations, University of California, 1960, for rich protocol materials drawn from a T Group throughout its life span, together with interspersed clinical comments.

. . . Gradually, we have moved from a strong emphasis on group variables to a relatively greater attention on individual dynamics and the unfolding of a more fully functioning personality. We have shifted from a stress on the development of interpersonal skills (narrowly defined) to a greater concern with an individual's understanding of himself and of his relations with others.

Our discussions in early training groups often dealt, at a rather superficial level, with there-and-then matters; but as time has passed there has been increasing involvement in "gut-level" here-and-now events. Whereas before, much effort was devoted to working on the specific, immediate, on-the-job problems of participants, now only minor emphasis on such matters remains. Rather, much greater attention is centered on broader, pervasive concerns of the group members, such as their central life values and their rarely faced feelings about themselves and others.

As attention came to be focused on the individual trainee, we noted that he began shifting his major emphasis from his neurotic tendencies to the release of his potential for richer, more constructive, satisfying living. Thus he appears to have become progressively less concerned with the discovery of short-run solutions to personal problems, and in turn exhibits more of an interest in long-range individual growth and development.[24]

The factors that have entered into their selection of this emphasis are not fully elucidated by the authors. Presumably, the selection was influenced by the basic importance they attach to personal growth as a central value in human affairs. Further, their selection seems influenced by a diagnosis of the vicissitudes of persons in contemporary culture. They see the crippling barriers which our culture puts in the way of "normals" in their attempts to achieve self-generated and self-directed personal growth. The prevailing definitions of "normal" behavior often lead men and women to a life of continuous role playing. Contrived façade and role meet contrived façade and role in much human interchange. Open and authentic encounter of person with person falls outside the rules of the "culture game."

"Normals" caught in the norms of the "culture game" are isolated and alienated within their interpersonal relations, and, since the urge toward personal authenticity seems to be an inherent motivation in healthy selves, "normals" become alienated also within themselves. Sensitivity training offers participants involvement in a régime of authentic interpersonal relations, in which processes of self-discovery through personal confrontation and human encounter are practiced and prized. It is a "respite from the culture game"—in the authors' words—or, more robustly stated, a deeply experienced alternative to that game. The immediate gains for the participant are a strengthened ego and an improved self-image. The continuing quest, beyond the

[24] *Ibid.*, pp. 33–34.

training, to which the participant is invited is a personal program of "long-range individual growth and development," not the short-run solution of personal or vocational problems. Finally, and this is speculative, the authors are associated with a human relations research group in a university school of business administration. In their work setting, they may well feel a deep responsibility to introduce humanistically oriented educative processes into the generally "vocational" and "technical" emphasis of a business school curriculum. At any rate, their educational emphasis is deeply and essentially humanistic in orientation.

What type of laboratory design is consistent with this orientation of T-Group training? The sensitivity training referred to in the published writings took place not in a laboratory but in a course on the campus of a university. Participants met in weekly sessions. The published statements permit only inferences as to the curriculum supports which the authors would provide for "sensitivity training" in a residential laboratory. It seems fair to infer, however, that the ideal laboratory design for them would be of type pattern number one with heavy emphasis on T-Group experience. Perhaps the experience in the original T Groups might be supplemented by experience, for part of the laboratory period, in a second T Group, sometimes called an N (New) Group. Activities outside T Groups would be designed to facilitate and deepen processes of T-Group learning. The authors mention such individual activities as periods of reflective silence and the writing out (for personal use) of personal experiences and impressions of others, and such general sessions as a session using films like *Eye of the Beholder,* a session in which a staff member reads anonymously and publicly individual accounts by participants of potent personal feelings about themselves which they tend to hide from others, theory presentations of "The Language of the Emotions." [25]

The authors stress the major role which trainer interventions play in determining the emphasis which develops in T-Group learning.

. . . In any group, much is said and done (both verbally and nonverbally) at the content level and in terms of feelings. The trainer—as well as the other group members—cannot possibly respond to all of it. He must make a choice from among alternatives in the selection of his interventions, any of which are likely to have much influence in determining the group's direction. . . . We feel it important that trainers face the impact of their actions (or inactions) rather than deny them. . . .

In the early life of almost any sensitivity training group, for example, the members begin to react in characteristic ways to the lack of both structure

[25] *Ibid.,* pp. 35–36.

and overt direction. The trainer can help the group to analyze and discuss the role of structure in effective group functioning and can assist it to find a pattern appropriate for its purposes, or he can help the members of the group to become aware of and try to understand the nature of their feelings as they have responded to the lack of structure. In our judgment, the former intervention (and subsequent ones like it) will lead to a concern with group variables; whereas the latter intervention (together with subsequent ones of like kind) will move the group in a direction of concern with individual variables.[26]

And, consistent with their emphasis on "personality," as contrasted with "intellectual" determination of behavior generally, the authors stress the personality dynamics of the trainer as influential in shaping the content and style of his interventions.

The nature of trainer-intervention, we feel strongly, is based on something more than intellectual considerations. The personality dynamics of the trainer undoubtedly are a key determining factor. A trainer who chooses the self-in-process direction must be willing and able to face, at least on occasion, intense emotional encounters which involve strong expressions of hostility, anger, love, fear, anxiety, hope, and the like. He must be able to face such feelings and deal with them, both as they occur in others and in himself, without becoming blocked, anxious, or confused. He must be able, on occasion, to share his own feelings with the group.[27]

Finally, the authors recognize the close kinship of their type of sensitivity training to psychotherapy.

By now it should be quite clear that major similarities exist between this type of sensitivity training and some forms of group psychotherapy. The rather distinct differences between training and therapy to which Jerome D. Frank was able to point a few years ago appear to be becoming more and more blurred. Both of these activities are concerned with increasing the sensitivity of the group members to their own functioning and that of others and with correcting blind spots and distortions. Sensitivity training shares with group psychotherapy the objective of ego-strengthening and improving the self-image. Both stress the development of insights and opportunities for reality-testing. Both attempt to examine pervasive central-life values and put emphasis on replacing old, hampering modes of behavior with more adaptive new ones. . . .

What is needed now is a general theory of the structure and dynamics of the interpersonal helping process which would bring under one single conceptual scheme the various psychotherapies, sensitivity training, psychiatric case work, counseling, guidance, and existential psychology. . . . This effort would represent a spelling out of the assumptions, techniques, and

[26] *Ibid.*, p. 36.
[27] *Ibid.*, pp. 36–37.

desired outcomes of a variety of helping activities, all designed to contribute, in one form or another, to the enhancement of the total person.[28]

Variation II: The Instrumented T Group

In sensitivity training on the model of "therapy for normals," as we have seen, the importance of the group trainer is emphasized. Realization of the potential for personal growth and reduction of the risk of personal damage in the group experience require trainers "with a high professional and clinical competence, a dedication of purpose, a genuine interest in the well-being of people, a constant commitment toward experimentation and evaluation, and an appreciation of the potential risks in this type of activity." [29]

In the instrumented T Group, the trainer is removed from direct participation in the group. In his place, a series of self-administered instruments are introduced. The feedback provided by the compilation and analysis of the data provided by all members in responding to these instruments serves as a principal steering mechanism in the group's development and in the learnings which members achieve. The rationale underlying the instrumented group is a "dilemma-invention theory" of learning. The instrumented T Group (or Development Group), like all T Groups, is initially confronted with a "dilemma" situation—familiar conditions and rules of group interaction are removed. As in other T Groups, participants try to meet the dilemma initially by imposing traditional ways of behavior on the group. When these ways fail, the group is moved to experiment, to invent, and to think through and reconstruct their assumptions.

How, precisely, does an instrumented T Group operate? [30] The general purpose is not unlike that of many trainer-helped groups: to aid participants in becoming more effective members of groups. The

[28] *Ibid.*, pp. 44–45.

[29] *Ibid.*, p. 46.

[30] A convenient brief account of this type of group training is provided by Robert R. Blake and Jane Srygley Mouton, "The Instrumented Training Laboratory" in Irving R. Weschler, and Edgar H. Schein. *Issues in Human Relations Training*, NTL Selected Readings Series, No. 5, 1962. In their historical note, Blake and Mouton date the first fully instrumented laboratory as the Fifth Southwest Human Relations Training Laboratory in Texas, 1959. They acknowledge help in the development of this variant of group training, from Muzafer and Carolyn Sherif, Herbert Shepard, Murray Horwitz, Frank Cassens, and J. H. Lumpkin. This laboratory pattern has been used in industrial, university, and hospital settings, as well as in cross-occupational laboratories, and in laboratories for religious workers.

groups are usually smaller than trainer-helped groups. Various principles may be employed in composing the groups—occupationally heterogeneous groupings have been used, and groups representing a diagonal slice through the hierarchy of one organization, as well as "family" groups (work teams) from the same organization, have also been trained in this way.

In the instrumented T Group (or Development Group, as the authors rename it), emphasis is placed upon the early establishment of a feedback model in the group. This is not different from the aim of trainer-helped groups. But the way in which the feedback mechanism is introduced and maintained is distinctly different. Blake and Mouton have the following to say about this difference:

Feedback is emphasized . . . as an important key to procedural, process, and personal learning. Here is where the difference between the two approaches becomes evident. In the trainer-directed group, the primary role of the trainer is to aid feedback by calling attention to critical events occurring within the group. He creates the conditions and provides the model for members to become participant-observers of group action. The trainer also can make significant contributions in helping members to explore ground rules appropriate for personal evaluation. In other words, in a trainer-directed group, one important focus of trainer-intervention is on establishing the feedback model.

In the instrumented group, the entry into feedback is aided by a set of scales and measures which are used to plot, on wall charts, the characteristics of group and personal action during each meeting. After the concept of feedback and examples of its use have been introduced, "direct" feedback is given by members themselves whenever they see it as appropriate. The frequency of face-to-face feedback is not lessened when instruments, rather than a trainer, are used to establish and apply the feedback model; instead, it appears to be enhanced. In comparison with the trainer-directed group, however, no one person is set apart to provide, to provoke, or to force the use of feedback for learning.[31]

The instruments introduced into the group by the laboratory staff are of three general sorts: rating scales, check lists, and rankings. The rating scales permit participants to rate quantitatively perceived variables in their group: the type of structure in the group, the level of mutual support and trust among members, the degree of leveling among members, group accomplishment, group development, group cohesion. Check lists provide an opportunity for participants to identify the actual procedures used by the group in making decisions, the words that best describe the climate of a group session, the types of agenda items dealt with during a group session. In the case of

[31] *Ibid.*, pp. 63–64.

both rating scales and check lists, quantitative data from all members are compiled, grouped, and charted by the group for its use. Ranges, as well as measures of central tendency, are determined and charted by the group and used as an aid to self-diagnosis and self-evaluation of the group condition.

Rankings are used in comparing members within a group on some aspect of personal behavior. Members rank themselves and one another from "most to least" in relation to some psychological factor—rankings of influence in the group are most often used. Ranks for each member are averaged. The average is fed back to the member, who usually ranks himself as well. Discrepancies between his self-perception and perception of others of his influence in the group can be evaluated and discussed. These rankings may be made several times during a laboratory session.

Actually, the model of training employed in the instrumented group (and laboratory) is an action research model. Members learn about their group and their membership by becoming "an active and integral part of the analyzing, gathering, and interpreting of data" [32] about themselves and their group. A very important part of the justification for this type of training model is that participants can readily make frequent and effective use of the model not only in the laboratory but also in their group and organizational life outside the laboratory. The belief of the proponents of the instrumented group is that members who assume responsibility for doing action research in effecting changes in themselves and their group will transfer laboratory methods more readily beyond the laboratory than members who have depended upon an "expert" trainer or therapist in learning how to learn.

Of course, an instrumented T Group is not deprived of expert guidance in other laboratory activities that condition and support its development. In general, the instrumented laboratory is integrated according to the second type pattern; i.e., the T Group is used as a medium for various kinds of learning. The staff intervenes, in words congenial to the instrumented laboratory's underlying theory of learning, by precipitating dilemmas and providing inquiry tools and conceptual tools to aid the group in inventing and experimenting with ways to handle these dilemmas.

The major staff intervention is, of course, in the provision of the instruments of action research and in training members to use the data gathered through their use. But the laboratory staff may use

[32] *Ibid.*, p. 70.

general sessions in modeling and in setting standards for giving and receiving feedback. One development group may be asked to conduct a brief session in the presence of another group who act as observers and feed back observations for discussion. The staff members who are conducting the session offer comments or ask questions regarding basic features of the intragroup and intergroup interactions.

Staff members also arrange for intergroup competitions and collaborations among development groups and help them to collect and analyze data about processes and problems in intergroup (organizational or community) relations. Theory sessions are also provided by the staff as needed by the participants. Thus in a variety of ways the laboratory staff make training contributions without "sitting in the group and controlling, or at least influencing or regulating, their interaction on a session-by-session basis." [33]

Summary Comment

The historical account of the development of the T Group in the context of the training laboratory has been brought up to date. This development is continuing. Some of the trends noted here in recent events may prove to be ephemeral and other more valid trends revealed by future developments. Prediction of the future is more appropriate to the prophet than to the historian. But perhaps it is within the prerogative of the historian to note in conclusion a few of the major issues which are actively engaging the attention of professional trainers today and are at times tending to divide their efforts. Whether these issues will be settled by autonomous parallel developments within the laboratory "movement" or whether they will be used as opportunities for creative syntheses in experimental training methodologies and designs will be determined by future events.

General Human Relations Laboratories and Vocational Laboratories

One set of issues focuses in differences between the simultaneous operation and organization of two kinds of laboratories. Cross-occupational laboratories, often called general human relations labora-

[33] *Ibid.*, p. 71.

tories, exist side by side with occupationally homogeneous laboratories. The latter kind of laboratory reaches its peak in family type laboratories in which work units from an organization are transplanted into laboratories for training. While many elements of methodology and technology are common to both, the differences in perceived learning needs and the directions resulting from efforts generated in participants to find common ground lead to marked and perhaps widening differences. In the general human relations laboratories the search for common ground among occupationally heterogeneous participants may lead to a focus on intrapersonal problems and disintegrities between role demands on the person "more intimate" than the demands of the vocational role. Trainers need not yield completely to differences in the empirical realities of these two kinds of laboratory situations. Trainers in occupationally homogeneous laboratories may deliberately institute experiences which tend to generalize beyond the vocational focus. And trainers in general human relations laboratories may deliberately seek to vocationalize the "general education" postures which such laboratories tend to assume. But the inherent educational dynamics of the two situations are different, and these differences have shown up in recent laboratory practice.

The T Group conceived as "therapy for normals" seems at home in general human relations laboratories, but other T-Group and laboratory experiences not so deeply oriented to therapy are equally so. Emphasis on task aspects of group functioning as well as emphasis on role and organizational functioning are reduced, however, to some extent. A humanistic general education emphasis in T Groups and in the laboratory built to support them fits the tendency in these laboratories. On the other hand, the emphasis, in occupational laboratories, on the task aspects of groups, means that T Groups and the supporting laboratory activities are more group-oriented. Instrumented T Groups are more commonly used in occupational laboratories.

This is no place to evaluate the values and disvalues of general education and vocational emphases in T Groups and training laboratories. Nor is it the place to speculate on possible integrations of the two emphases. But the issues have been drawn within the profession of trainers and need to be faced.

Action Research Models Versus Clinical Models of Training

Some of the issues between the action research model of training and more clinical models have been noted throughout this account. Particularly, differences in the conception of the role of the trainer in the two models were noted. The conception of T-Group experience as "therapy for normals" and the conception of the instrumented T Group bring this issue into clear relief.

What, more specifically, are the differences between the two?

1. In the clinical model, problems for attention in the T Group arise out of the existential encounters of member with member and of members with trainer. The specific character of these problems cannot be anticipated in advance. The problems emerge out of deeply felt difficulties inherent both in the life histories of individual members and in the encounters between unique individuals in the group setting. Data at the feeling level of experience are collected and out of these data problems can be clarified. On the other hand, the action research model, as illustrated in the instrumented T Group, presupposes that the areas of significant data for group inquiry and learning can be anticipated, at least in general terms, in advance. Trainer-led T Groups also use instruments for data collection, whether planned in advance or developed as a group begins to take an action research approach to its difficulties. The instruments are shaped by the assumption that certain kinds of data will be important for members to collect and analyze. Where the clinical model stresses the amassing of qualitative data, the action research model seeks for quantifiable data as well.

2. In the clinical model, abstract concepts drawn from experience outside the developing group situation are weighed with great caution. Trust is placed in concepts developed in and near to the "gut-level" experiences of members which emerge in the group and demand more or less immediate clarification. In groups functioning with an action research model, on the other hand, concepts and related skills of data collection, analysis, and application, are provided as a necessary ingredient of thoughtful action-oriented research by group members into the problems that they encounter.

3. Actually, the hope in both kinds of groups is that learning and growth achieved in the laboratory experience will be transferred to improve the quality of personal functioning of members in their outside associations. But the assumptions about how such transfer of

learning best takes place seems to be quite different in the two models. In the clinical model, what is likely to transfer effectively are growth in integrity and wholeness within the person of the member. The assumption seems to be that a person who can achieve a more authentic revelation of himself to himself and a way of relating authentically to others will transfer these personal achievements into the various relationships of his life. This transfer is conceived as a continuing process of personal growth in other associations. In the action research model more dependence is placed upon the acquisition of appropriate concepts and skills and of a developing habit of using these concepts and skills in clarifying and diagnosing problems in interpersonal, group, and intergroup situations.

The distinctions between these two models of training are perhaps more sharply differentiated here than examination of training-learning processes in groups organized according to each model would support. In fact, most laboratory sessions successfully utilize concepts underlying both models. However, the two models have attained an admirable degree of differentiation in the two variations of T-Group training reviewed in the final section of this chapter. Clear differentiation is an advantage if the different models can be sympathetically yet rigorously tested and evaluated in future laboratories. As such evaluations occur, it seems clear now that professional trainers will have to give attention to their differences with respect to the goals of training as well as to the effectiveness of varying techniques. This further growth in the understanding of T Groups and their place in the re-education of human relationships belongs to the future.

5

Trainer-Intervention:

Case Episodes

Leland P. Bradford

Chapter 3 gave a very brief glimpse into a T Group in action. This chapter will attempt to give a more inclusive, firsthand feeling for the events in a T Group, so that later chapters may have more meaning. The six episodes presented here, together with reflections by the trainers or the trainer, are taken from different T Groups, with different compositions and at different points in a T Group's total experience. Together, they hopefully give a picture of the T Group in action.

Obviously there are many other recurring critical episodes that might have been examined here had there been space. For example, most groups at one time or another respond to problems with "fight" or "flight." Frequently, the group is unable to work on the problem facing it directly and must find some off-target topic to cover its real concern. The trainer's difficulty lies in knowing how to help a group recognize its many patterns of behavior and decide when and how to tackle its central problem. Most groups also face, from time to time, problems stemming from difficulties individual members may have in relating to others and "taking out group membership." Individual problems of working through intimacy with others, hostility toward others, and degrees of distrust about others, have a way of becoming group problems.

Generally, the episodes selected below present crucial situations which test the trainer's diagnostic skill, his ability to integrate his own actions into the group process, the extent to which his own personality presents problems to the group, his ability to make intervention decisions, the consistency of his behavior, and its congruence with his beliefs. Lest these episodes seem consistently to picture only groups in turmoil, it should be said that other episodes could depict many moments in almost any T Group in which openness and trust prevail and in which data collection and feedback were effectively utilized.

Episode 1

Group Opening. The trainer opened the group by stating that they would be together many hours during the laboratory session; that this provided an opportunity for each to increase learning and skill in knowing more about himself, in carrying out many of the functions expected of him in other situations, in being a more effective group member, in understanding group behavior; that these learnings could best be accomplished by analyzing whatever happened as they continued to meet together; and that he did not intend to serve as a group leader. He then stopped. There was a silence, while tension mounted, of nearly fifty seconds. Individuals looked around the table at other individuals, but nobody spoke. The trainer assumed a relaxed posture and expression and, while he did not focus on specific individuals, he gave the impression of looking at the group.

The silence was broken by one individual who said that he had not understood all the trainer had said and would he repeat himself. The trainer said he would be glad to and, using about the same phraseology but more briefly, said again that he felt the group could learn from examining its own interactions and process and that he did not propose to serve as leader.

Another member asked the trainer just what the group was supposed to work on and how it was to get started. The other trainer responded by saying that these decisions would need to be made by the group.

Silence again settled down, this time for about thirty seconds. It was broken rather violently by one individual who said that all of this was a waste of time. If it were true they would learn something by getting the group organized, he proposed they get started. Every group had a leader. Why did they not pick a leader? Then they could select a topic and get rolling.

This outburst was met by complete silence. Seeking reaction and support, the speaker looked around the table. He could find none in the frozen faces confronting him. Possibly he assumed no one else wanted a leader. In all probability, others wanted some leadership almost as desperately as he did, but wondered why he suggested the idea. Did he want to be leader? They did not know him well enough to judge what he would do. Probably the violence of his outburst added to the tension in the group.

After a few seconds of silence someone else very mildly suggested that perhaps they might introduce themselves, adding that this seemed customary in groups of his experience.

This was considered by other individuals, and a few spoke up rather timidly to support the idea. The originator of the suggestion, gaining boldness from the support of two or three others, suddenly turned to the person on his right and said, "You start by introducing yourself. Then we'll go around the table."

Galvanized by the direct request, this individual gave his name and the organization and city from which he came. (Later one of the trainers would recall the incident to the group and suggest that perhaps this was an ineffective way to make decisions—by one individual's assuming responsibility and ordering another person to act. The trainer would also ask how people felt. Did they resent or welcome the action of the individual who directed the movement, and why?)

At the moment, however, the trainer merely said that if the group members planned to introduce themselves, he wondered what they wanted to know about one another in order to work more effectively together. The group had difficulty hearing the intervention, not to mention understanding its implications, partly because of anxiety about what the trainers thought of them and partly because of irritation that the movement of the group—any movement—had been stopped. A number of members said that they wanted to know who others were—their names and where they came from, where they worked, and what their titles or job descriptions were. One member said she would like to know how large a family each person had.

With this much reassurance, the members went around the table introducing themselves. The introductions differed in style and content. Some were reticent; some expansive. Some gave status symbols. Others were more factual about their roles. One woman, who followed an official in a national organization who had mentioned an imposing title, said that she hesitated to say that she was just a school teacher, but she had no other title to recommend her.

At the end of the introductions one trainer said that he felt that he knew more about the organizations from which people came, but he had not heard too much about the persons themselves. It seemed to him that people were introducing their organizations rather than themselves. Were they, he asked, trying to use their organizations to give themselves status or acceptance? Were they hiding behind their organizations—not yet ready to bring themselves out until they saw what the situation would be like?

This statement was ignored by most of the group. One person, however, took the trouble to point out to the trainer that (1) it was traditional to tell where you worked and what you did, (2) that you could "place" a person if you knew his kind of work and what position he held, and (3) that such introductions told the group what resources it had. The trainer did not think the time was appropriate to question these statements. Further questions would appear as attack or as establishing authority over the group.

However, the trainer did ask the group whether, now that the introductions were completed, people had thought of things they would like to know about other members, or other things they would like to have told others so that they could work more effectively together in this group.

After hearing some of the experiences and responsibilities of others, one or two comments touched upon personal feelings of inadequacy. Before this could be carried very far, one member turned to the trainer and accused him of deliberately blocking the group.

"You both," he said, "have given us no help in what we are supposed to do. You've let us drift. When we did accomplish something, even though it was only introducing ourselves, you've indicated you didn't like what we did. If you don't like what we do, tell us what to do; otherwise you have no right to criticize us."

There was a stunned silence. The trainer who had been spoken to said that he could understand how the member felt. Other members joined in to defend the trainers, saying that they had not criticized them, that they were right in whatever they did, that they would "come out" at the proper time with help to the group. A couple of other members, however, also felt that the trainers had criticized the group. The subject was then dropped.

For a while discussion was sporadic, multi-directioned, with no great push for group movement. The group seemed more apathetic, as if the emotional intensity of the statement by the one individual and his attack on the trainers had somewhat immobilized the group. Suggestions for discussion topics were made, but none was picked up. Individuals who made comments seemed to look around the table as if to find someone who would respond. When responses did come, these individuals would direct their next comments to the person who had shown some verbal or facial response. Pairs of relationships were established momentarily around the table.

During this period a number of questions were directed toward the trainers—obviously asking them to give directions to the group. In some instances a trainer merely smiled in response. Once a trainer responded by saying that the question put him in a dilemma. He had to be sure, he said, that any response on his part did not cause the group to expect him to carry out some of the group responsibilities. In this instance, he felt that any direct response to the question would be beyond his functions and would only increase the dependency of the group upon him.

Toward the end of the session, the group began to discuss some of the reasons why they had come to the training laboratory and what they expected to get out of it. Interspersed with these observations were punishing statements directed at the trainers. Members wondered how they were going to learn something if the trainers did as little as they had thus far. One member asked how trainers were selected. Another member said he had heard that the trainers in another group had very fine reputations.

The discussion on expectations seemed to indicate that everybody wanted to learn how to handle certain specific persons who constituted problems for them and how to get their group to function better. They were eager to be taught these things. The consensus was that they had not learned much during the first meeting, and on this note the meeting ended.

TRAINER ANALYSIS. In the clinic meeting that the trainers had at the end of the session, the previous two hours were pretty thoroughly rehashed. They noted the efforts of the group members to reduce tension by producing a traditional group, with standard introductions, a selected leader, and imposed discussion topics. They talked about the difficulties in getting group movement because of the anxieties experienced and the lack of trust that members had in one another. They went around the group, discussing each member in terms of anxiety level and the way anxiety was handled. They discussed who might need more support so that every individual could learn and so that the group would not be blocked or immobilized by any one member's undue anxiety. They commented upon the extent to which efforts to build status by some individuals in the introductions would come back to haunt them later, and the extent to which some people were made more timid, as a consequence. They wondered how they could have worked toward building a more permissive and supportive climate. Some of the comments they could have made, they thought, would have been heard as punishing, and thus were inappropriate at the time. Even though some of the trainers' interventions elicited no response, they felt that they had been partially heard and that they would help in developing readiness to explore individual and group action.

They noted the "handclasping" efforts between members, as individuals sought someone who would respond to them. The trainers discussed how these handclasping experiences would gradually widen as members gained more trust in other members and could enlarge the number of persons with whom they felt comfortable or protected. They also noted various competitive relationships that were beginning to emerge: already patterns of participation were discernible in which certain pairs of individuals always spoke after each other, subtly counteracting the other's statement. The trainers discussed at length how and when these competitions might develop and erupt and what their actions should be. On the one hand, group conflict belonged to the group. For the trainers to enter too soon, they said, would be both to deprive the group and to create more dependency. On the other hand, if the conflict and competition became immovable and blocked further group action, the trainer would need to bring it to a head, one trainer felt. This led them to discuss ways in which the trainers could work toward helping the group develop ways of facing and handling conflict by periodically reminding the group of problems it had but had not worked on. This led to a further discussion in which the trainers explored the need for group strength, inter-member trust, and methods of facing and solving problems before tackling major group problems and giving much feedback to individuals. At the same time, they recognized that much of this learning came from dealing with issues successfully. While they could not exactly define any line between the two, they did remind each other of the need for them to help the group build internal strength and an atmosphere of trust and peer support so that facing interpersonal problems and giving feedback from member to member would lead to learning rather than to inhibition and increased distrust.

The trainers noted the efforts of some group members to test them in terms of their reaction to attack and punishment. It was extremely important, they felt, that group members should see how the trainers reacted to attack and to bids for special friendship. As members learned that the trainers would not be "thrown" by emotional episodes, the group could better work through its anxieties about leadership and authority. They talked about trainer style and the consequences of their different personalities on the group. They talked about whether they were providing additional problems to the group. They recognized that they might individually add problems from time to time but if they did, it could be turned into a group learning experience.

Having discussed and reached agreement about their perceptions of some of the emerging characteristics of the group, the trainers turned their attention to the interventions that they had made. They recalled and discussed each separately. One offered reasons for making the interventions, and the other trainer added his diagnosis of the situation and his observation of the way in which the trainer intervened and its consequences.

The first intervention, after the opening and the replies to immediate questions, was one in which one trainer asked the group what they wanted to know about one another from their introductions that would help them to work together later in the group. While he did not expect that the responses he might get would be too insightful at this early stage, he did hope that the intervention might have certain values. It might help to emphasize the importance of member-responsibility for group progress. It might underscore differences between this group and other groups. And it might serve as a base point to utilize in considering later consequences.

The lack of response to the intervention surprised neither of the trainers. Both felt that its impact was not negligible.

Following the introductions, the other trainer shared with the group his perception that individuals had introduced their organizations rather than themselves. The implication of building status by so doing was apparent and did elicit a strongly defensive remark by one member. The trainer recognized that his comment could, and probably did, sound punishing to the group. Nevertheless, he felt the need to help to establish a pattern of exploring the consequence of any action in the group. His associate said that, in his judgment, this intervention did make it possible for some members to talk openly about their reactions to power and status symbols after the trainer's next intervention.

They discussed the beginning dependency and counterdependency statements directed toward the trainer. They agreed that, from the group's standpoint, the trainer's interventions would necessarily have appeared as disruptive; but they felt that the requirement of questioning why action took place should be established early in the group. They predicted that in a few days a deep cleavage would develop in the group between those who needed more structure and were more dependent upon leadership and those who were less in need of structure and less dependent upon imposed leadership; and they perceived the vehement reaction of one member to the trainer as one evidence of the growing anxiety in some persons which would lead to a cleavage. They talked about the way in which the trainer accepted the attack calmly and with expressed understanding of how the member had felt. While this could serve as a model of the manner in which expression of feeling could be handled, they discussed various other ways in which they could help develop a learning approach rather than merely a fight approach, which might be unproductive.

The final intervention they discussed was that in which the trainer shared with the group his dilemma as to whether and how to respond to a direct question. The trainer had tried to accomplish two things by this response. He had tried to make it easier to talk about dependent and counterdependent reactions to him later, and he had tried to model open expression of personal motivation when this was important for the group to know. Both the trainer and the associate trainer felt that this intervention could be important to the group.

Episode 2

Group Cleavages. Most T Groups, within three or four sessions, face a sharp cleavage. On one side are those members who have come to realize that group problems of communication, standard setting, and decision making will be solved, and that individuals will learn, only as the problems are squarely faced and action in the group is adequately explored and studied. On the other side are those individuals who, for a variety of reasons, are bothered or threatened by efforts to understand group action or individual behavior. This cleavage grows slowly, usually comes to a crisis, and is resolved sufficiently for the group to move ahead—although it is never solved for all members. Sometimes one or more members continue for days to try to keep the group on "safe" topics dealing with issues far away from the present experience of the group. The cleavage is seldom clear-cut, because so many different struggles and anxieties are part of it; and the crises may occur and recur as different events help to shape the direction of the group.

In one T Group, composed entirely of industrial managers from a number of companies, the purposes and anxieties of three separate individuals—all differently motivated—combined after the second session both to highlight and to further complicate a cleavage in the group. The second session had witnessed more realistic discussion than had the opening session. Specific interpersonal problems emerged in the group, and some members showed evidence of wanting to dig into them. As a result, there were brief efforts to look at group process, interspersed with discussions on generalized topics.

The third session opened with comments by a few members who noted that they felt clearer about the purpose of the T Group. They had just listened to a theory session concerned with emotional patterns and group behavior, and they now felt that the task was to bring out on the table and discuss some of the emotional feelings of various group members so that the group could better understand its problem.

From the beginning, Don, an intense, eager, apparently anxious member, had rushed in with suggestions for group action. He had been the first to move on the opening day with a suggestion leading toward introductions. However, as the sessions continued, his interventions had decreased in relevancy to what was happening in the group. Most of his contributions were lengthy, and all of them dealt with some topic that was far from the group and usually rooted in some personal situation he faced in his work back home. His interventions came at times when the group was moving toward a decision—usually toward a decision to discuss behavior within the group. One member of the group asked Don directly why he always brought up something of his own just when the group was beginning to discuss a group problem. Don hotly denied that he had deliberately done so. He said he had been sitting there, thinking both about the group and his own problems, and it seemed to him the questions he had in his own situation were ones that would interest and help the group. After all, he added, his company was sending him here to get something out of the program.

At this point, another member asked, "If you spend all the time bringing your problem in, how will the rest of us get any help on ours? It seems to me that we will get the most help as we figure out what we are doing here and how we can improve the situation."

A third member rushed in, however, to defend Don. "Everybody," he said, "must have the right to speak. If Don has something to say to the group, no matter what it is, we should all listen to it. I, for one, think that Don's problems are very serious problems, and I would like to hear him talk about them at greater length."

Don took this as sanction to continue describing a particular back-home situation. His description continued for nearly five minutes. Attention in the group continued to fade, and restlessness became apparent.

After Don had finished his statement, one trainer commented on the growing lack of attention when individual back-home problems were discussed, as compared with the greater attention when present group problems were being discussed. At the same time, he added, a number of group members specifically stated that they did not wish to work on present group problems. The trainer indicated that this seemed to present a dilemma to the group.

At this point Bill re-entered the discussion. Bill had pushed for a designated leader from the beginning of the first session. He had said, flatly, that every group had to have a leader, that it was impossible to proceed without a leader, and that this group particularly needed one. He had then offered his services as leader. The fact that he so openly offered his own services shocked and somewhat embarrassed the group, and, while there was some movement to accept, his open bid died for lack of support.

Bill now said, in response to the trainer's intervention, that clearly the reason for all of the difficulty was the lack of an established agenda and a leader. There was no one to discipline group members and keep them from wandering from point to point.

A considerable number of voices rose in Bill's support, seemingly because the group was uncertain as to what to do about Don and was fearful of conflict. Bill urged that a leader be selected to choose a topic and to insist on everyone's following it. He again offered himself as leader.

At first there were a few statements, from those least fearful of exploring the causes of group difficulty, to the effect that they did not really feel the need for a leader. Movement of the group, however, toward naming a leader became apparent, and those who were unhappy about this merely stated that they had nothing against having a leader. They just wanted to get a few things (unspecified) clarified before they decided upon a leader.

Bill, sensing movement to his side, loudly demanded a vote. A few rapidly—others slowly—raised their hands, until eleven out of the twelve group members (not including the trainers) had voted. One individual did not vote. Bill immediately declared that a consensus had been reached and that he was the leader.

The member who had not voted said, "I didn't vote, and therefore there is no consensus. You're trying to railroad us." There was a sigh of relief from one member. It was as if the group, which had almost made a decision having many consequences, marched down the hill again.

There was expressed criticism of Bill for trying to override the group; there was also expressed criticism of the individual who had not voted. There was a prolonged discussion as to whether such abstention was a vote against, and whether, in fact, Bill did not have consensus. This argument gradually faded.

One member accused the abstainer of blocking the group's will. One trainer asked whether the group had a will. Was this merely an assumption? How could the group tell whether it had a will? This precipitated a discussion which centered for a time on group decision making, on consensus, on conformity pressures, on tendencies for individuals not to say what they really felt.

Gradually the discussion turned back to the present issue and the abstainer was asked why he had abstained. He responded by saying that while he was not really against a leader, he felt the group had not thoroughly thought through what the leader would do, and he was uncertain whether the leader should select the topic for the group or, in fact, whether the group should have a topic at all. He said that he personally was enjoying the discussion, did not consider it a random one, and felt that the group was getting somewhere, particularly when it tried to understand feelings and when it felt able to talk openly about what various members of the group had done. He said, for example, that he felt that Don was using the group for his own purposes, irrespective of what other members wanted. Group members were letting him get away with it because they were afraid to tackle the situation. They did not know exactly what to do.

It was at this point that Harry came into the discussion. By far the biggest man in the group and with the loudest voice, Harry had not participated much during the preceding three sessions. When he did participate, his booming voice and aggressive body action stopped the group in its tracks. Already two or three members were agreeing with Harry even when their agreement reversed previous statements they had made. They seemed to be traumatized by Harry's overpowering masculinity.

In this instance, Harry said he was astonished and shocked by what was happening. This was worse than brainwashing. It clearly was an invasion of privacy. People had no right to speak to other people in the way that they they had spoken to Don. He, for one, was not going to permit this kind of behavior. Definite lines should be established in the group as to what should be discussed, and these should certainly exclude any discussion of individuals or what they did.

A number of people agreed, including some who had been most interested in discussing the here-and-now feelings and behavior of the group.

One of the trainers raised the question as to whether Harry was setting standards for the group and whether the group sanctioned it. Some members of the group said it was all right for Harry to set these boundaries for the group because it was good for them. Others were less certain. They seemed to be on the horns of a dilemma. On the one hand, as one of them put it, he did not come here just to talk about somebody else's work situation. He was interested in exploring what was actually happening in the group. On the other hand, he did not want to see anyone hurt. (The assumption seemed to be building that Don had been deeply hurt.) So, perhaps Harry was right.

The issues became more clearly joined. What should be the area of discussion of the group? Should topics suggested by various members be discussed? Someone suggested that each member contribute a topic on a piece of paper, that they elect Bill chairman, and that he arrange the topics in the order to be discussed.

Another person suggested that Harry be appointed leader. Harry said he preferred to sit back for a while.

Even against the rather devastating force of Harry's behavior, a couple of members kept alive the desirability of trying to understand the struggles they were having. When was it all right to talk about the group? How could they talk about the group without talking about members in the group? Was this really brainwashing?

Thus the cleavage between those who wanted assigned topics and those who were interested in exploring behavior deepened and widened. The cleavage was further complicated by a variety of issues of personal concern. It was at this point that the group session came to an indecisive and frustrating conclusion.

TRAINER ANALYSIS. In the clinic meeting of the two trainers there was much to be discussed. What were the forces operating in the group? It was clear that the group was slowly—and with much backtracking—working toward facing some of its major problems. Could the group, as a group, tolerate sufficient ambiguity and lack of structure to tackle fundamental problems of group building? Or would the anxiety and need for clear structure among some members keep the group in flight to safe discussions of generalized topics or vaguely described situations back home? If the group moved, would it find ways of moving effectively? Here, the trainers saw the need for care-fully timed modeling on their part to aid the group in moving. Could they find the right time to point up a group-process problem which the group was studiously ignoring, describe the group behavior symp-tomatic of the problem, and discuss calmly some of the emotional content of the issues?

A second major problem facing the group was that of membership. How could the group help various individuals to decide to take out membership in the group? Again, the trainers wondered whether, if they identified the problem of developing open pathways to member-ship, the group would be able to use these pathways on its own. The trainers saw these basic problems further complicated by the actions and anxieties of three individuals—Don, Bill, and Harry. They dis-cussed each along the following lines.

Don seemed anxious about his place and influence in the group, but more worried about his typical relations to people and fearful that the group discussion might reach his own actions. As a consequence, he seemed to alternate between periods of withdrawal and periods of monopolizing the group's time in an effort to keep it from focusing on an individual or group problem. His anxiety was communicated to the group and left members uncertain as to how to relate to him and to his contradictory behavior. On the one hand, he invoked a standard of fairness in letting a person talk when he had something to say. On the other, he admitted trying to induce the group to do what he wanted it to do and to pay attention to him. The group members were caught between concern for his anxiety and hostility because of his manipulation.

Bill presented a different problem. On the surface he showed none of Don's anxieties. Although he seemed concerned for the group, he seemed rigid in his belief that the group needed a designated leader and a set agenda and that he could provide the leadership. Was Bill fearful of a discussion of emotional, interpersonal, and intragroup prob-lems, or was he merely uncomfortable with lack of structure, or did he wish to control the group? Was he reacting to past patterns of behavior, or was there a deeper anxiety? The trainers were inclined to believe the latter. At all events, his calmness, assurance, and seem-ing stability actually served to keep the group uncertain about its own direction.

Harry presented a third force. While he was the most masculine and aggressive member of the group in outward behavior and domi-nated it with his physical proportions and his tone of voice, his be-havior indicated to the trainers his own very definite anxieties about discussing personal feelings, even though he took the position of protecting weaker members in the group. His protective efforts actually created more anxiety and a greater tendency on their part to submit to his edicts. The trainers discussed what they could and should do to help Harry become able to bring out on the surface and talk about his anxieties about closeness or intimacy, about others' perceptions of himself and particularly about his own feelings of inadequacy. At the same time, the trainers discussed what they could do to help the group gain strength, both as individuals and as a group, to withstand Harry's efforts to control them. Tackling Harry immediately themselves would polarize the group, create fears in the group as to the outcome, increase dependency. At the same time, the situation would have to be faced if not by the group alone, then by the trainers. The trainers agreed that their first efforts should be to keep the issue on the table. The group might free itself from undue influence by Harry, but still invite Harry into membership. Later, if they were to tackle Harry directly, as was very probable, it should be in terms of later reacting as a group member, with the intention of helping Harry be aware of what he was doing to the group. Before proceeding further, they examined in some detail three interventions they had made.

The first came after Don's long monologue. At this point, one trainer referred to the dilemma evidenced by the lack of attention to there-and-then discussions but, at the same time, the expressed desire to keep away from the here-and-now. The trainer had tried to couch the intervention in such a way as to draw attention to the behavior in the group, and not only to Don. He had also tried to focus group attention on the decision as to whether to discuss back-home situations or here-and-now behavior.

The trainers felt that the intervention did open the issue, but that Bill had tried to close it again. They realized that in some eyes, especially Harry's, the intervention struck too close to Don and, by implication, to him. They expected this intervention to be referred to a number of times, particularly as a horrible example of how someone could be hurt. They discussed other interventions that might have been made. One less direct intervention might have been to ask whether the group wished to analyze what had happened to the group and within members over the incident.

The second intervention was made toward the end of the discussion on leadership and after the vote had been taken. One of the trainers had asked the group to what extent a leader, if they had selected one, would have been able to solve all of the group's problems. Was a leader a crutch upon which the group could lean? Did they need a crutch?

This intervention had aroused some discussion within the group. Those who did not particularly want a leader had been encouraged to speak up. Those who did became defensive. The trainers understood that the intervention appeared to place them on the side of some people and against others, even though the intervention was directed toward a group problem. They knew, however, that interventions will frequently be interpreted as supporting one faction or another, but that issues change as well as adherents. They held firmly to the realization of their responsibility to help create a learning group and to aid individual learning. Therefore, they should continuously stress the desirability of questioning the behavior in the group.

The third intervention raised the question as to whether Harry was setting standards for the group and where his sanction had come from. This seemed, to the trainers, a crucial point. Standards imposed by one strong person can immobilize the group. Whether or not the group would be able to face the important issue of how standards are set, it seemed important that the question be raised. The intervention produced no immediate effect, but the trainers felt that it would be picked up later in the group.

The trainers then considered the dilemmas facing the group and the movements which should occur if the group were to grow and if individual learning were to take place.

Certainly it would be a loss to the group and a prevention of learning if Harry succeeded in building strong boundaries around the group and kept it from analyzing its own process. While the group could ultimately accept leadership which was sensitive to the group's needs, Bill's present assumption as to how the leader should behave would prevent the group from moving into an analysis of its own problems. It seemed necessary to have Bill examine with the group why he sought leadership so strongly. The trainers talked about appropriate timing and ways of opening up the issue with Bill.

Don's anxieties about himself and his tendencies to manipulate the group might well block the group if members did not learn how to help Don become a more effective member. This would not be easy to do. Efforts to help Don to look at his anxieties would be very threatening to him. Don would need much tolerance and patience, but not sanction to block the group. The trainers felt that Don needed emotional support to join the group, but not sanction to manipulate the group.

Harry presented still a third problem. Until the group members could gain courage to face Harry, he could not be helped.   The train-ers faced a difficult task.

Clearly, the issue of there-and-then and here-and-now discussion had to be seen by the group and some of the confusions surrounding it removed.   The group needed to see that discussing the process of the group itself was not brainwashing or too great an invasion of privacy. Only as the group did analyze its own process and the behavior of its members, including the trainers (public property, because the be-havior was present for everybody to see), could the group develop and much learning take place.

The trainers felt that forces in the group would move toward facing this problem.   They were prepared, however, to intervene where necessary, to keep the issue clarified in the group and open for group solution.

Episode 3

Private Manipulation.   As the ambiguity of the T Group becomes apparent to the participants, the width of the boundaries of possible actions, the apparent freedom to behave as one wishes, the pressures to "get the show on the road," and the lack of exerted control by the trainer—all provide an open invitation for private manipulation of the group by an individual or clique.   It is at this point that the reactions and interventions of the trainer have much to do with the ultimate degree of trust generated in the group.   Obviously, if the group im-mediately deals with the manipulative situation openly and effectively, there is little for the trainer to do except to make sure that the group has made explicit, or at least is obviously implicitly aware of, a group norm concerning private manipulation.   However, if the group does not meet the situation openly, the trainer needs to keep the issue open and help the group to handle the problem.   For the trainer not to be ready to take a strong stand on the issue of manipulation, if required, would be to give tacit approval to the jungle situation where values are not examined, and would prevent the development of healthy trust in the trainer as well as in other members.

Sometimes an individual who has been active—and has been rebuffed or ignored—sits back for a session to "observe the group," but in reality to see how much guilt or concern he can generate in the group.   Some-times a subgroup between sessions plans ways of controlling the next day's sessions and of "railroading" its desired goal for the group.

The issue of private manipulation is a crucial one for the group.

Because few, if any, values have usually been discussed or confirmed, there are no guidelines to determine behavior. The line between private and unsanctioned manipulation, and public and sanctioned experimentation, usually is not perceived. Yet future issues of trust and openness, the possible development of the group, and effective individual learning rest, in large part, on whether the issue of private manipulation and sanctioned experimentation is raised, and how it is resolved.

George had been a strong and rather dominating member during the first three meetings of the T Group. However, he had not been overly participative. He had given the appearance of being under wraps, of waiting, of withholding. When he did come in, he did so powerfully and effectively, and usually with the result of stopping forward movement of the group. His attraction was greatest to the more dependent members. The attraction seemed to contain as much fear as liking.

During the first three sessions, the seating arrangement accidentally developed at the opening meeting was rigidly maintained. Name cards were propped up in front of each chair, and each member took his accustomed place behind his card.

When members arrived at the fourth session, they found the name cards shifted around so that a new seating pattern was formed. Members, including the trainers, took their seats quietly, but tension could be felt.

At first there was silence. Then a few tentative jokes were made about who sat next to whom. After a bit, one member wondered aloud what the trainers had in mind in shifting the name cards. Another member said he had just got used to sitting where he was. He was not certain he liked his new place. Another member countered by saying he was very happy with the change and quite pleased that the trainers had seen fit to change the seating arrangements.

Both trainers said that they had not changed the cards and were equally at a loss as to who had done so.

This statement was met with polite skepticism. One member, apparently trying to help the trainers, suggested that the Administration had changed the cards. Perhaps this was part of a master design of which even the trainers were unaware.

This suggestion seemed too unlikely to be given much credence. After a few moments, there was some tentative probing as to whether any member had been the agent.

Suddenly one of the members—one of the least dominating—admitted he had moved the cards. The group was shocked. Here was the least likely member of the group confessing to the act. Shock was mixed with disbelief. What were his motives?

He said, weakly, that he just thought it was a good idea. Someone asked if he had done it on his own. Before he could respond, another member, about as retiring and unassuming as the first, said that he also helped to move the cards. Both said, upon further questioning, that the idea had occurred to them that morning when they arrived early at the meeting room.

The group still felt disbelief, mingled now with some openly stated resentment. Probing continued.

At this point George spoke up. He also, he said, had arrived early. He had suggested to the others that it might be a good idea, in order to stir the group up, to shift the name cards around to "see what would happen." They had fallen in with the suggestion and had carried out the action.

George defended strongly the actions of the other two. Was this not an experimental group? Certainly the trainers had stressed the need for the group to conduct its own affairs and to learn from the experience. How else could the group learn unless it experimented? Besides, it was good for the group. They needed stirring up. Cliques and subgroups needed breaking up. People could learn more about one another if they sat next to different people and looked at new faces across the table.

George said he could not understand what all the fuss and resentment were about. The group was helped. Those who did it should be praised and not blamed. This should end the discussion.

There was a rush of voices, including some previously raised in resentment, agreeing with George. His statements were defended, and those who had expressed resentment were criticized.

Some who had expressed resentment now admitted they had been wrong. No one spoke up against George's reasoning.

One of the trainers asked how people had felt when they first saw the change in name cards. Some said they felt pleased. Others said momentary resentment was quickly washed away. The trainer persisted. He asked if anyone felt pushed around by the incident. There was silence. One member spoke up and said that he had and, furthermore, he still did. The other trainer said that he also felt pushed around. There were a few nods of agreement; but others strongly criticized the trainer for feeling "pushed around," for attacking George and the other two members, for interfering in the group, and for seeming to imply that all was not well with the group.

Two members mildly supported the trainer, and a discussion began that took the rest of the two-hour period. One of the members who moved the cards finally said he had not felt quite right about the action at the time, but did not want to say anything because George had seemed to feel it was all right.

There was silence for a moment. Then another member said he really had felt pushed around, but he had come to expect that in life, and so he had learned not to object too strenuously. Everybody tried to manipulate others, he said.

Gradually the issue became clearer. A group value began to emerge. There should be public discussion of efforts to experiment before the event, with a sharing of motives. There should not be private experimentation with motives not openly expressed.

During the discussion some rather direct statements were made to George concerning his motives in the whole affair. Was he trying to manipulate and control the group? Why had he encouraged the other two to carry out the act rather than doing it himself? Was he trying to hide behind the others while he controlled the group?

George hotly denied the suggestions, but there was evidence he had heard them and had been surprised and shocked that his actions were not acceptable. Certainly there was evidence that other members of the group had become aware of some of the ethical issues involved in manipulation. They had identified more openly than before the resentments growing out of feeling manipulated, had seemingly thought more seriously than before about value postures. And they had reduced some of their fear of George.

TRAINER ANALYSIS. The trainers felt that several milestones had been passed in the group's development and in the learning of individual members. First, the group had met and successfully handled—with trainer help—a major value test. If this issue had not been met and solved, the group would have had continuing difficulty in differentiating between public experimentation and private manipulation. A jungle situation might have prevailed, with the more aggressive and manipulative members able to control more dependent members. Standards, and the value bases of standards, would not have been set.

Again, the development of adequate decision methods for handling group problems might have been delayed. Norms of openness, of tracking down and solving problems, of legitimately expressing feelings, of standing out against pressures toward conformity, might not have emerged. The trainers thought it was particularly important, since the group did not do so, for them to open and keep opened, the issue of values, openness, and public decision making. Individuals frequently are highly ambivalent about manipulation. While ethics and human feelings are against manipulation of other people, social acceptance rewards it as a way of "getting things done." The socially accepted dichotomy between Sunday and daily behavior made this a difficult area for the group to handle.

The trainers' decision to take a stand on the issue of appropriate values helped the group to form further value standards. If the group had handled the issue, there would, of course, have been no need for the trainers to intervene. But the trainers felt they could not have let this issue pass without urging the group to identify and solve it. The trainers discussed a further reason why it was, and generally would be, important for them to be forthright and open in the issue of manipulation. Participants very frequently ascribe to trainer acts manipulative purposes. Helping the group to examine manipulative acts may help to build more open and trusting relationships between members and trainers.

Another basic milestone for the group lay in facing George and reducing some of the fear some members had of him. So long as this fear endured, the group was largely inhibited in its movement and growth. Finding a solid position of sanctioned values enabled the group to control the devastating aspects of George's behavior and at the same time to grow in its ability to help George. The trainers spent some time in discussing some of the forces that were very probably affecting his behavior. As they saw it, his personality dynamics resulted in a need to control individuals and situations in which he was involved. At the same time, George came from an intensively competitive situation where the cultural norms would support manipulation as a "smart" way to keep ahead. The trainers wondered whether he basically sought dependency relations with authority figures and was cautiously testing the strength of the trainers and the boundaries they would set. Or they wondered whether George was seeking assurance from equally strong peers and was endeavoring to determine strength and weakness among members. With these various hypotheses, the trainers planned to observe George carefully to gather more data.

The trainers recognized the difficult position they had been in with their intervention. They recalled the punishment directed by most of the group at the trainer who intervened. They felt that by absorbing this punishment without producing a further conflict between themselves and the group they had helped the first member to admit feelings of guilt about his part in the manipulation. On the other hand, they wondered if the intervention had not taken action from the group. Perhaps it deflected the group's attention from member behavior and made the trainers the focal issue. It might have been better merely to have kept the issue alive rather than to have expressed trainer feelings.

The trainers hoped that the situation, which had shocked many members by making them aware of how indifferent they had been about manipulative action and of how unaware they had been of the consequences of such acts, would increase measurably the sensitivity of the total group. They speculated about George's future behavior. They were well aware that behavioral change is seldom miraculously sudden and not necessarily enduring. They felt that the shock George had received might increase his sensitivity to others sufficiently for him to continue to learn. They felt that the fact that the group had partially reduced its fear of George might cause them to face him with any future inadequate behavior and to support more helpful behavior. But they agreed that George would continue to be somewhat difficult for the group and that he had further learning to achieve.

Episode 4

Establishing an Effective Feedback Process. Most T Groups begin to recognize fairly soon that the development of the group will require some modifications in the behavior of some members. In addition, hearsay knowledge defines the T Group as a place in which people learn by "baring their souls" or "getting clobbered by feedback." For most, this supposed knowledge has been both titillating and anxiety-producing, bearing similarities to the sensations of one's first roller coaster experience As sessions pass, some of the initial fears about exposing oneself for learning are reduced. However, the group faces difficulties in developing an effective feedback system for individual learning. There is latent anxiety ready to alert defenses. There is uncertainty about what others can "take"; there is uncertainty about how one can go about giving feedback without appearing to attack. There are no familiar models to follow.

In one T Group, a number of events relating to feedback had occurred. Early in the T Group, one anxious member had asked the group members to tell him anything they wished about himself. He was here to learn all he could. He could "take" anything they said. His anxiety communicated clearly, however, and the group did not respond, except to show increased uneasiness.

Later, another member recounted an anecdote which was told to her about another T Group. This described a horrendous situation in which one member was "badly hurt" by feedback.

This stimulated a long, abstract discussion about the value of feedback in learning. The more anxious members in the group pressed for the establishment of rules, supposedly to protect members from dangerous feedback, but actually to ban any kind of feedback. No difficult situation had occurred in the group, and this move was not accepted.

Still later, a member who had been monopolizing the time and attempting to hold the group's attention on herself was sharply spoken to by another member. She became defensive and said that she had been "hurt" by the attack. Some members, anxious to prevent discussion of damaging interpersonal here-and-now situations, then pushed for rigid rules preventing interpersonal feedback. Words like "head-shrinking" and "brainwashing" were used, and fantasies were spun about depth interpretation and the shattering of individuals. The fight this time was intense. The trainers tried, from time to time, to relate the discussion to the actual data about the event, but these interventions were brushed aside.

Finally, the issue was temporarily settled, with no restricting rules, but with a general group caution to be careful not to hurt anyone.

In the meantime, forces in the group were building up for acceptance of feedback and a way of carrying it out. Members' problems needed to be dealt with. The group needed to be able to talk realistically about its activities and process, if development was to occur. Little learning would come to individuals if all data about their performance were withheld from them. Even some of the more anxious members were becoming restive over a need for more candid conversation. Trust had been building in the group. Fantasies about couches and bloody attacks were seen as unrealistic.

At the same time, past cautions hung over the group. There was no accepted model by which individuals could pattern efforts toward feedback. The trainers had opened up group issues and had reported their own internal feelings about various events, but group members did not think that they could be so skillful. Thus, they did not take trainer behavior as a model.

The T Group needed to find a way out of its dilemma.

Finally, a path emerged. Earlier in the group history, when the leadership struggle had been at its height, the group had accepted as a pattern that a different member would start the session off each time and would serve as "leader" for the meeting. In actuality, the group neither expected nor would allow anyone to serve as leader for an entire session. However, they maintained the function by having each member take his turn in opening the meeting. Usually this took the form of asking what the group wanted to discuss.

One day, about midway through the T-Group life, the leader for the day started in a different way. He begged the indulgence of the group to permit him to tell them something more about himself than they could have seen merely from his behavior in the group. With the knowledge of how he saw himself and of some of the things that had been meaningful to him in his life, added to the knowledge they had gained from assessing him in the group, members of the group might have enough knowledge to help him to understand himself better.

He had obviously thought through very carefully what he wanted to say. For nearly a half hour he sketched out much of his background—the things that had meant much to him during his life—to a quiet and attentive group. At the end, very simply, he asked them to respond in any way they pleased, but in ways they thought would give him more knowledge of himself. He particularly asked that they comb through their memories of events in the group in which he had been involved, and to give him their perceptions of his behavior in those situations. He said that the kindest and most helpful thing they could do would be *not* to hold back their reactions to him.

Only slowly did responses come. But, as they came, they were thoughtful and penetrating. The leader (for the day) did not merely listen. Interacting with the other members, he drew out those who spoke in terms of their perception of what actions on his part had produced their reactions. He was asking for and receiving help. And the help was being given thoughtfully and warmly.

During the last half hour of the T Group, there was an excellent discussion of the day's activities and of the way feedback could be effectively used. The group saw that the person, by talking about himself, in a sense controlled the area in which feedback would likely occur. In addition, the extra information provided enabled the group to understand the individual and thus to be of real help. There was some discussion as to what would happen if some members used the opportunity to be destructive rather than helpful. While they saw that this could not totally be prevented, they did see four safeguards: the climate of helpfulness, the ability of the volunteer to cut the feedback off, the support of most of the group, and the group members' being alertly sensitive to purely destructive feedback. One of the trainers reminded the group that the leader of the day had said that the most helpful thing members could do would be to be honest and open with their feedback. Otherwise there was the presumption that they did not care enough about the person to give him information he might need and did not trust him enough to think he could handle it.

The group decided to continue the pattern of individual reporting and acceptances of feedback it had initiated with this meeting.

At this point, one of the trainers sensed a stir of uneasiness in the group. He immediately raised the point that perhaps everyone was not ready to report about himself, did not want to, or felt he could not do it so successfully as the first member did. If the group set up a rigid and demanding pattern, would this not be utilizing conformity pressure?

The comment sobered the group, and they thoughtfully discussed how they could make it as inviting and easy as possible for each person to seek feedback, but not to demand or expect the same reaction from everyone. It was decided that the group would not select a leader each day but would let anyone volunteer who wished to.

TRAINER ANALYSIS. At the time, the trainers felt that this had been an excellent breakthrough in the group, and they were particularly pleased that it had emerged so spontaneously and naturally in the group. Each trainer resolved, himself, to remember the incident. Perhaps in other groups they might find it desirable to suggest it to the group as a possible process.

Later, the trainers looked back on this incident as one of the major turning points in the group. While not all efforts were so open or helpful as the first, all were helpful, and a growing climate of openness and trust resulted. Almost all the group members took their turns. Those who did not volunteer had the face-saving excuse that there had not been time in the days remaining for everyone to have a chance.

The trainers thought some rather tremendous results came from this process. An attitude of greater understanding, concern, and caring for others emerged. As a result, members felt freer to disclose thoughts, perceptions, and anxieties they had. One or two essentially lonely persons were able to gain much from closer contact with other group members. At the same time, the trainers thought that it would be desirable for the group to develop alternate methods of feedback. They decided to suggest to the group that, along with the planned feedback process, the group might wish to establish a standard encouraging immediate feedback at the time of an event.

The occasion enabled the trainers to look back at the group history and examine the restraining forces that needed to be removed before individuals would feel free to reveal much of their internal concept of themselves, to discuss without defensiveness reactions to their behavior, or to admit to their feelings. They also discussed desirable strategies that a trainer might follow in helping to remove restraining forces of fear, distrust, competition, cultural cautions, formal procedures, and caution about interpersonal closeness. They discussed the ways in which trainer-behavior can honestly and clearly communicate openness and sharing. They looked at ways in which—by showing their own feelings openly—others would be encouraged to do so also. They also saw that their modeling was not effective because they appeared to possess too much skill. Perhaps raising the need for feedback close to the event, discussing more freely the ways it could be successfully accomplished, and encouraging trials might have proved more effective in this instance.

Episode 5

Building a Work Organization.   The process by which a group builds a competent work organization is a slow and complex one. In building an effective organization, one of the barriers which must be overcome is the fact that most members have no experience with organization which is really effective. The goal toward which they struggle in the early days of the T Group is patterned on traditional organization and attempts to build a group structure and rules for activity before there is clear awareness of the complexities of the group task, of the idiosyncrasies of the group composition, and of latent problems of relationships among members. The result is a controlling and confining organization that inhibits and misuses its resources. An effective organization is forged so slowly that it is frequently unrecognized as being so, even when it is achieved.

T Group 4 was a typical group in the way it worked toward organization. In the beginning session, there was loud demand for a full-blown organization to be magically delivered to the group, but there was no evidence that they could work in an organized way. Member-interventions were seldom heard or utilized. Charting the group discussions would have shown violently zigzagging lines as the conversation jumped from point to irrelevant point. Contributions were thrown out on the table aggressively, only to "plop." Other contributions were pushed timidly forward, to die almost before being heard. The group had no clearly stated goal, or any way to reach a goal if they had had one.

Members firmly declared that all that was needed were a leader and rules of order. The goals would then appear and all would be well. No group could even get going, they said, without first selecting a leader who could ascertain what topics were desirable, decide among them, and guide the group as it systematically discussed the topics. Many leadership plans were suggested—the nomination of a permanent leader, the rotation of leadership by chance, the abdication of responsibility to the leader, inhibiting controls on the leader, and a formal agenda accepted for the week.

As no proposals could get acceptance, and as frustration reached new heights, individuals—gradually, almost in desperation, and with some help from the trainer—began to explore one another's feelings, their purposes in being in the group, their desires for learning. They began to check original stereotypes about other group members against the reality of present behavior. Gradually, they began to hear one another on levels on which they had not listened before.

Slowly, too, a few group norms began to build. There seemed to be an implicit decision that everyone should be given a chance to speak. There seemed to be an accepted assumption that loud voices did not necessarily mean weighty contributions and that putting issues to a vote too rapidly was not the best way to reach effective decisions.

People began to produce an organization. It was true that a number of crucial group problems were swept under the rug, while the members pretended these group and interpersonal problems did not exist. It was true also that discussion did not flow freely. Many feelings and perceptions, as it turned out later, were withheld. Also, for long periods, the discussion was disjointed.

But a semblance of organization had developed, and no longer were there bald statements to the effect that no group could exist without a selected leader and a prearranged task.

The organization, such as it was, limped along for a few sessions. The members felt very well pleased with their accomplishment. When the trainer raised questions, from time to time, concerning what was going on in the group, this was often interpreted by the group members as an attack upon their accomplishment.

Finally the submerged issues erupted. A competition for power and leadership which had been present from the first hour of the T Group came to the surface, and members in the group were asked to choose sides and line up.

To the trainer, the issue was almost traditional in all T Groups, even though it often appeared in different guises. It dealt with individual differences in tolerance for ambiguity and lack of clearly defined structures and predictability. It also dealt with individual insecurity and anxiety about reactions of others and the fear that feedback would be destructive rather than helpful. It dealt with competition for leadership and control between members, and it dealt with relations to authority in the person of the trainer.

In this case, as usual, each segment of the group had a strong leader. Further, while efforts were made to force the group into two camps, in actuality there was a larger group who lay somewhere between the extremes. This subcollection (not organized or cohesive in any way) was the prize for which the other two subgroups struggled. The issue, as the group perceived it, dealt with two ways in which the group members could approach helping one another to learn from the experience. One suggestion was that each person describe to the group a specific back-home problem he had, and the group would spend some time advising him on it. The other suggestion urged that each member spend a little time in trying to describe to the group some of the ways in which he saw himself. The group would then help him to see himself more accurately or help him to improve those aspects that he wished to change.

The conflict became heated. Arguments pointing out lurid dangers resulting from suggestions made by the other side were flung across the table. Efforts were made to cajole members of the middle group. Charges and countercharges took place between members of the extreme groups. One course promised danger. The other course would surely mean that the group would disintegrate from apathy. Individuals who tried to steer a middle ground were attacked by both extremes.

The previous organization began to disintegrate under the stress. Group norms proved not to have the strength expected. Emotionally charged words, spoken loudly, substituted for listening.

After the group situation had regressed rather far, the trainer suggested that the group might want to stop to look at and analyze what was happening and ask how it occurred. He bluntly described a couple of characteristics he saw in the present behavior of the group which were opposite to the way they had described themselves earlier. He wondered to what extent they had tried to get at the real purposes underneath the two suggestions.

Because the group members were anxious to get out of the situation they had created, they listened to his comments. Gradually a few, not those on the extreme fringes, commented on what they saw happening and how concerned they were that the group was being shattered by polarization and conflict. Another comment from the trainer attempted to remove any idea that conflict was necessarily bad and to stress that what the group did with conflict was what was important.

Others entered into the description of the present group behavior. Gradually, the group traced its history backwards. They began to see the places in which they had tried to bury an incipient conflict rather than to attempt to resolve it. They saw that they had been unable to express their anxieties openly. They saw that they had rushed ahead too rapidly, which resulted in their preventing some people from expressing feelings and perceptions that would have been helpful to the group. They discovered that, through poor listening, the real feelings and motivations of one member had been almost completely misinterpreted. They realized that all the individual purposes had to be recognized and somehow integrated into the over-all goal of the group.

As far as the present issue was concerned, after people felt free to express their concern relative to talking about themselves, and even though, at the same time, they longed to be able to relate more closely to the others and to get help from them, the group decided not to force any pattern on the group, but to encourage each person to seek help in a way possible to him.

It was a sobering analysis. Gone were the naïve assumptions about inevitable progress. In their place were individual intentions to listen more keenly to one another and to face up to group and interpersonal problems and try to work through them.

In the following session, after a quiet start, the group did begin to work at a high level of group efficiency. The trainer watched it with great interest. Items of work flowed from one to another with an integrity of connection. Each area of discussion was explored thoroughly and unhurriedly. The trainer noted to himself that each suggestion for group movement seemed to come at the right time—and only after all who wished to express themselves had done so—and with great sensitivity to the direction of change the group desired.

Later, the trainer checked his impressions with the group. No one reported feeling blocked or shut off from expressing his ideas or feelings, and all felt that the group movement was so natural as to be almost unnoticed.

No one felt pressure to agree or conform, and such disagreements as ensued were constructive and did not polarize the discussion. Individual contributions were explored or expanded. Where procedures for group movement were needed, someone seemed to come up with a pertinent suggestion. Support was freely, but not overly, extended from member to member. The group saw that good organization implied opportunity for each person to be listened to and to learn. They also saw that it was less important that everyone agree on a common goal than that there be group awareness of the necessity to balance between meeting individual needs and continuity on group tasks, and that several group goals might be accomplished during the same period.

It was a satisfying and swift-moving session. Toward its end, the trainer suggested that the group look back on the session, first to express their feelings about it and then to examine it in terms of effective group action. The group saw that they had created a very effective work organization. They saw that it had emerged from the growing trust developing in the group, the increased acceptance of one another, the climate of support they had created, the willingness to be open and candid about feelings and ideas. Someone recalled that they had once thought that the group had to be formally organized, whereupon several members laughed ruefully.

TRAINER ANALYSIS. The trainer later reflected on this session. It was markedly evident that group members had not only learned to organize and direct their own activities but also had successfully taken over responsibilities for teaching themselves from their experiences. Many of the areas of concern that had initially been the trainer's had now been accepted effectively by the group. The trainer felt he need worry less about their ability and willingness to learn. He could continue to try to work with the group in their further learning.

The trainer speculated about what work organization meant in a group like this versus one in which some product is being completed. While both have problems to solve, the fact that in the present case individual learning and change were the ultimate products meant that the group must go more slowly both to create an effective climate and to remove individual blocks to learning.

Episode 6

Ending the T Group. Most groups begin to move toward closure during the last two or three sessions. Individuals who have been somewhat hesitant to participate actively or to seek much feedback from the group are subtly encouraged and helped to do so. Usually, there is a considerable amount of empathy and understanding present. Cohesion is high. Sometimes special T-Group dinners, parties, or other events are planned and carried out. Discussion usually centers on the re-entry problem of going back home with new insights and understandings. What will the situation look like? How can new insights be utilized effectively in a different situation? Time may be spent in the waning hours of the T Group in helping one another with these problems.

If the laboratory has been held in a residential setting, and if more than one T Group has been present, the night before the closing session may witness a total laboratory party which effectively expresses the many emotional feelings present in individuals and in groups. The last session then—as part of the separation process—becomes a quiet and sober review of the history of the group and its meaning for various members. The group ends quietly, with each member carrying away that image of the group which will be most meaningful and supportive as he faces new situations elsewhere.

But all T Groups do not end this way. Sometimes a conflict or a personal problem is so difficult that the group cannot handle it. In such cases, efforts are made by the group to keep the problem sufficiently covered that it does not overtly intrude upon the group. Members are tense during the closing session, fearful that the problem may burst forth and shatter the group or that the group may not be able to help the individual concerned. Usually, the opening of the last session is especially tense, as members wonder whether the pressure of the closing moments will force the difficulty onto the table. However, with the actual approach of the last few minutes of the session, the group generally relaxes.

T Group 3 faced this type of situation. One member had worried the group from the middle of the first week onward. Cy seemed to have one topic that he wished the group to discuss. During the early days, his had been only one of the there-and-then topics urged for group consideration. In Cy's case, however, he never relinquished urging the acceptance of his topic, even after the rest of the group had long since passed the need for external topics for discussion. Cy urged the group, in emotional and dramatic terms, to follow his lead. As his topic became more and more irrelevant to the group's interests, the rejection of his ideas became greater and more obvious; but nothing the group could do modified his perseverance. His response to rejection was to urge his plan in even more emotional tones. Group members first became irritated and punitive. Sharp questions as to why he was blocking the group seemed not to be heard by Cy as he patiently explained he was doing what was best for the group. In one instance he was told bluntly to keep quiet for a while. He did withdraw temporarily from the group, and there was evidence in terms of glances toward Cy that his withdrawal made them uneasy. Later, members appeared embarrassed when he spoke—and then worried and tense. They listened politely when he talked and then, after a tense silence, moved on to another area of discussion.

On Sunday night, at the beginning of the second week, Cy reported how much the week end at home had meant to him, how good he felt about the T Group, and how he was not angry with anyone in the group, even though no one had had the wisdom to follow his lead. The group, not knowing how to handle this, did nothing. The trainer came in to say that he thought he was reflecting what others in the group might be feeling. He said that he felt Cy's warm comments about the group indicated his desire to be accepted by the group, particularly after the rather difficult time he had seemed to be having during the first week. The trainer said also that perhaps Cy now realized that what he wished the group to do might not be what the group wanted to do or what would even be best. The group itself had become pretty wise about its own affairs. Perhaps Cy, he said, was signaling that his own behavior would be different during the second week. (Privately the trainer was not at all certain that Cy's autism would permit him to hear anything he had said except that Cy liked the group.)

The trainer made a point of having a number of talks with Cy outside the group. He also asked the laboratory counselor to find an informal way to talk to Cy. It was the judgment of both the counselor and the trainer that the group could not be very helpful to Cy, and that the best thing would be to encourage Cy to get some therapeutic help after the sessions were completed. They also thought that it would be very unwise to remove Cy from the group. The trainer gave Cy what support he could during the sessions, and the group was careful not to appear to attack him. During the second week, Cy appeared more quiet, more reflective, and less inclined to push his pet idea, although when he did speak it was in the general vein of his first week's comments. As various members sought feedback, there was always the concern that Cy might do so also, and group members were not at all certain what they could say.

Cy made no move, however, to direct the conversation toward himself. At the beginning of the final session, only three persons, including Cy, had not sought helpful reactions from the group.

During the first hour, two of the members did talk about themselves with the group. There was still half an hour to go. Conversation became general, as everyone hoped that Cy would maintain his silence for the final few moments.

The final moments approached, the session closed, and members started toward the door. As they reached it, Cy spoke out and said that he did not want to be the only one not to get help from the group, and would they come back and tell him their reactions to him. There was a stunned silence. A final closing session for the entire laboratory was to start immediately.

The trainer turned back to the table. He told Cy quietly, and without hesitation, that he was sorry Cy had chosen this time to ask such a question, because it made it extremely difficult for the group to respond. He felt that Cy did not really want help from the group or he would not have waited until the group ended. The trainer said he would be glad to talk with Cy immediately after the final closing session, which the trainer had to lead, but he did want Cy to recognize his behavior was difficult for the group to respond to at this point in time.

The trainer hoped that this intervention would help the group recover its poise and not end the session with too shattering an experience. At the same time, he hoped it would get through to Cy and help him recognize forces outside himself. The trainer resolved to talk further to Cy after the closing laboratory session.

TRAINER ANALYSIS. The trainer thought quite a bit about this situation later. He talked it over with another trainer, to check his perceptions and actions. He reflected that there was no good answer to the dilemma. There was a very serious discrepancy between Cy's needs and the needs of the other members of the group, and there was insufficient time even to attempt to reconcile the differences in needs. The trainer did not feel at all happy about the way he had handled the particular situation, but he was equally uncertain as to what else he might have done. He reflected about the problems of special members—the autistic person, the crying female, the hostile psychopath—who cannot be appreciably helped, if at all, given the short time restrictions of the T Group. This led him to ponder on the role of the trainer in arranging both therapeutic encapsulation of the individual so that he is not hurt by the group and protection of the group so that it is not destroyed by the worries produced by the individual.

6

The Present Status

of T-Group Theory

Jack R. Gibb

In this section eight behavioral scientists present their individual views of the T Group. These viewpoints contain essential background material for emerging theories of the process of learning through group interaction. Each of the writers has had extensive experience in leading T Groups. Each chapter represents an amalgamation of the writer's experience, speculation, research, and systematic background in behavioral science theory.

Theory may exist at all levels of complexity and formality. It may be a formal and logically consistent system of postulates and theorems designed to impose order upon a whole constellation of phenomena. At another extreme it may exist as a loosely related and only partially articulated body of assumptions, intuitive impressions, and hypotheses derived from a blend of experience and speculation. In education, therapy, and training, as in other engineering fields, practice tends to outstrip theory. Practice is refined from a series of gradualistic innovations which grow out of some blending of miniature models, intuitive impressions, empirical data, opportunistic considerations, and systematic thinking.

T-Group theories are useful to at least four overlapping classes of people. The *theorist* in a wide variety of fields that border on the T-Group experience is interested in building a systematic and consistent picture of behavior that will have maximal predictive and explanatory power. The *researcher* is interested in creating hypotheses that will guide field or laboratory tests of critical issues in the field of behavior change. The *trainer* is interested in examining his own behavior as a T-Group leader and in increasing his proficiency in practicing his art. The *participant* in T Groups is interested in maximal understanding of the processes which influence his behavior. Any reader may take one or more of these four stances in examining the following chapters.

Of the many functions that theory might perform for these classes of recipients, we propose to examine three critical and central ones: the selective, heuristic, and illuminative functions. Table 1 provides a summary of the major functions that an applied science theory might perform for the above-mentioned four classes of recipients. These functions are elaborated at some length in the following sections.

From the Viewpoint of the Theorist

Engineering theory probably develops in many different ways. Most of such theory originates in the practice of the art, arises out of problems met in practice. Practitioners try out various ways of educating, training, or practicing therapy, and some of them make self-conscious articulation of their rationale. The theorist borrows from whatever background of theory about the process that exists at the time. The writers of the following eight chapters have borrowed from their backgrounds in the disciplines of psychology, sociology, anthropology, group behavior, and learning theory. They have also borrowed from emerging engineering theory in psychiatry, education, social work, and other fields of practice. As engineering and engineering theory become more highly developed, a group is emerging who are doing research and theory building as an area of professional specialization. One can see these processes at work in the viewpoints presented in these papers, which provide an informative documentary to students who are interested in the emergence of applied science theory in a field undergoing rapidly accelerating change.

One often sees spurts in growth of scientific theory when disciplines intrude upon one another. Often it is the press of "practical" problems of engineering that has forced growth upon relatively dormant areas of scientific theory. Thus we see dramatic bursts of progress in physiological chemistry, psychosomatics, humoral chemistry, or astronautics. Because practitioners became increasingly interested in the possibilities of inducing behavioral and social change through process-oriented training in groups, there occurred a fresh look at the reciprocal intrusions of group dynamics, learning theory, psychiatry, edu-

Table 1   Functions of an Engineering Theory for Four Classes of Recipients

Functions	Recipient Groups			
	Participants	Trainers-Technologists	Researchers	Theorists
Selective	Indicates direction of focus	Provides diagnostic categories	Provides independent variables for manipulation	Selects phenomena central to his miniature model
Heuristic	Gives direction to provisional behavior	Provides intervention alternatives	Indicates operations for empirical test	Places stress on theory boundaries
Illuminative	Provides integrative frame of reference	Provides framework for examining his total assumption-attitude complex	Provides significance hierarchy for variables	Relates to behavioral science reservoir of theory

cational psychology, and other areas upon one another. This process has forced a fresh look at the adequacy of various kinds of engineering theory for understanding the T Group.

The Selective Function. Each of the following students of the T Group selects out certain aspects of the total experience as being of special significance in theory building. Thus, Bennis looks at the dynamics of dependence and interdependence, Benne at the formation and management of polarization, Gibb at the processes of defense reduction and trust formation, Bradford at the problem of membership attainment, Blake at the trainer-member relationship, Horwitz at the process of legitimation, Shepard at the influence properties of the training milieu, and Whitman at the dynamics of focal conflict. In a sense, each writer, in his role as practitioner-theorist, is saying to the theorist: "This process I see is in some way central to what is happening in the T Group. Examine the phenomena and incorporate them into your theory."

The Heuristic Function. It is a function of the immaturity of the field that these formulations have as yet led to few productive empirical tests. A theory performs a heuristic function when constructs and relationships among variables are so defined as to lead almost immediately to operational statements that are susceptible to ready empirical or experimental test. This process of testing demands an operational rigor of statement that is in little evidence in the following papers. An examination of the Stock chapter (Chapter 15) reveals that the research done in T Groups tends to be upon hypotheses that derive directly from theories of perception, learning, growth, emotionality, and other areas relatively independent of emerging T-Group theories as represented here. Few studies (e.g., Bennis, 1956; Gibb and Gorman, 1954) seem to be derived directly from the theories as formulated in the present chapters. Some of the studies have indirect implications for the theory, and all of the findings must be in some way incorporated into a full and mature T-Group theory. At a later stage of development of T-Group theory it is likely that theory will be stated in such a way as to be more directly susceptible to empirical test and resulting modification through research.

It is perhaps healthy that in most fields of psychological engineering (e.g., therapy, education, child rearing, training) there is a relatively independent growth of practice, research, and theory building. Only at certain times do these processes engage one another with the kind of confrontation that requires change in practice, in theory, or in research. As such engagement occurs, each process is enriched and modified. It is hoped that books like the present one will facilitate the reciprocal modifications necessary for vigorous growth of theory and resulting change in practice. Child-rearing practices tend to be little modified by psychiatric and educational theory and research. Parents who do the child rearing seldom do the research and theory building. Such is also the case to a lesser degree in educational and psychiatric practice. Because, with few exceptions, the people who do T-Group training are behavioral scientists and theoreticians in their fields of specialty, it is possible to predict that there will be increasingly productive confrontations of practice and research.

An examination of the papers reveals some apparent assumptions as to the subject-matter content of T-Group theory. It is possible to distinguish four constellations of subject matter: the processes of interpersonal relationship and influence; the dynamics of intrapersonal change; the processes of group development; and the dynamics of intergroup and community processes. These areas, of course, touch on the whole gamut of concerns of the behavioral and social sciences. An "adequate" theory of behavior change would be imbedded in a mature body of behavioral science theory. The limitations of T-Group theory in one sense are representative of the inadequacies, truncations, conflicts, and other limitations of current behavioral science theory. This is certainly not to say that there has been as yet an adequate attempt to synthesize the implications of all of behavioral science theory for the T-Group processes.

One central area of concern is the *dynamics of the relationships among persons* who are engaged in confronting one another for purposes of learning. The writers are thus concerned with the relationships of influence, feedback, leadership, communication, conflict resolution, trust formation, giving and receiving help, intervention, power, control, and legitimation. Thus Bradford examines the relationship aspects of the process of human learning. The process of learning has perhaps been examined as intensively and systematically as any other single topic in behavioral science. For historical reasons, studies have focused upon physiological and other intrapersonal processes represented in the learning process. Relatively neglected has been the relationship properties of the total learning process. Bradford analyzes the dynamics of perceptions that others hold of the learner, the process of live feedback and "learning from peers," and the influence of the relationship properties of membership upon the learning process. Blake examines in detail the relationship between a trainer and individual group members. Whitman focuses upon the dynamics of trainer entry into the relationship system of the T Group. Gibb looks at the process of trust formation as a relationship that changes during group development.

Central concerns in some of the theories are around the *dynamics of intrapersonal behavior*. Theorists examine the intrapersonal aspects of management of hostility, goal formation, integration of emotionality and work, withdrawal, identity stress, management of tension, language formation, predispositions to polarize, and other aspects of personal development. Thus Bennis examines the role behavior of the trainer at various levels. Bradford looks at individual reactions to ambiguity, concern for identity, and investment of self. Gibb looks at façade production as an aspect of the defense system. Benne examines the intrapersonal aspects of language production. Whitman brings focus on the impact of conflicting dynamic forces within the individual.

Another concern is with *group dynamics*. Both research and experience in practice have demonstrated the powerful influence of group variables upon the significant dimensions of personal change. Much of the research on group problems has been motivated by an interest in the change-induction properties of group life. Bennis presents a systematic view, developed by Bennis and Shepard, of group development changes on the dependency dimension. Changes on this dimension are seen as underlying many other interrelated changes in group development. Starting from the proposition that "the movement of training-group life, when it is successful, seems to be from polarization to paradox," Benne traces the processes incident to the management of these polarities. Gibb describes the development of a group as a product of the resolution of four primary modal concerns: acceptance, flow of data, formation of goal, and development of a control system. Horwitz gives a developmental account of three sequential phases in the growth of legitimation structure. Bradford and Mallinson describe the cyclic processes "in which learning recurs in increasing depth" as the T Group "approaches and reapproaches" the central problems of its group life. Whitman looks at the role of work on "group focal conflict" as central to group development.

The properties of group action interest all of the writers. They are interested in norms and standards, legitimacy structures, emotionality and work, membership, decision making, goal formation, communication patterns, control systems, problem solving, and other aspects of behavior which describe group conditions or properties.

Blake describes the intermember problems incident to group formation: getting acquainted, setting up procedural standards, interpersonal alliances, subgroup development, cohesion, and differential verbal participation. The fusion of process and work, of task and need, of emotionality and problem solving, are treated at length by Horwitz, by Benne, and by each of the other writers to a lesser degree.

Somewhat less attention has been paid by the writers to *community variables* such as the nature and effect of the "therapeutic community," the intergroup relationships in the training or institutional community, and the presence of the following as community variables: conflict resolution, power, trust formation, norms, and standards. Presumably, many of the generalizations made by the writers about the dynamics of small groups would apply to the dynamics of the larger training community. Shepard and Gibb make explicit a concern for the training properties of the larger community: the organizational setting, composition by organizational role, the community atmosphere that generates trainerless groups, and the atmosphere in the training team as it relates to the effects of the training community.

To perform the heuristic function for the general theorist, an analysis should stimulate a set of cognitive and/or logical operations which lead to continual mathematical, deductive, or other logical tests of the constructs and relationships within the concern area of the theorist: A theorist's theory, to have heuristic value for other theorists, should juxtapose constructs and suggest relationships among constructs in such a way as to invite, perhaps to force, logical analysis and experiential consonance. Thus Bradford's analysis forces the theorist to take a look at identity stress as produced by situational ambiguity and as arousing further sequential stresses that may be productive of learning. Shepard and Blake suggest a new perspective and force a new examination of assumptions about heterogeneous composition of T Groups. Gibb's speculations about the trainer role and the trainerless group force the logical testing of previously comfortable assumptions about the dynamics of trainer-intervention. Benne's analyses of polarities and paradoxes suggest new ways of theorizing about the dramatic member conflicts that ebb and flow during T-Group life. Horwitz's detailed examination of the effects of legitimation upon the dynamics of the learning group at various stages suggests, among other things, a logical examination of power and influence as developmental phenomena. Whitman and Stock provide heuristic impetus to re-examine the dynamics of conflict and goal formation. Bennis and Shepard provide a rich source of hypotheses from their detailed examination of the longitudinal trends in the dynamics of dependency.

The Illuminative Function. Each writer attempts to explore, clarify, and place in perspective the processes that he sees as relatively central in the total experience. The limited state of our knowledge makes it impossible for the theorist to build a comprehensive theory that would meet the many tests of adequacy of a full theory, such as power and economy of constructs, internal consistency, and logical elegance. What we seem to have is a series of fragments, points of view, and constructs which must be given consideration and have great potential in the process of theory building. The informality of these considerations is probably appropriate to the level of development of the area of knowledge under surveillance. Greater refinement and elegance would probably be incommensurate with the state of relevant research and theory from the areas in which these theories are imbedded.

It is somewhat difficult at this stage of development to determine what the essential content of a T-Group theory should be. Perhaps because many of the scientists who have been instrumental in developing the T Group as a method of inducing learning have been especially interested in the dynamics of the small group, one sees in these papers a disproportionate emphasis upon the structure and functions of the developing group. Students of personality theory, learning theory, and person-development theory have not been so often attracted to the T-Group arena. The following chapters, as a consequence, tend to be considerably less rich and less differentiated in these fields. A full theory of the T-Group processes will illuminate more fully the spectrum of relationships between intrapersonal and small-group dynamics. Taken in total perspective, these eight chapters and the research summary chapter written by Stock provide a structure which is beginning to tell us where the gaps are and to tell theorist and researcher alike where to look next.

From the Viewpoint of the Researcher

The Selective Function. In Chapter 15, Stock indicates that researchers have distilled variables from many sources. It reveals that early research done on T Groups was generated by concerns coming from well-developed lines of interest in psychology and sociology—interests in perception theory, role theory, learning theory, and sociometric theory. As interest in and theorizing about T Groups have developed, a change has come about. Research is increasingly done upon issues generated by essentially T-Group concerns. A summary of this research is contained in Chapter 15. An analysis by the researcher of the differential coverage of constructs in the following chapters and in the studies summarized in Chapter 15 indicates where the theorists, as well as the researchers, might look.

The Heuristic Function. To be of maximum usefulness in research, a theory must pose the statement of relationships in such a way that predictions from the theory can be subjected to experiential, field, statistical, or laboratory test. The papers as they now stand are filled with clinical insights, descriptions of events and processes, speculations about underlying dynamics, and implicit assumptions about the relative induction-of-learning effects of certain group states or trainer behaviors. The next steps would entail refinement of the statements of the theories in such a way as to clarify the experimental manipulations necessary to make a test probe. An effective and useful theory must have within itself the mechanisms for survival or lack of survival. The theory must change or die. In a sense, an effective theory makes provision for the lineage of succession and specifies the rules under which lineage is determined.

Some examples from the chapters are relevant. For instance, Whitman predicts that focal conflicts must be dealt with before the group can move on to productive work on the explicit goal of therapy or training. Whitman and Stock are making empirical tests of this and related predictions. Bennis makes a number of well-differentiated and testable predictions about sequences in developing groups. The specificity of the predictions facilitates the process of empirical assessment. However, there is an apparent and discouragingly negative correlation between the significance and generality of a statement and its susceptibility to immediate empirical test. Obvious problems lie as barriers to a satisfying assessment of maturity and growth in a group situation. It seems obvious to trainers and participants alike that groups in training undergo radical change. The problems that confront the researcher are, however, formidable. Lack of correlation between latent and manifest evidence of change reduces the correlations found on one-level analyses. Students of individual growth have found growth jags, dormant periods, great differences in rate and manifestation of growth among individuals, and other phenomena that complicate the research problem.

Shepard makes a number of statements contrasting the effects of various kinds of influence milieu and inductivity in a T Group. A statement such as the following is susceptible to test: ". . . simultaneous replication of small-group experiments is more meaningful to participants [than demonstration role playing]. . . ." Many practical questions of method and composition are settled in practice

by gradualistic or sudden changes in practice, with trainers often settling for impressionistic data. Without adequate measurement, however, there are obvious dangers of prolongation of impressionistic error.

Gibb makes the statement that ". . . immediate attempts at handling
the control function arise out of distrust and are essentially directed at
resolution of the acceptance concern." This chapter, along with others
in the series, makes use of constructs taken from depth psychology.
These constructs and hypothetical relationships inherit the mensura-
tion difficulties along with the richness of the constructs.

Productive research questions can be formulated from statements
such as Blake's: "If, from the standpoint of training rationale, the
behavior is regarded as inappropriate, and particularly if it is destructive, intervention is indicated." One might specify the operations that
would indicate whether behavior was "appropriate" or "destructive."
If one specified a relevant dependent variable (e.g., later effective
behavior in the T Group) and devised adequate measures of the independent and dependent variables, one could set up a series of
representative-design experiments which could examine the impact
of various such elements of trainer style.

Many assumptions are held in common by T-Group trainers. One is
stated by Bradford: "People generally approach learning and change
with ambivalence." The statement has face validity for people with
T-Group experience. Further empirical assessment of the prevalence
and depth of ambivalence and its effects as a barrier or facilitator of
learning would be helpful. Bradford's statement that "investment of
self requires considerable awareness of one's own motivations and
personal defenses" is in part a definition of self and in part a statement
about the relationship between two independently definable constructs
and thus is a statement susceptible to test at least at one significant
level.

The Illuminative Function. Adequate theory helps to pinpoint and
differentiate the attack of the researcher upon an empirical problem.
Adequate theory facilitates the performance of the empirical test.
Adequate theory also performs an integrative and illuminative function of placing test probes into perspective with other tests. Theory
and research are interrelated, cumulative, and reciprocally influential
processes. To be maximally productive each effort must in some way
build upon other efforts.

The T Group was a brilliant invention that has forced stresses upon
many fields of theory and has stimulated some research. Developments in the T Group have come largely through innovations in prac-

tice, less from theory, and still less from empirical research. Stock clarifies areas in which this state of affairs is changing.

Development of the T Group, then, is a kind of cross-illumination among the above three processes. Examples may be helpful. The centrality of perceptual and feeling feedback to the T-Group process was noted in early experiences in the T Groups. Modifications in practice of feedback have occurred as a result of experiential innovation (dyads, participative groups, triangulation groups, induced stress, and instrumented groups, among others); as a result of research on feedback (Miles, Gibb, and others); and as a result of inference from personality theory (Jeanne Watson, R. Lippitt, and others). Developments in intergroup variations on the original T-Group design have resulted from innovations in practice by Blake, Shepard, and others; from examination of the theories of Muzafer Sherif and other social psychologists; and from continual gathering of empirical data during the designs.

Theories derived from a blending of social psychology and personality theory have rich possibilities for modification of T-Group theory. J. R. P. French, Jr., for instance, is examining the implications of identity theory and reference-group theory for T-Group behavior and is gathering data which will test derivations from these bodies of theory, the results of which may have direct implications for forcing design innovation in the T Group.

Theories about influence relationships are contained in the voluminous literature on counseling, therapy, consulting, education, group work, and other change-induction fields. The implications of these fields for T-Group practice is inadequately explored. A barrier to such reciprocal influence is the diversity of clinical and empirical literature using different terminologies, different operations for independent variables, different measurements of dependent variables, and widely varying language systems for communicating results.

From the Viewpoint of the Trainer

Theories may have immediate technological effects. A well-formulated and internalized theory may be a powerful determiner of trainer behavior.

The Selective Function. The trainer cannot attend to all of the events in the T Group. Theory can be useful to the trainer in helping him to select out from the mass of experience available those aspects which are most relevant to the productive work of the T Group. Dissertations such as those contained in the following chapters can be helpful to the trainer in causing him to examine his assumptions and to go about the business of building a consistent effect upon his practice. The trainer who is sensitized to the meanings of polarities, focal conflicts, trust formation, legitimacy structures, dependency patterns, membership attainment, and group maintenance functions may, with learning, be able to increase his role repertoire, his empathy range, and his perceptions of self-adequacy by following what he sees to be significant theory of training. The function of these chapters might be to increase the range of phenomena out of which the trainer might select for focus at a particular time in the T Group.

The Heuristic Function. The trainer is a learner who continually subjects his own behavior to empirical test, who continually makes hypotheses about his intervention behavior and tests the adequacy of the hypothesis against the effects of the intervention. In a sense, the adequate trainer is one who takes "research" stances toward his job in the T Group. Indeed, one of the implicit assumptions common to most of the papers is that experimentation with one's own behavior will lead to growth and continual learning. Although there is some independent evidence for its validity, this assumption deserves further empirical test.

The theory can bring to awareness of the trainer the alternatives available to him in working with the T Group. One set of alternatives has to do with the nature and range of interventions in the group activities. The trainer must have thought through such questions as the following ones: With what range of consciousness do I work? How much do I work at the individual level and how much at the group process level? How often do I work with the here-and-now and how much with the there-and-then? With what kinds of feelings do I work and at what level? How often and how much do I work at the content and at the process levels? How much hostility do I deliberately arouse in myself and in others? How do I handle this hostility? How much do I rely upon emergent properties of the group, and how much responsibility do I feel in guidance and direction? At what level of reality or irreality do I work? How open can I be about my own feelings, attitudes, and motivations? How protective am I of members and of myself?

A second kind of option that is brought to awareness by the papers has to do with the alternative purposes of the T Group. To what degree is the training oriented toward therapy, skill development, or behavior change? Is the training primarily preventive or remedial and to what degree?

A third area of alternatives has to do with the formation of the training community. How is the T Group imbedded in the training community and to what degree? How much and how do I use ancillary stimulus techniques (data-gathering instruments, feedback methods, role playing, simulation experiments, demonstrations, subgrouping)? How is the T Group imbedded into the design and methodology of the laboratory and to what degree? How much a part of training is research *qua* research?

There is little solid research to help the trainer in taking his options on such dimensions. Also, it is difficult to find explicit formulations in the chapters that follow which specify solutions to these trainer dilemmas. Some statements are helpful, general formulations which probably provide guidelines but certainly do not provide the level of specificity necessary to allow a trainer to "follow the theory" in practice. The purpose of the papers is not to provide a training manual but to provide a discussion of considerations that the trainer must take into account in developing his own style.

One might legitimately hope that, as theory becomes more differentiated and adequate in this human engineering area, theories will become sufficiently explicit to specify in some detail the nature and kinds of interventions that trainers might make in specified situations. On this level of assessment the papers do not differ greatly from writings in the fields of therapy, educational method, and child rearing. Engineering theory is unable, for a vast array of reasons, to specify what parents, trainers, and therapists might do in specific situations.

Well-differentiated statements from the standpoint of this heuristic criterion are contained in the chapters written by Blake and by Whitman (Chapters 11 and 12). Sufficient detail is given in certain instances by each writer to provide cognitive clarity for the trainer who may be attempting to understand the position. For instance, it is clear what is meant when Blake states that "I do not participate in topical discussions," or ". . . my interventions decrease as member participant-observer contributions increase." It is comparably clear when Whitman states that he ". . . should make his interpretations in the form of questions or hypotheses that he wishes the group to examine and test," or that the trainer "should try to make wide, generalizing remarks which are pertinent to many members of the group." Somewhat less clear in the cases of the two papers just mentioned are the relationships between these intervention operations and an integrated body of engineering theory. Each of the writers gives reasons for such intervention styles, but the reasons tend not to flow unambiguously from the theory.

The Illuminative Function. The trainer might hope that a training theory would put things in such perspective as to help him arrive at a theory that would fit his understandings of the whole body of knowledge in the behavioral and social sciences, and somehow synthesize his own value system and ontology with this body of knowledge. Because the trainer invests so much of his person in the process of interaction in the T Group it is perhaps more necessary that he make this synthesis than that the therapist, educator, or parent do so. Ideally, such a synthesis is helpful in any interpersonal role and is probably essential to maximal growth and mental health.

Several of the following papers deal with aspects of this problem. Thus Whitman is helpful in integrating his view of the T Group with some considerations taken from psychiatric theory. Benne makes integrative speculations about the management of work, the development of a time perspective, and the development of language. Bennis brings in some psychiatric and clinical considerations to his account of the development of interdependence in a group. Gibb employs some concepts derived from the literature on mental and organizational health in his discussion of trust formation. Bradford injects considerations from the social psychology of learning. Space prevents the writers from making further attempts to integrate their considerations with the larger body of behavioral science theory. Development of the theories of the T Group in the future may well move a greater distance along the dimension of integration with widely growing bodies of theory.

From the Viewpoint of the Participant

The participant in the T Group may find some help in reading the following set of chapters. As some theorists have it, the participant is in a sense his own trainer, theorist, and researcher. That is, the participant looks at his own behavior and the behavior of others, builds feelings of responsibility in directing his own search for more effective behavior patterns, examines his own set of assumptions (his theory), constructs more or less systematic hypotheses about the roles that he might take in the group, and conducts continual miniature experiments upon his relationship with this world of experience. Well-formulated theory can be potentially very helpful to the participant in the accomplishment of these tasks.

The Selective Function. Most observers agree that one significant change from T-Group experience is a widening and deepening of the sensitivities of the learner. Again, the participant is able to look at only a small fraction of the significant things that happen in the T Group. Perceptual work is difficult and there is much work on inhibition as well as defensive resistance that prevents the participant from looking at dimensions of experience in the group. To the extent that the blockage comes from lack of focus, a theory can be a kind of observer guide to the participant in his journey through the T Group.

Blake's discussion, for instance, of the mechanical or formal procedures for achieving direction would be a useful road map for the participant in looking at some of the significant procedural devices used by groups in handling control and decision-making problems. The chapter is written with sufficient concreteness to be helpful to all participants. It performs the pointing function very effectively. The same can be said for his discussion of the familiar phenomena of hand-clasping, topic jumping, gate keeping, bids for personality analysis, silences, and other socio-emotional reactions in the group. Somewhat less concrete, but perhaps equally helpful in contributing to insights and to directions of perceptual exploration are the notable discussion of the development of legitimacy structure (Horwitz), the detailed journey through the dependency cycles (Bennis), the comfort-growth, authority-freedom, and group–versus–self-maintenance polarities and paradoxes (Benne), and such passages as the description of stereotyping by Whitman, norm centering by Gibb, and self-investment by Bradford.

The Heuristic Function. An adequate theory can assist the participant in his experimentations in the T Group. Early experimentation in the T Group is likely to be fortuitous, manipulative, self-need meeting, and relatively ineffective in accomplishing either personal or group goals. As the member comes to recognize and sense the importance of a group focal conflict (Whitman) between the wish to trust the group and examine the interpersonal relations in the group, on the one hand, and the fear of group members' getting hurt, on the other, he may be able to attempt a helpful interpretation of this conflict at a time which would open up the conflict for analysis and at least partial resolution. Thus, selective sensitivity could be integrated into his provisional behavior in an effective and, what might be for him, a new and exciting way. The participant might come to greater awareness of the perceptions of his minimal-trust behavior (Gibb) and, through behaving in a more open way, reduce his own distrusts and those of others. The participant might gain a new insight into the significance of here-and-now descriptions (Bennis) as contrasted with there-and-then concerns in such a way as to enable him to attempt whatever here-and-now interventions might "feel" comfortable to him. The member might gain a new insight into his ambivalences about membership (Bradford) and be able to devise an entry into the group that would reduce his resistance to membership by giving him a satisfying experience with influence and relevance. The member might become aware of his linguistic dissonance with the group and make the necessary adjustment in some of his language to facilitate the flow of feeling and perceptual data in the group.

As the participant experiments with his own behavior, he learns to make hypotheses about the effects of his entries into the membership life of the group and to test in various ways the effects of these entries. The trainer is a continuously experimenting person, and the effective participant is also. The participant-experimenter learns to make use of intervening group-variable constructs to simplify his conceptual task. He thus may aim, in his entry, to change a group state which will make it possible for him and for other members to relate more effectively. In order to be an autonomous learner it is necessary for him to articulate and internalize a functional theory of learning. Examination of the theories of the trainers about the inductive properties of the small group, for instance, will aid him in building his own theory of learning-in-a-group.

Whitman's theory of group learning encompasses the concepts of optimal ambiguity for the purpose of maximizing projection; optimal anxiety and discomfort, because "too much anxiety is disintegrating to the organism," and conversely, "too little anxiety makes a person unwilling to abandon his usual approach"; optimal visibility of the leader's and presumably the member's motivations and self-properties; optimal regression; and progressive removal of the focal group conflicts because they serve "as a resistance against the exploration of the individual personality or the dynamics of the group." This provides a model that the participant might use as an inaugural point for his experimentation with his own behavior.

Horwitz's theory of group learning encompasses such concepts as optimal congruence of member needs and group activity; optimal awareness of individual needs and openness of feeling and need expression; presence of a legitimacy structure; and optimal satisfaction for each member in the expressed and functional group goal. Such a theory would focus the participant's attention and efforts upon the exploration of needs, feelings, and goals and upon efforts to precipitate some kind of adequate congruency tests.

Gibb's theory of group learning includes such concepts as optimal trust and confidence; optimal exploration of feelings and perceptions appropriate to the trust level; open testing of intrinsic member goals against continual tests of group goals; and optimal reduction of interpersonal threat. Such a theory focuses the attention of the participant upon the defense-reduction and trust dimensions of the T-Group experience and tends to guide member entries in directions commensurate with such norm building.

Each of the eight writers charts a possible, though not always operationally clear, course toward attainment of group membership and member effectiveness and provides multiple options available for the participant-experimenter in the performance of his continual miniature experiments upon his own behavior in the group. Theory performs the function of stating these options in a manner that facilitates immediate test and minimally distorted incorporation of the theory by the learner.

The Illuminative Function. The participant comes to the T-Group experience with a frame of reference and a cognitive and attitudinal background that may be quite dissonant with the apparent and visible aspects of the T Group. In one sense, what the T-Group experience asks is that the participant take a larger vantage point, a broader frame of reference that will include multiple aspects of process. He lacks the kind of cognitive integration and synthesis that would frame the experiences for him and give a larger integrative meaning to his life. The presentations in the following chapters will aid in this process. The presentations probably perform this function less well than they do other functions. It is suggested that the participant examine the other parts of the book for this wider perspective, particularly the early chapters dealing with the laboratory method—its functions and its history.

General Considerations

The following eight chapters present some viewpoints and considerations that must be examined in the development of a full and adequate theory of T-Group action. They represent rationalizations of practices that are growing up in a rapidly expanding field of professional activity. The level of refinement and elegance of these fragmentary theories represents the current state of the practice of the art and the development of research and theory.

T-Group theory is not a theory of group development, of influence, or of personal dynamics, but a peculiar, emergent *Gestalt* which deals with the phenomena that occur when persons meet in groups with intent to learn and to change through increasing process awareness.

The discerning reader can see in the papers the seeds of future development along many lines:

1. There is an increasing tendency to integrate speculations and hypotheses with research findings.
2. There is increasing innovation in directions that are changing the patterns of T-Group training.
3. There is an increasing, healthy diversity in practice and theory, a diversity not fully represented by the small sample of T-Group theories given here.
4. There is a growing integration with findings from other professional fields dealing with the dynamics of interpersonal learning, personality development, dynamics of planned change, psychiatric and clinical theory, and because behavior is imbedded in organizational life, emerging theories of organization and management.
5. There is a blurring and fusion of the lines between training and education, on the one hand, and between training and greater depth therapy, on the other.

Unfinished Tasks

No attempt will be made here to assess individual chapters. This evaluation is best done by the consumer. It may not be amiss, however, to indicate some strengths and limitations that seem evident. Each aspect of the analysis points up a kind of unfinished task for the theorist.

Integration of Theory and Data from the Behavioral Sciences. A strength of the following papers is the blending of a great diversity of both scientific and engineering concepts from a variety of disciplines. The traditional boundaries of historically diverse and sometimes antithetical fields of study have been violated. Concepts from theories of conflict, equilibrium, subliminal behavior, linguistic development, group dynamics, human learning, work inhibition, problem solving, labor-management relations, self-concept, power and influence, and other diverse fields have been used at various points by the writers.

A related limitation is the resulting lack of integration of behavioral science concepts into a unified theory of behavior-change-in-group phenomena. Such integration is a continuing task of the student of T-Group learning.

The Experiential Nature of T-Group Training. A strength of the papers is that they clearly grow from authentic experience in practice. They are written by persons who have had long experience in T Groups and whose insights are imbedded in such experience. The experiential components of the formulations overshadow the logical and theoretical structure of the conceptualization. This is perhaps as it should be with engineering theory. The backgrounds and personalities of the writers are reflected in the choice of constructs, the selection of emphasis, and the choice of examples. The face validity of the presentations for those who have participated in process-oriented groups is thus very high.

This experiential imbedding occurs at some cost. Several writers emphasize that persons must experience the T Group in order to participate fully in the trainer role. This statement has a familiar ring to those who have interviewed persons who have recently emerged from the T-Group experience. A full theory of the training group, to be useful to theorists and researchers as well as to trainers and participants, must disengage itself from its experiential origins and become public property susceptible to the usual experimental as well as logico-deductive tests. This criterion is a severe one for engineering theories of education, therapy, training, and child rearing. To a significant degree, such theory *is* imbedded in the therapist, trainer, and parent—and appropriately and necessarily so.

Vulnerability to Empirical Test. A strength of each of the theories presented is that they have been demonstrated and modified through years of experience by successful T-Group trainers. Greater formality and elegance would be inappropriate and would overstep the data. There is little pretense in these statements of theory. Each presentation is clearly an effort to present thoughts, considerations, experiences, comments, and fragments.

This strength points up an area of further development. To be most useful, a theory must be stated in such a way that the formulations are susceptible to immediate empirical test. Because such statements are seldom made in the following chapters it is not always clear how one might go about demonstrating that the formulations are correct or false. Moreover, there is inadequate integration of the presentations with bodies of research. This is not to say that there has been no such integration. Most of the writers are behavioral scientists familiar with the research literature, and their formulations have been derived in varying degrees from their own personal integration of research results. But the reader is seldom provided with direct references to existing research even when it is relevant. The process of further development of the theories would be aided by such an explicit integration.

Dynamics of the Learning Process. A clear strength of the presentations is that they are grounded in "learning-in-a-group" phenomena. There is an effort to understand the relationships between the dynamics of the group and the dynamics of the learner. This is less true of other engineering disciplines where practitioners use groups to facilitate the learning process. In group therapy and in educational classrooms, therapists and teachers often do therapy and education *in* a group, as Whitman points out in his paper, and fail to do therapy and education *with* a group, thus failing to use the inductive properties of the group as the medium of learning. The educational classroom is often a place where teachers build a series of dyadic and often polar relationships between the teacher and individuals in the group. Classroom learning and group therapy often use a multiple-and-overlapping-pair situation to which the dynamics of the dyad are more appropriate than the dynamics of the group. T-Group theory, in contrast, is a valid theory of *group* experience.

A commensurate and resulting aspect of the above strength is the failure to deal more than superficially with the dynamics of the learning process *in the person.* If one looks at the traditional textbook in psychology of learning or educational psychology, he finds a correlative neglect of what might be called the psychodynamics of individual learning. It is unfortunate for each of the three areas that there is so little cross-fertilization among the three fields of (1) traditional learning theory, (2) the psychodynamics of personality, and (3) the dynamics of in-a-group learning. T-Group theory has much to contribute to the dynamics of personality and to the dynamics of the learning process but also much to learn from historical studies in each of these areas.

Diversity and Power of Constructs. One strength of the presentations is the presence of a great diversity of constructs and a wide range of problems being dealt with in the theories. The T Group is a slice of life, a group which presents significant and generalizable similarities to all groups, and a group in which, in either direct, surrogate, or symbolic fashion, all phenomena of living are encapsulated. This inclusiveness presents the theorist with the necessity of building a complete and unified theory of social science to deal with and account for all levels of such experience. This is, of course, an impossible task. The task encourages theorists to present a wide array of constructs and concerns. This diversity and richness is a strength. There is something for everyone.

At the same time there is a sense in which these somethings are dissatisfying. For a theory to be maximally useful it must deal with a wide range of behavior through use of a minimum of constructs. The model must have power and economy. For a theory to be of maximal use it must be presented as a compact road map, it must provide a straightforward guide to all of the terrain, and the traveler must know almost immediately when he has arrived at his destination.

The Art and the Science. There is a helpful and realistic recognition that T-Group experience contains elements of art, technology, and science. The T-Group trainer is something of an intuitive artist, something of a technician and professional, and something of a scientist.

Analogies with physical sciences are only partially suggestive. Many disciplines, for instance, contribute to the care and feeding of a radio. The physicist, the engineer, and the radio technician all contribute knowledge and insight to the repairman who deals directly with the radio. The theorist and researcher, the professional engineer and trainer, and the skilled training leader all contribute analogously to the knowledge and insight of the specific trainer who deals with a specific person in the group. The group learner-member is qualitatively more complex than the radio. He interacts with his interpersonal environment in a manner that the radio does not. He grows and changes with interaction. The trainer usually sees his task as interacting with the *whole* person at various levels of consciousness and intrapersonal integration. The trainer usually sees his task as developmental and creative rather than as remedial. The trainer usually sees his task as at least a quasi-scientific one in which there is a joint miniature experiment in data collection upon jointly determined hypotheses. Thus the leading of a T Group is a process which is an emergent blend of artistic, intuitive, technological, professional, scientific, and highly personal elements. The theories presented below have made many imaginative adjustments to this complexity.

At the same time it is true that, to a degree, the above paragraph contains a rationalization for all T-Group trainers. The concepts of behavioral sciences and the "hard" variables of behavioral engineering can go much further than is apparently now possible to reduce the mystique of training, to bring into empirical examination the inarticulate assumptions of the T-Group trainer, to increase the likelihood that a given T-Group experience can be replicated, that T-Group trainers can know when they have made an error and when they have been correct, and how they might go about correcting an "error," once made.   Science will eventually contribute much more to the technology, and technology, much more to the art.

7

Membership and the
Learning Process[1]

Leland P. Bradford

Experience in social creativity provided by the T Group has learning values difficult to secure elsewhere. Seldom in life does one share in the creation of a segment of society. Individuals are born into families where a structure and organization are already present. They enter school, go to a church, become part of a community. In each instance, they confront and accept (or resist) rules, customs, and laws set down for them. Even marriage, where a new family group is created, has relatively established role expectations and cultural traditions; and even when one is a founding member of a new organization, the pattern of organization is largely set through precedent and tradition.

Few people have the opportunity to be tossed, figuratively, from the sky to face the necessity of hacking their way collaboratively out of a social jungle. Given such an opportunity, they might come to understand, on cognitive, feeling, and behavioral levels, the great need for both order and change and the delicate relationship and balance that must lie between them. If in the process they have to re-earn position through present accomplishments rather than to rely on previously

[1] The author has been helped by a number of individuals in thinking through the materials in this chapter. He particularly wishes to acknowledge the contributions of Chris Argyris, Kenneth Benne, Warren Bennis, Douglas Bunker, Jack Gibb, Edgar Schein, and Ronald Lippitt. Dorothy Mial helped greatly in its final expression.

secured status symbols, they might become more innovative and creative in other social situations.   If through this same process they learn to test assumptions about social organizations, they might refuse to perpetuate archaic organizational models.   If they have to create a new kind of organization, they might develop more of the wide range of skills required for responsible membership.

If they examine the interpersonal difficulties encountered in their collaborative struggle out of the social jungle, they might learn important truths about themselves and their relations with others.   Each person exists in a network of human interrelationships and a mixture of cultural forces which place conflicting strains on his ability to adjust, to utilize his potential resources, and to grow.   As a result, people adjust only partially to their worlds.   They allow abilities to atrophy.   They secure less than adequate understanding of themselves.   Fearful of upsetting the precarious balance of internal-external relationships, they find little opportunity to become more aware of themselves, to find greater meaning in living.

The unstructured nature of the T Group provides opportunity for these kinds of learnings.   Methods of observation and data collection on the complex processes involved in the development of a group help to make sense of these processes.   Norms that support an experimental approach to individual and group problems help to give range to what can be learned.   The intense personal nature of involvement in the T Group provides the energy—the motivation—for learning of considerable depth.

Learning may be focused on a number of emphases: on the development of cultural norms in the group; on the process of social organization; on the dynamics of group behavior; on interpersonal relationships; on individual perceptions and motivations; or on individual and group values.   Data about all of these aspects of human behavior—far more than can be utilized—are generated in the T Group.

The very fact that so many interrelated learnings are available makes some order and organization of learning goals essential if the trainer is to develop and hold to a set of consistent premises guiding his behavior.

A First Goal: Learning How To Learn

A first purpose of the T Group is to help individuals to learn how to learn from their continuing experience in the areas of self-awareness, sensitivity to phenomena of interpersonal behavior, and understanding of the consequences of behavior—one's own and others'. Learning in these areas requires willingness to explore openly one's motivations and one's feelings; to utilize the reactions of others as feedback about the consequences of one's behavior; and to experiment with new ways of behaving. Since each of these steps requires emotional support, the T Group faces the dual task of creating a supportive climate and of developing situations in which members can learn through examining their own experience.

The essence of this learning experience is a transactional process in which the members negotiate as each attempts to influence or control the stream of events and to satisfy his personal needs. Individuals learn to the extent that they expose their needs, values, and behavior patterns so that perceptions and reactions can be exchanged. Behavior thus becomes the currency for transaction. The amount each invests helps to determine the return.

Through this negotiating, the individual can validate or correct his assumptions. He can learn to recognize and use feelings, and he can evaluate his behavior and learn to make it more consistent with his intentions. As individual members grow in these directions, the group itself grows in its capacity to encourage still further individual learning. Through a very genuine experience the group learns that barriers to learning—defensiveness, withdrawal, fear, distrust—can be reduced so that problems of interrelationships can be dealt with on deeper and more realistic levels.

In the process of learning how to learn, the concept of interdependence takes on new meaning. Learning as a transactional process implies *active* negotiation among peers rather than dependence on superiors. It implies mutual help in coping with problems that cannot be solved by "teacher." The trainer is himself a party to the transaction. He, too, must be willing to receive reactions as well as to give—to be taught as well as to teach. Indeed, this is one part of the trainer's reward.

In helping individuals to learn how to learn, usually certain attitudes about learning must be changed. Typically, learning is assumed to take place only in formal learning situations. Individuals seek to repeat previous behavior, even if only moderately satisfying, rather than deliberately to seek to change. Most individuals seem unaware that they themselves can engage in a deliberate process of learning from everyday events.

A Second Goal: Learning How To Give Help

The transactional nature of the learning process is illustrated by the fact that individuals can most effectively seek and use feedback about their own behavior as they help others in the same process. Resistance to learning may be more clearly seen in others than in oneself. The individual does not feel so alone if others are involved with him in learning. Observing others who are working on problems similar to one's own stimulates ideas for improving one's own behavior. Finally, joint collaboration lessens the possibility that an offer of help will be interpreted as an attack. As these discoveries are made, individuals learn that giving help and receiving help are extremely difficult—but that they can help one another more than they had thought possible.

A Third Goal: Developing Effective Membership

A successful transaction requires an association, however temporary, of those persons involved. The more difficult and delicate the transaction, the more carefully developed the association must be, and the more open, stable, and trusting it must become. To build and maintain such an association requires membership skills. Members must develop diagnostic sensitivity to difficulties facing the group, increase their ability to communicate so that diagnostic suggestions will be heard, and learn to behave in ways that will help the group move forward. These membership skills are not easily acquired. Their acquisition is a major goal of the T Group—in fact, a key to the accomplishment of the other goals.

There are also other reasons why the development of membership ability is important. Each individual needs the satisfaction of participating with others and of being accepted by them. Each discovers part of his own identity as he relates to others. Each should both influence others and be influenced by them if, together, they are to solve problems collaboratively. All of these needs call for the ability to carry out membership functions effectively.

In any association, each member brings many differences: different past experiences and present problems; different fears and anxieties about possible consequences of membership; different pressures to learn and to change; different degrees of pain in the process; different assumptions, values, and perceptual screens; different self-concepts;

different patterns of relationships to others and to authority; and different approaches to learning. All of these differences must somehow be accommodated by the members if a learning association is to be created.

Maintaining the association is also a membership responsibility. Barriers to openness and trust must be located and reduced; differences in premises about goals and methods discovered and resolved; motivations of individual members understood; normative structures for communication and problem solving developed.

The T Group provides opportunity for developing insights and skills, at successively deeper levels, necessary for carrying out these membership responsibilities. Participants learn through experience that apathetic, irresponsible, or ineffective membership reduces the effectiveness of the group; that silent or withdrawing members withhold from the group the resources needed for individual and group growth; that irresponsible members distort the group to serve their own purposes. Participants learn that full membership necessitates continuing questioning of assumptions and values underlying behavior and continuing validation of perceptions and diagnoses.

The T-Group Process

The T Group, then, is a crucible in which personal interactions are so fused that learning results. The members provide the data for their own learning as they interact and construct a learning group. In a sense, members write their own textbook as they read it. The trainer faces the task of encouraging and occasionally helping the group members to supply sufficient relevant data, to learn *how* to read the book they are writing, and to utilize the results of the reading in experimenting with new ways of behaving.

The T-Group process accomplishes a substantive goal as well as the methodological goal of developing sensitivity and skill. Learnings about group process, group behavior, and group development are gained from analyzing the dynamics of the T Group. Thus, the process of group development, with all of the attendant problems of individual change, is itself a part of the content of learning.

The goals of learning to learn and to help others to learn, of developing membership skills, and of increasing sensitivity are gradually approached as individuals gain more self-awareness, sensitivity to others, diagnostic and problem-solving abilities in group development, and the ability to seek and to accept realistic and responsible membership functions. They are learned in the heat of the transactional process of the T Group.

This, then, is the T Group: a group formed for individual learning purposes where the data are created and analyzed by the work of the group and not fed in from outside and interpreted by a teacher, where learning is a group task entered into jointly, where the trainer does not deny the group members the experience of creating and maintaining their own group even though this experience will be difficult and may produce anxiety, and where the motivation for learning comes from the high degree of emotional involvement of the members.

These characteristics suggest dimensions for examining the T Group more thoroughly. They deal with eight central learning factors, around which the remainder of this chapter is built: (1) the ambiguous situation; (2) the identity stress; (3) self-investment or participation; (4) collaboration and learning from peers; (5) motivation for learning; (6) experienced behavior and feedback; (7) group growth and development; (8) trainer-intervention.

Factors of the Ambiguous Situation and the Identity Stress

Anyone who has observed or participated in a T Group has been struck by the extraordinary amount of emotional involvement and energy expenditure. After a two-hour session, people frequently feel drained but still eager to continue. Extra sessions often are held. Small clusters of T-Group members continue to talk about the T Group during meals and recreation periods. Various members sit through long evening hours, playing back the tape recording of the previous session to squeeze out further meaning. This degree of involvement seems to continue throughout the life of the T Group. What are the causes of such involvement? Does involvement result in learning or does it inhibit learning? Or both?

One source of emotional involvement, particularly in the early days of the T Group, lies in the ambiguous situation created by the unstructured beginning. This ambiguity seems to produce stresses related to individual identity and group survival. The question as to whether one wants to be a member of the group, the uncertainty as to how to proceed, the very unpredictability of the situation, cause people to forget much of their learning purposes and to become deeply concerned, first about their own identity and position in the group and then about the survival of the group itself.

The group opens with ambiguity and uncertainty about power and leadership, about goals and pathways to goals, about norms to guide behavior, about which status symbols or efforts will secure a place in the group, about rewards and punishments, and about what will happen to each individual. This situation mobilizes individual defense systems to operate until greater predictability is secured. To some degree an identity stress is created for each individual. People gain identity partially in relationship to other people, in differentiation from them, and in relationship to position and function in the social organization. In a situation with few boundaries and very little structure and direction, each person is uncertain as to what he is supposed to do and, consequently, who he is to be. Frequently, the identity stress generated in the T Group motivates individuals to examine many more areas of their lives than the ones involved in the immediate situation.

Each individual is not only uncertain as to how he should behave, as he would be if he were entering an extremely foreign but already formed culture; he is also unable to find, in the beginning T Group, any obvious pattern of membership through which to discover what is expected of him. The group has not yet established ways to evaluate or utilize contributions. It has developed no way to confer membership. It has not even determined what constitutes membership. What appears to be a rejection to an individual making a suggestion may be merely inability to do anything because no conscious group goal or pattern of procedure is present (in reality, the basic goal of the group in the beginning is the survival of the members). Contributions "die on the table" for lack of a procedure for testing or accepting. Perceived rejection of what the individual sees as a logical suggestion increases his uncertainty. He interprets the rejection as a reflection upon his ability or as an indication that he is not liked. Increased individual anxiety causes him to listen more to his "internal noises" than to what others are actually feeling and saying.

The uncertainty with which individuals enter any new situation is thus compounded in the T Group. Individuals react in a variety of ways. Some deny that there is an uncomfortable and unpredictable situation. Members will say, with hands clenched, that they are relaxed and comfortable. Others seek to handle the situation by withdrawing into the role of an observer. They are here, they say, to learn by watching others behave. Others attempt to work out their own survival by trying to force the group to become a traditional and predictable group. Still others try to coerce the trainer into saving them. When this fails, they may punish him.

An early basic problem facing the T Group, therefore, is how to handle individual anxiety. The early hours of a T Group are spent in trying to "place" other people in relation to self; in discovering their motives, their power or superiority, and their ability to hurt; in endeavoring to find comfortable and familiar situations; in finding out whether one is liked; or in trying to win power or approval. Some of the dependent and counterdependent reactions to the trainer grow out of the desire to have him, as the one known power figure, reduce the discomfort.

Essentially, then, the individual is trying to bring order and security out of chaos. When his first move to get help from the trainer fails, he usually tries to relate the situation to known familiar patterns. He may, for instance, suggest that a leader be appointed. The fact that he does not perceive that his suggestion is seen as a desire to take leadership himself reflects the poor perceptual communication in the beginning hours of the group.

Since members differ in their perceptions of what is desirable and what is uncomfortable, early efforts to lead the group around the shoals of discomfort generally result in a clash over leadership. The individual contender may seek out one or more other members who appear to feel the way he does. By attempting to form relationships with them he seeks support and some validation of his own perceptions. The group forms or takes shape as these efforts to look for support and to confirm perceptions succeed and continue.

In the early days of the T Group, members are concerned almost exclusively, but not consciously, about individual anxiety. Can I survive? What will happen to me? What will be demanded of me? Can I accept feedback from others? Dare I give it? Yet discussion usually wanders in apparent aimlessness from descriptions of events back home to discussions of abstract or harmless topics and thence to suggestions for immediate group actions without adequate diagnosis. Discussion, interestingly, centers on group procedures or events not overtly related to individual concerns and anxieties.

There are many reasons why this is true. Even under stress over identity there seems to be awareness, or at least hope, that individual anxiety may be reduced by group formation. There are many suggestions for group development—from having formal introductions to electing a leader, developing a formal agenda, or imposing rigid procedures—but little effort to diagnose group problems. If the trainer suggests that diagnosis would be helpful, the group does not hear him—or heed him. This may be because members have had little experience in examining group actions, and there has been little cultural legitimacy for doing so; or it may be because diagnosis, if it means digging into interpersonal relations, could open up areas of personal anxiety.

Yet even in the early hours there is desire to communicate with other people about oneself—but it has to be done in "safe" ways and it must not reveal too much. Members tend to discuss themselves in terms of their organizations or events back home. Only much later does it come out how little of this early effort to communicate is really heard.

There is a paradox in the history of the T Group. When individuals are feeling their own anxieties and fears most keenly, they seem to conspire to keep the discussion centered on group action or on events unrelated to the present anxiety. Later, when some predictability has developed, some norms for sharing feelings and perceptions have been constructed, and greater understanding of one another has been established, concern centers on the group and its developmental problems. But now there is much more discussion of individual feelings, perceptions, and needs. Indeed, group problems are resolved through open discussion of individual reactions. A problem of group movement is examined not only in terms of suggestions for group action, but also in terms of individual perceptions and individual needs.

The stress over problems of individual identity and of group survival is never relieved once and for all, because new events present new threats. Gradually, however, individuals learn that they need to alert their defenses less frequently. Gradually they see that openness in sharing feelings and motives and willingness to give and receive feedback are not only less dangerous than imagined but can be extremely helpful if one's goal is to improve interpersonal behavior and to discover more fully one's own identity.

Factor of Self-Investment or Participation

People generally approach learning and change with ambivalence. They would like to improve—provided change is not too threatening. But any learning situation does imply a threat to the individual's perception of himself and to the perception others have of him. The potentiality of failure, the unpredictability of what the future may be like if change is undertaken produce ambivalence. Therefore, people approach learning and change with positive motivation but also with a considerable defense against going too far. This ambivalence toward personal investment is heightened in the T Group because its ambiguity creates anxiety, and the involvement demanded is not clear.

Here each individual faces, in heightened form, his own personal problems of membership in a group. As in any other group, he is asking: How important is this group to me? What will its consequences be for me? What gain—at what pain—may I expect? How close do I want to be to these people? How much am I willing to invest? He is concerned, too, about whether he will be accepted and whether he can measure up to expectations. He is uncertain what to contribute or how to measure its effectiveness. His defenses against correction are high.

Learning and improvement follow in large part from the individual's struggle to find membership which both satisfies him and contributes to the group. Satisfying membership implies more than acceptance. It also implies caring behavior. Membership entails the opportunity for growth through contributing out of one's own resources and through concern that others also have an opportunity to grow. When this is achieved, there is less need for individual defenses. The needs and resources of all can be used freely.

In struggling to achieve such membership, individuals acquire new insights into self, into others, and into the group itself. They gain new skills of cooperative action and new ways of learning. They discover in clearer terms the problems blocking learning and growth. Gradually individuals find that they can open themselves up to learn and to help others in learning. A group for learning—that is to say, a group whose members are willing to consider the possibility of personal change—gradually emerges. It takes shape as members learn that they can both influence others and be influenced by them in collaborative problem solving.

This movement, however, is not easily achieved. Entering an interchange of influence can be extremely threatening; hence the necessity, first, for personal security that the individual's integrity and identity will be maintained, and second, for willingness to invest self—to take out membership, even if this involves risk of exposure and of change.

Effective membership means that the individual has achieved a healthy balance between investment of self and withholding of self. With help from others, he has reduced his anxieties so that he can determine the investment he will make on the basis of relevancy to group concern and to his own interest. He invests himself sufficiently to assume his share (but not more than his share) of responsibility for group movement. He accords others the same opportunity.

Investment of self requires considerable awareness of one's own motivations and personal defenses. It also requires awareness of personal identity and sufficient ego strength to relate to others interdependently rather than dependently or counterdependently. Finally, to invest himself constructively, the individual has to be able to diagnose what is happening in the group. As these learnings take place in the T Group, members come to see that membership is something to be worked at and earned. They begin to see that through experimentation they may learn how to become more effective members.

Many events in the life of the T Group can be understood in the light of membership problems. If, for example, the group can be formed into a familiar pattern, and if the individual member can control the group so that it does not go off in threatening directions, then he can feel safe. It is for this reason that T Groups often struggle vehemently over issues seemingly of little importance. The struggle is not over the expressed issues, but over the larger issue of group direction and its implications for the personal safety and comfort of the members involved.

The classic split which first separates most T Groups into those members who wish more imposed structure of goal and procedures and those who are willing to venture down uncharted pathways is part of the battle over membership and group direction. The struggle over this split sometimes takes on epic proportions. The struggle between group and trainer is also in large measure an aspect of the struggle over membership. The push and pull on the trainer may be efforts to resolve the problems of membership by utilizing the trainer as a surrogate for unresolved power struggles among members.

Each individual works on the problem of how much he will invest of himself throughout most of the T Group. The group forms and re-forms as each individual makes his initial resolution of this question —some dramatically through a major conflict, others quietly as they slip into more active membership. No two individuals make it in the same way or to the same extent. Even after initial decisions by individuals to invest, there are continuous changes in the membership contract for each individual. Premature joining may cause persons to draw back from the group, to seek membership more thoughtfully later. As the group proves to be less threatening and more supportive and as satisfactions and learnings accrue, most individuals are able gradually to invest more. In turn, greater membership investment means greater resources for group development and individual learning. As learning increases, membership becomes easier to accept. And so a cycle of growth continues.

In the beginning, T-Group members generally are operating under the assumption that the group will move without much investment on their part. They find it difficult to believe that the trainer does not have it all arranged and that at the proper time he will resolve their problems for them. In one T Group, an individual summed up the group wish with a colorful analogy. "Don't worry," he said. "When my children are watching Lassie on television and are biting their fingernails as they see her surrounded by fire on all sides, I don't worry. I know that the advertising agency has too much money invested in Lassie to let her burn."

Only gradually do the members recognize that the show is not rigged, that the group will move and individuals will learn only from their own efforts and that without these efforts "Lassie *could* burn."

Factor of Collaboration and Learning from Peers

The T Group is perhaps unique in the extent to which learning influences come from peer members rather than from a teacher. There are many reasons why peer influence can be effective in learning. Because the individual is seeking a place in the group, peer efforts to influence him may be more clearly heard than efforts from "outside." Because the peer is perceived to be "in the same boat," defensiveness resulting from fear of exposure is reduced. A group of peers has more sources of data, more refractory mirrors for feedback, more possibilities for identification than has the trainer. Peers do not raise the authority problems that frequently distort or inhibit learning in a superior-subordinate relationship. Finally, since behavioral change must be carried out with peers in the outside world, learning through the influence of peers has the advantage of setting in motion processes likely to continue.

One of the basic purposes of the T Group is to enable people to communicate with one another in more areas of thought and feeling than are usually attempted. The underlying assumption is that people can come to "know" one another better through such communication and that, with knowledge, they will reduce the distrust separating them, increase their desire to give help, and feel freer in giving it. With less fear of being misinterpreted, less fear that they will hurt or be hurt, they are able to listen to one another better. With better communication, collaboration increases. Energy often used in inhibiting feelings is released for joint problem solving.

Factor of Motivation for Learning

The identity stress and the group survival stress growing out of the unstructured nature of the T Group and the resultant ambiguities have been seen as motivating considerable emotional involvement (not necessarily immediately satisfying) and the release of considerable emotional energy for the defense of the individual. As members gradually identify their common problems, learn to express and utilize observational and feeling data, and build a group organization, individual anxieties reduce somewhat and the individual moves toward less defensive behavior.

Closely intertwined with identity stress is concern with group survival and organization. Indeed, the development of some kind of organization to hold the members together and the emergence of a supportive group climate are seen as means of reducing anxiety. In the early stages of the T Group, motivation directed toward group survival leads toward the development of rigid controls. Deviancy is met by punishment, efforts to enforce conformity, or rejection. In later stages of maturity, group defensive behavior is reduced. Instead of strong pressures for conformity there is acceptance of deviancy. The group is more secure, and efforts are directed toward improving conditions conducive to individual growth, group achievement, and individual freedom and belonging.

As the T Group continues, the energy generated from early defensive motivations is increasingly expended in identifying basic individual and group problems, collecting and using relevant data about present behavior in the problem area, trying out new ways of perceiving and behaving, and generalizing from this process. This is a formula for learning.

As a learning group is constructed with a high level of trust, individuals are able to lower their defenses and develop satisfying relationships with others. They become freer in expressing and accepting caring feelings. Because it satisfies and rewards the individual, each venture toward accepting the reaction of others and expressing helpful feelings toward others reinforces the next venture. As the group grows in its capacity to support experimentation, risk taking becomes easier.

As defensive motivation is reduced, other driving forces lead toward continued high expenditure of emotion and behavior. Increasing trust in the group and in other members and the desire to grow as an individual and to help others, serve as driving forces that encourage openness, acceptance of feedback, acceptance of feelings, and readiness to experiment with new ways of behaving.

Like waves on a beach one set of motives follows on the reduction of others. One crests early and then breaks, making way for the others to increase in force. And the same pattern recurs at changing height and depth.   The following model may help depict the order of these interrelated motivational learning waves.

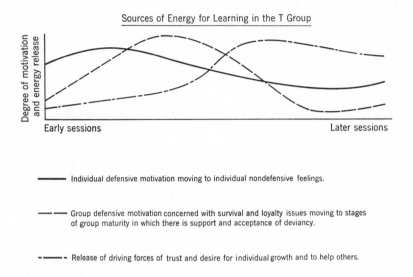

Sources of Energy for Learning in the T Group

——————— Individual defensive motivation moving to individual nondefensive feelings.

— — — Group defensive motivation concerned with survival and loyalty issues moving to stages of group maturity in which there is support and acceptance of deviancy.

▪——▪ Release of driving forces of trust and desire for individual growth and to help others.

Factor of Experienced Behavior and Feedback

The mature and effective group needs to build into its structure and processes a School for Members as well as a Clinic for Group Difficulties.   A School for Members implies the development by the group of a norm that legitimizes and a process that encourages open, experimental behavior and feedback of data about the consequence of behavior.   The individual widens his repertoire of member skills through participation and feedback.   In the process he collaborates with others to create a group which will encourage still further individual learning.

As the T Group progresses through its early concerns over survival, changes gradually occur in individual behavior.   Increasingly, individuals bring out for consensual validation their perceptions of what is happening.   They test whether what they see is what others see, and they begin to collect data about the discrepancies between their own perceptions and the perceptions of others.   With anxiety about their own identity reduced, they find they can listen to other people with less interference of personal "static."   They begin to compare observational data reported by others with the data of their own feelings.

They develop some willingness to explore the behavior of the group as well as their own behavior and attitudes. They gradually look at what they do and its consequences for the group and for individual members. They develop a willingness to receive feedback from the group. They learn to check what other people say about them against their own self-perception. They come to see that feelings and perceptions represent information important to improvement of individual and group performance. They see that improvement can occur only if information is reported, listened to, and tested.

As the group accepts the need for a Clinic for Group Difficulties, it develops a norm for analyzing and diagnosing problems blocking group progress. An experimental approach—the "provisional try"—becomes an accepted norm for the group when confronted with problems. The group learns to generalize from present experiences to future events. As all this occurs, individuals also can learn much about the behavior and development of groups.

The value of the T Group lies in the fact that the process by which individuals develop a group in which they can participate effectively is the process of learning. The conditions include exposure of problem areas, collection of data, analysis, experimentation, generalization, and application to other situations. Its genius lies in the deep involvement and expenditure of energy called forth by its unstructured nature coupled with a process of inquiry, action, and evaluation.

Factor of Group Growth and Development [2]

The T Group's function is to construct itself into a mechanism for learning in which the process of group development and the process of individual learning are intertwined and in which the method of inquiry serves both processes.

Because the T Group does not start with a fully formed structure and accepted procedures for learning, these must be developed by the learners to conform with their readiness for learning. The T Group can develop only as the individual members learn. It must be sufficiently flexible so that it changes as their readiness and abilities to learn change. With a minimum assistance from the trainer the learners are themselves creating the group through which learning takes

[2] Much of this section has been developed from a paper by Leland P. Bradford and Thomas Mallinson, "Group Formation and Development," 1951. Reprinted in *Dynamics of Group Life*. Washington, D.C.: National Training Laboratories, NEA, 1958.

place. The content of their learning comprises the methods and processes they employ, the feelings produced, and the results achieved.

Group growth does not occur in a straight line. One way of looking
at the T Group is to see it as a cyclic process in which learning recurs
in increasing depth. The T Group approaches and reapproaches the
same basic problems of relationships to authority, of interpersonal distance and relationships, of goal formation, of decision making, of norm
setting, of communication. Growth lies not in ultimate "solutions" but
in the readiness to face up to basic problems and in the improvement
of methods by which the group approaches them.

Part of the problem of group growth lies in the fact that while the
group must proceed from dissatisfaction to satisfaction to dissatisfaction to satisfaction it is very easy to become frozen at some point of
satisfaction. The impetus for growth comes from dissatisfaction with
an organization previously effective but now impeding action. Difficulties arise when past successes serve to perpetuate a structure that
does not fit changing goals and competencies. A T Group which has
won in a planned competition with another T Group in producing a
specific product, for example, usually considers its organization validated and resists examination of its continuing effectiveness. The
problem facing the T Group therefore is that of learning how to study
its structure so that it can recognize, change, or discard previously
useful parts.

No two T Groups grow at identical rates, nor does any T Group
grow at a constant rate. Variation in ability to solve problems arises in
part from the fact that the T Group, probably more than other groups,
re-forms and is a different group each time it meets. This is not to
say that its history does not have impact upon it. Rather, in its new
formation the T Group deliberately utilizes the consequences of previous activities, but its unstructured nature means that events from the
previous day are not forced on the next session. The group task shifts
each day as different individuals take focal positions, and the group
re-forms to meet the new task. Efforts to control the group come from
various people and in different guises, each presenting different problems. Efforts to work out authority problems with the trainer also
continue in different forms because the trainer's role shifts with the
change and growth of the group. The significant development through
this shifting situation is the accomplishment of a difficult task—that of
bringing more and more reactions to the surface of group awareness
and of learning better ways of handling these reactions.

The T Group rather quickly develops some structure (often arbitrarily imposed by an individual or a small subgroup), some tenta-

tively accepted norms about what constitutes areas of discussion and acceptable levels of communication, some efforts to encompass or control a few members perceived as deviants. Once the group has organized itself sufficiently to tackle a problem successfully, a greater sense of cohesion develops. Members often compare the group favorably with other groups that are perceived as not being so "good."

Somewhere in the relatively early life of the T Group, however, the group generally encounters a major barrier that tests the strength of this cohesiveness. The group faces an unexpected situation and is unable to react to it adequately. The federation of members, precariously built despite lack of understanding of one another, gaps in communication, and false assumptions about group behavior, crumbles and falls apart. The group must reconstruct itself on a firmer basis.

A variety of problems and events may precipitate the first major barrier. Sometimes it is an apparently minor problem for which the group is unprepared. Sometimes it is the emergence of a problem the group has tried to keep covered or a behavioral consequence of a decision reached in an earlier meeting (e.g., a plan to rotate leaders every hour or to impose time limits on participation). Sometimes it is a result of overconfidence; the group attempts a problem beyond its present competence. Sometimes it is an imposed task in competition with another group in which the first group is the loser.

Frequently a barrier results from some interpersonal event. This may be a severe attack by some member on the trainer, threatening previously established norms of how one reacts to authority and creating fear among dependent members as to what will happen if a member can destroy the leader. Part of the group may be immobilized by anxiety, while others join the attack or grapple with the attacker.

Sometimes a member who has been inhibiting or controlling the group is spoken to sharply. If he leaves the room, becomes overnice, or gives other evidence of feeling punished, the group may be badly disrupted. Feelings of guilt, fear of a situation in which anyone can attack anyone, and feelings that the punished member deserved the treatment he received may be mixed together. Some may turn on the punishing member, who very probably did everyone a good turn, if somewhat ineptly, and attack him. Others may move to establish group boundaries, straitjacketing the group and preventing reactions from member to member.

Sometimes a conflict between two members who are competing for leadership spills over in an overt clash. The group may be immobilized by the fight. Peaceful members, afraid to seek peace by working on the conflict itself, would like to pretend that nothing has happened.

The group has no methods to control fight; it is possessed by fears of the consequences of widespread fight.

At times a manipulative situation occurs. Overnight, two or three members gang up to direct or control the group. If the manipulation is carried out by relatively dominant individuals, the group may have no way to control or prevent private experimentation at group expense. Sometimes a dominant individual, fearful that feedback might reach him, may succeed in preventing the group from any but the most innocuous there-and-then discussion.

Sometimes the cleavage between those who seek structure and dependency and those who can tolerate greater ambiguity splits the group. The two sides polarize, and without adequate group problem-solving methods, each issue or topic is treated as a battlefield.

At times the group is disrupted by the speed with which it moves into new and uncharted areas. The border zone in which learning goes on represents continual oscillation between fantasy and actual daring. As movement takes place, newly found skill and insight make yesterday's daring today's commonplace; but seeing other people jump into real or fancied danger may arouse anxiety in those not ready for such daring. Thus, in meeting a major problem the group may be disrupted by those who wish to move ahead aggressively and those who fear the consequences.[3]

In the face of such barriers, hard-won effectiveness may disintegrate. Like pioneers who have gained some distance on their trek only to face what looks like an insurmountable mountain, the group now faces a major task of reorganization.

At this point of "failure shock," group members begin to look for causes or targets for blame. After hopelessness, "scapegoating" appears, generally focused on the behavior of an individual—whether member or trainer. The permissiveness of the trainer has "allowed" the group to get into a mess—or he has been too directive and has led the group into trouble. If a member is blamed, it may be for leading the group farther than it wanted to go, for punishing weaker members, or for being unconcerned about the welfare of the group. Punishment is liberally distributed.

A second pattern of behavior at the point of group disintegration is to regress to far more structured standards of behavior with reduced learning goals, more formalized procedures, more autocratic use of power. The group may set rules that no one may say anything even remotely critical of others, that discussion shall deal with outside-the-

[3] *Ibid.*, p. 78.

group topics, that formal leadership shall be rotated, that each person may have so many seconds to talk, that a leader shall be appointed and given authority. In one group, under shock from the attack of one member, it was almost unanimously agreed to select a leader by lot and give him authority to make *all* decisions concerning the areas and procedures of discussion and the behavior of members. This classic picture of abdication of all power and control to a single leader as a result of fear does not always appear so clearly. However, the ingredients are usually present.

Whatever the pattern of reaction to the barrier, it generates a great deal of behavior. There may be violent disagreement about past events and about decisions made. Past decisions are distorted. There may be compulsive doubting that the group can make any decision whatsoever. The members may defer abjectly to authority. Argument, persuasion, manipulation, creation of false data, emotional appeals, and coercive social pressure take the place of other methods of problem solving. Communication decreases. The purposes of others are misperceived. Undisclosed personal agendas increase. Discrepancies between individual perceptions and reality multiply. Subgroups tend to form to a greater extent than formerly. There is flight from the group problem.

This is a critical period—one in which group members learn, almost for the first time, that structure and organization will not come miraculously or easily. As they work through their initial needs to "scapegoat," to fight, or to run away, they come to learn that the group will develop only as it utilizes scientific methods of inquiry and problem solving. This means collecting relevant data, evaluating and analyzing these data, establishing and testing hypotheses, and planning and taking joint action. At this point, members may realize that group development and their own growth will come only through facing and surmounting a series of major barriers and through continuously reorganizing available forces. The further realization may come that there is no final group organization which will be discovered and bring peace forever after.

Yesterday's problems do not appear to be problems today. The group faces new problems with increasing courage and security and with increasing ability.

Looking back, the members often see the period in which they faced their first major crisis as a dark valley of despair and frequently wonder how they came through it. This crisis; the regression that followed; and the slow, painful process of re-forming and repair may, however, be seen as the major event in their learning.

Factor of Trainer-Intervention

Through this complex process of discovery, failure, reorganization, and achievement, the position of the T-Group trainer is a difficult one involving a seeming contradiction. His interventions, or lack of interventions, have much to do with the process of the group, the problems analyzed, and the learning that results; yet the trainer is neither a teacher, in the usual sense, nor a discussion leader. He does not predetermine the specific learnings or direct the work of the group, but neither is he passive and without responsibility for helping learning to take place. He does not hold the clear-cut authority of the teacher or leader; neither does he become a complete member of the group, although he usually approaches full membership more closely than does the teacher or leader.

The trainer does not have the easy security of knowing what the curriculum content will be, because this must emerge each day from the problems of the group. The trainer who enters a given meeting of the T Group with assurance that he can predict what will happen that day will probably find himself blocking group movement as he tries to force what he has predicted, or he will be unable to "read" the group process and to determine which, among the many issues and problems before the group, is presently focal.

In the T Group it is not the trainer who controls process and gives direction to interaction; rather, it is the method of inquiry itself. The trainer's concern is to help the group to develop adequate methods of inquiry. He is himself involved in interaction in the group, and he needs to work on the emergence of his role just as do other members. For trainer as for group member, roles must grow out of what the group requires and out of the perception, abilities, and behavior patterns within the group.

The trainer, however, should and does have certain advantages in the emergence of his role. He may not know more about the individual needs and problems than do other members, but he has the security of knowing better how to discover them. He should have a clearer image of the functions and process flow of the T Group and thus be more constantly aware of the basic purposes. Through work with other T Groups, he may anticipate some aspects of the general experience, the broad problems groups face, even though he cannot predict specific interactions or prevent himself (nor should he) from receiving feedback about his own behavior. He cannot escape involvement in new situations from which he must learn either to extricate himself or to use creatively. One of his rewards is his own learning.

The trainer does not predetermine group goals, but it is highly important that he have a general sense of direction to aid the group as it moves toward its goals. Otherwise he tends to be immobilized and to rationalize his immobility to the point of shirking his responsibility for the training. Or, uncertain of ultimate purposes, he intervenes under different assumptions each day and ends up by becoming a major group problem himself.

The trainer's purposes might be summarized as follows:

1. *To help to develop a group whose purpose is to learn about the sensitivities, understandings, and skills necessary for membership in social situations.* To accomplish this the trainer needs to help members break off continuity with the outside or "back-home" world. By helping to establish a "cultural island," as opposed to a "mainland culture," he helps the group to examine new facets of behavior in new ways.

The ambivalence with which most individuals approach learning has already been discussed. In the T Group, where heightened ambiguity creates initial tension, members tend to subordinate the learning purposes they brought with them to the perceived need to survive. At this point probably only the trainer is holding onto learning purposes. If he, like the others, allows himself to be swept into the struggle for survival, of which the first moves are toward tradition and safety, he may lose sight of the real problem facing the group.

Members and the trainer probably see different needs in the beginning of the T Group:

Group Needs as Participants See Them	*Group Needs as the Trainer Sees Them*
For structure	For exposure of member-behavior
For predictability	For permissiveness to reduce defensiveness
For security	
For measurable progress	For sanction and support to explore feelings and behavior
For safe position	
	For methods of data collection, feedback, study, and experimentation

This difference in perceived needs means that the trainer should help to develop a learning group that will be unlike customary groups on the "mainland." In his initial contract with the group his assumption that a different group will emerge and his belief that members can learn from their experiences if they will study these experiences, help to keep present the task of developing a group as a way to learn.

2. *To help to remove blocks to learning about self, about others, and about the group.* Most individuals have barriers to learning that need to be overcome. They may have to remove self-imposed restrictions on participation in learning experiences. They may have to reduce anxiety about revealing their assumptions and feelings. They may have to overcome their resistance to observing their own behavior or to become more diagnostic about their own and others' behavior. They may have to become more willing to consider feedback.

In the early stages of the T Group the trainer should take certain definite steps to help group members to develop learning processes. He should first legitimize the expression and analysis of feeling. If members are not encouraged to express their real reactions, important information may be withheld and no patterns of collecting data established. The trainer can help by showing calmness rather than tension as feeling begins to be expressed in conflicting behavior. He can accept an explosion of feeling as normal. He can use such words as "feeling" and "emotion" in the same tone of voice as when speaking of other phenomena. He can keep himself from exerting control when a conflict breaks out. He can resist punishing individuals or the group. He can feel free to express his own feelings as objective data, if he does not endeavor to impose his feelings on others. He can speak of diagnosis and analysis of group barriers. ("What is happening in the group now?" "How are we feeling now?") In his efforts to help the group to face its feeling problems, he may himself react to a group event by expressing his own reactions as a part of the group.

Second, he can model a participant-observer behavior as he reports observation of the consequence of his behavior or of the behavior of the group. Again, he can accept reactions to his behavior from the group in a manner which invites such reactions, and after considering and testing their validity and the possibility of change, he can mend his behavior.

3. *To help to develop a group climate in which learning can take place.* There must be a norm of permissiveness that makes it easy to express feelings and reactions without fear of punishment or rejection. There must be emotional support for members who undergo sometimes painful reassessment of attitudes and behavior. There must be standards that encourage members to invest themselves in learning situations and foster willingness to explore new attitudes and behavior. There must be sufficient interpersonal trust, acceptance and care, and group cohesiveness so that individuals can give and accept influence.

The trainer can help to build such a climate in many ways, but he cannot alone build climate. If he could, he would control the group and thus prevent learning.

He can make explicit, from time to time, evidences of climate building, and he may wish to raise to the level of discussion the consequences of an inadequate climate. He can help to bring about mutual understanding by testing for misunderstanding. He can try to keep issues open between persons and within the group until they are worked through so that mutual trust can grow as members learn that problems can be faced and dealt with rather than concealed.

4. *To help the group to discover and utilize methods of inquiry— action, observation, feedback, analysis, experimentation—as ways of group development and individual growth.* The trainer should encourage the group to focus on here-and-now experience during the early part of the T Group. He should indicate dimensions of behavior for observations. He may want to support courage in each member to assess and diagnose his own behavior and to experiment with new approaches. He may feel it desirable to support and model various methods of self-inquiry and inquiry into group behavior. He may wish to encourage and support collaborative problem-solving efforts and methods. Unless the group can develop and use methods of inquiry, experiences may be filled with feeling, whether comforting or threatening, but little learning will result.

5. *To help the group to learn how to internalize, to generalize, and to apply learnings to other situations.* An insight is not used until it results in change in the way events are perceived and in the way the individual responds. The role of the trainer includes responsibility for encouraging individuals to explore and test new perceptions until they become part of the pattern of the thinking and behavior of the group. Equally, he should help in the process of generalization so that learning can be utilized in other situations. Otherwise the group may pass from experience to experience, gaining understandings about the specific experiences without enlarging the understandings to apply to other situations. With no planned curriculum events in the T Group and no set times for generalizing from immediate learnings, it becomes important that the trainer recognize opportunities when the group may profitably, and with the least interruption to the flow of experiences, discuss their learnings in relation to other situations. With practice and encouragement, the group itself learns to generalize its learnings.

The trainer must be systematically understanding and aware of the problems of effective learning that the learning group faces. He must be aware of the points at which the group needs help. He must be aware of the seduction of resolving current difficulties without learning from these difficulties. Perhaps most important of all, he must endeavor to help group members become equally sensitive to their problems so that they grow in ability to direct their own continuing learning. Otherwise he subtly maintains the reins in his own hands.

The questions continuously facing the trainer are whether or not he should intervene at any given point and, if so, in what role and for what purpose. His intervention should aid the group and not do work that the group itself is ready to do.

The trainer has three roles in which he may make interventions. As an observer and, occasionally, as an interpreter it may be appropriate for him to ask the group to report their observations of a given event or to report his own observations to stimulate further thought and discussion. He may think it appropriate to give his interpretation concerning some of the possible causes and consequences of the event and to invite others' interpretation also.

In his member role, the trainer may occasionally intervene by contributing his own feelings as part of the needed data when the group is dealing with their relations to him, or to work with the group on other events in which his behavior is involved. To be unwilling to participate in a releasing way when group members discuss his behavior would be to inhibit their effective dealing with his presence and behavior.

As a source of resources for the group, the trainer may feel it appropriate to suggest or to model ways of data collection or study so that the group interactions may be effectively utilized for learning.

Behind trainer decisions about interventions should lie a personal theory of learning and change and a set of values concerning his relations to other individuals. Hopefully, these values would include the desirability of being empathic as well as discerning and the willingness to be open as to his own motives and purposes to the extent that individuals and the group need these perceptions and have the ability to utilize them.

Purposes Reviewed

Having followed the T Group through the intricacies of its intensive life, it may be helpful to review the purposes of this invention for learning.

The first major purpose of the T Group is to help individuals to learn how to learn in the areas of self-understanding and relationship with others. The T Group builds on the concept that learning about self and about others comes best from experiences with others and the analysis of these experiences. Analysis of experience, however, requires access to the data about the experience, much of which lies in feelings and perceptions which the individual should recognize and understand. Some of these data, however, are in the possession of others—their perceptions and feelings about a given situation. Learning how to make these data available so that the individuals and the group can learn from them is a major task of the T Group. Each individual in the group should invite and utilize help from others and give help in return.

Thus, the first two T-Group goals of learning better how to learn from continuing experiences and learning how to give help to others in their learning and growth experiences are interactive and reciprocal. The relationship may be expressed thus:

Learning how to learn ←——————————→ Learning how to give help

The third purpose of the T Group is to develop skills of effective membership. The raw data for learning these skills are the actions the group takes toward its goals. As the individual invests himself in group membership, he learns better how to give and accept influence and how to work with others in creating a climate that encourages collaborative problem solving and a process by which it can take place. In so doing, he creates conditions for learning about himself and about others, about the processes of continued learning, and about ways of helping others to learn and grow. He is learning how to become a more effective member. Thus a third dimension is added to the model:

Growth in effective membership

Learning how to learn   Learning how to give help

The unstructured T Group is the crucible in which learning goals can be realized. Through a living and very real experience in earning and bestowing membership and through analyzing this experience, individuals develop sensitivity to group processes and to individual behavior. In so doing they are developing skill for continued learning and for continuing help to others. And they are learning about membership behavior and group process. Thus, the purposes of the T Group interact in the following manner:

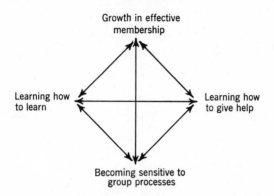

The integration of these purposes and their interactive influence on one another comprise some of the major purposes of the T Group.

8

From Polarization to Paradox

Kenneth D. Benne

The remarks which follow are clinical comments based on experience with some fifty T Groups in which I have functioned as trainer during the past seventeen years. The comments are hung around a framework of nine selected aspects of T-Group development and functioning. The first four of these are "sociological" aspects, in the sense that they isolate various social-system characteristics, or member-relationship patternings, that can be accurately noted and described from time to time but ordinarily change observably during the course of a T Group's career. The remaining five are "cultural" aspects of group life, in the sense of "normative," "ideological," or "world-outlook" elements that crystallize out of the history of the group and function with varying changeability to give meaning, value, and control to the experiences of the group and of its members.

These comments frequently fall into the form of a statement of some polarization which group members encounter as they seek to bring order out of the initial chaos of T-Group life. The discussion goes on to show how further experience in the group tends to convert the polarization into a paradox which can be handled by the group, if not always eliminated. The movement of T-Group life, when it is successful, seems to be from polarization to paradox.

Paradoxes of Goals and Goallessness

The most obvious characteristic of a T Group is the absence of any prearranged or externally assigned task. If we were to interview members of a T Group during its early sessions concerning the then current goal of the group, we would find two modal perceptions. One is a perception of goallessness—"We have been floundering around with no direction." The other is that the group goal is what "I" and a few other members have stated it should be and that most of the other members are aimlessly (or willfully) wandering from this goal.

If, on the other hand, we think of the goal aspect of group behavior as that which an observer might see to be the focal direction of member-efforts and energies during any unit of time, the T Group is never devoid of a goal. For member-effort and energy are channeled by the situational requirements confronting the people around the table. And these requirements in the early stages of the T Group are common, however differently they may be seen, interpreted, or handled behaviorally by different individuals in the group. The "realities" of the situation which require treatment inhere in the *ambiguities* and *uncertainties* of an unformed group. These include not only, or primarily, indefiniteness in the verbally stated task or goal of the group. They extend to role definitions of "member" and of "trainer," to standards of appropriate and inappropriate participation, including emotional expression as well as work contributions, to authority and power relations in the group, and to procedures for consensually validating or invalidating (judging) member and group choices and decisions. The resultant group goal, the direction in which member efforts are actually channeled, is toward the dispelling of these uncertainties.

The goal, on this view, is to give form to an unformed group of people. And as we observe with detachment the early behavior of a T Group, or as the group subsequently, from the vantage point of comfort if not paradise regained, reconstructs its early history, there is seen to be goal direction in even the earliest overtures to participation, however chaotic or arbitrary these overtures may have seemed consciously to most members living through the throes of group formation.

But the problem of goals in the group is still more complex and paradoxical than the above discussion indicates. The ideal goal of the T Group, in the minds of those who organized it and of those who have paid tuition to take part in it, is to help members in achieving learnings (more or less objective insights and clarifications) concerning processes and problems of group formation and functioning and about themselves as members of groups. Nor is it enough for them to learn their "way around" in this particular group. Rather, learnings which generalize reliably and validly to other groups and to themselves in other social situations, define the rational purpose for participation in the T Group. The central goal of the T Group is, therefore, not the more or less conscious contriving of work products— verbalized public conclusions growing out of consecutive discussion of agenda items or written-down policies and decisions. *Yet the T Group must do work in order to accomplish its learning goal.* Nor is the central goal to build and maintain a group—to construct a social system in which members can participate with relative comfort and satisfaction. *Yet the members must build, maintain, and rebuild a social system if they are to learn about group building and maintenance and about their participation as members in these processes.* So problems of work and problems of group formation and re-formation do set complex goals which become engrossing to group members, though rationally they are always instrumental to the over-all goal of learning.

It is my custom as a trainer to state at the beginning of the first session what I believe to be the "contract" between me and the group, to use Dr. Semrad's term.[1] The ideal goal of learning about groups and group membership is reviewed. A general definition of my role as helper to the group and to group members in finding ways of learning from their experience is stated. The two sources of data for learning which are available to the group are noted: (1) the pooling and analysis of knowledge about and experience with groups other than this one which members bring to it; and (2) the observation and clarification of behavioral events, and the relationships that emerge in this group as we deal with one another. It is proposed that my special function as a trainer in the group is primarily to help the group collect, interpret, and use the second kind of data for member learning. Special responsibilities of the trainer for setting the direction of work or for organizing the group for work or for prescribing the forms or patterns of group life are denied.

This early, general delineation of the role of the trainer is not normally understood or accepted fully by group members. Yet the early statement of it seems important for two reasons. It serves as a point

---

[1] Dr. Elvin Semrad is a Boston psychiatrist who has done pioneering work in group psychotherapy. I learned his ideas about "contract" in conversations with him.

of reference in later struggles by the group to give concrete shape and definition to the role of the trainer. It helps to differentiate the complexities actually inherent in the goal structure of the T Group and the co-related complexities in member-responsibilities for contributing to these goals.

This discussion of the goals of the T Group underlines what seems to be a fact. Its goals are complicated, diverse, and not always capable of easy integration. One way of seeing "maturation" in the T Group is in terms of progressive differentiation and integration of these various kinds of goals—goals of conscious work production, goals of group formation and re-formation, and goals of learning. The early tendency in many groups is, in effect, to select one of these as *the* goal and to attempt to deny the others. Of course, such "abstract" selection of one facet of the concrete group "reality" will not work for long. For the fiction involved leaves whole areas of the experiences and the goal systems of members unattended to and uncontrolled. Such abstraction falsifies the reality which the group and its members must somehow recognize, negotiate, control, live with, or reconstruct, and so is unviable—cognitively, aesthetically, and practically.

These unviable abstractions concerning *the purpose* of the group frequently maintain themselves for some time when they become slogans and platforms in the power struggles of factions in the group. One faction may become a "production" faction. They will try to treat the group as if it were really a work group, with work to get done and a brief time in which to do it. They may seek to impose well-defined agenda upon the group, with well-defined management offices and working procedures to match. Another faction may emerge as a "feeling" or "process" faction. They will resist agenda, officials, and defined procedures. They may wish only to probe member-feelings and interpersonal relations. Often they resist going beyond the expression of feelings and perceptions, since the selection or development of a system of concepts for sorting, relating, and interpreting feelings and perceptions is seen as structure, and as such is seen on the side of the "production" faction. These untenable positions about what *the goal* of the group really is or should be may persist, because the viewpoints involved and the rationalizations of them are functioning as weapons in struggles to impose a partisan control over the group's thought and action. (The motivations in such power struggles, defensive or aggressive or both, are various and will be treated more fully in the next section of this chapter.)

In such struggles, other members may point out the untenability of both production and feeling slogans and platforms. They may point out the common basis in reality out of which both polarized abstractions emerge—the lack of form and legitimacy within the life of the group—with one faction seeking to impose a familiar but inadequate form upon this formlessness, and the other faction resisting any effort to invent and test forms for managing the group's life. Or they may point out the common forms that are emerging in the group willy-nilly in the very struggle between "familiar form" versus "no form."

The task of training leadership is to support efforts to bring the group to accept and to understand the concrete realities in which their struggles are set. It is only as the group comes to work in a way which incorporates as relevant data the expression and exploration of member-feelings and relationships that workable common goals will emerge. It is only as the group comes to combine such work with clarification and interpretation of what is happening to the group and its members now, and of how this is related to what has happened before and to what may happen next, that the group can learn how to handle paradoxes with respect to its complex goals. The purposes of work, of group formation, and of learning can be furthered best through realistic recognition, clarification, and interpretation of the plight of the group and of its members. Only through such realism can unworkable polarizations about goals and goallessness be converted into manageable paradoxes about goal complexities.

Problems of Growth and Maintenance of the Group and of its Members

Three kinds of goal-directed activities in the T Group have been identified—activities directed toward forming and re-forming the group and its membership as a social system; activities directed toward objective accomplishment of work tasks; and activities directed toward learning. Problems encountered in relation to each of these three kinds of group activities will be dealt with in this and the two succeeding sections.

Three sets of polarities confront the group as it encounters and deals with problems of system maintenance. The first has to do with the different and sometimes conflicting demands upon behavior for maintaining the social system of the group and those for maintaining the self-systems of the members. The second has to do with the differential demands upon the group for group and member maintenance (comfort) on the one hand, and for group and member change (growth) on the other. The third has to do with the interrelations of authority and freedom in the group.

Group Maintenance Versus Member Self-Maintenance

This polarity may confront the group in a variety of concrete ways. Sometimes it arises out of anxiety about silence and nonparticipation on the part of some members. The problem may be considered first in connection with a case of nonparticipation in an outside group. It may then be talked about in general terms as a question of the responsibilities of individual members to the group and of the group to individual members. Finally, names of members may be mentioned and pressure brought to bear upon the silent ones to explain their silence. (Such indirect and oblique circling toward direct recognition of a maintenance problem occurs frequently in a T Group.) Usually such pressure evokes defensiveness on the part of and (or) on behalf of the silent members, in terms of their right to be silent. Or again, the polarity may be confronted through a post hoc discovery that some members went along with a "group decision" to explore some topic, or to adopt some procedure, even though these members were uninterested in the topic, thought some other procedure better, or were actually threatened by the topic or procedure undertaken. Usually such a post hoc discovery brings guilt to those who pushed the others into activity against their will, whether the guilt takes the behavioral form of self-attack or of attack on the acquiescent ones for not speaking up at the time.

Whatever the concrete circumstances, the common element is the apparent irreconcilability of the demands of "the group" for movement, for order, or for data from or about members and the demands of the "selves" of some members for noninvolvement, privacy, or peace. And, at any one time, the two (or more) sets of demands may be not only apparently but actually irreconcilable. Abstract and partial "solutions" may be sloganized as weapons in factional struggles within the group. Some may urge the rightness of self-sacrifice or self-denial on the part of members to the demands of the group, which are taken for granted as "right" and "prior." Others may urge the rightness of adamant resistance on the part of individual members in protecting themselves against the encroachment of group demands, which are taken for granted as "inferior" and "secondary." Neither principle, of course, offers a resolution of the polarity.

If the differing demands of the group and of different members within the situation can be faced realistically, usually some compromise can be worked out. Certain topics may be rejected (at least temporarily), protections for member privacy and rights may be built into procedures which the group adopts, new topics or new procedures may be adopted experimentally. The trainer may be useful to the group by supporting those members who are seeking to move the group past the crippling polarity, without denying the differences among members in their valuations of member duties and privileges in the group. He must be careful not to deny the reality of any member's feelings or valuations. For to do so would violate the standard of recognizing, accepting, and talking openly about member differences.

As compromises which prove successful are analyzed in retrospective evaluation, new paradoxical principles usually come to replace the original polarization of group versus individual rights and responsibilities. It comes to be seen and accepted that the more threats of group compulsion and invasion of member individuality and privacy are reduced, the more members give of themselves to the group—in terms of ideas, feelings, and imagination. As members contribute more freely to the common work of the group, it becomes stronger and more cohesive, and members are better able to be themselves. This new paradox, when adopted as a standard, tends to be more effective in moving group and members into mutually acceptable changes and resolutions of conflict than was the original polarity. Since it works better, the new paradox tends to be assimilated into the emerging culture of the T Group.

It is no negligible learning to see that group support to the selves of members in their differential demands upon their social environment may strengthen both the individuality of members and the solidarity of the group. The trainer does not moralistically verbalize such a point. His responsibility is rather to help members enact and verbalize experiences which illuminate and reinforce the insight. To do so, he must accept the point for himself as well as for others in the group.

Comfort Versus Growth

As the group moves out of its early ambiguities and attains some workable patterns of group functioning, it moves typically into a "honeymoon" period of sweetness and self-congratulation. Members or factions who threaten the equilibrium which has been attained, often with some pain and discomfort, are frowned upon as trouble-makers. Group comfort and stability become the tacit touchstones by which group or member conduct is judged acceptable or unacceptable. Yet this comfortable equilibrium is necessarily unstable. For it is built on a denial of negative affect on the part of members toward themselves, toward other members, and toward the group. Yet such negative affect is present, however inhibited its expression may be. Some individual or factional concerns of members almost certainly are denied by the compromise arrangements which led the group out of its initial wilderness of uncertainty and ambiguity. And these concerns must somehow find their way into overt expression and action. Whatever the actual occasion of the unfreezing of the group equilibrium may be, unfreezing does come. The group must seek again a new set of workable patterns and relationships, hopefully one which permits satisfaction of deeper concerns and denies fewer realities.

Usually, after the attainment of a freer and stronger set of mutual relationships, the issue of comfort versus growth can be formulated as an issue for group consideration. Here, as elsewhere, the first tendency is to polarize verbally the claims of comfort and the counter-claims of change and growth. It is an index of increasing maturity that group members become able to concretize the issue in terms of what established arrangements in the group are to be maintained and what arrangements are to be altered. Do we, for example, want to continue discussing general and safe issues about leadership, or do we want to analyze the leadership problem in our own group? Do we want to spell out a list of blackboard agenda and stick to it, or do we want freedom to deal with behavioral events in the group as they arise and demand attention?

There is a general drive toward stable self-systems on the part of the members. But there are also specific drives toward upsetting existing equilibria stemming from the operation of self-defenses which are threatened by the present group equilibrium or from interest in fuller and freer expression of ideas and feelings and in growth by members and by the group. Both are facts of life, and the more mature the group and its members the more able they become to recognize, accept, and assess these often-conflicting drives and to effect working compromises or syntheses among them. The trainer is interested in releasing and supporting motivations toward growth; but he knows that specific ventures toward growth (change) will be made only if members are secure in some established relationships not involved in the change.

Authority Versus Freedom in the Group

In another connection, I wrote of the dialectic of competing authorities during crises in group life. This dialectic seems well illustrated in the struggle of the T Group to achieve a workable basis of legitimacy in the control of its life and career. Basic group instability "is marked by attempts on the part of each of various competing 'parties' to capture the dominant authority symbols of a social group for its own use in control of that group. In the stress of the conflict, confirmed partisan constructions on 'proper' authority tend to grow fixed and dogmatic. The 'masses' of the group membership tend to grow confused and insecure as various partisan 'authorities' compete for control of their minds and hearts, for the 'legitimacy' which, in the long run, only popular acceptance can give. An ever-present danger in such competition of 'authorities' is that the social group will seek to purchase a restored clarity and security too cheaply by accepting the control of some 'strong man' or 'strong party' which promises security through the imposition of order and the suppression of conflict. A clearheaded understanding by people of the nature of authority, its virtues and limitations, might help to offset this danger." [2]

Certainly, the refusal of the trainer to act as a traditional authority figure throws the group into an authority vacuum. Early unsuccessful efforts to impose authoritative patterns which have functioned legitimately in back-home groups only underline the fact of this vacuum. As insecurity mounts, various attempts are made to seduce the trainer into acting as a familiar authority figure. Usually these attempts are countered by other members who resent domination by any and all authority figures. Sometimes, though not invariably, the earliest factionalization in the T Group swings around this issue. Typically, both parties refuse to believe that the trainer is actually rejecting the functions of authority in setting goals for the group or in determining its social organization, whatever his statements and deeds may imply to the contrary. Frequently, elaborate myths about the mysterious and omnipotent manipulation exercised by the trainer in controlling the group are projected into the situation by both the partisans of authority and of freedom. Members more affectively neutral toward problems of leadership and authority are often unheard in pointing out the irreality in many of these projections. And the trainer's attempts

[2] Kenneth D. Benne. *A Conception of Authority.* New York: Teachers College Bureau of Publications, Columbia University, 1943, p. iii.

similarly to clarify the situation are frequently twisted into a pattern of partisan support or attack on the side of freedom or of authority.

Within this struggle, various contrived authorities may be accepted temporarily by the group. Elaborate agenda may be rammed through by one faction. Officers may be selected who are followed slavishly for a time by some and sooner or later ignored or attacked by others. Elaborate sets of rules or laws may be adopted temporarily in the search for legitimate order. Usually, none of these makeshift authorities lasts for long. More workable patterns of relationship and control typically get hammered out under the surface within the very partisan struggles that occur. These patterns give some measure of security out of which the authority problem in the group can be recognized and diagnosed by the members. Such clarification often becomes possible when new alignments or factions form on a more realistic basis of common and conflicting interests.

Recognition by a group of the unviable character of opposing authority in general to freedom in general does not solve automatically all the concrete problems of authority and freedom which group life presents more or less recurrently. But it does permit the working out of provisional compromises, whether in terms of acceptable standards, procedures, or offices, or in terms of consensus about permissible and valuable areas of member spontaneity, variation, and change within these patterns of control. It does permit assessment of specific patterns of conscious control and of free member-spontaneity and the experimental testing of proposed changes in such arrangements. As a group becomes more mature, patterns which permit the interpretation of specific authorities and freedoms tend to become the rule rather than the exception.

No other issue in the group taxes the personal stability or the ingenuity of the trainer more heavily than the issue of freedom and authority. For the trainer becomes inescapably the personal symbol of authority for many members of the group. He is simultaneously attacked, whatever his behavior, both for being dominant and for being derelict in his proper duties. Some members find less need than others to project distorted perceptions on the trainer. They are able to point out what the behavior of the trainer actually is. The trainer's job is to reinforce the reality elements in the perceptions of members and, at the same time, to help those who are distorting the situation to recognize the character and source of the twisted perceptions that thrive under conditions of no legitimate order within the group. It is easy for him, when he is attacked for what he is not doing or thinking, to become defensive and by his defensiveness to reinforce distorted perceptions and to suppress rather than to bring up for conscious examination the assumptions and conceptions of authority and freedom which bolster and rationalize these distorted perceptions.

Nondefensiveness is the attitude which the trainer attempts to achieve. Does this mean that he remains impassive and enigmatic, intervening only to clarify and question, but not to join the fray? At times this seems the best strategy. Members will detect their own projections better if the trainer maintains his objective clarifying role under threat either of seduction or attack. However, if there are few nonconflicted members in the group or if they are not strong enough to be heard, the interventions of the trainer may have to be more direct, whatever the risks involved. He may share his own feelings of discomfort, anger, uncertainty, and helplessness with the group. This means that the group is challenged to deal with him as a person as well as a symbol and a role. The main risk is that the challenge will be too great and that unproductive flight from the authority problem will ensue. The advantage is that the reality elements in the perceptions of less-conflicted members will come to be expressed openly, as the trainer has expressed his own, and that the authority problem can then be clarified.

Learning from Problems of Group Building and Maintenance

Maintenance and building problems, as they emerge, exercise a prepotent demand upon the energies of the T Group. The group finds it impossible to work effectively on an "objective" task or to analyze adequately its experiences for purposes of learning so long as severe and unsolved difficulties in member self-maintenance or in group maintenance are present. Often, such hidden difficulties are revealed by the way they tincture or twist, preconsciously or unconsciously, the content of work undertaken or the manner of working, either through indirect infiltration of irrelevancies into the group's discussions or through studied evasion of certain areas of group life. It is as if the group needs to build up confidence in its ability to bring into the open, for analysis and treatment, the difficulties of a disaffected member or of a disaffected faction in the group. Often, successful dealing with a maintenance problem is followed by an upsurge in group self-confidence and in the quality of work and learning accomplished. Even open and accurate recognition in the group that a member's difficulty or a faction's special plight is beyond the power of the group to remedy can have this tonic effect on subsequent work and learning.

What may members learn from dealing with maintenance problems? On the "group side," members may learn to accept some of the difficulties inherent in all social living, the inescapable paradoxes of individual and group relations, of stability and change, of authority and freedom. They may learn further the limitations of attempts to solve these paradoxes through the dialectical manipulation of abstract concepts alone. And they may learn to bring abstract principles, through which the paradoxes are clarified cognitively, into relationship with the concrete empirical conditions where the principles must be applied and tested, if they are to be applied and tested at all. Moreover, they may learn the inescapability of maintenance problems in any attempt to use groups either for purposes of work or of learning. Such problems cannot be ignored. If they can be faced and assessed openly and realistically in the group, the quality of both work and learning can be enhanced.

On the "self side," a member may discover personal quirks and blind spots in his system of defenses which interfere both with adequate self-defense and with self-growth. He may learn to accept such personal qualities where they are unchangeable; he may begin to change them; or he may be led toward appropriate therapy beyond the training experience when such help seems to be indicated. These learnings about self, since they are by their very nature more idiosyncratic than learnings about groups and social situations, are hard to codify. Nevertheless, such learnings are among the most important to be achieved in T-Group experience and also among those learnings most dependably transferable by members to other group and social situations.

Problems of Work-Management Functions and Their Allocation

Some trainers tend to minimize the importance and relevance of developing work-patterns involving analysis and solution of objective problems in the career of the T Group. There is a relative lack in group life in our culture, and correspondingly in social education generally and leadership training specifically, the argument goes, of conscious attention to "human relations" problems internal to group and interpersonal relations. Or, put the other way around, there is commonly a relative overemphasis upon task functions and objective work in group life. In the limited time available for T-Group experiences, this emphasis should be reversed. T-Group members sometimes rationalize ineffectiveness in task operation in their group by a similar argument: "We have an almost unique opportunity here to learn about ourselves as group members and about the internal operation of groups. Let's not waste time in doing over again what we already know very well how to do in the groups we work in outside the T Groups." There is considerable cogency and plausibility in this practical economic argument. Here again paradox confronts the group and its training leadership. First of all, if a group is to work on maintenance difficulties effectively, they must be constructed as "problems" with some objective and external quality. For those parts of the personalities of members not given to the group in expression and behavior are truly outside the group. And the outside groups to which members belong, even as these outside associations influence problems of membership in the T Group, are external to this group. Data from these external dimensions of member personality and association are invoked, explicitly or implicitly, as members objectify their outcropping difficulties in the group. In essence, what they say is, "My behavior here is like or unlike my behavior there." Out of such comparisons and contrasts come conscious construction of problems and, hopefully, generalizations for further testing within the laboratory of the T Group.

In a T Group which works at maintenance problems, the problems themselves become tasks, and the ways in which the group works on them display task properties. Relevant information, both from within and from without the present association, must be sought, organized, and interpreted; more or less adequate criteria for defining "better" and "worse" by way of a solution must be formulated (or borrowed) and applied; and experimental testing of the adequacy of solutions to the problem must be attempted and carried through. The alternative to conscious work in dealing with maintenance problems is passive dependence on drift, time, history, or providence—call it what you will. And this is precisely to reproduce the neglect which marks so much of the handling of maintenance problems in group and organizational life outside the T Group. If their experiences are to help reduce effectively the alleged imbalance of run-of-the-mill group and organizational life in outside society, T-Group members must learn to *work consciously* on problems of group and member maintenance and growth.

This paradox is underlined when we recall the trainer's responsibility to help members in transferring learnings accomplished in the training group to their back-home life as citizens, workers, teachers, or parents. Most of the group situations in which members work in these outside roles involve tasks imposed, at least in part, by the external environment in which the groups operate. The urgency and emergency of these problems often means that maintenance and growth problems are thrust to one side and left to the untender mercies of time, chance, absenteeism, sabotage, group disease, or death, to resolve. The T Group provides a social environment protected by design from the impositions and pressures upon the ordinary work or action group: maintenance and growth problems can come to the fore and be dealt with consciously, in order that members may learn better how to diagnose and to deal with such problems as they occur in outside groups and in organizations. The T Group cannot be expected to reproduce all the conditions of the outside world. Precisely in the interest of more valid generalization of learning beyond the laboratory, the T Group—like the laboratories of the physical scientist and the engineer—seeks to produce a special, protected, and controlled environment. The valid question is really: Is the goal to learn how to deal with maintenance and growth problems in isolation from work problems, or is it to learn how to combine effective handling of maintenance, growth, and work problems in their interrelationships? Effective transfer of T-Group learnings seems to me to underline the latter learning goal.

In any event, a T Group cannot help bringing into being some work structure in the process of its development. Common goals do emerge, and the group seeks and finds ways of organizing movement toward them. Alternative goals present themselves, and the group seeks and finds ways of reducing or combining alternatives to some manageable number and order—in brief, of making decisions. Ways of organizing for goal achievement and of deciding involve more or less effective and consistent patternings and distributions of functional contributions by members. A decision by the T Group and/or by the trainer not to interpret or clarify problems of task organization is, therefore, a decision *not* to clarify and interpret selected aspects of group structure and functioning that are part of the group's reality. Not infrequently in my experience with T Groups, the part of the group's "reality" which becomes problematic and thwarting to further development is some aspect of its work structure. The group, for example, may have developed no adequate decision-making structure to make the choices it needs to make in order to move forward as a group. Certain functional member roles are missing. Or they have become the "inalienable property" of members who are not able adequately to perform them. The member frustrations which occur in such a situation may lead to a deterioration of interpersonal or interclique relationships in the group. To seek to clarify and treat difficulties in these relationships without reference to the inadequate work structure of the group is a treatment of symptoms, not of causes. This is not to deny the converse, i.e., that faulty interpersonal or interclique relationships may at times lead to failure by a group to use adequate decision-making methods and structures available to it.

The dichotomization of efficiency versus effectiveness, to use Barnard's terms, is a paradox deeply imbedded in current organizational life, industrial and nonindustrial.[3] The hope of the T Group is not that this paradox be magically eliminated but rather that members can learn to see, study, and treat the poles of the paradox together within the concrete and more or less controllable reality of an ongoing group experience.

Science, Art, and Politics in the T Group

The T Group is a species of the genus, learning group. Its distinctive characteristic is the degree to which it uses clarification and interpretation of events in the group's own ongoing experiences as data for learning and as part of the dynamism of learning. This presupposes, of course, that the *primary* subject matter of learning in the training group is social and interpersonal relations.

Clarification of the group's own experiences calls for more or less objectified, or at least publicly checkable, sources of observational data about what actually takes place in the group, as well as a common language system, more or less impersonal and disinterested, for classifying and interrelating the observations.

The problems encountered in adopting and adapting a commonly acceptable and usable language of interpretation will be discussed in a later section. It may be enough here to say that the requirements upon this language of interpretation are complex, partaking of the required characteristics of the language of social science, the language of art, and the language of social policy. For the uses of data interpretations in a T Group are not alone to verify or disverify hypotheses formed independently of (but relevantly to) the value choices or actions of the group or to make post hoc sense of historic events in group life. Interpretations serve also to clarify and guide the current choices of action policies and of procedures in and by the group. It is only as interpretations are translated into action policies and tried

[3] Chester I. Barnard. *The Function of the Executive.* Cambridge: Harvard University Press, 1938.

out by the group that they are effectively tested, corrected, and qualified in the minds and experiences of T-Group members.

These combined functions of post hoc reconstruction of events, of
prediction, and of action planning served by data that are fed back,
organized, and interpreted by the T Group help to illuminate some
of the paradoxes which the goal of learning through personal experience introduces into the life and career of the group. If primary
stress is placed upon the immediate usefulness of observation and
feedback in confronting problems of maintenance or work, "moral"
and "political" considerations will narrow the scope of learning
achieved and so prejudice the probability of its generalization to other
situations. Yet, without some such practical reference in the selection and interpretation of observations, motivation to use data from
personal experience is reduced, at least initially, and the habit of observing and analyzing one's own experience is not reinforced.

On the other hand, if primary stress is placed upon elegant and
convincing post hoc reconstructions of group history, the danger is
that the aesthetic satisfactions of plausible, clever, and relief-giving
verbal dramatizations of past frustrating and painful events will override considerations both of "practicality" and of "truth" in the meanings that are lifted out of and built back into the group's ongoing
experience. However, without "artistic" reconstruction of its past,
the group develops no common self-image, no mythology, no unique
conscious ethos and character—in brief, no living culture. Finally,
if the group were to become completely "scientific" in its self-observa-
tions, concerned only with verifiable statements about groups and
group membership, it would dry up its sources of data drawn from its
own actions and decisions. Conversely, a T Group that fails to put
important emphasis on striving for "truth-value" in its statements
about itself will, in all probability, leave its members with little *validly*
generalizable knowledge.

None of these abstract alternatives is likely to occur in pure form
in a training group, and certainly not throughout its career. But I
have seen training groups attempt to approximate each of them for
limited periods. Different T Groups do emphasize different aspects
of self-interpretation and attain different characters in the process:
the practical group, which maneuvers adroitly and circumspectly
through its difficulties with little imagination or deep introspection;
the aesthetic group, which builds a rich and flavorful mythology out
of its successes and failures; and the scientific group, cautious, even
awkward, in its choices and movement, sparse in imaginative constructions upon its experiences, but ever hygienic and tight in its manipula-

tions of language and observation. The more mature group cultivates a balance among the three modes of interpreting its experiences and, in the most happy instances, achieves some degree of synthesis among the three.

Part of this process of maturation comes through increasing assumption of responsibility for observation and interpretation by more and more of its members. It may be found that the spread of training responsibilities is seldom, if ever, mechanically even among the members. Perhaps, too, it will be found that the group achieves a balance through some informal allocation of practical, aesthetic, and scientific interpretations to different members. A mature group may need to develop more or less specialized "managers and politicians," "poet laureates," and "research scientists" among its membership, as well as a common language and orientation.

Much has been written about the resistance of group members to observation and interpretation of their behavior. This resistance has been attributed to defensiveness of members toward exposing feelings and motives to others who, it is feared, may use such knowledge to hurt and destroy. The disarming of such resistances is believed, on this view, to come from the development of nonjudgmental attitudes by members toward themselves and toward other members and by the development of a climate of mutual trust and confidence among the members. There is no doubt a considerable truth in this prescription. Some members want to "judge" adversely, whether justly and rationally or not. Some members are highly uncomfortable in a climate of confidence and trust. Also, a group which chooses among alternative actions and alternative standards of conduct must make judgments and apply sanctions. In order to grow, a group must make action choices and develop criteria for choosing and acting. In order to reduce irrational resistances to accurate self-observation and interpretation, a standard of accepting and encouraging members in expressing and enacting their individualities must become one of the powerful standards in an effective T Group. Nevertheless, the group must judge ideas and behavior and develop standards to guide such judgments in the course of its development.

This principle, however, hardly goes the whole way in explaining either the motivation toward self-observation and self-interpretation in a training group, or the resistances to them. All members want to achieve greater consistency and integrity in their own behavior and in their group environment, even as they resist exposure that is perceived as painful and destructive to self and/or to the group as currently maintained. It is this strain toward greater consistency and integrity of behavior and perception that training leadership supports as it helps the group to face and accept and understand the empirical realities of their experiences. At least some of the resistances to observations and interpretations attempted by the training leader or by others may come, not from personal defensiveness primarily or alone, but rather from inappropriateness of the interpretation attempt to the need of the group for interpretation and clarification at the time. Perhaps the three functions of interpretation already distinguished—practical, aesthetic, and scientific—give some mindhold toward locating and identifying the group's changing needs for self-clarification from time to time.

Shifts in Time Perspective and the Accumulation of a Group Culture [4]

Up to this point, the discussion of the T Group has been largely "sociological" in the sense that it has dealt with problems of social organization, structure, change, and control within the developing social system of the group. The discussion has been "quasi-sociological" in the sense that it has trespassed into areas usually reserved by sociologists to psychology and to the academic limbo of pedagogical and managerial wisdom and technology. The sections which follow are more "anthropological" in the sense that they focus on aspects of the normative ordering of its social world, the group's culture, as this is accomplished and accepted by the group over time. Perhaps "quasi-anthropological" would be a better description, since intrusions of pedagogical and managerial wisdom and technology seem to be inevitable in any formulation which I attempt.

The culture of the "small group" is a relatively neglected study. Cultural anthropologists generally have kept their eyes on the life patternings of larger social units. The social psychologists and sociologists who have pre-empted the small-group field typically have not raised anthropological questions about the groups they have researched. So the discussion here probably will move farther beyond the pale of academic respectability than my sociological discussion which, whatever its possible appearance to the contrary, was written with the growing body of small-group research in mind.

The T Group begins its career with a life expectancy of ten to forty hours. The fact that the group is foredoomed to early extinction plays an important part in the economy of its cultural development. The

[4] This discussion of time perspective in the T Group has been influenced and enriched by a number of discussions with Warren G. Bennis.

certainty that the association will not be prolonged lends to members a freedom of expression and sharing that is harder to achieve in a group where the tenure of continued association is indefinite.

This initial time perspective lends a related quality to the association—a motivation to live the association intensively and to the hilt, with some relaxation of anxieties for the consequences. As members begin to realize positive values in their T-Group experience, a resolution to actualize to the full its unique potential becomes a spoken or unspoken assumption in their participations.

These effects of predated group death facilitate in some measure the purposes of the T Group. But they also present problems with respect to the development of robust learnings which will transfer out of the T Group into the continuities of life. Associations on a shipboard excursion, while often marked by unwonted intimacy and intensity, are notorious for leaving little imprint. The lasting impress is a faded memory, framed in lavender (or perhaps in purple) and reviewed only covertly in moments of sentimental escape and unguarded fantasy, or perhaps more overtly on other week-end excursions. How can the T Group use the "advantages" of predated death and yet help members achieve learnings which will tincture and alter their "real" associations?

The answer seems to lie in the development of a time perspective, alternative to that of calendar time, within the associations of the T Group—a time perspective which comes to rival in "reality" that of everyday life, and, in some sense, comes to intermesh with the time which stretches beyond the dissolution of the group. The achievement of such an alternative time perspective seems to be related to the accumulation and formulation by the T Group of its own distinctive, meaningful culture and to the internalization of this culture by its members.

To save this broad generalization from an aura of mysticism, let me try to illustrate more concretely what this accumulation of a group culture means.

A T Group, meeting indoors during the twenty mornings of a summer workshop session, began, during its seventh meeting, to attach great symbolic significance to the question of whether they should move the table into the outdoor sunlight and continue to meet there. This choice gathered into it several current ambiguities about the development of the group. The stilted politeness of their early honeymoon period had grown thin and was becoming a burden. The inability to reach a conscious decision which carried the group continuously through any extended period of activity had become a matter of concern to several members. The question of moving the table had come up originally as a way of testing the trainer's willingness to let the group make its own decisions. His refusal to rule *ex cathedra* had made his relationship to the members a matter of general concern among them. No one could quite believe in his acceptance of his role as described to them—as helper to the group in clarifying and diagnosing the processes of its own development and functioning. Some members had adopted the attitude that the T Group was a pawn within an assumed master plan. Members variously feared, hoped for, and resented the idea that they were powerless to modify the larger workshop environment.

When the table was actually moved outdoors, many aspects of their group life up to that time fell into a new shape. Members became freer and more confident—to express their feelings about the trainer and his role, to look at widely varying member images and evaluations of the group, to share both negative and positive feelings toward one another, to think about and decide inventively and readily how to deal with different members' preferences. The prevailing immediate mood was one of exhilaration and celebration. The group contrasted their daring and independence with the craven conservatism of the other groups who had stayed indoors.

After celebration came analysis and some historical reconstruction of the event. In the assessment of previous and subsequent events, this event became a mountain-peak experience within the group's subsequent time perspective. It had developed a sense of its own historic past and, in the same act, some sense of its potential future destiny—a destiny over which, within limits, members felt confident they might exercise collective and individual control. In other words, they had accumulated and constructed a conscious culture for themselves.

It was not the event alone which developed significant culture for the group. It was the event *plus* the group's "artistic" reconstruction of it, the "scientific" analysis of its generalizable meanings, and the "practical" translation of its significance into new, more livable policies for the control of ongoing adjustments and adaptations.

At this point, the reader may be feeling as some members do when they come in late to a T Group. They encounter a sense of history and of destiny in the group, but the events supporting this compelling common outlook seem too trivial to bear the weight of significance with which the group has endowed them. A deeper look reveals that the events were not so trivial after all.

The case-example used involves some of the deepest dilemmas of personal and social life, the dilemmas of self and society, of authority and freedom, of conservation and change. It involves the odyssey of human loneliness and of apartness partially overcome in an association which, while firm and security-giving, yet enhances and affirms rather than eclipses and derogates individual variation and difference. Although such dilemmas are part of the lot of all men, in the T Group they can be dramatized on a stage small enough so that they can be enacted as well as seen, worked through to some acceptable outcome, and the experience of their working out criticized and evaluated in terms of personally significant ideas.

In our own larger culture, which for many incorporates much vocational and personal loneliness in confronting the basic dilemmas of personal and organizational life, it is not surprising that the discovery and achievement of uncoerced community in facing and clarifying them should be of profound significance to the persons involved in such discovery and achievement. This community is the more significant because it is achieved not in opposition to the exercise of individual and collective intelligence, but primarily through the application of intelligence to immediately confronting problems of one's relationships with others. It is this sense of significant discovery and achievement that makes successful T-Group experience a genuine alternative, in part, to a member's outside organizational life, rather than a willful escape or vacation from it; and it is in being seen, at least in part, as a practical alternative that some transfer of learnings from the training group to other social situations is made possible.

Focus on the Here-and-Now

One implication of the discussion of the accumulation and construction of a distinctive culture by the T Group is that it is achieved as members come to focus upon the control, appreciation, and understanding of the concrete realities of their immediate group experiences. It is only as the group learns to focus upon its present experience that its own past and future attain clarity and significance and that members' outside experiences can be related meaningfully to experiences within the group.

Nevertheless, learning to face and to examine the here-and-now is a learning not easy to achieve. Members interpose a screen of assumptions, concepts, attitudes, and evaluations between themselves and what is actually taking place in themselves and between themselves and others. These patterns are drawn from members' outside experiences with other people, other groups and organizations. These are *transferred* to the T Group. Since it is set up differently, attempts to impose familiar forms upon what takes place there tend to compound rather than to clarify confusion. It is through factoring out the actualities of the here-and-now from the importations of the there-and-then that personal and collective patternings are opened up to conscious examination.

The phenomenon of status stripping has frequently been observed in the T Group. Outside statuses of members tend to be irrelevant. Members must establish anew their statuses, appropriate to the here-and-now social system of the T Group as it emerges. It is out of the shock of this stripping off of familiar statuses and the challenge of having to achieve new statuses that significant learnings both about self and about social systems may emerge.

Actually, status stripping is only one aspect of a more general primitivization of member-behavior that ordinarily occurs within the T Group. A whole range of familiar sophistications fail to work for members as they seek to negotiate a new and unfamiliar social environment. This phenomenon of primitivization of behavior extends not only to patterns of overt response and verbalization but to patterns of perception and evaluation as well. In many ways, members come to act in ways similar to ways in which adolescents act in our culture.[5] Questions concerning personal identity, vocational choice, sexual role, and world view, thought to be settled once for all during adolescence, are opened up for re-examination. Much of this re-examination goes on covertly but, in some measure, it comes to be acted out and verbalized publicly in the interactions of the T Group. As members turn to one another for help in redefining who they are and what they stand for, they are thrown back to the behavior evinced in the here-and-now of the T Group for dependable empirical evidence to validate their interpretations. And, confronted by various interpretations of "the same" behavioral events, they are driven further to distinguish idiosyncratic from common perceptions and evaluations of these events.

What is achieved at least by some members, as familiar sophistications are stripped away, is a kind of Socratic ignorance and humility before the complexities of human behavior. Of course, such "constructive" ignorance and humility are not achieved equally by all

[5] This observation of the "adolescent" quality of T-Group behavior was worked out by Dr. Roy Whitman and myself during our collaboration in a T Group in Bethel, Maine, in 1952. We hesitated to label the phenomenon "regression," in its usual psychiatric sense. The more neutral term, "primitivization" of perception, evaluation, and response, seems to me now a better label for it.

members. Nor do they extend to all areas of conduct and behavior for any member. But where members become secure enough to recognize limitations in their familiar sophistications about self and others, some processes of inquiry do take place and some willing use is made of other members in consensually validating or invalidating the results of personal observations and interpretations.

To be sure, a new sophistication develops in the group. This development was described in the previous section as the development and formulation of a group culture. The hope is that this new sophistication is based, not upon ignoring or explaining away the data of immediate experience when they clash with the "certainties" of previous indoctrinations, but rather upon respect for these data as potential levers in a "reality-oriented" extension, refinement, and revision of a cultural heritage. Taking account of the here-and-now, both when it fulfills and when it violates familiar and favored prophecies and predictions, becomes a part of the life-orientation, the "method" of the group.

It is this respect for the present, in its pains and frustrations as well as its fulfillments, which, seen as potentially an avenue toward the sober revision and improvement of the history and the destiny of the group, is among the learnings most beneficially transferable by members from the T Group to their other areas of social and organizational life. A sophistication which continually seeks learning from the here-and-now, which accepts "rebarbarization" of experience as a condition of significant personal and social growth, rather than one which attempts willfully to impose its familiar forms upon the facts, feelings, and potentialities of the present, is a sophistication become a tool of growth and change rather than an instrument either of dogmatic conservatism or of doctrinaire reform.

The Language of Action and the Language of Observation [6]

An adequate language of interpretation has been said to partake of the linguistic requirements of "social science," "social policy," and of epic or dramatic "art." A part of the initial struggles of the T Group for security-giving patterns of organization centers in a struggle to define the "official" language of the group. In a group where the trainer is seen as a social scientist, struggles over the proper relationship be-

[6] So far as I know, only one careful report of language shifts in a T Group has been attempted. Herbert Thelen and Watson Dickerman, "Stereotypes and the Growth of Groups," *Educational Leadership*, 6:5:309–316, February 1949.

tween the trainer and the group frequently involve related struggles over the place of social science jargon within the language to be employed habitually in the group. Those who attack the leadership, even when their training is in social science, may parody and satirize the *outré* language of the leadership of the group. Failures to "hear" the trainer's interpretations or comments frequently are attributed to his cruel and unusual vocabulary. Those who want more forceful leadership frequently copy the trainer's language. If he uses social science jargon, his words are not only used, but overused and misused, so far as their precise meanings are concerned. "Cohesion" or "role" or "power" function at least as much as weapons in the struggles for control of the group as they do as instruments for precise explaining of observations of behavior.

Members attempt to express questions in language systems which they can handle effectively and with authority. In a heterogeneous group, various vocational and academic jargons may struggle for supremacy as members jockey for statuses within the group. Attacks by some members on the unintelligibility or inadequacy of the special languages of other members are closely related to factional struggles within the group.

An assumption that underlies early factional struggles over language is that there should be *an* official language in the group. Just as the group often attempts to impose order on the chaos of noncommunal struggle through precisely listed agenda, carefully codified procedures, or a proliferation of group officials, so does it often assume that the group should have an authoritative dictionary to control the "correct" usages of words. Sometimes attempts are made to develop a more or less elaborate glossary of key terms.

It is only as the group loses its need for the security of an official language that language begins to function imaginatively and flexibly as an instrument for establishing communications among members. Often this is seen first in a profusion of metaphorical expressions. Frequently, these come out as members try to *express* with some vividness how they felt during a certain event. A training group of industrialists in which I recently participated provides examples of what I mean. "I felt yesterday, when I was all alone, like a pygmy among giants. And all the giants had their faces turned away so I couldn't see which were friendly and which were angry with me"; and, "When Bill told me that he thought I disapproved of everything he stood for, when I thought I was supporting him, I felt suddenly like all of my clothing had been taken off. I guess I wasn't just supporting him, but actually trying to make him over in my image so I could feel more comfortable with him." Or as an observation of another's characteristic relations to the group: "Jack looks to me like a little Indian peering out from behind trees at us as we work in an open space in a forest. He dashes in occasionally to touch one of us. Or I guess maybe he shoots an arrow at us occasionally—usually one with a soft point"; and "I feel like Ted sees himself as always presiding at our meetings, even when he is eagerly pressing the gavel into the hands of someone else—Murray usually. And I feel Murray doesn't exactly like being made king by somebody else."

This profusion of more or less apt metaphors is likely to come during or following the "second" equilibrium period, which the group achieves following the breakup of its honeymoon ("first" equilibrium) period. Group members, with anxieties about "correct" and "official" language stilled, begin to "talk poetry" in efforts to achieve a more concentrated and concrete communication of feeling and perception than either the "morally" tinctured language of common sense or the designedly unambiguous and aseptic language of science can achieve. (This is not to say that there is no moral concern or concern for precision implicit in the disciplined use of poetic language.) As "experimental" exploitation of the "poetic" resources of language is achieved in some degree, both common preferences and valuations and a common appreciation of individual variations in preference and valuation are achieved by members. Without them, common action which is at the same time sensitive to the individualities of members cannot be accomplished.

The language of action must be "poetic" in the sense that it is inescapably a language of persuasion, mobilizing common attitudes, preferences, feelings, and motivations in relation to compelling images of "member" and of "group," or of group goal and of individual and group efforts to reach the goal. If the community of action is to be uncoerced and respectful of valid differences in individual orientation and valuation, each member—not one or a few—must use poetic language to get openly and tellingly before the others his "subjective" interest and stake in whatever is being considered and decided. This calls for mutual exploitation of the expressive and persuasive resources of language—not just its resources for unambiguous pointing and for logically consistent argument and demonstration. Feelings and attitudes cannot become "evidence" to a group until they are tellingly and convincingly expressed in the same processes of deliberation in which objective evidence is marshaled, and evaluated.

Yet, in a T Group, the goal is not action alone or primarily, but learning through action. Members are expected to function alternately as participants in full-bodied action and as observers and analysts of their joint and individual actions. And the reporting and joint analysis of observations call also for a common language. In the language of observation and analysis, where valid cognition of what is happening in the group is a requirement, the linguistic virtues of unambiguous reference, of clear and precise definition, of logical consistency, become necessary.

To the observer and analyst, the very poetic expressions which informed, influenced, and shaped group- and member-actions become data to be named and sorted. Let us suppose a group is analyzing a member's expressed feeling of being a pygmy in the presence of giants with averted faces. Here one talks about a member's inability to perceive the affect of other members toward his disagreement with them. Were cues of negative or positive feeling toward his disagreement given by other members? If so, why could not the disagreeing member see them or interpret them? If not, why did the other members hide their affective reactions? How far are personal and how far are group factors involved in "explaining" the event? These represent scientific approaches to the happening.

The event may be interpreted also by placing it in historical perspective. Has the member experienced similar difficulties in getting feedback from the T Group in the past? If so, under what conditions? Does this event show similarities with comparable events in the past life of the group? If not, how has the group or the member changed? How do we evaluate any changes that may have occurred?

The event may be assessed also for its "practical" significance. Do we need more adequate ways of giving feedback to an uncertain member? Should we have a standard that a member may ask others how they are reacting to him when he feels uncertain? This last type of question pulls the group back again into a framework of choice, decision, and action. In settling these questions, the language of action again becomes appropriate.

It seems hardly necessary to state that in actual group situations the language of action blurs and at times merges into the language of observation. But the distinction between the two is still an important one to make and to learn in a T Group, granted its professed goals.

A Look into the Abyss

"And in this staggering disproportion between man and no-man . . . men build their cultures by huddling together, nervously loquacious, at the edge of an abyss." Thus vividly, Kenneth Burke characterized the precariousness of the *human* régime within the world of *no-man*.[7]

In the régime of ordinary life, men are protected by largely unquestioned routines and cultural patternings, and by unquestioning acceptance of them, from looking into the abyss of fundamental insecurity that stretches beyond the man-maintained securities of social existence. Individual men glimpse at times their basic dependence, for order and meaningfulness in their personal lives, upon the order provided by the institutions and ideological assumptions of their social group(s). They glimpse this dependence, and the prospect of individual loneliness and un-sanity outside it, most readily in moments of radical personal decision or when caught teetering and compelled to choose between radically differing group demands and loyalties. But this bleak vision for most men is difficult to maintain for long and, typically, myth-making loquacity quickly patches all frightening breaches in their personal-social systems of meaning and security.

In a T Group, members catch more than a glimpse of the personal insecurity that accompanies the absence of stable, common criteria for judging the rightness of actions and transactions, criteria of the sort that lend certainty and security to their judgments, evaluations, and responses in the everyday round of familiar associations. The most frightening insecurities come when the group-sanctioned ways of settling doubts imported and invoked by some members, encounter alternative group-sanctioned ways of other members, and neither is able to lend decisiveness to the choices of an unformed group.

It is as if the group were operating in that precontractual human state postulated by some political theorists which, taken literally as a datable historic (or prehistoric) condition of man, is mythical anthropology but, taken as an ever-threatening condition of human existence, embodies a profound truth.[8] Group members are thrust back upon their own resources to legislate and maintain a viable order of relationships. Men, as I have noted, typically take for granted the going patterns of their associational life. Some mythical "they" or "he" has fixed the orders of associational life as they are, and their legitimacy is acknowledged even in rebellion against them.

In the T Group, valiant efforts, like those of Kafka's "K" in *The Castle,* are made to detect the order which "he" or "they" really want for the group and tantalizingly are refusing to divulge. When these efforts fail, the group seeks to impose a rigid order which will shut out

[7] Kenneth Burke. *Permanence and Change.* Los Altos, California: Hermes Publications, 1954, p. 272.

[8] On numerous occasions I have explored with Leland Bradford this way of describing the early conditions of a T Group.

ambiguity. When these external and inappropriate social arrangements fail, as they must, members may try willfully to be good and kind to one another in what I have called a honeymoon period. But this effort must also fail, because it attempts to solve what is in part a social as well as an individual problem by individual restraints alone and because it rests on a *denial* of irrepressible psychological "facts" (of negative affect, differential feelings toward one another, or aggressive impulses, among others) and social "facts" (such as lack of viable patterns of social control, lack of mechanisms for consensually validating decisions and judgments). Group members finally come to accept, at least in part, the empirical reality of their plight. If they are to be saved from the threatening abyss of meaninglessness and ambiguity, they must save themselves through their own personal *and* collective "legislations." Commitment to an "experimental" quest for meaning, control, and communication, as it comes and is evaluated, is found to yield its own common security and authority, a security and authority based on affirmation rather than denial of member individuality, of personal and collective intelligence, and of the enduring paradoxes of social-personal life.

Why should contemporary "organization men" be brought to look into the abyss which lies beyond the conventional and parochial certainties of unquestioned group identifications and loyalties? Perhaps it is enough of an answer for the present to say that contemporary men cannot achieve a viable combination of "freedom" and "security," both of which they claim to prize, through rejection of group and organizational life in a spree of romantic individualism. But their affirmation of its practical necessity must not be a blind acceptance of the contemporary and traditional patterns in which their lives happen to be set historically. In affirming the inescapability of grappling with the demands of groups and organizations, contemporary men must at the same time learn how to alter, how to build and rebuild group and organizational patterns, even as they participate in them, with an eye to the values of personal freedom and spontaneity. Such learning is facilitated by the kind of clear-eyed and socially supported look into the abyss which T-Group experience provides.

The Clash of Methodologies

The T Group, I have said, finally finds or, better, constructs a basis of security and community in commonly acceptable ways of treating "experimentally" the concrete empirical "realities" of its here-and-now situation. These ways include approaches for eliciting honest evidence from all members relative to failures, disaffections, and conflicts, as well as to victories, euphorias, and resolutions, which occur in the course of group life. They include methods and mechanisms for analyzing and assessing the evidence in terms of its practical significance in the ordering and reordering of group activities and structures, in terms of its generalizable import as "knowledge" to be tested in various ways, and in terms of its meaning for imaginative and artistic construction and reconstruction of historic events and future destinies in the emerging culture of the group. They include the ways of managing, with increasing linguistic and behavioral skills, required shifts of membership between the postures and orientations appropriate to participant-actors and those appropriate to observer-analysts. These ways of group life do not eliminate pain and paradox, loneliness and suffering. But they do help members to sort the pain and paradox, the loneliness and suffering, which are self-imposed and organizationally imposed, from those which must be accepted as inherent—though not, therefore, incapable of future diminution—within the tragic human situation. The methodology developed for achieving consensual validations of perception and response should help members to distill from these latter limitations some measure of personal and collective clarity and wisdom.

The basic security of group members comes to be invested in this composite and complex methodology. The methodology is designed to support both individual and group growth in an inherently pluralistic community of constructive and reconstructive effort.

The nature of the "consensus" and "community," here described and normatively affirmed as "right," seems difficult for many contemporaries to envision and, so, to understand. The "positivist" mentality, draped in the robes of "scientific" sanctimoniousness, either denies rational meaning to the very notion of a community of ethical agreement or identifies it erroneously or perversely with a psychologically factual agreement attained by whatever means and resting on whatever grounds—spurious, fantastic, or perhaps by chance, correct. Arthur Murphy's statement seems to be particularly cogent at this point. "To maintain the ethical agreement vital to such community it is indeed essential that its members think alike on fundamentals. That does not mean, however, that they must hold identical opinions on controversial issues, opinions maintained by indoctrination in all the various media of managed mass credulity. That is not to think alike, for so far it is not to think at all. It is, rather, the way in which men agree when they do not think, when their minds are the passive instruments of social forces they do not understand. To think alike, where doubt has arisen and a justification is called for, we must first of all think, and to think is to judge, to submit divergent claims and opinions to the test of examinable reasons and to decide, not arbitrarily, but fairly, on the merits of the case. An agreement thus maintained is an ethical agreement and the society that preserves and defends it a community. . . . The morally authoritative verdict of the community is the consensus maintained and validated in this process." [9]

Contemporary society is devoid of "community" in many of its parts. The T Group seeks to provide an experience in building and managing a "community," in the hope that through transfer of learning the normative drought of contemporary society can be reduced.

This involves, of course, an ideal, but hopefully not a sentimental, view of member maturity and of group maturity. It is not achieved equally by all members in the same training group or to the same degree by different groups. Nor are all areas of member experience opened equally to public examination. This is as it should be. Privacy is also a value within a well-organized community when not purchased at too high a price in terms of personal and social dis-ease. But some glimpse of such an ideal of social and personal organization and of its dependence upon the achievement, both at group and at member levels, of an adequate methodology for facing and dealing honestly and creatively with difference and conflict, comes to each member of a successful T Group.

A methodology adequate to the conditions and goals of training-group life ordinarily makes its way against two sorts of methodological alternatives in the characters of its members. One kind of alternative is contradictory at some points to the rational-empirical-experimental methodology described above. One illustration is a thoroughgoing commitment to the method of authority in validating one's own critical judgments, valuations, and behaviors. Cognitively, this view denies the possibility of finding within the processes of personal and collective experience any norms for judging whether to believe this or that, whether to do this or that. Behaviorally, this view means a tenacious clinging to some authority outside the T Group as infallible, or a search within the group for an infallible authority-surrogate. The demands of a developing T Group upon a member with such a methodological commitment are excruciatingly difficult to meet.

The other sort of alternative is to take one part or aspect of the re-

[9] "The Common Good." Sidney Hook (Ed.). *American Philosophers at Work.* New York: Criterion Books, Inc., 1956, p. 436.

quired methodology and to treat it as if it were the whole. An illustration would be a commitment to some strict version of "scientific method" as defining completely the necessary intellectual discipline of effective group membership. Consistent with this view, the stance of observer and analyst, not of participant, is the only proper stance for a member to take in the group. If this point of view were to be generalized to all members, the T Group would have no subject-participants to observe and analyze; or the group would be brought perforce to make of its observations and analyses *actions* for further analysis and observation. (This sometimes happens.) Again, this view tends to limit the function of observation and analysis to the formulation and checking of precise predictions about relations between isolable elements of group and member experience. The equally important "artistic" and "practical" (moral and political) functions of observation and interpretation, if I have been right in my argument, tend to be ignored and, thus, deprived of any conscious and critical cultivation in the group. The adaptation of the "scientistic" member to the full methodological demands of training-group experience is, when healthy, not to foresake his commitment to "scientific method" but to learn to reconcile its legitimate demands with the equally exacting requirements of "historical-artistic" and of "practical" methods.

The clash of methodologies is never fully resolved. However, as some measure of genuine community is attained, these differences and conflicts among the members, as do others, may become accepted as sources of potential creativity, rather than proscribed as threats and blemishes to a soullessly efficient régime of social stability and order.

What, Then, of the Role of the Trainer?

Perhaps some comment on the attitudes and values which the trainer requires in giving help to others in learning for themselves will provide a useful conclusion to this essay. St. Thomas Aquinas, in his *De Magistro,* poses and discusses a question which all trainers should have pondered seriously before undertaking their roles. Can one be taught by another?

St. Thomas considers all of the then current arguments for and against the proposition that one can teach another and draws a qualified and conditionally affirmative conclusion. One can teach another only if he can enlist the other in thinking and learning for himself.

Whether or not the trainer reaches the conclusion which St. Thomas reached, he should have worked on the question seriously and should have attained the humility about helping someone else to learn for himself to which such serious consideration is certain to lead. This humility is needed by the trainer. Some people he probably cannot teach. Others he may be able to teach, but no two persons will learn in exactly the same way. Similarly, no two T Groups will develop in exactly the same way or present the same learning opportunities to their members.

What the trainer can predict are some of the major dilemmas and paradoxes of personal and social life which the group will encounter. What he cannot predict is the concrete form these problems will take in the life of a particular group or the distinctive shape they will take in the perceptions, feelings, and thinking of particular members. The trainer must be ready to let the group, and the individuals in it, find their own tortuous ways toward insight. He must be willing to let them try and fail as well as succeed. He cannot protect them from reality if his goal is to support them in facing the reality of self and others in all of its complexity and in handling such reality more rationally than before. What he can insist on is that realities be recognized, named, and analyzed, rather than ignored, denied, or oversimplified. But his version of reality is not reality, and he must be strong enough to have his version of reality challenged and changed if he is to be permitted to challenge the versions of others.

The main value that sustains him in his desperate resolve is that it is better for people to learn than to remain ignorant, that it is better for people (himself included) to change toward less distorted ways of perceiving and reflecting on themselves and their world than it is for them to remain chained to the comfort of false perceptions and crippled thinking processes. The faith that supports this value is a faith that he and others, through genuinely common efforts, can attain greater clarification in their insights and working assumptions than if they depend on their own unchecked perceptions alone. He must be ready to be used by others, and this frequently involves abuse, in order that they may discover how they are seeing and relating to others.

The trainer's ultimate reliance is on the institutionalizing of a methodology of participant-observation in a group as a self-correcting way for members to learn about themselves and about other people. His reward is increased insight into how this institutionalization can better be accomplished so that he and others can better teach and be taught by one another.

9

Patterns and Vicissitudes

in T-Group Development

Warren G. Bennis

Someone once compared the first days in a T Group with a group of blindfolded individuals, all strangers, entering a completely darkened room. Milling about in chaotic fashion, some overstepping cautiously, others creeping along the floor as the one certain support, the "group" moves gingerly and with exaggerated defensiveness toward the physical boundaries of the room as if the walls might contain some clue to the location of the light-switch. As the walls are touched, so the description goes, they, too, start moving in an unpredictable manner. This analogy, even if not bizarre exaggeration, fails to describe fully the suspense of the situation. For, very likely, the first days in a T Group present a new member with an experience which is certain, paradoxically, only in its uncertainty.

The usual factors we associate with organizational life and tend to ignore because of their immanence are conspicuously absent. Thus, the début of a T Group evokes an elemental situation where the control mechanisms we take so much for granted in traditional group settings—orderliness, precision, specified degrees of intimacy, control, authority—are indeterminate.[1] The major activity of group life, then,

[1] This statement must be qualified. Members bring to the T Group certain goals, expectations, and wishes, some of which are explicit and others of which are not. Other participants have delved into the available literature of T Groups and are as sophisticated as one can be from an intellectual preparation. Many members have discussed the "Bethel experience" with intimates and workmates and know a good deal about the training methodology. Thus, for some members, the

concerns the development of a "work" structure and "emotional" structure from a virtually undifferentiated life-space, as well as the management of anxiety which the inchoate situation engenders. Section I of this chapter will be devoted to a theory and description of how a T Group responds to the assortment of unsolved problems it confronts. The vicissitudes and phases in the complex problem-solving process constitute the major pattern of group development.[2]

Section II will treat the role strategy of the trainer as well as the purposes and methodology of human relations training by group methods. It might be said as a preview to this section that the major efforts of the trainer are directed toward exploiting the tensions and anxieties present in the situation so that group members can experiment with different responses which may be translatable and useful in other, more traditional, organizational settings.

SECTION I.   GROUP DEVELOPMENT: THEORY AND DESCRIPTION

The Two Major Areas of Internal Uncertainty: Dependence (Authority Relations) and Interdependence (Personal Relations)

.To construct a broadly useful theory of group development, it is necessary to identify major areas of internal uncertainty, or obstacles to valid communication,[3] which are common to and important in all group

situation may not be so dramatic or suspenseful as for others. In addition, varying styles of training methodology (see Section II of this chapter) contain differential degrees of structuring in the initial situation; some trainers afford a good deal of structure, while others tend to rely on ambiguity for evoking certain group responses. One of the most important research areas would be to measure the degrees of ambiguity present in the initial structuring of the T Group.

[2] Section I has been adapted from and is a revised version of "A Theory of Group Development," by the author and Herbert A. Shepard. *Human Relations,* 9:4:415–438, 1956. In the writing of the second section, I have profited from the ideas and influence of William C. Schutz and Kenneth D. Benne. Acknowledgments are also in order to the Harvard Medical School Group Research Project, which has stimulated some of the ideas presented here. Elvin Semrad, in particular, has influenced several aspects of the chapter, especially the role of "intimidation" in group process. (See page 255.) Finally, I have profited from and am grateful for discussion with my students at Boston University who are taking a group dynamics seminar. They have sharpened and added refinements to the chapter.

[3] By valid communication, we mean that group members are armed with "referential tools for analyzing interpersonal experience, so that its significant differ-

meetings under a given set of environmental conditions. These areas must be strategic in the sense that until the group has developed methods for reducing uncertainty in them, it cannot reduce uncertainty in other areas and in its external relations. Two major areas of uncertainty can be identified by induction from common experience, at least within our own culture. The first is the area of group members' orientations toward authority or, more generally, toward the handling and distribution of power in the group. The second is the area of members' orientations toward one another. These areas are not independent of each other: a particular set of intermember orientations will be associated with a particular authority structure. But the two sets of orientations are as distinct from each other as are the concepts of power and love. A number of authorities have used them as a starting point for the analysis of group behavior.

In his *Group Psychology and the Analysis of the Ego,* Freud noted that "each member is bound by libidinal ties on the one hand to the leader . . . and on the other hand to the other members of the group." Although he described both ties as libidinal, he was uncertain "how these two ties are related to each other, whether they are of the same kind and the same value, and how they are to be described psychologically." [4] Without resolving this question, he noted that (for the Church and the Army) "one of these, the tie with the leader, seems . . . to be more of a ruling factor than the other, which holds between members of the group." [5]

Bion [6] conceptualizes the major dimensions of the group into "dependency" and "pairing" modalities which correspond to our "dependence" and "interdependence" areas; to them he adds a "fight-flight" modality. For him, these modalities are simply alternative modes of behavior; for us, the fight-flight categorization has been useful for characterizing the means used by the group for maintaining a

ences from, as well as its resemblances to, past experience, are discriminable, and the foresight of relatively near future events will be adequate and appropriate to maintaining one's security and securing one's satisfactions without useless or ultimately troublesome disturbance of self-esteem." H. S. Sullivan, "Tensions, Interpersonal, International," in *Tensions That Cause Wars.* Edited by Hadley Cantril, University of Illinois Press, 1950, p. 111.

[4] S. Freud. *Group Psychology and the Analysis of the Ego* (translated by J. Strachey). New York: Liveright Publishing Corp., 1949, p. 45.

[5] *Ibid.,* p. 52.

[6] W. R. Bion. "Experiences in Groups: I, II." *Human Relations,* 3:314–320, 1948; and 4:487–496, 1948. For an abbreviated account of Bion's theory, see his "Group Dynamics; A Re-view," *International Journal of Psychoanalysis,* 33:235–247, 1952.

stereotyped orientation during a given subphase. Thelen and others,[7] using the Bionic dimensions, devised a behavioral rating scheme which correlates to the work and emotional structures of the group. More recently, Schutz [8] has made these two dimensions central to his theory of group compatibility. For him, the strategic determinant of compatibility is the particular blend of orientations toward authority and toward personal intimacy.

The core of the theory of group development is that the principal problems or issues the group must solve are to be found in the orientations toward authority and intimacy which members bring to the group. Rebelliousness, submissiveness, or withdrawal, as the characteristic response to authority figures; destructive competitiveness, emotional exploitiveness, or withdrawal, as the characteristic response to peers, prevent consensual validation of experience. The behaviors determined by these orientations are directed toward enslavement of the other in the service of the self, enslavement of the self in the service of the other, or disintegration of the situation. Hence, they prevent the setting and clarification of, and movement toward, group-shared goals.

In accord with Freud's observation, the orientations toward authority are regarded as being prior to, or partially determining of, orientations toward other members. In its development, the group moves from preoccupation with authority relations to preoccupation with personal relations. This movement defines the two major phases of group development. Within each phase are three subphases, determined by the ambivalence of orientations in each area. That is, during the authority (dependence) phase, the group moves from preoccupation with submission to preoccupation with rebellion to resolution of the dependence problem. Within the personal (or interdependence) phase, the group moves from preoccupation with intermember identification to preoccupation with individual identity to a resolution of the interdependence problem.

[7] H. Thelen, and others. *Methods for Studying Work and Emotionality in Group Operation.* Human Dynamics Laboratory, The University of Chicago, 1954.

[8] W. C. Schutz. "What Makes Groups Productive?" *Human Relations,* 8:429–466, November 1955. Since this article, Schutz has been devoting his time to developing a theory of interpersonal needs based on these dimensions and one other which he calls "inclusion," or the degree to which an individual may be conflicted about "prominence" (as distinct from dominance) in group life.

The Relevant Aspects of Personality in Group Development

The aspects of member-personality most heavily involved in group development are called, in Schutz's terminology, the dependence and personal aspects.

The dependence aspect is comprised of the members' characteristic patterns related to a leader or structure of rules. Members who find comfort in rules of procedure, an agenda, an expert, and the like, are called dependent. Members who are discomfited by authoritative structures are called counterdependent.

The personal aspect is comprised of the members' characteristic patterns with respect to interpersonal intimacy. Members who cannot rest until they have stabilized a relatively high degree of intimacy with all the others are called overpersonal. Members who tend to avoid intimacy with any of the others are called counterpersonal.

Psychodynamically, members who evidence some compulsiveness in the adoption of highly dependent, highly counterdependent, highly overpersonal, or highly counterpersonal roles, are regarded as conflicted. Thus, the person who persists in being dependent upon any and all authorities thereby provides himself with ample evidence that authorities should not be so trustingly relied upon; yet he cannot profit from this experience in governing his future action. Hence, a deep, but unrecognized, distrust is likely to accompany the manifestly submissive behavior, and the highly dependent or highly counterdependent person is thus a person in conflict. The existence of the conflict accounts for the sometimes dramatic movement from extreme dependence to extreme rebelliousness. In this way, counterdependence and dependence, while logically the extremes of a scale, are psychologically very close together.

The unconflicted person, or independent, who is better able to profit from his experience and assess the present situation more adequately, may, of course, act at times in rebellious or submissive ways. Psychodynamically, the differences between him and the conflicted are easy to understand. In terms of observable behavior, he lacks the compulsiveness and, significantly, does not create the communicative confusion so characteristic of, say, the conflicted dependent, who manifests submission in that part of his communication of which he is aware and distrust or rebellion in that part of his communication of which he is unaware.

It is the actions of members unconflicted with respect to the problems of a given phase of group development that move the group to the next phase. Such actions are called barometric events, and the initiators are called catalysts. This part of the theory of group development is based on Redl's thesis concerning the "infectiousness of the unconflicted on the conflicted personality constellation." [9] The catalysts (Redl calls them central persons) are the persons capable of reducing the uncertainty characterizing a given phase. Leadership, from the standpoint of group development, can be defined in terms of the catalysts responsible for group movement from one phase to the next. This consideration provides a basis for determining what membership roles are needed for group development.[10]

Phase Movements

The foregoing summary has introduced the major propositions in the theory of group development. While it is not possible to reproduce the concrete group experience from which the theory is drawn, we can take a step in this direction by discussing in some detail what seem to be the dominant features of each phase.

Most importantly, the significance of the role and personality of the trainer must be emphasized. What is outlined here as a theory of development may exist only because the particular training style highlights one or two group problems from a wide range of possibilities. The whole dependence modality may be submerged by certain styles of trainer-behavior. Thus, it is important that we distinguish at the outset a "natural" development from the one set forth here, which is a

[9] For a brilliant discussion, see Fritz Redl, "Group Emotion and Leadership," *Psychiatry*, **5**:573–596, 1942. Redl, following Freud's formulation, illustrates that it is possible for group action to come about as a result of the exculpation of guilt as the unconflicted frees the conflicted personality by the magic of the initiatory act. It is also probably true that individuals may like and feel more compatible with those individuals who do not stir up defended areas. For example, the highly ambivalent person who polarizes his conduct along unswervingly submissive lines may react negatively to an individual who represents the opposite pole of the ambivalence, the highly rebellious person. On this latter point, many interesting leads can be found in George Kelly's *Psychology of Personal Constructs*.

[10] Schutz has developed a test, Fundamental Interpersonal Relations Orientation (FIRO), which measures "conflictedness" and "independence" with respect to our two dimensions of dependence and intimacy. This equips us with a measure which makes possible predictions about leadership. Mention will be made below of some research undertaken at the National Training Laboratories' Summer Laboratory in Human Relations Training (1956), Bethel, Maine, where this instrument was used.

programmed attentiveness to what are considered the major areas of group uncertainties.

Phase I: Dependence

SUBPHASE 1: DEPENDENCE-FLIGHT. The first days of group life are filled with behavior whose remote, as well as immediate, aim is to ward off anxiety. Much of the discussion content consists of fruitless searching for a common goal. Some of the security-seeking behavior is group-shared; for example, members may reassure one another by providing interesting and harmless facts about themselves. Some is idiosyncratic—for example, doodling, yawning, intellectualizing.

The search for a common goal is aimed at reducing the cause of anxiety, thus going beyond the satisfaction of immediate security needs. But group-goal seeking is not quite what it is claimed to be. It can be understood best as a dependence plea. The trainer, not the lack of a goal, is the cause of insecurity. He is presumed to know what the goals are or ought to be. Hence, his behavior is regarded as a technique; he is merely playing "hard to get." The group's pretense of a fruitless search for goals is a plea for him to tell the group what to do.

We are talking here about the dominant theme in group life. Many minor themes are present, and even in connection with the major theme, there are differences among members. For some, testing the power of the trainer to affect their futures is the major concern. In others, anxiety may be aroused through a sense of helplessness in a situation made threatening by the protector's desertion. These alternatives can be seen as the beginnings of the counterdependent and dependent adaptations. Those with a dependent orientation look vainly for cues from the trainer for procedure and direction; sometimes, paradoxically, they infer that the trainer must "want it that way." Those with a counterdependent orientation strive to detect, in the trainer's action, elements which would offer ground for rebellion, and—paradoxically—may even demand rules and leadership from him because he is failing to provide them.

This phase is characterized by behavior which has gained approval from authorities in the past. Since the meetings are to be concerned with groups or human relations, members offer information on these topics to satisfy the presumed expectations of the trainer and to indicate expertise, interest, or achievement in these topics (ex-officers from the armed services, from fraternities, among others, have the floor).

Past experience often becomes the intimidating agent early in group life. It serves a useful function for group members in that it is based on the false but comfortable expectation that past authorities (such as status positions, experience) can substitute for present relationships. A subtitle of Subphase 1 might be "intimidation through experience." These initial power moves are usually doomed to failure.

Leadership bids based on the assumption of past leadership and experience fail because no one yet is willing to share leadership functions, and they fail because it becomes painfully obvious that those who dare to covet a leader role are quickly disposed of by the group. Group members who have claimed to have previous "group" experience are turned to, at first, as resource people, are regarded later as incompetent for not being capable of solving the group's problems, and finally are waved into the limbo where it is problematical whether they can ever become good group members because they have had previous experience. This is seen often when the intern-trainer becomes the focal figure. The disenchantment which is first focused on him, as a visible apprentice to the trainer (sorcerer), presages the eventual return of the problem to the doorstep of the trainer.

Topics such as business or political leadership, discrimination, and desegregation, are likely to be discussed. During this phase, the contributions made by members are designed to gain approval from the trainer, whose reaction to each comment is surreptitiously watched. If the trainer comments that these behaviors seem to occur, or if he notes that the subject under discussion (say, discrimination) may be related to some concerns about membership in this group, again he fails to satisfy the needs of members. Not that anyone is misled by the "flight" behavior involved in discussing problems external to the group. Discussion of these matters is filled with perilous uncertainties, however, and so the trainer's observation is politely ignored, as one would ignore a *faux pas* at a tea party. The attempts to gain approval based on implicit hypotheses about the potential power of the trainer for good and evil are continued until the active members have run through the repertoire of behaviors effective in the past.

SUBPHASE 2: COUNTERDEPENDENCE-FIGHT. As the trainer continues to fail miserably in satisfying the needs of the group, counterdependency begins to replace the overdependency phase. In many ways this subphase is the most stressful and unpleasant in the life of the group. It is marked by a paradoxical development of the trainer's role into one of omnipotence and powerlessness and by division of the group into two warring subgroups. Power is much more overtly the concern of group members. A topic such as leadership again may be discussed, but the undertones are no longer dependence pleas. Discussion of leadership is partly a vehicle for making explicit the trainer's failure as a leader. In part, it is perceived by other members as a bid for leadership.

The major themes of this subphase are as follows:

1. Two opposed subgroups emerge, together incorporating most of the group members. One subgroup attempts to elect a chairman, nominate working committees, establish agenda, or otherwise structure the meetings; the other subgroup opposes all such efforts. What appears first to be an intellectual disagreement soon becomes the basis for destroying any semblance of group unity. Voting is a favorite way of dramatizing the schism; suggestions that the group is too large and should be divided into subgroups for the meetings are frequent; a chairman may be elected and then ignored. No one is willing to relinquish the right of leadership and control to anyone else. The trainer's abdication has created a power gap, but no one is allowed to fill it.

2. Disenthrallment with the trainer proceeds rapidly. Group members see him as at best ineffectual, at worst damaging, to group progress. He is ignored and bullied almost simultaneously. His interventions are perceived by the counterdependents as attempts to interrupt group progress; by the dependents, as weak and incorrect statements. His silences are regarded by the dependents as desertion; by the counterdependents, as manipulation. Much of the group activity is to be understood as punishment of the trainer, for his failure to meet needs and expectations, for getting the group into an unpleasant situation, for being the worst kind of authority figure—a weak and incompetent one, or a manipulative, insincere one.

In the first subphase the trainer's wisdom, power, and competence are overtly unquestioned, but secretly suspected; in the second subphase the conviction that he is incompetent and helpless is clearly dramatized, but secretly doubted. Out of this secret doubt arises the belief in the trainer's omnipotence. None of the punishments meted out to the trainer is recognized as such by the group members; in fact, if the trainer suggests that the members feel a need to punish him, they are most likely to respond in injured tones or tones of contempt that what is going on had nothing to do with him and that he had better stay out of it. The trainer is still too imposing and threatening to challenge directly. There is a secret hope that the chaos in the group is, in fact, part of the master plan—that he really is leading them in the direction in which they should be going. That he really may be helpless, as they imply, or that the failure may be *theirs* rather than his, are frightening possibilities.   For this reason, Subphase 2 differs very little in its fundamental dynamics from Subphase 1.

The trainer has failed consistently to meet the group's needs.   Not daring to turn directly on him, the group members engage in mutually destructive behavior; in fact, the group threatens suicide as the most extreme expression of dependence.[11]   The need to punish the trainer is so strong, however, that his act of salvation would have to be magical indeed.

SUBPHASE 3: RESOLUTION-CATHARSIS.   So far, only the degenerative aspects of the chain of events in Subphases 1 and 2 have been presented, and they are, in fact, the salient ones.   But there has been a simultaneous, though less obvious, mobilization of constructive forces. First, within each of the warring subgroups bonds of mutual support have grown.   The group member no longer feels helpless and isolated. Second, the trainer's role, seen as weak or manipulative in the dependence orientation, can be perceived as also permissive.   Third, his interpretations, though openly ignored, have been secretly attended to. And, as the second and third points imply, some members of the group are less the prisoners of the dependence-counterdependence dilemma than others.   These members, called the independents, have been relatively ineffective in the group for two reasons.   First, they have not developed firm bonds with other members in either of the warring subgroups, because they have not identified with either cause.   They have accepted the alleged reason for disagreement in the group (for example, whether a chairman should be elected) at face value and have tried to mediate.   Similarly, they have tended to accept the trainer's role and interpretations more nearly at face value.   However, his interpretations have seemed inaccurate to them, since in fact the interpretations have applied much less to them than to the rest of the group.

Subphase 3 is the most crucial and fragile in group life up to this point.   It is truly a bridging phase; if it occurs at all, it is so rapid and mercurial that the end of Subphase 2 appears to give way directly to the first subphase of Phase II.   If it does not occur this rapidly and dramatically, a halting and arduous process of vacillation between Phases I and II is likely to persist for a long period.

As the group enters Subphase 3, it is moving rapidly toward extinction—that is, splintering into two or three subgroups.   The independ-

---

[11] Frequently, groups select issues which are capable of fragmenting the group, e.g., desegregation in a group of Northern liberals and conventional Southerners. Thus we see evidence of what is so typical during this subphase, the "self-fulfilling prophecy."   That is to say, certain strategic topics are predestined to splinter the group, which only serves to confirm its uselessness and disparateness.

ents, who until now have been passive or ineffectual, become the only hope for survival, since they have thus far avoided polarization and stereotypic behavior. The imminence of dissolution forces them to recognize the fruitlessness of their attempts at mediation. For this reason, the trainer's hypothesis that fighting one another is off-target behavior is likely to be acted upon at this time. A group member may express openly the opinion that the trainer's presence and comments are holding the group back, suggest that "as an experiment" the trainer leave the group "to see how things go without him." When the trainer is challenged thus directly, the whole atmosphere of the meeting changes. There is a sudden increase in alertness and in tension. Previously, there had been much acting out of the wish that the trainer were absent, but at the same time a conviction that he was the *raison d'être* of the group's existence, that it would fall apart without him.

Challenging the trainer can be done in a surprising variety of ways, both direct and indirect; it emerges in many guises. In some groups, members decide that it would be interesting to experiment with his removal in order to assess the consequences. In other situations, the group may challenge a member who represents a replica of the trainer, perhaps the "doctor's assistant" or a similar role indistinguishable psychologically from the trainer. There are some cases where a group met outside the regular meeting hours in order to plot an "overthrow of the present régime"—all in jest, of course. Whatever method the group uses, and however the trainer exploits the revolt, it tends to develop a new leadership orientation in the group.

In the discussion which follows the trainer-challenge, the group finally is freed to bring into awareness the hitherto carefully ignored feelings toward the trainer as an authority figure, and toward the group activity as an off-target dramatization of the ambivalence toward authority. How ambivalent members acquire such transferable insight from this experience is difficult to assess, but from now on, the problems of submission and domination rarely emerge as significant group problems. The power problem is finally resolved by being defined in terms of member responsibilities, and the terms of the trainer's acceptance are settled by the requirement that he behave as "just another member of the group." The outcome is autonomy for the group.

The criterion for evaluating a contribution is no longer who said it, but what is said. The illusion that there is a struggle for power is somewhat dissipated, and the contributions of members are evaluated in terms of their relevance to shared group goals. From this subphase the trainer emerges perceived as being a more experienced "technologist," with possibly useful resources for the group.

Why this trainer-challenge effects the changes in the group structure is not altogether clear. Some Freudian allusions to its similarity to the primal killing of the tribal chief and the formation of the group are more provocative than explanatory. Probably, several intervening components exist in its success. For one thing, the confrontation of the trainer unifies the rivaling subgroups against a common enemy. Keying into this is the emergence of those independents who until the present time have exerted little noticeable impact. In fact, the distinguishing element between the trainer-testing of Subphases 1 and 2 and the trainer-challenge of Subphase 3 is that the initiator of the challenge represents the hitherto-unheard rational questioning of the leader role.

Subphase 3 clarifies Freud's remark concerning the libidinal ties to the leader and to the other group members. Libidinal ties toward the other group members cannot be developed adequately until there is a resolution—no matter what form it takes—with the leader. In our terms, those components of group life having to do with intimacy and interdependence cannot be dealt with until those having to do with authority and dependence have been resolved.

Chart I summarizes the major events of Phase I, as it proceeds typically. This phase has dealt primarily with the resolution of dependence needs. It ends with acceptance of mutual responsibility for the fate of the group and a sense of solidarity, but the implications of shared responsibility have yet to be explored.

Phase II: Interdependence

While the distribution of power was the cardinal issue during Phase I, the distribution of affection occupies the group during Phase II. The main member orientations affected by this problem are those associated with attitudes toward interdependence and sharing, i.e., intimacy, friendship, identification, cohesiveness, cooperation.

SUBPHASE 4: ENCHANTMENT-FLIGHT. At the outset of Subphase 4, the atmosphere is one of "sweetness and light." Any slight increase in tension is instantly dissipated by joking and laughter. Efforts are devoted to patching up differences and healing wounds. Typically, this is a time of merrymaking and group minstrelsy. Coffee and cake may be served at the meetings. Hours may be passed in organizing a group party. Poetry or songs commemorating the important events and persons in the group's history may be composed, often as a group

Chart I   Phase 1: Dependence–Authority Relations

	Subphase 1 *Dependence–Submission*	*Subphase 2* *Counterdependence*	*Subphase 3* *Resolution*
Emotional modality	Dependence—Flight.	Counterdependence—Fight. Off-target fighting among members. Distrust of staff member. Ambivalence.	Pairing, Intense involvement in group task.
Content themes	Discussion of interpersonal problems external to T Groups.	Discussion of group organization, i.e., What degree of structuring devices is needed for "effective" group behavior?	Discussion and definition of trainer role.
Dominant roles (Central persons)	Assertive, aggressive members with rich, previous organizational or social science experience.	Most assertive counterdependent and dependent members. Withdrawal of *less* assertive independents and dependents.	Assertive independents.

Group structure	Organized mainly into multi-subgroups based on members' past experiences.	Two tight subcliques consisting of leaders and members of counterdependents and dependents.	Group unifies in pursuit of goal and develops internal authority system.
Group activity	Self-oriented behavior reminiscent of most new social gatherings.	Search for consensus mechanism: voting, setting up chairmen, search for "valid" content subjects.	Group members take over leadership roles formerly perceived as held by trainer.
Group movement	Staff member abnegation of traditional role of structuring situation, setting up rules of fair play, regulation of participation.	Disenthrallment with staff member, coupled with absorption of uncertainty by most assertive counterdependent and dependent individuals. Subgroups form to ward off anxiety.	Revolt by assertive independents (catalysts) who fuse subgroups by initiating and engineering trainer-challenge (barometric event).

(Group moves into Phase II)

project. All decisions must be unanimous, since everyone must be° happy; but the issues are mostly ones about which group members have no strong feelings. Soon the pleasures begin to wear thin.

The myth of universal harmony eventually must be recognized for what it is. From the beginning of this phase there are frequent evidences of underlying hostilities and unresolved issues. But they are quickly, nervously, smoothed over by laughter or misinterpretation. Subphase 4 begins with catharsis, but that is followed by the development of a rigid norm to which all members are forced to conform: "Nothing must be allowed to disturb our harmony; we must avoid the mistakes of the painful past." Not that members have forgotten that the painful past was a necessary preliminary to the autonomous and (it is said) delightful present, though that fact is carefully overlooked. Rather, there is a dim realization that all members must have an experience somewhat analogous to the trainer's in Subphase 3, before a realistic definition of their own roles in the group can be arrived at.

The solidarity and harmony become more and more illusory, but the group still clings to the illusion. This perseverance is, in a way, a consequence of the deprivation that members have experienced in maintaining the atmosphere of harmony. Maintaining it forces members to behave in ways alien to their own feelings; to go still further in group involvement would mean a complete loss of self. The group is therefore torn by a new ambivalence: (1) "We all love one another and, therefore, we must maintain the solidarity of the group and give up whatever is necessary of our selfish desires." (2) "The group demands that I sacrifice my identity as a person; but the group is an evil mechanism which satisfies no dominant needs." As this subphase comes to a close, the happiness which marked its beginning is maintained only as a mask. The "innocent" splitting of the group into subgroups has gone so far that members will even walk around the meeting table to join in the conversation of a subgroup, rather than speak across the table at the risk of bringing the whole group together. There is a certain uneasiness about the group; there is a feeling that "we should work together but cannot." There may be a tendency to regress to the orientation of Subphase 1: group members would like the trainer to take over.

SUBPHASE 5: DISENCHANTMENT-FIGHT. This subphase is marked by a division into two subgroups—paralleling the experience of Subphase 2—but this time based upon orientations toward the degree of intimacy required by group membership. Membership in the two subgroups is not necessarily the same as in Subphase 2: for now the fragmentation occurs as a result of opposite and extreme attitudes toward the degree of intimacy desired in interpersonal relations. The counterpersonal members band together to resist further involvement. The overpersonal members band together in a demand for unconditional love. Yet a common theme underlies them. For the one group, the only means seen for maintaining self-esteem is to avoid any real commitment to others; for the other group, the only way to maintain self-esteem is to obtain a commitment from others to forgive everything. The subgroups share the fear that intimacy breeds contempt.

This anxiety is reflected in many ways. For the first time, openly disparaging remarks are made about the group. Invidious comparisons are made between it and other groups. Similarly, psychology and social science may be attacked. The inadequacy of the group as a basis for self-esteem is dramatized in many ways—from stating, "I don't care what you think," to boredom, to absenteeism. The overpersonals insist that they are happy and comfortable, while the counterpersonals complain about the lack of group morale. Intellectualization by the overpersonals frequently takes on religious overtones concerning Christian love, consideration for others, and the like. The counterpersonal members account for member behavior in terms of motives having nothing to do with the present group; the overpersonals explain all in terms of acceptance and rejection in the present group.

Subphase 4 might be caricatured as hiding in the womb of the group; Subphase 5, as hiding out of sight of the group. It seems probable that both of these modalities serve to ward off anxieties associated with intimate interpersonal relations. "If others really knew me, they would reject me." The overpersonal's formula for avoiding this rejection seems to be to accept all others in order to be protected by the others' guilt; the counterpersonal's way is to reject all others before they have a chance to reject him.

We now can look back on the past two subphases as countermeasures against loss of self-esteem, what Sullivan once referred to as the greatest inhibition to the understanding of what is distinctly human, "the overwhelming conviction of selfhood—this amounts to a delusion of unique individuality." The sharp fluctuations which occurred between the euphoria of Subphase 4 and the disenchantment of Subphase 5 can be seen as a struggle between the "institutionalization of complacency," on the one hand, and anxiety associated with fantasy speculations about intimacy and involvement, on the other. This dissociative behavior serves a purpose of its own: a generalized denial of the group and its meaning for individuals. For if the group is important and valid, then it has to be taken seriously. If it can wallow in the enchantment of Subphase 4, it is safe; if it can vilify continually the goals and objectives of the group, it is also safe. The disenchantment theme in Subphase 5 is perhaps a less skillful and more desperate security provision, with its elaborate wall of defenses, than the "group mind" theme of Subphase 4. What should be stressed is that both subphase defenses were created almost entirely on fantastic expectations about the consequences of group involvement. These defenses are homologous to anxiety as it is experienced by the individual, i.e., the state of "anxiety arises as a response to a situation of danger and will be reproduced thenceforward whenever such a situation recurs." [12]

SUBPHASE 6: CONSENSUAL VALIDATION. Two forces combine to press the group toward a resolution of the interdependency problem: the approaching end of the training program and the need to establish a method of role evaluation. (In some T Groups, a "contract" is made whereby the group agrees to develop some system of role evaluation or merit rating.)

At first, the characteristic defenses of the two subgroups fuse to prevent any movement toward the accomplishment of the evaluation or grading task. The counterpersonals resist evaluation as an invasion of privacy; they foresee catastrophe if members begin to say what they think of one another. The overpersonals resist it since it involves discriminating among group members. Members of each subgroup are perceived by members of the other as "rationalizing," and the group becomes involved in a vicious circle of mutual disparagement. In this process, the fear of loss of self-esteem through group involvement is near to being realized. As in Subphase 3, it is the independents, whose self-esteem is not threatened by the prospect of intimacy, who restore the members' confidence in the group. Sometimes all that is required to reverse the vicious circle quite dramatically is a request by an independent for assessment of his own role.

The fear of rejection fades when tested against reality. The tensions which developed as a result of these fears diminish in the light of actual discussion of member-roles. What ensures this diminution is a serious attempt by each member to verbalize his private conceptual schemes for understanding human behavior—his own and others'. Bringing these assumptions into explicit communication is the main work of Subphase 6. This activity demands a high level of work and of communicative skill. Some of the values which appear to underlie the group's work during this subphase are as follows: (1) Members can accept one another's differences without associating "good" and "bad"

[12] S. Freud. *The Problem of Anxiety.* New York: Psychoanalytic Quarterly Press and W. W. Norton and Co. (translated by H. A. Bunker), p. 72, 1936.

with the differences.   (2) Conflict exists, but it is over substantive issues rather than emotional issues.   (3) Consensus is reached as a result of rational discussion rather than through a compulsive attempt at unanimity.   (4) Members are aware of their own involvement and other aspects of group process, without being overwhelmed or alarmed. (5) Through the evaluation process, members take on greater personal meaning to one another.   This facilitates communication and creates a deeper understanding of how the other person thinks, feels, behaves; it creates a series of personal expectations, as distinguished from the previous, more stereotyped, role expectations.

The above values, and some concomitant values are, of course, very close to the author's conception of a "good group."   In actuality they are not always achieved by the end of the group life.   The prospect of the death of the group, after much procrastination in the secret hope that it will be over before anything can be done, is likely to force the group into strenuous last-minute efforts to overcome the obstacles that have blocked its progress.   As a result, the sixth subphase is too often hurried and incomplete.   And if role evaluation is attempted, either the initial evaluations contain so much hostile material that they block further efforts, or evaluations are so flowery and vacuous that no one, least of all the recipient, believes them.

In the resolution of interdependence problems, member personalities count for even more than they do in the resolution of dependence problems.   The trainer's behavior is crucial in determining the group's ability to resolve the dependence issue, but in the interdependence issue the group is, so to speak, only as strong as its weakest link.   The exceedingly dependent group member can ride through Phase I with a fixed belief in the existence of a private relationship between himself and the trainer; but the person whose anxieties are intense under the threats associated with intimacy can immobilize the group (Chart II summarizes the major events of Phase II).

Conclusions

Dependence and interdependence—power and love, authority and intimacy—are regarded as the central problems of group life.   In most organizations and societies, the rules governing the distribution of authority and the degree of intimacy among members are prescribed. In the human relations training group, they are major areas of uncertainty.   While the choice of these matters as the focus of group attention and experience rests to some extent with the trainer, his choice is

Chart II Phase II: Interdependence—Personal Relations

	Subphase 4 *Enchantment—Flight*	*Subphase 5* *Disenchantment—Fight*	*Subphase 6* *Consensual Validation*
Emotional modality	Pairing—Flight. Group becomes a respected icon beyond further analysis.	Fight—Flight. Anxiety reactions. Distrust and suspicion of various group members.	Pairing, understanding, acceptance.
Content themes	Discussion of "group history," and generally salutary aspects of program, group, and membership.	Revival of content themes used in Subphase 1: What is a group? What are we doing here? What are the goals of the group? What do I have to give up, personally, to belong to this group? How much intimacy and affection are required? Invasion of privacy versus group giving. Setting up proper codes of social behavior.	Discussion and assessment of member roles.
Dominant roles (Central persons)	General distribution of participation for first time. Overpersonals have salience.	Most assertive counterpersonal and overpersonal individuals, with counterpersonals especially salient.	Assertive independents.

Group structure	Solidarity, fusion. High degree of camaraderie and suggestibility. LeBon's description of "group mind" would apply here.[13]	Restructuring of membership into two competing predominant subgroups made up of individuals who share similar attitudes concerning degree of intimacy required in social interaction, i.e., the counterpersonal and overpersonal groups. The independent individuals remain uncommitted, but act according to needs of situation.	Diminishing of ties based on personal orientation. Group structure now presumably appropriate to needs of situation based on predominantly substantive rather than emotional orientations. Consensus significantly easier on important issues.
Group activity	Laughter, joking, humor. Planning out-of-class activities, such as parties. The institutionalization of happiness to be accomplished by "fun" activities. High rate of interaction and participation.	Disparagement of group in a variety of ways: high rate of absenteeism, tardiness, balkiness in initiating total group interaction, frequent statements concerning worthlessness of group, denial of importance of group. Occasional member asking for individual help finally rejected by the group.	Communication to others of self-system of interpersonal relations, i.e., making conscious to self and aware to others of conceptual system one uses to predict consequences of personal behavior. Acceptance of group on reality terms.

[13] Gustave LeBon. *The Crowd.* New York: Viking Press, 1960.

Chart II Phase II: Interdependence—Personal Relations (Continued)

	Subphase 4 *Enchantment—Flight* (Cont'd)	*Subphase 5* *Disenchantment—Fight* (Cont'd)	*Subphase 6* *Consensual Validation* (Cont'd)
Group movement	Independence and achievement attained by trainer-challenge and its concomitant, deriving consensually some effective means for authority and control. (Subphase 3 rebellion bridges gap between Subphases 2 and 4.)	Disenchantment of group as a result of fantasied expectations of group life. The perceived threat to self-esteem which further group involvement signifies, creates schism of group according to amount of affection and intimacy desired. The counterpersonal and overpersonal assertive individuals alleviate source of anxiety by disparaging or abnegating further group involvement. Subgroups form to ward off anxiety.	The external realities, group termination, and the need for some role-assessment system comprise the barometric event. Led by the independent individuals, the group tests reality and reduces autistic convictions concerning group involvement.
Main defenses	Denial, isolation, intellectualization, and alienation.		

predicated on the belief that they are the core of interpersonal experience. As such, the principal obstacles to valid interpersonal communication lie in rigidities of interpretation and response carried over from the anxious experiences with particular love or power figures into new situations in which they are inappropriate. The existence of such autisms complicates all discussion unduly and in some instances makes impossible an exchange of meanings.

Stating the training goal as the establishment of valid communication means that the relevance of the autistic response to authority and intimacy on the part of any member can be examined explicitly and at least a provisional alternative formulated by him. Whether this makes a lasting change in the member's flexibility or whether he will return to his more restricted formula when confronted with a new situation, remains unsolved; but it probably varies with the success of his group experience—particularly his success in understanding it.

Several final qualifications are necessary. In this attempt to generalize into a systematic theory the sequential relations of group life, there has been a tendency to force into categories behaviors and actions which are more indeterminate and overlapping than the theory implies. Life in a T Group is more of a "puzzlement" than any such simple classification suggests. Rather than the thesis-antithesis-synthesis dialectic presented here, where one phase movement chronologically follows another and inexorably erases all traces of the past, the process more closely resembles a cyclical movement, where the major problems evolve at different points in time—the group's attempting a deeper understanding each time around.

A useful analogy is to think of development as a wheel-changing process. After the mechanic places the wheel onto the base, he adjusts all the lug bolts tightly enough to hold the tire in place. Then he adjusts each lug a little tighter. If one lug screws in too tightly, the entire wheel is in imbalance until the lug is sufficiently loosened. Then he goes around threading each lug into the socket until the various lugs are tightened. Group life may proceed in this way with certain basic interpersonal tensions more salient in one period than in another but with complete resolutions impossible until other tensions are managed to about the same tolerance and, finally, the entire system is equilibrated.[14]

[14] For this metaphor I am grateful to William C. Schutz. It may be useful here to make a distinction between a "phase" and a "cycle." A phase is described in terms of a certain invariant interpersonal tension which the group must solve. Thus, in this section I have specified two major phases based on dependence and interdependence. A cycle, on the other hand, represents a process by which the

Another important question concerns the unique contribution of the trainer to the training situation and to what extent group development is independent of his particular personality and habits. Each trainer has in mind—either explicitly or implicitly—some general notion of development, i.e., where the group is going and an assessment of the consequences of the direction. In a survey of the pertinent literature on phases, we have discovered some fifteen such phase-movement theories ranging from task-oriented groups to therapy for psychotic patients. For the trainer, the sequential relations constitute helpful bench marks, and to him it appears the phases are clearly discernible. However, with only two exceptions, all the statements lacked any clear-cut operations capable of testing the trainer's perceptions. Whether the developmental theories exist as self-fulfilling prophecies which unfold as inductions of the trainer obtain the desired results or whether the trainer selectively disregards problems external to his own theoretical leanings, remains as yet a vexing and open question.

SECTION II.   GOALS AND STRATEGY OF THE T GROUP

The T Group emerged out of the needs of our particular historical period to learn something about group process and behaviors in groups. The T Group, which originated at the National Training Laboratory in Group Development,[15] held at Bethel, Maine, in 1947, was a brilliant invention devised to foster knowledge in this direction. It is interesting to note that this book of theory was conceived and written after fifteen years of laboratory practice and many years of thought. In this respect, the development of a systematic theory approximates the development of theoretical thought in the social sciences in general. Theoretical systems, more often than not, stem from the applied social scientists' confrontation of a problem for which there is no adequate body of theory. Out of this practical approach to a critical problem, theoretical advances often are made.[16]

Thus, we have seen the field of industrial sociology emerge from

group solves the problem. An example of a cycle may be characteristic subgroup clusters which ensue during certain problem areas.

[15] Now known as the National Training Laboratories' Annual Summer Laboratory in Human Relations Training.

[16] For an elaboration of this point, see Alvin Gouldner, "Some Explorations in Applied Social Science." *Social Problems,* January 1956.

the Western Electric researches of Mayo; [17] the development of psychoanalytic theory from Freud's treatment of middle-class hysterics; group therapy arising from the pressing need for relief from combat tensions; sociometry as a device capable of housing Allied soldiers in World War I with minimum housekeeping problems. Although there are many other examples, it is not the author's intent to claim primacy for the applied or basic researcher or practitioner. More likely, the process resembles cross-fertilization where applied problems feed into the main stream of theoretical thought, which, in turn, spills back to the practitioner in a more refined form, with the process repeated again and again. This short excursion into the sociology of knowledge is made in order to clarify the position which this section takes with regard to the goals and strategy of the T Group. It is the chief contention here that if, in an attempt to theorize about the nature of T Groups, we rely too heavily on conceptions from standard social science literature, we shall bog down into a debate as to whether the T Group is a therapy group—that is, dealing with the reorganization of the *personality*—or a training group, which is concerned with the reorganization of a *role*. A good deal of time and effort is spent in maintaining this false dichotomy between role and personality and its group derivatives, training and therapy, and there is a plethora of ethical customs which attempt to outlaw any jurisdictional trespasses from either side.[18] Out of this dilemma develop two general approaches to groups: groups which are psychoanalytically oriented and have as their main goal the reconstitution of interpersonal behaviors; and training groups which have as their main goal learning about group behavior.[19] Actually, the T Group by its very nature must involve both relevant personality and role relationships. Attention by the trainer to one, to the exclusion of the other, will limit the richness of the group experience.

[17] Eton Mayo. "The Social Problems of an Industrial Civilization." Division of Research, Graduate School of Business Administration. Boston: Harvard University, 1945.

[18] See J. D. Frank's chapter in this volume for a careful analysis of some differences between T Groups and therapy groups.

[19] A good example of the difficulty in distinguishing between the clinical and social orientations can be seen if we compare the British psychoanalyst, Bion, and an interpersonal specialist such as Timothy Leary. The former refuses to make an intervention specifying a single individual's behavior, yet his theoretic-group model is based on psychoanalytic dimensions; while the latter is concerned with less "depthy" interpretations, yet focuses almost primarily on the individual. In one case—that of Bion—we observe a psychoanalytic frame of reference based on group formation; in the case of Leary, the model follows a more social-behavioral approach, yet with more attention on the individual.

Human Relations Goals in the T Group

The very complexity of the T Group creates a variety of unanticipated consequences which, as the action unfolds, would be impossible
to take into account. To some extent, however, the trainer's goals and
methodology structure the situation; and while his operations, as in
science, determine the results, consideration will be given first to the
desired results and goals.

There are two major goals of the T Group which can be indivisible
in operation: (1) that group members become more aware of the
enabling and disabling factors in decision making in groups and of
their own behaviors and feelings in groups; (2) that group members
utilize the group as a crucible for increasing their repertoire of skills
in managing group processes and their own behaviors in groups. To
the extent that one is stressed at the sacrifice of the other, the training
loses effectiveness.[20]

On the awareness dimension, we hope that the trainee gains sophistication in teasing out of the total group behavior "process" problems
from "content" problems, so that interpersonal tensions can be isolated
from the specific work goals of the group. We should also hope that
he derives a feeling for the "work" structure of the group problems
dealing with decision making, achievements, goals, tangible results,
modes of consensus, as well as the "emotional" structure of the group
problems dealing with member feelings (sensitivity to tolerance limits
of other members in terms of intimacy, cohesiveness, and morale).
As the group matures from a heterogeneous assemblage to a moderately interdependent unit, trainees may derive some sense of the
proper social mix of work components and emotional components
necessary for effective group functioning.[21]   As attention to group
processes increases, the individual finds it impossible not to become
a keener observer of his own self-processes and more particularly his
"face-work"—that is, his unique pattern of verbal and nonverbal acts
by which he expresses his view of the group situation.[22]

[20] That social sensitivity may be dysfunctional to the system and incapacitating
to the individual is discussed fully by Ivan D. Steiner, "Interpersonal Behavior
Influenced by Accuracy of Social Perception." *Psychological Review*, 62:4:1955.

[21] That self-knowledge and interpersonal and/or group knowledge may not proceed independently is brought to mind by a statement made by a mythical
analysand.   When he was asked whether his four years of analysis changed him,
he responded, "No, I didn't change, but my friends sure got better."

[22] I am indebted for this particular idea to the brilliant work of Erving Goffman.
See his "On Face-Work," in *Psychiatry*, 18:213–231, August 1955.

Along the action dimension, the T Group provides a magnificent crucible for attempting new behaviors. To the extent that the group builds in an adequate feedback mechanism for group members to obtain new information in order to experiment with new behaviors, the group will succeed as a change agent. All organizations provide feedback mechanisms of one sort or another. The chief differentiating factor is that the T Group provides almost simultaneous data, while natural organizations prefer longer time-lags which take the form of promotions, salary increases, or, negatively, of termination of membership. In short, feedback (or methods of evaluation and reward and punishment) more often than not comes as a terminal point in natural organizations; while in the T Group, evaluation emerges at a time when new responses are still possible.

Strategy and Methodology of the Trainer

The major strategy employed by the trainer is the exclusive use of and attention to material which emerges from the unique relationships and experiences evoked in the T Group and solely in the T Group. The degree to which the trainer "permits" [23] reference to external contexts, contrasted with the degree to which the trainer encourages attention to the here-and-now, provides a convenient dimension for analyzing various types of training methods.[24]

Naturally, it is difficult to place all the training methods in this linear fashion, because to some extent it would depend upon the particular style of the trainer. Conceivably, a therapy group of Dr. Bion's at Tavistock, in London, might not differ very much from a T Group at Bethel. Similarly, many practitioners of the case-study method utilize role playing as an intrinsic part of the case. The most controversial ordering on the list probably is placing a T Group over a therapy group. This is done in order to stress that members in therapy groups are encouraged to bring into the sessions material about past relationships, about unconscious fantasies, about various external relationships. The T Group makes no such demands, and the trainer is

---

[23] The trainer may, of course, be helpless to enforce this rule. He can work toward the goal of here-and-now attention only by monotonously making interpretations on that level.

[24] Kenneth Benne points out that the here-and-now actually includes a time dimension of the "past" and the "future." The history of the group, while occurring in the past, is incorporated in the here-and-now; and the future, insofar as it concerns members' expectations about future events, also is contained in the here-and-now.

Chart III

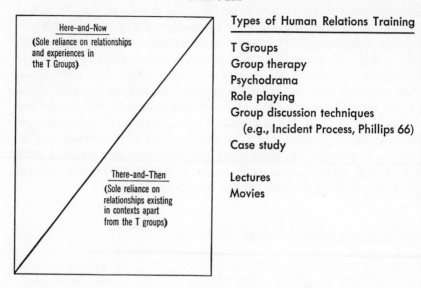

Here-and-Now
(Sole reliance on relationships
and experiences in
the T Groups)

There-and-Then
(Sole reliance on
relationships existing
in contexts apart
from the T groups)

Types of Human Relations Training

T Groups
Group therapy
Psychodrama
Role playing
Group discussion techniques
    (e.g., Incident Process, Phillips 66)
Case study

Lectures
Movies

more interested in how the direct expression of unconscious material (like a dream) would affect the group processes and the individual's integration in the group than in the symbolic content of the dream itself.

As we proceed up the list we encounter training settings with more ambiguity. In witnessing a movie, for example, there is very little doubt about how group members are supposed to behave. Aside from a rare and surreptitious pinch in a darkened movie theater, one can make accurate predictions about the degree of intimacy required. In role playing, serious attention is given to spelling out to the actor the role requirements. The therapy group provides a substantial goal, a curative process, to the individuals. The T Group, by stressing the here-and-now phenomena, violates typical member-expectations about a training situation and, at best, sets up a vague and unfamiliar goal. Second, in addition to dealing with this ambiguity, it is possible that the member has to participate more in the group itself than he would need to do in any of the other groups. Third, it appears that the T Group brings about more of a convergence of role and personality attributes than do the other methods. Without any particular structure or clear-cut goals to begin with, the group must develop its own muscles and structure; and this demands sophistication about the group formative processes, as well as sensitivity to the self as a result of this maturation process.

To clarify the issue, let us examine a fairly typical event which might occur early in group life. The group is discussing some aspects of leadership. A member goes to the blackboard and begins to make an outline of the salient problems involved in leadership as the members discuss them. Another member attempts to interpose his view on the group by stating the way in which his organization deals with leadership matters; a third member argues that the second member's suggestion may not be the appropriate way to deal with the problems of leadership in this situation; and various other members support one or another point of view. The member at the blackboard, diligently taking notes, finds himself completely ignored or out of field. He tries as best he can to slide back to his seat unnoticed. The leading contenders on the leadership issue continue their pace, attempting to gain supporters by pitching their arguments to the uncommitted members of the group. At this point, it might be appropriate for the trainer to ask the group whether the events in the group over the past several minutes have yielded any light on the question of leadership and whether the discussion of leadership might be related to how this group intends to resolve the problem. The general contention here is that the content of the discussion on leadership is shadow play for the underlying issue facing the group at this time.

Another example might be that which takes place when group members introduce themselves—a ritual practically unfailing in its appearance at the first meeting. The introduction ritual serves many purposes, least of all its main intent, which is members' "locating" one another in terms of background. It does serve to provide a task for the group, a breaking of the ice, and some general introduction to others in the group. The major activities at this time, however, are the "sizing up" and the method the group uses for the introductions. Evidence for the idea that members are more concerned about what the other person is like, rather than who he is, can be seen when members discuss the first day's experience with almost total amnesia as to what members actually said about themselves. After the introductions, the trainer might say—using the here-and-now methodology—that the group already has established a norm (say, going around the table) and that perhaps we might want to look back and determine how the act developed. Usually, this intervention serves to acquaint the group members with the technique of the here-and-now and to evoke responses from members as to how they perceived the action which up to this point has been perceived either only dimly or as inappropriate to bring up.

There are several advantages to this approach. First, the trainer utilizes data which can be checked and clarified against distortions and possible errors in reporting. A discussion of leadership in external organizations cannot provide equal reliability of reporting. When questions arise about distortions, about correct data, about perceptions, we have only to rely on the direct sources of the information—the group members.

A more strategic advantage is that in a T Group we extrapolate from experiences in the group to external organizations and groups—that is, from internal to external phenomena. In most other methods of human relations training the process is reversed. A T Group provides experiential referents which can be generalized to non-T Groups, whereas other approaches more typically generalize without any direct experiential element.

Trainer-intervention—the style and timing of making explicit certain observations—provides the trainer with his second major device, which keys into the here-and-now approach. Generally, there are four levels of group behavior which the trainer attends to: Level 1, the content; Level 2, the behaviors; Level 3, the defenses members characteristically play in relation to interpersonal threat (these can be called "roles"); Level 4, the anxieties. Chart IV presents an example for each level with respect to the major dimensions of group life.[25]

If the trainer is aware of the four levels simultaneously, he has to select one of the levels appropriate at a particular point in time for the group; that is, the level which the group is ready to assimilate and use in relation to clarifying its interpersonal problems. It is probably fair to say that interventions on the content level are more acceptable (and most sanitary) at the beginning of the group experience than are statements about the anxieties. As the group continues meeting, it may be possible for greater understandings to take place at Level 4, but it remains problematical as to whether a two-week period is long enough for adequate understandings at this level.

The *content* provides one of the best indicators for the more under-

[25] The use of the terms "defenses" and "anxieties" may be unfortunate here inasmuch as they connote intrapersonal meanings. This is not intended. By defense, I mean the characteristic role the individual plays with respect to a certain group problem. Anxiety is the designation of the fears and difficulties involved in solving the particular *group* problem, e.g., interdependence. I am grateful to William C. Schutz for this suggestion of levels, as well as his insight on the analysis of content relationships. (See page 277.)

Chart IV   Four Levels of Interventions

Dimension	1 *Content*	2 *Behaviors*	3 *Defenses*	4 *Anxieties*
Dependence	Intellectual discussion on leadership.	Voting. Difficulty in arriving at decision.	Off-target fighting. Contending for leader role.	Ambivalence with respect to authority.
Interdependence	Discussion on "When is a group a group?"	Setting up rules of appropriate interpersonal behaviors.	Withdrawal. Isolation.	Anxiety about closeness.

lying tensions. If the content of the discussion involves peer-group or colleague relations, cohesiveness may be the issue; superior-subordinate relationships as a content issue possibly may be related to leadership and authority problems. For example, if the group is discussing attitudes toward the training administration, possibly what is at stake is the members' concerns in the authority area. Henry Ezriel, the British group psychotherapist, provides a good example of this. One day his group was discussing whether the Christian God were a punishing or benevolent deity. He suggested that the content might have something to do with attitudes toward him, the leader. While the content of the group discussion is not often so thinly disguised as in this example, the content serves as a useful cue to the more underlying issues.

Above all, the trainer's interventions must focus exclusively on relationships, not properties. He must never make an intervention to or about a single individual. His remarks will be relevant insofar as they concentrate on the group process and interpersonal relationships, and not on the properties which exist within a person or subgroup of persons. This is not to say that his comments will not have meaning for a particular individual. For example, the trainer may remark that the group has yet to develop a satisfactory decision-making apparatus. Now this intervention on the group level can resonate—at differing rates of speed—to various individuals and to various regions of personality. If there is a peculiarly skewed distribution of interaction and talking in the group, the trainer might inquire as to the nature of this distribution, but certainly not in the form of questioning individual members as to their avoidant or ascendant behavior.

By focusing on the group-relevant phenomena, the trainer sets certain limits on group activity. Individuals who attempt to exploit the group for private therapy or for depth interpretations of others' motivations are not encouraged. In addition, by stressing the *group* process the trainer is free to remain somewhat detached from the prominent intragroup tensions and is able to utilize better his intellectual resources to discern what is going on.

Two other considerations should be mentioned. From time to time, the trainer, as a methodologist, is called on to comment upon group observation techniques and group process. While at times this referral to authority may be a desire to avoid problems, at other times it may be an appropriate response to the trainer as a resource person. If the help is desired for the latter reason, there is no reason for the trainer to withhold help if indeed he believes that it will serve a purpose. Finally, it should be said that, with these rules of thumb, perhaps the critical determinant of the trainer role is how useful a role-model he is to the group members. It may be that one of the chief characteristics of the successful trainer is that group members may find in him a suitable model for imitation.

10

Climate for Trust Formation

Jack R. Gibb

A person learns to grow through his increasing acceptance of himself and others. Serving as the primary block to such acceptance are the defensive feelings of fear and distrust that arise from the prevailing defensive climates in most cultures. In order to participate consciously in his own growth a person must learn to create for himself, in his dyadic and group relationships, defense-reductive climates that will continue to reduce his own fears and distrusts.

Arising inevitably from all social interaction are four modal concerns: acceptance, data-flow, goal formation, and social control. These modal concerns arise in all social structure. They are brought into focus of awareness and are articulated by orientation toward process in the T Group. These concerns generate intrinsic motivations to reduce the concerns, and this reduction produces movement and growth. Significant and enduring movement toward concern-reduction in the last three areas can be made only as movement is made on the acceptance dimension.

A person can learn to grow as a person through learning how to create for himself defense-reductive climates that continue to reduce his fears and distrusts; he thus makes change possible along the other three dimensions. The critical function of the T Group is to augment this process of personal learning. The person learns to participate with others in creating a defense-reductive climate, becomes aware of the processes of such creation, and learns how to generalize these learnings to other dyadic and group situations. That is, he learns how to create the interpersonal situations which will help him to accept himself and others—to grow and to help others to grow.[1]

It is possible to describe effective behavior for T-Group members and trainers in terms of the above theory. Two hypothetical, idealized models for member- or trainer-behavior are outlined below. A "persuasive behavior" model leads to minimal growth along the four dimensions, and a "participative behavior" model leads to maximal growth.

The Four Modal Concerns

Our research on a wide variety of groups in various life settings indicates the apparent validity of the assumption that there are four basic concerns that arise inevitably from all social interaction. As indicated in Table 1, these modal concerns specify four dimensions of personal and group growth. These concerns generate intrinsic forces that reduce the concerns and produce personal and group movement. The categories are in no sense discrete, but are highly interdependent.

The *acceptance* concern has to do with the formation of trust and acceptance of self and of others, the reduction of fear of self and of others, and the consequent growth of confidence. This concern becomes differentiated into concerns about degrees of *membership* in the various groups of which the person is a part. The *data*-flow concern has to do with the flow of feeling and perceptual data through the person or through the group; the system output of behavioral

[1] The theory is derived from (a) a continuing program of laboratory and field experimentation conducted between 1937 and 1956 at Brigham Young University, Michigan State University, and the University of Colorado, and from (b) a concurrent and subsequent series of field studies conducted in industrial and organizational settings. A major share of the research has been financed through a series of grants from the Group Psychology Branch of the Office of Naval Research. The theory, certain derivations from the theory, supporting empirical studies, and applications to problems in teaching, child rearing, and management are presented in detail in a forthcoming publication by Jack R. Gibb and Lorraine M. Gibb titled *Participative Action*. Credit is given in the publication to the many colleagues and students who participated in the formation of the theory. We are particularly indebted to many insights contributed by Professor M. Wilford Poulson. It was through the help of his insights that we arrived at the concept of the genetic antecedence and functional prepotence of data processing and goal formation over leader control in the formation of group structure. This concept forms a basic postulate of the theory and led us to the experimentation on "leaderless" groups.

Table 1   Modal Concerns in Group Development

Primary Modal Concerns	Derivative Modal Concerns	Symptoms of Unresolved Concern	Symptoms of Resolved Concern
Acceptance	Membership	Fear Distrust	Acceptance Trust
Data	Decision	Polite façade Caution strategy	Spontaneity Process feedback
Goal	Productivity	Apathy Competition	Creative work or play
Control	Organization	Dependency Counterdependency	Interdependence Role distribution

cues and all communicative evidence of attitudes, feelings, and perceptions; and the system input of such data. This concern finds its expression in *decision* making and choice behavior in the group. The *goal*-formation concern has to do with the continuing assessment of intrinsic motivations in the person or the group and the integration of motivations at various levels into action sequences, problem solving, and decision making. This concern becomes differentiated into a concern about *productivity*, about doing work, having fun, creating ideas, learning, or growing. The *control* dimension has to do with intrapersonal and interpersonal control or regulatory mechanisms that lead to coordinated sequences of behavior in the person, sequential flow of behavior in the group, formation of roles and expectancies, and integration of function into structure at all levels of social behavior. This process becomes a concern about *organization*, which, in the sense we are using the term, has all degrees of formality, stability, awareness, and complexity in all variety of social relationships.

The Modal Concerns as Methodological Tools. These four concerns are the continually recurring themes or processes of all groups. They are modal in the sense of being the most common concerns of the greatest number of group members at the time of analysis. The concerns exist at all levels of awareness. A member may have deeply unconscious or barely subliminal fears about self-adequacy or distrusts of self and others (acceptance concern). He may have a deep sense of depersonalization and isolation from the groups in which he has ambivalence about membership (data concern). The member may feel a loss of identity, a feeling of not knowing who he is or what he wants from life (goal concern). He could develop a deep feeling that he cannot get himself to do what he wants to do or exert any significant influence on the world of which he is a part (control concern).

The concerns pervade all interpersonal relationships. At other, more conscious, levels of awareness a person may build elaborate checks and balances in his social world to keep from accepting full membership (acceptance concern); deliberately distort his output of feelings and thoughts to maintain personal or corporate images (data concern); engage in frenetic off-target work in an effort to find himself or to keep from finding himself (goal concern); or engage in various kinds of personable or persuasive behavior to get others to conform to his control demands (control concern).

In groups and organizations one sees the rise and persistence of inspection systems, policing functions, and membership regulations (acceptance concern); of parliamentary rules and an elaborate grapevine (data concern); or merit badges and work incentive systems (goal concern); and of committee chairmen, organization charts, and job specification sheets (control concern).

There is some evidence for the methodological usefulness of this four-unit categorization:

1. The concerns are apparently universal in occurrence in work, action, training, and therapy groups. They continually recur in the verbal and nonverbal behavior of group members.

2. The categories show a relatively good fit with categories of mental health and personality development as seen in the clinical literature (cf. Table 2).

3. Experimental manipulation of each of the four major variables seems to produce increments or decrements in group effectiveness.

4. Our studies of group growth indicate that significant changes occur along each of the four dimensions with prolonged training or therapy.

5. Examination of the anthropological studies of group behavior and organizational structure indicates the prevalence of these four concerns.

6. Handling of the concern by a group is frequently accompanied by high emotionality, neurotic persistence, or neurotic denial.

7. The categories have high validity for trainees in group therapy, group education, or group training.

8. The categories have face validity for naïve group members, who

can easily identify, from their own experiences, instances of change along each of the four dimensions.

The Contingency Hierarchy. Our studies strongly suggest a consistent genetic sequence in the rise of the four concerns in social structure. The deepest and earliest concerns arise in the following order: acceptance, data-flow, goal formation, and control. Development of each factor in this order seems to facilitate subsequent development of the other factors. Growth of all social structure occurs as a concurrent and interdependent development on each of the four dimensions, but optimal growth occurs when the factors "lead" one another in the optimal sequence. The basic order of development is often camouflaged at the phenotypical or manifest level. For example, immediate attempts at handling the control function arise out of distrust and are essentially directed at resolution of the acceptance concern. Early attempts at goal setting may be strategies to manipulate the flow of data and are made sensible when seen as attempts at resolution of the data-flow concern.

Growth in each dimension is contingent upon growth in each of the dimensions higher in the hierarchy. Each factor in the hierarchy provides a pace-setting or boundary function for the factors lower in the hierarchy. Thus, data-flow is possible only within the limits of trust formation. A free flow of data is possible only with antecedent or concurrent reduction of distrusts and fears. Defense mechanisms and organizational demands prevent functional processing of data beyond the trust limits. A person can look at his goals only as he begins to trust himself. This growing self-trust makes self-awareness possible. Integration of group goals occurs only as rapidly as members build sufficient trust and awareness to verbalize openly their intrinsic goals. Premature goal formulation beyond the trust and data boundaries leads to unrealistic, overaspirational, or formalized goals, the pursuit or lack of pursuit of which leads to apathy or various other forms of resistance. Stable and functional organizational structure is possible only as goals have been achieved through adequate reality processing of data within the trust boundaries of the organization. In the early stages of group growth, organization is maintained by an appropriate degree of formalization of control mechanisms, imposition of extrinsic goals, filtering of the communication system, and checks and balances appropriate to the trust level. In the later stages of group growth, the organization, growing from a free flow of data in relatively high trust, becomes spontaneously generated through integration of intrinsic motivations. In early stages of organization, the structure is to some degree maintained by fear, strategy, persuasion, and power. In later stages, the structure comes to be maintained by trust, reality-data, intrinsic motivations, and interdependence of roles.

ACCEPTANCE. It became dramatically evident in our early experimentation with groups that members come with unresolved feelings of fear and distrust. These feelings are often denied and deeply buried. Sometimes they are fairly near the surface. They are apparently rooted in lack of acceptance of the self and consequent lack of acceptance of others. The façades produced by socialization make it difficult for a person to find himself, accept himself, or trust himself.

One sees many symptoms of distrust, particularly in the early stages of group formation: persistent defense of one's public image, attempts to change attitudes and beliefs of others, attempts to make decisions for others, avoidance of feeling, avoidance of conflict, advice giving, flattery, cynicism about the powers of the group, derogation of the group's abilities, maintenance of formality in behavior and in control mechanisms, lack of confidence in the product of the group, and denial of membership. In action groups where distrust is strong, one sees insistence upon control, rigid preplanning of the group agenda, preservation of social distance, or fear of controversy.

Under the frequent defense-productive climates in social groups, members and leaders maintain fear and distrust. Lacking confidence in what the group can do, they try to find strong or expert leaders. Fearing the exposure that comes from informality and intimate social action, they insist upon formal rules. Believing that "familiarity breeds contempt," they insist that things be kept on an impersonal basis. Feeling that the group cannot be trusted to make progress on its own, they try to set up rigid procedural specifications. Assuming that other members cannot make decisions for themselves, they attempt to persuade, influence, and control the beliefs of others. Feeling that they will be unable to handle conflict and chaos, they appoint strong leaders to whom they assign the critical functions of problem solving and group maintenance.

The problem of acceptance becomes further differentiated into a concern for membership in the group. Individuals become concerned with the questions of how they can attain membership, how they can be heard, how they can be seen as important by the other members. With productive work in certain social situations, persons earn membership by coming to lose their fears of one another and to trust one another in the situation. With process awareness in group training or therapy, members come to find that membership is a matter of fear reduction and trust formation. Experiences which produce trust tend to reduce the incidence of the symptoms cited above.

DATA-FLOW. After a T Group has attempted to move in some direction and has thwarted itself to some degree, it runs into a complex problem that is largely buried beneath the surface of natural groups. This is the problem of finding out how group members feel, how they see things, and what their attitudes are about the relevant concerns of the group. How do we know what we want to do? Even if we as individuals know our own intrinsic motivations, how do we find out what others think and what their motivations are?

A kind of datalessness is present in most natural work groups that finds expression in many symptoms. The process of socialization produces a façade which camouflages data output. Members develop many mannerisms for covering up feelings and perceptions. They deny feelings, flatter others, speak with artificial politeness, show great concern over hurting someone's feelings, and engage in much polite "weather" talk. With socialization, people develop great skills at covering up data output. Data input is also reduced under the defensive climates of ordinary living. People who are defensive produce their own screens that prevent them from seeing the data that are present, and from responding to the cues that do exist.

Under the extrinsic control systems of high-defense groups, people often do not find out that they lack data. When groups make decisions, they make inappropriate assumptions, such as "silence means consent," or that the reverse is true. Such assumptions lead to inadequate data-flow, which, in turn, causes groups to continue to operate with partial efficiency or without knowledge that they are operating with partial efficiency. When, through some form of data collection, the group finds out some of the previously hidden data, a partial paralysis often slows down the group efficiency while the members learn how to handle the new data and the complacency shock which comes from the realization that unseen and relevant data were present all the time.

With training and growth, the group learns to collect data more effectively. In varying degrees people can learn to listen, to express feelings and perceptions with candor and honesty, to be somewhat more spontaneous in their actions, and to integrate emotionality into work.

The problem of data processing ramifies into the problem of decision making and choice. Indeed, it is usually in the process of making decisions that the group becomes aware that data are inadequate for the purposes toward which the group is marshaling force. The group becomes concerned with how decisions are made, how members feel about various alternatives that arise, and how members can produce other verbalized alternatives.

With group development, these symptoms are reduced and data become more adequately processed.

GOAL. Groups soon find that people will not accept goals imposed by others. Groups find that goals must be created in interaction. An early problem in group formation is the determination of joint goals. What do we want to work at? What do we want to do? Can we find something that we want to do together? The more freedom that is allowed to the group, the more blurred this problem becomes and the more clear the magnitude of it.

There are many signs of the existence of this unresolved concern in groups. In natural groups, goals are always to some degree imposed by leaders or peers. People impose goals upon others by various coercive or persuasive methods. People who have only partial commitment to joint purposes are often apathetic or bored. Others may work from a sense of duty or loyalty to the leaders, to friends in the group, or to the general aims of the group. People who work from such extrinsic motivations may engage in spurts of frenetic activity, perhaps to "get it over with" or perhaps to show themselves that they are loyal, competitive, or "good members" of the organization.

In natural, high-defense groups, a fabric of external controls is often imposed by administering extrinsic rewards in the forms of grades, money, approval, or other kudos. Activity under extrinsic motivation is less than full commitment of the person to the task. In T Groups, where people are forced by the nature of the social contract to examine goals and to *create* goals, as it were, the fragile nature of the extrinsic commitments is revealed.

Groups, because they are unable to assess own motivations, will ask the trainer to give them goals. Lacking visible and verbalized common goals, they may decide to do something "just to get something done." Like the airline pilot in the popular joke, they may not be sure where they are going but they are making good speed getting there. People have acquired the habit of working—to be working. Once the group has made the decision to move in some direction it may then proceed to move but may show many signs of passive resistance in the form of out-of-field activity, whispering, irrelevant debate, or semantic quibbling.

Derived from the concern about purpose is the problem of being productive. What is productivity for us? How can we grow, be creative, learn, achieve something related to our intrinsic selves? What are we? and What do we want out of life? are questions to which the unresolved answers cause tension and concern. That people have not achieved for themselves an adequate working solution to these questions is revealed in the chaotic escape work that they create when given freedom in the T Group.

Natural groups and T Groups may achieve, with growth, a kind of development to the state where the group is engaged in sustained, meaningful, and creative activity which is close to the intrinsic motivations of the participants. High interest and greater spread of participation accompany this kind of work. External controls or rewards in the form of competition or trainer-approval are not necessary under these circumstances and, indeed, have little effect upon performance.

CONTROL. Early in the T Group, the members become confronted with the problems of exerting influence in the group. "How can I exert some control over what happens?" "How can I control my own impulses and internal forces?" "How can I influence others in the group?"

This problem grows into the problem of organization. "How can we organize to do what we want to do?" "Supposing we have found out our purposes through adequate data processing, how can we exert control over one another and the forces we produce through our interaction?"

In a very real sense, the control problem disappears when data-collection and interpersonal-acceptance problems are solved. When people are doing what they want to do, know that they are doing what they want to do, and have developed some trust and acceptance in the group situation, the control and organization problems become relatively simple or disappear.

Indications that there are unresolved control problems in the group are prevalent in natural groups as well as in T Groups. People who have unresolved control concerns will engage in various persuasive methods for controlling others: advice giving, debate, argument, or constructive fight. A power struggle may develop among members who desire to have things move their way or enjoy leadership, control, or power. Strategies for manipulation may be developed. These may follow rules of debate and be in the open or may be developed by subgroups outside the total group. People may appeal to the leader or trainer to control them. People may fight all forms of control and rather enjoy the luxury of lack of organization.

As groups develop, signs of resolving the concerns occur. Problem-solving roles become distributed in the group and may arise spontaneously in response to immediate problem-solving needs. Conflict may disappear, or may become more productive and directed toward problem solution. Activity may become more smoothly regulated. Regulatory functions in the group are performed more effectively. Interdependence is increased.

Group Development

Implicit in the foregoing section is a theory of group development. The critical dimensions upon which groups change are specified by the four modal concerns. As suggested in Table 2, growth is an interdependent process. As persons develop, they are better able to participate in group growth. Persons are better able to grow when they are attaining membership in a developing group. This is not to say that healthy individuals necessarily produce healthy groups or that a healthy group necessarily produces healthy individuals. In the natural state, individuals and groups are in the processes of change. Healthy individuals and groups show directionality in this change—interdependent movement along the four dimensions specified.

Table 2   Dimensions in Group and Personal Growth

Primary Modal Concerns	Derivative Modal Concerns	Signs of Personal Growth	Signs of Group Growth
Acceptance	Membership	Acceptance of self and others	Supportive climate, climate of trust
Data	Decision	Spontaneity, awareness	Reality communication, functional feedback
Goal	Productivity	Integration, directionality	Goal integration, tractability level
Control	Organization	Interdependence	Interdependence, participative action and structure

Many theorists have made analogies describing the process of group formation as a spiral, a series of cycles, or a series of stages which succeed one another as new phases occur in growth. Our studies suggest that group growth is no more saltatory than individual growth. What seems most likely is that group growth is a gradualistic and global process, in which themes and subthemes may intertwine but in which the dramatic quality is the wholeness, or the *Gestalt*. The modal concerns we describe are products of analysis—methodological tools which simplify the task of the diagnostician but bring an artifactitious quality to the flow of processes in the developing group. To say that there are probably no *stages* of development is not to say that there are no consistent sequential changes in looking at groups over a time span. In the Colorado studies, for example, we brought both naïve and trained observers in to observe the third and fifty-eighth hours of the T Groups. All observers agreed on the presence of dramatic changes on the four modal dimensions. In contrast to this high agreement, there was low interobserver agreement in identifying interim "stages" of growth on the four dimensions.

In the last section, we saw certain symptoms of immature groups in early stages of formation. The symptoms of what a theoretical model of a mature group might be are difficult to predict. According to our theory, such a group would have optimal interpersonal trust and acceptance, functional feedback of all relevant data, creative activity that was satisfying intrinsic motivations, and an interdependent function and structure. Bennis (see Chapter 9) has done a careful and helpful job of describing many of the changes that often take place along the control dimension during group development. Space prevents our detailing in a similar way the changes that take place along the other three dimensions.[2]

Analysis of the tapes and coded observations of the T Groups on the Office of Naval Research program indicates that change on some of the dimensions does occur in all cases. It is impossible from our data for us to build at this point a completely satisfying sequential model. It does seem clear that, in some groups, change is in cyclic or spiral form, with movement back and forth across dimensions. In other groups, change seems to proceed in dramatic and unpredictable spurts. In other groups, long periods pass with either regressive movement or plateaus of no progress, with occasional dramatic spurts at the end. Most of the data we have are on groups of two or three weeks' duration, making a total of 20 to 30 hours in group time. In some cases,

[2] An attempt is made in *Participative Action* to spell out in detail the changes that occur on all four dimensions.

our Colorado groups continued for as long as 240 hours, over a period of nine months. In all cases, groups that continued for over 60 hours made significant progress on the measures we used.

Major symptoms of what a hypothetical group in a high state of development might be are presented in Table 2. Elaborations and additional symptoms are presented in the paragraphs below and are summarized in Table 6. The symptoms are all derived from our observations of groups that had been under intensive T-Group training for more than 60 hours. Not all symptoms were present in all groups in comparable degree. The statements made below represent extrapolations from empirical data and are characteristic of what a composite, idealized model would be. The language problems here are very difficult, and the statements made below represent a high degree of abstraction from the operational data coming from the various research instruments.

ACCEPTANCE. Groups with high acceptance show a reduction of fear and distrust. There is a reduction of humor and an increase of warmth that are perceived by members as genuine and often characterized as "nothing like what I have seen before." Deviations from the norm are accepted, often encouraged. There is a high amount of confidence in the ability of the group, with minimal concern about comparing the group with other groups.

DATA-FLOW. Communication is free and open. Data are available for processing and use by members. Expert resources in and out of the group are used in problem solving or action. Conflict is recognized, dealt with, and used in problem solving or creative action. Feedback is used to continually modify goal formation and decision making. People are tolerant of interruptions and deviations. Activities are related to goals or can be made to be so. A person with the data can be heard. Decisions in the group are based upon processed data. Methodological and technological decisions are made by consensus or near-consensus. Decisions can be reversed with focus on new data.

GOAL. When the concerns about purpose and productivity have been appreciably resolved, there is a high degree of goal integration. People who have been able to integrate their many intrinsic goals into a common goal show purposeful, meaningful, and creative work or productivity. Conflict at various levels is minimal. Goals are explicit and verbalized, and they change as the tasks become accomplished. An optimal number of people are interested in the ongoing activity of the group and can change the direction of the group when this no longer becomes the case. The intrinsic goals of individuals are tied in with the goals of the group, or should they cease to be so meshed, the individual is free to leave the group, temporarily or permanently, depending upon the nature of the group role-prescriptions. People are learning, growing, and changing.

CONTROL. Legitimate influence is easily exerted. There is optimal interchangeability of critical roles in the group. The power structure is relatively open and manageable and varies in nature with expertness, the nature of the problem, and the nature of the situation. There is an optimal distribution of member roles at any cross-sectional analysis of group activity. Organization is relatively spontaneous and occurs in response to the needs of the problem. Organization is easily changed. There is maximal flow of communication. Formal channeling is not necessary in problem solving. Control is exerted by the nature of the goal, the intrinsic motivations, and the objectives of the group. There is a participative structure.

Because of the changing nature of the external environment of groups and the demands of new goals as these become differentiated, there is no single readily visible organizational format that is preferable to another. For instance, formal appointment of a leader or recorder makes little difference in the role interdependence called for by the demands of data processing, goal formation, and problem solving. Many organizational functions disappear. Conventional concepts of span of control, channeling of information, and group composition seem to be appropriate to high-defense groups, and less appropriate and perhaps dysfunctional in more mature groups.

Growth of the Person

Implicit in the material already presented is a theory of personality development. The critical dimensions of growth of the personality are assumed to be those identified by the four primary modal concerns. The primary block to continuing personal growth lies in the defense level—in the lack of acceptance by the person of himself and of other persons. Significant progress along each dimension makes possible or directs change in the lower dimensions on the contingency hierarchy.

In building an informal theory of change, we have examined the clinical literature on personality growth, analyzed interviews of individuals undergoing group training, and made logical extrapolations of the processes we noted in training groups. Our four dimensions are a tentative "best fit" of all these observations.

The healthy personality has growing awareness of himself and of his own motivations and can live with this awareness. Just as he accepts himself, it is possible for him to accept others and to trust them. He is able to attain and to accept membership in mature groups. He permits others to deviate from his own attitudes and ideas without strong needs to change them. As a father, teacher, or manager, he is able to be permissive, accepting. He is able to love himself and is free to love others.

The healthy person is able to behave with spontaneity. In doing so, he participates with others in giving and receiving data. The spontaneous person can act interdependently by being an effective participant-observer. He is able to integrate input of data into his actions *as he acts* and to modify his actions with feedback. He maintains his person, with integrity and unity, but communicates openly with others. He expresses feelings, perceptions, and attitudes freely when relevant to the dyadic or group situation to which he gives membership. There is low disparity between his inner thoughts and his verbalized speech. He is able to act spontaneously without undue concern as to how his speech will be heard—without undue concern for his social image. There is high congruity between the self-image and the image others have of him. He can make interpersonal and intrapersonal decisions with relative ease because of the free flow of data relevant to such decisions. He is thus able to live with reality with minimal need to distort reality.

The healthy person has a high degree of integration of needs and actions at all levels of awareness. The multiple aspects of the person are in optimal congruence. He has minimal intrapersonal conflict. He is able to determine his own intrinsic motivations, to create new ones as he grows, and to find a work life and a play life that will maximize his intrinsic growth patterns. He is able to work effectively with others to create group goals that will be actualizing for himself and for the others. Because growth is a process of change, this process of integration or congruity is never static. As the person grows, his intrinsic motivations change. But as they change he is able to attain new memberships and seek new activities, goals, or jobs.

The healthy person can participate with others in solving problems, without an undue expenditure of energy either in depending upon others or in fighting them in counterdependent ways. He imposes his own controls from within with a minimum of external controls. He can live with the authority problem. He works well in joint inquiry and joint problem solving, as well as in independent inquiry. He is flexible in roles he can take. He works well with or without organizational structure.

Persuasive and Participative Models of Action

As has been seen, group formation occurs as a continuing set of solutions to the problems deriving from the four focal concerns of acceptance, data, goal, and control. A person who attains or is given a focal role in the group formation (e.g., father, teacher, manager, or trainer) tends to develop some consistencies in his technology of operation in the group. The "theory" he uses is based upon some more or less systematic set of attitudes, beliefs, and assumptions about group formation, person formation, and his relationship to such formation. For purposes of our analysis, we have distinguished two clusters of theories about group leadership or management.

One technology, the "persuasive technology," tends to arise predictably and somewhat systematically when a group has failed to make great movements on the acceptance dimension. When the group has made great progress on the acceptance dimension, another technology, the "participative," tends to arise. In practice, of course, fathers, teachers, managers, and trainers tend to exhibit mixed and inconsistent technologies. We are concerned with certain predictions that can be made from such a systematic treatment of leadership technology and have derived a theory of trainer-behavior from this analysis.

As indicated in Tables 3 and 5, the persuasion technology is defined by certain clusters of behavior which arise as resolutions of the focal concern problems. The behavior of the manager is derived from fear, distrust, and lack of confidence in the capacities, attitudes, and maturity of the members of the group. Resolutions of the other three concerns arise out of this distrust and fear. In handling the purpose and productivity concerns, the manager or father tends to use command, persuasion, influence, guidance, or training in an effort to give motivations to members of the group and to influence productivity (learning, work, or growth). Thus educators tend to try to develop appropriate goals in the student and to train students to become creative, to learn, and to be effective according to the preconceived model viewed by the teacher. The parent attempts to get the child to be conscientious, loving, ambitious, or to fit into the culture of the group as the parent sees it. The trainer tends to motivate the group members to look at themselves and to want to change. Under this technology,

Table 3   Early, "Persuasive" Technologies in Groups

Modal Concern	Entry Behavior	Reaction in Group
Acceptance (Membership)	Fear Distrust	Façade building Cynicism, suspicion
Data (Decision)	Strategy Façade	Circumvention Distortion
Goal (Productivity)	Manipulation Persuasion	Apathy, flight Suspicion, cynicism
Control (Organization)	Control Bargaining	Dependency Hostility

Table 4   Later, "Participative" Technologies in Groups

Modal Concern	Entry Behavior	Reaction in Group
Acceptance (Membership)	Confidence Trust	Trust Diversity, exploitation
Data (Decision)	Openness Spontaneity	Feedback, exposure Consensus potential
Goal (Productivity)	Self-assessment Problem solving	Ego strength Creativity
Control (Organization)	Permissiveness Interdependence	Participative form Participative function

Table 5   Reactions to Persuasive Technologies

Modal Concern	Persuasive Mode of Entry	Modal Reactions to Persuasive Technologies (Symptoms of Unresolved Concerns)
Acceptance (Membership)	Fear Distrust	Distrust and accompanying denial Fears of personal inadequacy Legalism; quibbling Resistance to initiation of action Bartering of personability; "polite" behavior Atrophy of affection Concern over motives Paranoia; suspicion; cynicism Concern over inclusion; protective pairing Controls; reporting requirements Specificity of channeling and structure Conformity; rituals; restriction of range of behavior
Data (Decision)	Strategy Secrecy Communication downward	Ambiguity; maximization of projection Strategy; gimmicks, tricks Fear of the unknown Façade building; secrecy Distortion of data through channels Caution; pretense; protective phraseology False assumptions; inadequate theory Extremes in slow or rapid decision making Circumvention; grapevine behavior Deceit; dishonesty; intrapersonal disparities Increased communication downward, with screening Rise of suppression skills
Goal (Productivity)	Manipulation of extrinsic motivations	Apathy, flight; withdrawal Resistance, passive or active Increased use of extrinsic rewards Increased approval and status needs Low commitment; overaspiration Extreme of frenetic or apathetic work Persuasion; advice; "helping" or changing others Manipulation; coercion Competition; rivalry; jealousy; favoritism Need for structure or personal leaders Displaced feelings of responsibility Atrophy of self; loss of identity; stereotypy Intrapersonal conflict "Pumping" of motivation by interpersonal conflict
Control (Organization)	High control Persuasion Guidance	Chaos; disorganization; cynicism about control Dependency; regressive behavior Counterdependency; resistance to control Hostility, often latent or consciously masked Power struggles; fight; symbolic fight; debate Bargaining; limited war Status and power concerns Formalization of rules and structure Concerns about leadership Formal job prescriptions, organizational positioning Allocation of work through power or barter

goal determination and assessment of motivation are usually done by the manager, teacher, or trainer.

In handling the data-flow concerns, the persuasion technologist is likely to use a "strategy" of some kind. He tends to make decisions about and to control the data output or input within the system. He tends to use various strategies in order to make decisions palatable or understood. He may initiate a great deal of clear communication downward in order to be sure that the policies of management, the teaching aims, or the trainer philosophy is clear to the members of the group. Under stress this technician will become more secretive. More planning will be done in private before working with the group.

The persuasion technologist uses varying degrees of control from the top in handling the organizational problem of the group. The father, teacher, or trainer acts in such a way as to maintain the dependency of the members. Under crisis the organization tends to become more formal. Lines of authority become more clear. Channels are specified. Job prescriptions and role specifications become increasingly formalized. Control of organizational functions is maintained by the leader. This process becomes more formalized with crisis and becomes modified greatly in the flow of everyday work. The control becomes more hidden and subtle and may become more palatable as things go more smoothly in the group.

In contrast with this persuasion technology is a "participative" technology, which is defined by the resolution of the four focal concern problems that are listed in Table 6. With personal growth and group growth come greater trust and respect in the group relationship—greater acceptance of self and others within the group. This trust and acceptance tend to be accompanied by another cluster of behaviors in response to movement on the other three dimensions. In the extreme manifestation of this theory, individuals in the group are allowed great freedom to assess their own goals, determine their own intrinsic motivations, and decide their own directions for learning, productivity, and creativity.

The participative technologist tends to develop open and free communication and decision making. In the extreme instance, all planning is done in or in front of the group. The group itself makes all decisions. A maximum of communication of feelings and perceptions goes through the system on all matters relevant to group locomotion and progress. The leader encourages spontaneous action, expresses his own feelings and perceptions easily, and acts in such a way as to permit optimal flow of data within the system. Interdependence is achieved through interaction in high acceptance, intrinsic goal forma-

Table 6   Reactions to Participative Technologies

Modal Concern	Participative Mode of Entry	Modal Reactions to Participative Technologies (Symptoms of Resolved Concerns)
Acceptance (Membership)	Confidence Trust	Trust and acceptance of distrust Greater feeling of personal adequacy Acceptance of legitimate influence Positive affect toward members Diversity and nonconformity Acceptance of motives of others Easy expression of feeling and conflict Façade reduction Acceptance of idiosyncratic behavior Controls over processes, not people
Data (Decision)	Openness Spontaneity Communication, all directions	Clarity; minimization of defense Problem-solving behavior Trust; reduction of suspicion Increased feedback upward Freedom of movement outside channels Reduction of intrapersonal disparities Open expression of feeling and conflict Increased permeability of boundaries Façade reduction
Goal (Productivity)	Problem solving Freedom for self-assessment	Work orientation Visibility of intrinsic motivations Reduction of competitive behavior Reduction of conflict Creativity in sustained work Increased involvement in tasks Reduction of apathy Reduced need for work structure Diversity of behavior and attitude Increasing congruence between work and play Reduced potency of extrinsic rewards Nonconformity High personal identity; ego strength
Control (Organization)	Permissiveness Interdependence Freedom of form	Interdependence Diversity and nonconformity Fluidity of organization Greater unpredictability of behavior Reduced latent hostility Allocation of work by consensus or ability Reduction of symbolic fight Open expression of feeling and conflict Informality Spontaneity of form Reduced concern over organization form

tion, and maximum freedom of data processing. The organization becomes as free and as informal as trust, size, and other relevant factors permit. Formalities of communication systems and of inter-role responsibility systems are determined by needs of coordination and data-flow rather than by needs for control, distrust, power, or strategy. These two ideal models are logical constructions which are derived

from experiment and empirical observation, followed by logical extrapolations of what seem to be the relevant dimensions in group and
personal development.   The relevant and critical dimensions of personal growth seem to be acceptance, spontaneity, integration, and interdependence.   The relevant dimensions of growth of groups seem to be
in the direction of supportive climate, reality communication and feedback, maximal goal integration, and functional interdependence in action and structure.

The T-Group Trainer

The theory of T-Group behavior that we are proposing is that the
trainer approximate the participative technology as closely as it is
possible for him to do at whatever state of personal growth he has
achieved along the four basic dimensions of growth.   In a sense, then,
the trainer who wishes to be maximally helpful should be as trusting,
as open, as permissive, and as interdependent as he is able to be.   Each
trainer will have a band-of-experimentation area in which he is making provisional attempts to adapt his own behavior to his intrinsic
need system.   Experimentation in an atmosphere of some degree of
trust and warmth, with process orientation, allows the trainer, within
his own limitations of growth, to become progressively more trusting,
open, permissive, and interdependent.

The trainer's permissiveness and trust are tested in situations of
crisis: a severe emotional breakdown; a bitterly hostile, personal attack by one member or another; prolonged periods when the group
seems to be working on something that the trainer does not feel leads
to learning; or strong dependence demands for the leader to solve the
problem for the group.   The taped analysis of the training behavior
of a number of T-Group trainers indicates that, irrespective of the
verbalized philosophy of the trainer, trainers differ greatly in their behavior under such crisis.   Some trainers jump in readily to protect
weak members, caution the group about dangers ahead, and exhibit
many aspects of persuasive technology.   There are strong reality-based
factors which determine fears and distrusts, but, in general, there is a
tendency for experienced trainers to become more trusting, accepting,
permissive, open, and freedom giving.   Each trainer must evaluate the
forces in the situation as best he can and behave as consistently as he
can with the theory that he is evolving.

Our many years of experience with "leaderless" groups in various settings lead us to feel that maximum participative behavior is attained more readily in training groups without trainers than with trainers. The groups are perhaps more aptly described as "leaderful," in that what occurs is not an abolition of leadership but a distribution of leadership roles in the group. It is perhaps even more accurate to describe the participative groups as "trainerless." Members learn to observe and to experiment upon their own behavior in increasingly creative ways. They learn that it is less adaptive to take a "trainer stance," that is, to advise, "help," teach, change, or persuade others. As one member put it: "I found that I came here to teach the others, and I learned to try to learn rather than to teach."

Trainerless groups are optimally effective when significant norm-inducing activities occur in the total training community that produce a participative and supportive climate for provisional learning. As the educational literature indicates, trainerless groups in other educational climates are often notably unsuccessful.

The evidence that trainerless groups, under certain conditions, produce notable change in the participants does not necessarily constitute evidence that a persuasion technology cannot be made to work as effectively as a participative technology. There are other, less direct, indications that a persuasion technology is not so effective. One of the assumptions of the theory is that there is maximal congruence between participative technology and personal growth. The technologist also grows maximally under this kind of technology. The persuasion technologist not only inhibits the growth of others but inhibits his own growth along the four dimensions cited above.

Trainer Behavior and Concern-Reduction

The theory presented in this paper has been used in a variety of settings: classrooms, industrial groups, community groups, and T Groups of various kinds. The relevance of the theory to T Groups was tested by analyzing sequential trends in T Groups conducted in various settings by a variety of trainers with different training styles. Various kinds of data were obtained from samplings of tapes or coded observations of 114 T Groups in which one or more trainers were present and active. Forty-nine of these groups were observed at various laboratories conducted by the National Training Laboratories; 43 in various industrial settings; 22 student and adult groups in the University of Colorado studies. Data from these trainer groups were compared with similar kinds of data obtained at the University of Colorado on 66 groups in which trainers were not present.[3]

The evidence is abundantly clear from these studies that, whether or not a trainer is present, groups work on the four primary modal concerns and the four derivative modal concerns listed in Table 1. The analysis of the trainer-group tapes indicates that some trainer behaviors are associated with group growth and personal learning and that some behaviors are associated with apparent reduction of such growth and learning. Because of the inadequacy of our measurements, it is not possible at this point to specify all of the helpful behaviors, but it is possible to draw some guide lines and to make suggestions to T-Group trainers. T-Group trainers can become problems in themselves just as can other members. Inexpert trainers do little harm and often are useful sources of data, because groups learn to handle such problems as they handle other member-problems. The suggestions that follow have been helpful in the training of T-Group trainers in industry and in student leadership training.

Building Acceptance. There are many evidences of fear and distrust that may appear in the trainer's attitudes and behaviors: feelings that he can let the group go only so far in chaos before he "bails them out"; feelings that his role is to protect the weaker members who might become hurt in the interaction; feelings that he is irreplaceable—that, without him, members would remain involved in unproductive "content" discussion or get into damaging therapeutic areas; feelings that only qualified professionals may become trainers; or feelings that he must set up a strategy or training plan before the group meets in order to guarantee group progress or individual learning. As with all fears and distrusts, these trainer concerns have bases in relative degrees of reality. With experience in T Groups, with greater acceptance of himself and others, the trainer can learn to reduce these fears and distrusts to a minimum.

Each person is limited by his own acquired and changing trust boundary. The trainer learns to be as trusting and loving as *he* can be

---

[3] Sixty-six of the eighty-eight T Groups used in the University of Colorado studies were "leaderless" in the sense that no leader or trainer was present in the groups. Between the years 1949 and 1956 various kinds of data were gathered on 1,144 students and adult members of these trainerless groups. The analysis of the data was financed by the Group Psychology Branch of the Office of Naval Research, and the research is reported in Jack R. Gibb, "Effects of Norm-Centered Training Upon Individual and Institutional Behavior." Mimeographed paper presented at the American Psychological Association annual meetings, September 1, 1958.

—as accepting as his level of personal growth permits. He must learn how trusting he is able to be in all groups and in each special group. As he becomes more trusting, he can free himself to become more spontaneous, more interdependent, and more freedom-giving. A training tool that we have found helpful is to suggest that the trainer imagine, in any conversation that he has with any group member or with another trainer, that the conversation is being taped for eventual playback to the group in question. When he first attempts this, he will find that his spontaneous comments are filled with evidences of his own distrust. Particularly prevalent in the talk of beginning trainers are remarks derogating the abilities and attitudes of group members, humor directed at ineptness of members, and clinical or personal analysis of the latent motivational structure of members. As the trainer begins to process these data about his own self-acceptance, he is working on his own personal growth. As he becomes more accepting, he is better able to behave spontaneously in a way that would allow his taped conversations to be fed back to the group. He can learn to be trusting, spontaneous, open, and interdependent with the T Group.

In our seven-year span of experimentation with leaderless groups at the University of Colorado, we were initially highly concerned about the effects of allowing a class of 60 college students to work in T Groups with no trainers, supervision, faculty controls, or standard curriculum, and we were especially concerned about all the forces of faculty and administrative disapproval of such a process. We therefore built in some controls on attendance, gave weekly demonstrations of training methods, and specified numerous data-gathering instruments (questionnaires, reaction sheets, observer forms) that groups were required to fill out before, during, or after each group session. The staff tabulated and fed these data back to the groups on the day following data collection. As we became less fearful and more trusting, we gradually experimented with reduced controls. We found that groups tended to take over direction of their own processes and to move more quickly along the dimensions of growth when given greatest freedom and least prescribed structure. Groups built their own attendance norms and reduced absence to nearly zero as they arrived at group-generated goals. Groups found they needed data and constructed their own instruments, which were in many cases more imaginative and certainly more relevant to emergent daily concerns than were the instruments provided by the staff in earlier years. Groups organized for work built internal and distributive leadership structure and worked with interpersonal data that were more significant and at greater depth than those dealt with in conventional trainer groups.

This experimentation led us to develop a great deal of confidence and trust in the abilities of a group of people to handle their own process problems in a significant way when given support and freedom. In other words, through experimentation we learned along the same modal dimensions as did group members. As we became more clear as to our own intrinsic motivations, our own purposes became clear to the group. Groups learned to trust staff aims. Greater productivity occurred in terms of learning outcomes. A continuing series of experiments, financed by the ONR grant through the seven years, indicated clearly that groups in later years made significantly greater gains in learnings than did groups in earlier years. Group members learned, for example, that staff motivations were not to change them but to allow them to create the conditions under which they might make their own decisions about change. Our intrinsic motivations changed as we learned more about the processes of learning and growth. With greater trust, we were then able to try trainerless groups in community and industrial settings, with even greater success in terms of measurable learning outcomes.

Working on the Membership Concern. The problem of membership for the trainer is similar in kind to the problem of membership for other group members. Differential expectations and role demands make the trainer a special person at the beginning of training. Members have special concerns about his omnipotence, his manipulativeness, and his wishes. The trainer can be helpful if he offers to the group, for data processing, his perceptions and feelings about his membership. His own self-role prescriptions increase his membership problems. As he learns skills and attitudes appropriate to interdependency he can work more effectively with the group in resolving membership concerns.

Data Processing and Decision Making. Groups find early that available data are inadequate for decision making and group movement. In the process of concern-reduction, group members devise procedures of various sorts to facilitate the processing of data present in the group. The Colorado experiments show clearly that groups can initiate highly adequate data-processing procedures without the help of skilled social scientists as trainers and that they also can learn effective use of technical help from professionals.

One helpful trainer entry on this dimension is for him to share his feelings and perceptions with the group and thus to participate in resolution of the data problem. Being open and spontaneous is perhaps the most difficult problem for the inexpert trainer. Because of the role-perceptions and role-expectations built in for the classic T-Group trainer, the inexpert trainer may become a data artifact. Group members may see him as knowing the answers, but as unwilling to share his answers with them; as knowing the solutions to the concern-resolutions, but as standing aloof from the group; as allowing them to find out for themselves, because it is somehow best for them to "learn it on their own." The common feeling among members that "there is no need asking the trainer, because he won't tell us anyway" is an example of an artifactitious data problem.

One rule of thumb for the trainer is that he should be as open *as it is possible for him to be* in the data processing and decision making of the group.

Creating Goals. One of the blocks to handling the purpose problem is the difficulty in determining the intrinsic motivations of group members. As the trainer explores his own purposes in being in the group and his own model of what a group might be, he serves as a model of one possible way of arriving at goal clarity. He should avoid setting up his behavior as *the* model.

Productivity. Growth and learning come to be accepted as the verbalized goals and the work tasks of most T Groups. Most groups start with an underlying assumption that people learn by talking and thus that the primary problem to be solved is to find a discussion topic, preferably one about which there will be lively argument. As the group explores this problem under process concern, it finds that other "theories" will lead to greater productivity. As trust and acceptance grow in the group, the group is better able to use the significant methodological resources of the trainer in this area of growth. Then the trainer, as he becomes more comfortable in the group and with himself, is better able to exhibit in his actions his own theory of learning. As the group works through its many concerns, it becomes better able to accept any member of the group, including the trainer, as a methodological or content resource.

At one level, the activities of the T Group may be seen as a series of *work cycles.* Each cycle will consist of the following sequences: planning → acting-observing → process analysis → generalization. Early in group life these sequences are barely discernible. Planning may not exist at the verbal level. Acting (conversation, agenda setting, role playing) may be random and unorganized. Process observing and analysis may be sporadic and casual and often will depend upon trainer-interventions, if a trainer is present. In trainerless groups, members tend to initiate process interventions earlier. Generalization is often private, informal, or truncated.

As the group evolves, each of these phases of the sequence becomes better organized, more under group control, more part of the formal agenda.

Trainer behavior may be differentiated, in part, by the degree to which each trainer directly intervenes at each of these phases. One trainer intervenes only at the process analysis phase; in this way he exerts control only indirectly upon the other three phases. Another acts as a consultant to the group in the formal "planning" phase, the setting up of systematic observing techniques, and at the process analysis phase. Another may directly intervene in all four phases.

It is clear that the trainer may contribute to learnings in the T Group from a great variety of roles. Often the trainer's powerful influence in early stages of groupship arises from his deliberate role restriction, although his effectiveness will depend upon factors other than the degree of such restriction. He will operate to maximal effectiveness if he operates at all stages of the work cycle. This style of training introduces some complications, however. The more complex the role of the trainer, the greater the difficulty in communicating the role to the group and the less his initial power.

Particularly at the planning and generalization stages, there is danger that the trainer, because he was introduced to the group in a special status role, might easily be trapped into supplying functions usually supplied by a discussion leader or teacher, with a resultant increase in dependency. The trainer has several options. He may withdraw from the group completely—a behavior pattern which induces the frustrations and tensions accompanying ambiguity and lack of satisfactory work organization. At a later stage he may use this withdrawal state as profitable material for process analysis. He may choose an opposite alternative of entering the group as a member. However, such behavior greatly weakens subsequent interventions and deprives the group of the dramatic effect of trainer-interventions which come from the trainer-as-process-analyst-only role.

One successful pattern is to enter into the planning in the very early stages at enough points to help the group set up useful training plans, to play an observer role during the "acting-observing" stage of the work cycle, to contribute to the process analysis, and to stay out of the generalization stages until the group has attained sufficient maturity to handle participation of the trainer at the content level.

The reactivation of dependency feelings produced by member-

trainer interaction makes it extremely difficult for the trainer to participate effectively in the productivity dimension. He can learn to act as
a methodological resource and to communicate his skills and resources
in this area where his contributions may loom large.

Control. As the trainer grows, he is able to act more interdependently
and to limit the amount of group behavior that he needs to control.
It is particularly important that he understand his own dependency
needs and the effects of these needs upon the groups with which he
works and that he be able to discuss his own behavior rather freely
with the group. Otherwise, he intrudes too many of his own needs
into the dependency resolution. It is our impression, based on the
Colorado data, that understandings of dependency processes are
greater where members work them out in relation to emergent group
leaders rather than in relation to appointed trainers.

Building an Organization. Growth on this dimension consists of a
series of miniature experiments in forming a social organism. The
trainer can participate in this organization building by interpreting
and describing the organizational norms, by helping to analyze the
experiments performed by the group, by participating in the analysis
of the informal data that are produced, and by calling attention to the
organizational functions of his own artifactitious role.

Provisionalism. Growth as a trainer is an experimental quest for increasingly adequate personal resolutions of the four modal concerns.
The trainer makes continuing provisional attempts to relate to the
group in a way that will lead to concern-resolution, group growth,
personal growth, and defense-reduction. Trainer needs will influence
trainer style. If the trainer's group behavior is consonant with his
articulated training philosophy and he can talk about occasional dissonance when it occurs, he is in a position to contribute his behavior
as data for group learning.

Norm Centering. The primary methodological contribution that the
trainer can make to the group is continually to express the norms of the
group as he sees them. Each group member can learn to reproduce
to some degree, in other groups of which he is a part, the concern-resolutions that occur in his training group. He learns, to some degree,
to participate with others in creating a defense-reductive climate,
goal integration, functional feedback, and creative interdependence.
He learns to become aware of the processes of personal and group
growth. He learns how to create the interpersonal situations which

will help him to accept himself and others and to have others accept him—to grow and to help others to grow. It is not sufficient that he experience these processes in an intuitive way—"something exciting happened, but I'm not sure what"—but that he be able to talk about the phenomena and the technologies that have produced them.

To share in the stating of norms is a primary medium for such learning. Any member of the group can participate in such verbalization. From one point of view, the most adaptive work of the learning group is the diagnosis and articulation of what is going on in the here-and-now. As people become increasingly aware of the many facets of what is happening, they can exert more influence upon the growth process.

Following is a selected list of central norm areas that concern groups as they consciously attend to their own processes.

RISK. The group develops more or less consistent ways of limiting risk, handling fears, testing level of risk, punishing or rewarding risk takers, or handling those who either expose too much or fail to share in what are seen as the common dangers.

TRUST. The group develops more or less stable trust levels. It develops norms about communicating trust, handling members who deviate from trust boundaries, viewing suspicions about motivations of trainers and other members, influencing what is said about the group outside the group, and building trust.

NONCONFORMITY. The group develops ways of handling members who deviate in attitude or behavior, of expressing differential tolerance for special areas of conformity and nonconformity, and of communicating rewards and punishments both for conformity and for nonconformity.

MEMBERSHIP. Norms emerge about the privileges of membership, the ways of attaining membership, the degrees and levels of membership, the importance of commitment, and the expression of acceptance, affection, or approval.

REJECTION. More or less consistent patterns arise in the manner of expressing rejection, ways of camouflaging rejection or disapproval, what rejectees may do, and what kinds of behavior will elicit rejection.

FEEDBACK. In working through the data-processing concerns, groups learn ways of giving feedback, receiving feedback, determining limits of feedback, determining who can give such data to whom, ignoring demands for feedback, and acceptable ways of reacting to such data.

CONSENSUS. Norms arise as to what is meant by full or partial agreement, whether silence means assent, dissent, or indecision, how much in agreement a person must feel in order to say he agrees, how decisions are made, how decisions are ignored, and how consensus is tested.

PROCESS. Groups develop more or less consistent habits about what kinds of process to look at, ways of looking at process, how it is integrated into action, how often it is looked at, and who is allowed to make process interventions under what conditions.

DIAGNOSIS. Habits develop around how diagnosis is integrated into action, how much moralizing or evaluation is allowed, how often and under what conditions diagnoses are made, and how diagnosticians are given approval or disapproval.

FEELING-PERCEPTION. Groups develop strong standards about whether feelings should be admitted as data, how often and by whom feelings and perceptions may be expressed, what kinds of feelings and perceptions are admissible in verbal interaction and what kinds admissible only as nonverbal data, and how significant such data are in making what kinds of decisions.

GOAL DETERMINATION. In working through goal-formation concerns, groups develop norms about how goals are formulated, what bearing goals have upon subsequent activity, what is done about goal diversity and incompatibility, and how explicit goals must be in order to create movement.

REWARD-PUNISHMENT. Norms emerge around how punishments and rewards are administered, what kinds of punishments and rewards are appropriate in the group, who can give what kinds of approval or disapproval, and how members should react to differential treatment.

LEARNING-GROWTH. Particularly significant in the T Group, but also present in action groups, are norms about how we learn, what things are seen as evidences of growth, what are acceptable ways of initiating and reacting to change, what effects conflict and exposure have in learning, from whom members are willing to learn, and how members who learn or do not learn are handled.

PROVISIONAL TRY. Consistent patterns emerge concerning how experimentation is carried on by individuals or by the group as a whole, to what degree decisions of the group are provisional or immutable, how formal and deliberate experimentation may be, how to punish and reward innovators, and in what areas of group life provisional behavior is sanctioned.

WORK. Consistent ideas and behavior emerge around the nature of work and play, how work is avoided or accomplished, what constitutes efficiency and how important it is, and what kinds of activities are treated as productive or nonproductive.

CONFLICT. In resolving control concerns, groups soon meet conflict and develop characteristic ways of determining how to handle it, how to produce what kinds of conflict, how to integrate it into work and creativity or how to avoid and repress it, and how to live with different reactions to conflict among members of the group.

PERMISSIVENESS. Norms emerge about how to give or refuse permission or sanction for what kinds of behavior or attitudes, how to handle variable reactions to existing boundaries, how to communicate the permissiveness that does exist, and how to allow and to live with freedoms that emerge.

BOUNDARIES. Groups develop boundaries of various kinds and develop norms about how boundaries arise, how they are violated, how permeable they are, how they are changed, how they are tested, and who is allowed to violate them under what conditions.

RESOURCES. Norms arise regarding the use of people resources in the group—who are permitted to serve as resources or to give information about what, how emergent experts are ignored or used, how much information of what kind a person is allowed to give how often, and what kinds of resource information are seen as special or professional.

ORGANIZATION. Groups learn ways of organizing for action, what kinds of leadership roles are needed from whom, what kinds of organization will be tolerated, how organization can be changed, and how permanent or stable organization must be for what purposes.

Growth Is a Learning Process. Growth is a process of learning. A person can change the significant aspects of his personality and his behavior. Any person can become appreciably more creative and productive than he is at any one given point. The process of learning is a continuing, open-ended one. People do not necessarily learn by doing but may learn through experience under certain conditions. People generalize learnings from the T Group when they can understand the processes that are happening on the four dimensions of growth, can verbalize and generalize about these processes, and can perceive their own roles and the roles of others in the development. Learnings are most effective when induced by intrinsic reward systems, when there is an appropriate degree of self-trust and acceptance, when there is spontaneous interplay of perceptual and feeling data, and when the person has a maximum of control over his own participation in the learning process.

11

Psychodynamic Principles
Underlying T-Group Processes

Roy M. Whitman

The T Group is a collection of heterogeneous individuals who gather for the purpose of examining the interpersonal relations and group dynamics that they themselves generate by their interaction. Its approach is both clinical and experimental, using the basic principles of action research in which the data are neither so controlled that there is no room for innovation nor so loose that principles and hypotheses cannot be constructed and tested.

Its purpose can be described best in terms of freedom of choice. Though there is a theoretical problem in the concept of free choice, it is axiomatic that the more significant data one has on which to base a decision, the better the decision one reaches. Training in groups and in human relations of this type sensitizes the individual to the group process affecting him, the influence of other individuals upon him, and his own role in causing the group and individuals to respond to him in a certain way. Since this is essentially a circular chain of events, the individual gains an insight into himself and others as they participate in the transactional process that is human living.

This chapter will consider only those aspects of the T Group which can be described best as "process." By process we mean the dynamic emotional developments and unfolding affective patterns of the group. T-Group process will be divided roughly into three phases: the beginning, the middle, and the end. Following this, there will be sections on trainer-interventions, qualifications of a trainer, the concept of group focal conflict, and finally, some of the limitations of this form of training.

The Beginning of the T Group

In describing a typical trainer introduction, one is immediately faced with the multiplicity of possibilities in initiating a T Group. This holds not only for different individual trainers but also for the same trainer from year to year and setting to setting.

Minimal Definition of the Situation

The initial remarks made by the T-Group trainer are extremely important in defining the character of the group. Some of the remarks of Redl (Redl, 1942) on the importance of the initiatory act in human relations (stated colloquially, "He did it first") are pertinent in this connection. The group often will refer back to these remarks, and all sorts of distortions will be read into them. It is well, therefore, that the trainer know not only what he is going to say but also that he note carefully what he has said. One approach is to begin the group with as little detail as possible so that the situation is barely defined. Such an introduction might go, "My name is _____. I am the appointed staff trainer of this group and am here to help you in the study of this group as best I can." This sentence does many things despite its brevity: it is a claim for leadership; it is a promise of the gratification of some sort of dependency needs; and finally, it sets as one important group task the study of the group itself. It is, nevertheless, only a very terse definition of his role and leads to a relatively ambiguous situation into which projection of individual perceptions of the group can take place easily.

The Projective Hypothesis

Derived from projective psychology, this hypothesis states that people will project into any situation their own needs, wishes, and fears. This projection is a function of the degree of ambiguity of the situation. Thus, if people are shown a cigarette at close distance, they are more than likely to state it is just that. However, if they are asked to describe what they see in a cloud outside the window, the number of responses may be quite varied. The two variables or poles of this process are the Perceiver and the Stimulus Material. This bipolar theory of perception suggests an inverse relationship between the sharpness of stimulus definition and the degree and variety of the projections made.

Thus, if the trainer makes a formal speech and acts in a very defined and structured way, there will be very little projection into this behavior; conversely, if he says nothing at all and shows no facial expression, people are likely to read into him a wide variety of motives and attitudes. Perhaps beginning somewhere between the two extremes is most useful to the group.

Optimal Visibility

Optimal visibility would imply that the trainer reveals himself somewhere between the extremes of a continuum ranging between complete openness and complete impassivity. This has implications not only for trainer behavior *in* the group but also for outside behavior and the degree and amount of social interaction with members of his group.

Optimal Visibility

Absence of visibility (i.e., no facial responses, no social intermingling, ⟷ and the like).	Complete visibility (i.e., explains each move, is completely open with himself, mingles with his group freely).

The question immediately comes up: Why is the group so concerned about cues from the trainer?

The Abdication of Authoritarian Leadership

The impetus for the drive to obtain responses from the trainer lies in the newness of the situation. When anyone comes into a new situation with unknown potentialities, he becomes anxious. This is, moreover, an extreme degree of anxiety, as illustrated by some studies from Michael Reese Hospital, in Chicago (Hamburg, 1955), which demonstrate that the amount of anxiety aroused by a new situation is equal to or greater than that stimulated by the most deliberately formulated stress interview. When someone is beset by anxiety in a new situation, the natural response is to seek help from experts or people who seem to know what is going on. Some of this is realistic dependency, and some of it is unrealistic. When the trainer fails to supply this help, anxiety and dependency increase. This becomes progressively more unrealistic, as the questions directed at the trainer take on more and more of the character of getting some response, *any* response, of a "giving" nature.

As dependency is frustrated, hostility increases. Both hostility and dependency are rarely expressed directly but are found in displaced references in the group discussion. Thus, the group may find itself talking about supervisors who do not give enough direction. This is a displaced expression of hostility about insufficient guidance from the trainer. Often, hostility is reacted against inside the individual, and such reaction formation leads to expressions of how capable the trainer is and how lucky the group is to have that particular trainer. (The trainer has said nothing but his opening remarks.) When there is a reaction against dependency by the group, one finds such remarks as (often subsumed under the label of counterdependency): "We don't need the trainer at all. . . . This really gives us an opportunity to see what we can do on our own," among others.

Rationale of This Approach

The general approach of optimal trainer visibility and nonparticipation in the socially expected leader role at the beginning of the T Group can be understood best in terms of anxiety and learning. Too much anxiety is disintegrating to the organism. Too little anxiety makes a person unwilling to abandon his usual approach. The concept of optimal anxiety implies discomfort somewhere between these extremes; some anxiety or discomfort is needed for change.

The concept of optimal anxiety is especially significant for the rationale of interpretation. If group members are uncomfortable in their bewilderment about the trainer's abnormal silence or withdrawal to the point where they are beginning to disintegrate, then there is some need for the trainer either to interpret this confusion or actually to reveal himself more to decrease the anxiety. For example, a group was made very anxious by a prolonged silence and showed evidences of random behavior and extreme discomfort on the part of the members. When they were discussing the silence and how anxious they felt about it, one member asked the trainer whether he had felt anxious. The trainer readily admitted that he had. He felt that it best served the purpose of the group at that time for the members to realize that the trainer shared the same anxieties that they did and was not the superman some of them had fantasied him to be. Understandably, the very next subject for discussion was that of how some of the group members had projected superhuman abilities and capacities into the trainer.

The same general principle of optimal anxiety holds for interpretation specifically in the area of dependency and hostility, the two chief vectors of the opening phase of the group. If the group, for example, is talking about trainers who are reluctant to take on the mantle of leadership, then a too direct interpretation by the present trainer of the hostility of the group to him, such as, "I think the group is angry with me for not helping them out more in the way they are used to!" might be too anxiety provoking to the group. They are not able to face their direct hostility to the trainer at that point. It goes without saying that timing is one of the most delicate tasks of the trainer.

Optimal Regression

The concept of optimal, used in relation to anxiety and visibility, also holds for the phenomenon of regression. Regression refers to the tendency of an organism, when faced with an anxiety-provoking situation, to go back to "tried-and-true" methods of adaptation that it has used successfully before. An unstructured situation like the T Group seems to evoke behavior comparable with that found in an adolescent gang situation (Benne and Whitman, 1953). There are a lot of jokes about sexuality, a great deal of delight in highly idiosyncratic jargon, much comfort in being an ingroup—all characterized by a sharp dichotomy between "we" (our group) and "they" (all nongroup members). This is a healthy and understandable thing. Two extremes are: (1) the absence of any regression in the highly cognitive person, who acts as if the whole group experience is an intellectual exercise; (2) the person who regresses too much and acts in an infantile way. The latter is so stimulated by the group that he continually talks about "the whole thing's being just too thrilling for words." The trainer should be constantly aware of this vector, since his interpretations and comments contribute so much to the degree of regression which occurs.

Some regression is necessary for learning. Psychoanalysis utilizes the couch to encourage regression. It is as if the person goes back to a stage in his life before he has adopted certain fixed types of behavior and responses and gets another chance to form them. This type of regression is far more than one wishes to encourage in a relatively brief group experience. The analyst makes himself almost completely invisible by sitting behind the patient and this, of course, stimulates anxiety and regression. As we have indicated, in the T Group the trainer does show himself as a person, and the group is comprised of face-to-face relationships which are reality-checks on too much regression.

The Middle of the T Group

Lest it appear that the beginning recommendations contain a "cookbook" approach to working with a T Group, it must be emphasized that almost all trainer behavior must be guided by an extreme amount of sensitivity and tact, for which there are no rules. This is especially true of the middle stage of group development, where Freud's analogy of the chess game is especially apt—one can teach the opening moves of a chess game and even the closing game, but during the middle game the person must use his own ingenuity and skill. However, there are certain broad trends and phenomena which can be delineated and where sensitization is helpful.

The Development of a New Culture

Just as the infant must be socialized from the very beginning of his life as if there had not been five thousand years of culture before him, so must the group, in a vastly attenuated form, find its own culture and laws from the beginning. While each group member, as an adult, shares an approximately equal cultural background, each must experience every other as an essentially new entity. The group forms its own history and constructs its own standards and modes of behavior and, once fixed, they are extremely difficult to alter. Such things as coming on time, the length of contributions to group discussion, not leaving the room on any errand whatsoever, all become modes of behavior upon which the group stamps its print. They have almost the binding effect of laws; for the social punishment when they are broken (such as disapproval, ostracism, and hostility) is as severe as its equivalent prison sentence in Western society.

Stereotyping

This particular social and interpersonal phenomenon is so universal and yet so destructive that it deserves careful scrutiny. In its psychological value, it is essentially an energy-saving device. But since it is destructive of individual uniqueness, it is always worth highlighting. It is partly this characteristic that makes the group want to know the occupation of each of its members, their age, marital status, political views, and so on. The hypothesis is that the more one knows these distinguishing social characteristics of another person, the more one can predict his responses. This is a vast oversimplification, for social behavior is so overdetermined that a much greater variety of facts than can be gathered by sheer enumeration is necessary to characterize a person. The best predictor of social behavior is behavior in a comparable situation. Therefore, the day-to-day behavior of the group member is the best predictor of what he will do tomorrow or next week.

One of the members in a group was a Japanese. Someone made the statement that he seemed inscrutable. After a discussion of the pros and cons of this characterization, the trainer raised the question as to whether other members of the group had not thought of "the inscrutable Oriental." [1] This seemed to be a fairly widespread thought, and the trainer then wondered whether the group were seeing an instance of stereotyping. Following a guilt-and-shame reaction on the part of the group even to the point of apologizing, many members were able to state that they had had this feeling about the Japanese member ever since the group started. The generalization was made and accepted by the group that we often see foreigners as having hidden motivations. The usual verbal and nonverbal cues are not apparent to us because of the cultural differences in the expression of affect. Then, strikingly enough, some members were able to admit that they had envisioned the Japanese as being vastly superior; while others thought that he was contemptuous of the group; and still others, that he was hostile.

Stereotyping is often more subtle than this, however. The alert trainer should be aware of its going on, especially in a heterogeneous group (and what group really is not, in some respects?) and should capitalize on any opportunity to alert the group to this phenomenon.

[1] The fact that this issue became so important to the group suggests some displacement from the "inscrutable leader." I am indebted to Dr. Stanley Kaplan for this observation.

Male-Female Differences

Differences in the way men and women participate in the group often can be delineated sharply. Very often at the beginning of the T Group, one becomes aware of the males clashing for the leadership of the group and the females hanging back, occasionally to appear as maternal supportive figures to momentary "losers" or·as allies to emerging power figures.

Frequently, it seems as though the males are vying with one another for leadership, for sheer mastery or competitive purposes. The analogy of the male bulls fighting among themselves suggests itself from the animal world. Perhaps more immediate as a parallel is the adolescent boy who competes exhibitionistically for the young girl, only to fall silent and uncomfortable with her once he has vanquished his opponent.

Fighting for fighting's sake is all too common in this culture. The male seems to operate along a passive-aggressive axis in which withdrawal from competition or competitive fight characterizes much of his behavior (Whitman, Trosman, and Koenig, 1954). It seems that he is so often commanded to be aggressive and masculine that he reacts with passivity. Or, if he does act in an aggressive way, he may then respond to counterattack by a passive defense. An even further possibility is a "counterphobic" response: "You guys can say anything you want to me—I can take it!" In other words, he protests and asks for the very thing which he fears.

Simultaneously, the female operates along a dependency axis, in which most of her responses have to do with her need for dependency or her assertion of her independence. The most striking cultural example of her primary orientation is the man taking care of the woman in the marital situation. Thus, as the males battle for supremacy, the females anxiously watch, nurture, and wonder with whom they will throw in their lot. This is, of course, a vast oversimplification, but it serves as a blueprint for watching group differences as interactions and relationships unfold.

Here is an example from a recent group. The training observer (the co-trainer of the group, in a sense) happened to sit next to one of the very attractive females in the group. At the beginning, the males watched him carefully and were alert to any byplay. From their remarks, they were essentially in competition with the observer in the sense of dominance rather than having any major interest in the female. Simultaneously, the females in the group either competed for the attention of the observer (i.e., dependency competition) or turned to others of the emerging leaders of the group for that gratification.

The topic of sexuality itself seems to find a fairly strong tabu in training groups. Often it is made apparent by jokes or joking behavior which almost always has an undercurrent of hostility toward the opposite sex. Again one is immediately struck by the similarity to the adolescent culture in which much the same type of teasing erotization goes on, but also where it is particularly shameful actually to reveal sexual interests in other than a joking or casual way. The females are most prone to use sexuality in the service of competition with other females and thus to achieve leadership. Of course, this is by no means limited to the women. In any event, sexuality is used most often in pursuit of other power operations and is usually of a verbal-seductive type.

The Concept of Levels

A group operates on a number of different levels simultaneously. For practical purposes, two levels is a useful division. Overt and covert, or manifest and latent, are ways of describing these levels. The analogy that suggests itself immediately is that of words and music. What the group is saying is one thing, but what is going on beneath the surface is another. Both the immediate music underlying the words and the underlying theme drifting through the material over a period of time are significant.

At the Veterans Administration Research Hospital in Chicago, a recent therapy group discussed the question of the uselessness of building large buildings and hospitals and then staffing them inadequately. (The Veterans Administration Research Hospital is a towering new structure which won an architectural award in Chicago in 1955.) The discussion, which seemingly dealt, at a rather intellectual level, with the problems of government building, really reflected some of the doubts that the patients had about the adequacy of their group leaders.

In addition to the usual sensitivity that the trainer gathers from his training and experience in diagnosing groups and making interpretations, an additional maneuver might be mentioned that is extremely useful when the group process seems muddy. He can ask himself how he is feeling and how much what is going on in the group is responsible for that particular feeling. For example, the trainer may feel that he is not helping the group enough and that he should be interpreting more or offering didactic teaching. There are two possibilities: one, that he *is* inadequate in this respect; and the other, that the group is subtly shaming him into feeling this way. Then he can use these introspectively captured data to determine what the group is trying to do and, finally, he can raise the question of why they are trying to do it.

Communication Problems

Communication problems invariably arise when people talk to one another. They are so significant that it is possible to center one's entire discussion of interpersonal and group relations on that area. Since we have chosen a different emphasis here, perhaps a few remarks will suffice.

Communication difficulties arise from both the sender and the receiver, separately or simultaneously. It is, therefore, a trainer responsibility to ensure that the person who speaks clarify his remarks and that the rest of the group understand what has been said. Very often, a powerful group standard then can be erected which favors clarifying questions, paraphrasing requests, and exercising constant concern that those who are listening are also understanding. In essence, this question of understanding involves the problem of feedback.

Feedback implies not only understanding what has been said. The crucial test of understanding is whether the person can utilize what has been said to create a new thought or insight. A unique contribution that the T Group has made to the study of small groups is the use of immediate process feedback not only by the designated observer, or trainer, but also by any group member. One of the evolving facets of the T Group is the increasing ability of each group member to act as observer as well as participant. These observations may involve not only several other members but also the entire group process. This might be expressed graphically by the following simple curve.

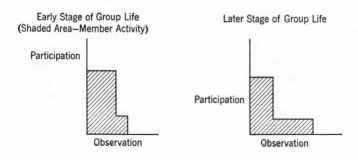

While members, because of their own predilections, may operate at each end of this continuum in a more or less consistent fashion, often they increase the areas of both their observation and participation. And certainly the group exerts a pressure for increasing these areas or balancing their relative proportions. Silent members are encouraged to speak or give their views, and active members are cautioned to become more reflective.

A typical example of this occurred in a group where the most active member was asked to be an observer for a while and was not permitted to say anything during the period of this observation. This was the group's way of silencing him, yet intuitively offering him a substitute role which would permit his self-esteem to accept a nonactive status.

Defenses Against Involvement

Variations in involvement show up all during the group meetings, but especially in the middle, when the height of involvement occurs for most people. Involvement is one of the crucial factors in group life and, indeed, in all relations among people. Noninvolvement is sometimes the chief and lifelong defense of people who go through life never involving themselves with anybody and living "as if" existences. These defenses may be divided into three clusters:

1. *Overintellectualization.* These people treat life and, therefore, the T Group, as an exercise of the intellect. Their use of the jargon and going through the motions of group interaction is often impressive, but their real involvement in the group is carefully guarded against. They may even boast of their success in keeping aloof as their ability not to get overwhelmed or even overcome by the group. Their most common rationalization is that they have come to observe and learn and watch the *others* interact.

2. *Overaffective Behavior.* These people are overidentified with the group and its process to the point where they really are not involved with any of the group at all. Their object relations with people are rather diffuse but very highly colored emotionally, so that they look as if they are the most avid group members; but on an ego level they are not participating. Their recall of the group experiment is that of an affective blur, with much feeling but no insight and no learning. An example that comes to mind in describing this type of person concerns a matron who is coming to visit a little boy. The mother tells him that this woman just *loves* children, and the little boy plain-

tively asks, "But if she loves *all* children, how will I know whether she likes me or not?"

3. *Selective Inattention.* This is a perceptual defense and, stated simply, means that a person sees what he wants to see. All facts and incidents that are intolerable to the self-system of the individual are not attended to (Stock and Whitman, 1957). It is very important, however, to distinguish this from adaptive perception. If there is a vicious interchange between two members of the group and one of the other group members has no recollection of the fracas at all, we can safely assume that there was something in the exchange which was not tolerable to that observer. However, if a person drives into a small town and sees the restaurant and the filling station immediately because he is hungry and the car needs gasoline, we can hardly say that he is defending himself against seeing the barbershop and the general store. He just is not oriented at that moment in his need system toward those supply sources.

The extreme type of perceptual defense is autistic perception. Here there is really no perception at all. Very often you see somebody in the group who has a dreamy look in his eyes or perhaps even listens interestedly, but a few minutes later will say, "Well, I've been thinking what was said to me (ten minutes ago!) and I have thought of this point. . . ." This is the person who most often is responsible for contributing a thud or a dud to the group discussion, because his remark is connected to his own ruminations but not to the thread of group discussion.

Stock and Whitman (1957) did a small experimental study using tape recordings to gauge perceptual defenses. They played a ten-minute excerpt of a crucial episode in group therapy and then asked each of the members of the group what they thought was going on during each segment of the interaction. Only when there was strong and unequivocal emotion being expressed was there even an approximation of unanimity of perception. During other times, selective inattention or autism prevailed, in which patients fastened on the most minute segments of group interaction and/or avoided the theme of the episode with astonishing facility.

The End of the T Group

An important difference between the T Group and the Therapy Group, or other types of face-to-face groups, is that the total time that the T Group will meet is specifically preplanned. This often results in a conscious or unconscious allotment of energy and involvement on the part of individuals to the span of the group time. People are hardly going to continue to increase the amount of involvement as the group draws to its conclusion, unless the group has become so meaningful to them that they are unable to disengage themselves. This leads us to make a comment distinguishing between the end of the T Group and the termination of the T Group. The end of the T Group is the reality of the physical separation which occurs when there are no more meetings. The termination of the T Group occurs when the people have withdrawn their affective investment in the group. This sometimes lasts for months and is evidenced by frequent correspondence and even planned meetings among the members. It is most helpful to work through this separation in the terminal phase of the group's meeting; although there is always a little lag (much as there is in any significant relationship among people) between the end and the termination.

Some people terminate their relationship to the T Group before it has ended. This is most clearly expressed in a popular song, "I Get the Blues in Advance." This person, in order to protect himself against the hurt of the too abrupt coming of the separation reaction, begins to withdraw emotionally from the group. This more or less happens with most of us and is one of the motivating factors in the increasing number of references to back-home situations that occur as the group draws to a close. Farewell parties are also attempts to master the separation by sublimation; if they occur prematurely, the group finds itself empty and dull, for it has terminated long before it has ended. Frequently, groups that find themselves in this uncomfortable situation decide to stop meeting, so that the end and termination coincide.

Action

In the final analysis, behavior of a coordinated and goal-directed nature is the *sine qua non* of both individual and group maturity. In the T Group, because of its essentially discussion-type methods, opportunities for action often are very few. This has led to the suggestion by some trainers that specific tasks be assigned to the group in the end phase, to test the maturity of the group and highlight its weak spots. However, if the trainer is alert, he can capitalize on seemingly trivial tasks of the group to point up difficulties in its action potential. These would be the coffee break, decisions to have parties, decisions to deal with other groups—particularly the central administration—and methods of selecting internal regulatory mechanisms, such as chairmen and committees. Modes of dealing with a new member, beginning with the decision to take him in or not and extending to methods evolved for dealing with him, might be generalized by the group trainer or other group members as examples of effective or ineffective action patterns. And, finally, the ways of setting up group discussions can be seen as involving successful or unsuccessful action by the group. Action is discussed in the end phase because, while the group attempts action throughout its duration, it is most likely to be successful when process problems have been worked through.

Member Roles

Most T Groups are not satisfied unless they examine interpersonal relations in the group as well as the group structure and dynamics. This is an ongoing need in the group but is probably more properly a task of the end phase, since patterns have there developed to the point where they may be delineated more accurately by the group members. Methods of examining this area are often potentially traumatic, and the trainer must be prepared to exercise a protective or even refereeing role if the occasion should arise.

One method of getting at this aspect of the group might be to have multiple role playing, in which each member is assigned another member's role to play. Then a discussion of the way the person felt who played the role is followed by a "rebuttal" by the person whose role was played. Finally, there is a general group discussion of the person's contribution to the group. The mechanism of role playing takes the edge off some of the criticisms that are expressed. But often groups are ready to look at their interpersonal relations without such an artificial facilitation. Then it is a task of the group to see that each member gets a turn, for, as always in the group, the most vocal and dominating members will prevail in this discussion, too.

It is worth noting that the group and its individuals occasionally are able to do and discuss things only because the end is in sight. Opportunities for learning are maximized because reactive fears of criticism are mitigated by the diminishing time element. Sometimes, groups make use of the time factor and the legitimization of "taking one another apart" to make irresponsible and cruel statements which have only destructive intent. These should be identified as being just that.

Trainer-Intervention and Training

Trainer-Intervention

The question is sometimes raised about the technique and form of interventions. While there is some difference of opinion, it seems to me that there is a certain similarity between this and psychoanalytic psychotherapy. In the early days of psychoanalysis, the analyst often made summarizing interpretations. He usually saved these until the end of the session when, with a marvelous degree of skill and organization, he would pull together all the varied themes that the patient had dealt with during the hour. Usually, the patient would fasten defensively on some small aspect of the therapist's remarks, however, because the process of integration of so much emotionally charged material was too difficult for him.

Today, there seems to be a drift in the direction of making much more succinct interpretations which deal with the patient's material on the spot. I think that this can serve as a model for T-Group intervention. The trainer should avoid long pronouncements which serve to enhance his status but are not so useful for learning.

While this may be too obvious to merit saying, interpretations should be couched in terms with which everybody in the group is familiar. If, however, the trainer finds it necessary to use a technical word (and this may be a legitimate part of learning), he should be very careful to explain it.

The trainer should try to make wide, generalizing remarks which are pertinent to many members of the group. Names of individuals in making group interpretations (in marked contrast to group therapy) should be used as little as possible, for the level of attention is being directed at the group process rather than individual interactions.

Frequently, he should make his interpretations in the form of questions or hypotheses that he wishes the group to examine and test. By no means should his interpretations conclude an hour when there is no opportunity for feedback from the group unless he wishes the group to do "homework" in response to a closing interpretation. He should try to set up a standard of confirming or denying his interpretations. One of the most difficult defenses to deal with is the group's ignoring the interpretation of the trainer (often when it is in a counter-dependency modality). His recourse then is to watch the ensuing behavior of the group and see how much his interpretation has been incorporated. The accuracy of an interpretation is shown by what comes after, not what has gone before. A phenomenon often seen is having one of his interpretations come up from a member of the group as if it has never been said before. At these times, it is difficult, but necessary, to restrain the impulse to claim credit for the contribution. At the other extreme, a group may be overaccepting of the trainer's interpretation in an effort to win his approval. This must be detected and interpreted to the group as a defensive maneuver against real insight.[2]

Finally, it has been my experience that the use of analogous reasoning is among the most effective methods of putting across an interpretation. Thus, when a group member is seeking to attack another group member by gradually attacking his clique, the analogy can be made with a similar phenomenon in Germany. During the rise of Hitler, the Storm Troopers were able to render helpless many individuals by destroying their primary-group membership. The individual alone is powerless. Fascist states know this, when they ban group meetings and thus decrease opportunities for communication and action.

The Education of a Trainer

What are the necessary qualifications for a good T-Group trainer? There are no arbitrary answers to this question, nor should there be, since the task of the trainer is so complex that there is no one set of traits that can be considered as necessary. Certain general suggestions can be made, however.

The trainer should have experience in two areas: his own inner life, and group dynamics. The former is achieved most easily by some sort of personal psychoanalytic or psychotherapeutic experience, though this is not essential. Experience of a clinical nature can be achieved by working with the unconscious and preconscious operations in other people, but a personal sense of conviction is achieved most firmly by exploring one's own unconscious. David Riesman has used the analogy of the Grand Tour of Europe so popular in finishing off the education of the generation of the early 1900's. Now it is more popular to take

---

[2] Recently, a psychiatrist from New Zealand, Dr. Brian McConville, brought to the Cincinnati Department of Psychiatry the novel idea of deliberately making an inaccurate observation to gauge the amount of individual propitiation. Such a technique, with both individuals and groups, should be used only if it will later be made explicit as a maneuver.

a journey through one's own unconscious and life. The aptness of this analogy is illustrated by the number of patients who, at the beginning of their analyses, dream so often of a trip to a foreign land.

In the area of working with groups, there is no substitute for actual experience. Groups have a uniqueness of their own which the clinician working with single patients alone cannot grasp. This is probably one reason why the individual psychotherapist doing group therapy so often does therapy *in* the group rather than therapy *with* the group. The field of group dynamics has a great deal to contribute to the field of group psychotherapy, although it is worth saying that this should be a cross-fertilization rather than a one-way street. The remarks that were made at the 1956 meeting of the American Psychological Association in Chicago (Whitman, Bach, Watson, Bennis, and others, 1956) were to the effect that it is actually more important for the group therapist to understand group dynamics than for the patient to do so. Paralleling this, it is more important for the T-Group trainer to understand personality dynamics than for the group members to do so.

Probably it is to be recommended that a potential trainer first participate as a group member, much as a potential therapist should participate as a patient. Failing this ideal, the idea of an intense preceptorship is a substitute, but this learning must be related to the actual situation and must not in any way be didactic and isolated.

The Concept of Group Focal Conflict

Following this over-all look at the T Group along a time dimension, it might be worthwhile to turn, in more detail, to a new conceptual scheme of looking at groups. The concept of *group focal conflict* (Whitman and Stock, 1958) has arisen from research done by Whitman and Stock in Chicago, supported by the United States Public Health Service. It is a product of both group dynamics concepts and psychoanalytic concepts and seems to be serviceable in both training and therapy groups.

The focal-conflict concept is one applied by Thomas French, of the Chicago Institute for Psychoanalysis, in his projected 5-volume work, *The Integration of Behavior* (French, 1952, 1954, 1958). Its most significant contribution comes from its empirical value in organizing the vast amount of data accumulating in individual psychotherapeutic sessions into two dynamic forces which are in conflict with each other, *the disturbing motive* and *the reactive motive*. All the material of the session can be seen as radiating from this conflict and as attempts at solution of this conflict. A further significance of this hypothesis is the contribution it potentially makes to the problem of consensus. If one conflict is assumed to be focal, this offers hope that a group of investigators can examine the same material and reach consensus (French, 1954).

The *focal conflict* is the conflict closest to the surface which will explain almost all the material of the session. Most common errors in constructing focal conflicts are to make them too deep or too superficial. In the early years of psychoanalysis, analysts tended to make too deep interpretations. "You are doing this because you don't like your father." On some level, this may have been correct, but it was often inappropriate and not very useful to the patient. Such interpretations have become almost a parlor game, and people loosely interpret one another's behavior as representing mother or father complexes. French's contribution emphasized that there is a level of interpretation which hits upon what is focal for the patient.

Topographically, this level of conflict lies somewhere in the preconscious, inasmuch as it is not conscious to the person nor is it at a deep unconscious level. Probably most T-Group learning takes place at conscious and preconscious levels and, therefore, the concept of focal conflict is particularly well suited to describe the process which occurs beneath the surface of the group. A schematic topographical chart follows, which relates the level of awareness of a concept to the type of learning involved.

Level of Consciousness	*Type of Learning or Process*
Consciousness	Traditional Education
	Perception
Preconscious	T-Group Training (Focal Conflict Concept)
	Ego-Oriented Psychoanalytic Psychotherapy
	Group Standards and Norms
Unconscious	Classical Psychoanalysis
	Group Analysis
	Dream Symbolization

There is overlapping here, of course, since the T Group deals somewhat with conscious processes and even some unconscious ones, just as psychoanalysis probably deals with all levels as well. Probably only the usual forms of education ignore the deeper levels of awareness in the individual.

The unconscious feeds into the focal conflict, and the conscious verbal and behavioral manifestations of the individual arise from it. It was given its name originally from its similarity, diagramatically, to the focus of a lens.

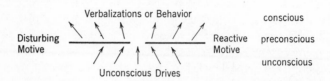

While the original work in formulating this concept was done with patient groups, it has proven applicable in other groups. A typical group focal conflict that seemed to be present in an experimental therapy group during the first ten sessions or so (and, therefore, more properly called the *group nuclear conflict*) was—

Group Focal Conflict (GFC):

Wish to trust the group and ⟷ Fear of betrayal by individual
reveal oneself to the group   members

In this conflict, a patient could ally himself with one side or the other of this conflict or attempt to participate in an amalgamation of the two sides. For operational purposes, we called the conflict arising, when members had committed themselves to a marked degree to one side of the conflict or another, a *group solutional conflict* (in contrast with the group focal conflict where no commitment has been made). Examples of participation on the left side of the conflict (above) would be the patient who talks freely, tells of painful personal material, and turns to the group for help and insight as to ways of dealing with his problems. The behavior which would characterize the other side of the conflict would be, in the extreme, to withdraw from the group, or to reveal almost nothing personal to the other members of the group and use such rationalizations as being able to trust only his personal psychotherapist. Members who utilized compromise solutions would reveal circumscribed areas of their lives, or they would insist that all members of the group move along at the same pace so that there would be an equality of revelation. An alternative solution suggested by this latter group was to ask the group leader to make a strict ruling that confidences were not to be carried outside the therapy room.

We have been impressed by the frequency of appearance of certain focal conflicts in the initial phases of group life. Almost exactly the same focal conflict (as above) was brought up in a recent T Group. This incident was initiated by a woman who had just received a back-home letter having to do with an interpersonal problem that she had with her boss. Her boss happened also to be in the training program. She wanted some help in dealing with the situation and so brought up the letter.

There ensued a vigorous discussion about the contents of the letter, which concerned the expression of hostility to the boss and how he would take it. It also involved opinion about her expressing hostility to another member of the office group with whom she worked. Most of the remarks contributed by members of the group concerned hostility and retaliation. One might be tempted to construct a focal conflict which dealt with hostility versus fear of retaliation and identify solutions as, "Don't reveal your hostility," or "The boss usually is much more understanding than one gives him credit for," and the like. But if you listened closely to the material and noted that the woman who brought up the letter never revealed the contents of the letter in other than a general way and that the group actually discouraged her from doing so, another conflict which was really focal for the group emerges—

Group Focal Conflict:

Wish to trust the group and   Fear of betrayal
to get help from the group ⟷
with problems of hostility

The individual focal conflict of the woman would be—

Focal Conflict:

Wish to get help with her   Fear that a member of the
office problem with the boss ⟷ group would betray her to
and her fellow worker   the boss

Her solution was that she would mention no names at all. The group used a variety of solutions of this same conflict. They encouraged generalization rather than examination of specific instances; the group felt that their main problem was hostility (really a displacement of focus). Since this was a displacement, they could engage in a vast amount of intellectualization about hostility, which became a defense, since at that point the topic of hostility was really not cathected (i.e., invested in). Subsequently, the group tried to formulate rules for behavior so that one topic that was suggested and adopted for discussion was, "How do you handle a hostile feeling?"; and the group suggested role playing to see "how you could handle a hostile boss."

In this particular incident, the suggestion of role playing was turned down by the group, but they did discuss an old role-playing scene which dynamically had the same meaning for them. Instead of dealing with the content of the former role playing, there evolved a discussion of role playing itself and its ethical meaning. What did it imply as to people's sincerity and reliability in behaving the way they usually do in the group if they could so easily behave otherwise? This gradually led to the theme of trustworthiness, so that the discussion led to the postulated focal conflict of trust versus betrayal. Most of the material of the session could be described in terms of this disturbing and reactive motive. The theme of trustworthiness inevitably is linked with whether the members of the group would betray one another in sensitive areas.

Another example from the same T Group might be helpful. At a certain point in the T Group, the members wished to examine their interpersonal relationships. This happens frequently during a T Group, and usually the group is in various stages of readiness to deal with it. At this particular time, the suggestion was made that the group do a sociogram so that they could examine the structure that so far they had set up in the group (about the middle, in length of time). Other members immediately became concerned that some people might be left out. The sociogram suggested concerned the typical questions asked in such investigations: "Whom do you like the most?" and "Whom do you like the least?" The possibility of people's feelings being hurt is obvious. Thus, a focal conflict could be set up which deals with and abstracts all the material of the discussion concerning the advisability of using a sociogram or not—

Group Focal Conflict:

Wish to trust the group and examine the interpersonal re- ⟷ getting hurt
lations in the group   Fear of members of the group

Those who were in favor of examination of the group and were willing to trust the group sufficiently were in favor of having a sociogram. Those who feared either getting hurt themselves or other members of the group getting hurt were not in favor of a sociogram at all and used cogent arguments in behalf of their point of view.

The compromise finally worked out to this group focal conflict was to have an anonymous sociogram administered by members of the training team (trainer, observer, and student trainees). As you look at the focal conflict and see how neatly the solution of an anonymous sociogram solves both sides of the conflict, you could have predicted, quite safely and correctly, that this compromise solution would meet with adoption.

It is important to emphasize that the concept of focal conflict is not applicable to every session of group activity. It is only a way of organizing those sessions in which the group is seeking a solution of a conflict. Often in the training group, discussion or action of some other type may be proceeding quite adequately. In therapy groups, patients may be bringing up and working through their intrapersonal and interpersonal problems, with the group's acting as a facilitating rather than a conflictual field of forces. In fact, there is some evidence to suggest that group sessions in which focal conflicts can be delineated seem to be bridge points that the group must deal with before they can move on to the goal that they have set themselves, i.e., therapy or training. In this sense, it has been suggested that the group focal conflict may be seen in the psychoanalytic sense as a resistance against the exploration of the individual personality or the dynamics of the group.

Relation of Focal Conflict Theory to Force Field Analysis

Some of the parallels between this method of looking at group interaction and Lewin's theory of "Force Field" (Lewin, 1951) are quite arresting. In both, there is hypothesized a field of forces fairly equally opposed which are in a dynamic equilibrium. Solutions of this problem of conflict most often unite the two opposing attitudes into a compromise solution, but also may shift in the direction of either side of the balance of forces.

This introduces the problem of how this field of forces may be altered. One method that we are especially concerned with is that of trainer-intervention. If we follow Lewin, we are led to the conclusion that interpreting the disturbing motive of the group and, in a sense, throwing the weight of the trainer on this side of the conflict seem to be of less value than decreasing the reactive fears that are involved in the conflict. Increasing the force of the disturbing motive increases the tension of the system, much as stepping on the accelerator of a car with the brake on increases the strain that the car is under. Decreasing the reactive motive relieves the tension on the system, much as taking one's foot off the brake takes the tension off the car and enables it to accelerate. (While this is a fairly good general rule, it must be kept in mind that sometimes the trainer wishes to increase the tension in the system for purposes of learning, for he may feel that the level of anxiety is not optimal for learning.) A possible interpretation of the reactive motive, when the group was in conflict about using the sociogram, might have been, "It seems that the group is afraid that someone's feelings will be injured," rather than interpreting the disturbing motive, "It seems that the group wants to examine their interpersonal relations more intensively in order to prove their trust of one another."

The concept of the group focal conflict is thus an extremely useful one for ordering the huge amount of data generated by groups and is further useful as a guide to trainer interpretation. It is a helpful adjunct in approaching the consensus problem, which requires similar frames of reference. And, finally, it is a useful guide to member selection, since the concept of heterogeneity (a usual criterion of selection for training) certainly involves the representation of a variety of focal conflicts. One of the learnings that this heterogeneity encourages is the comparison of alternative methods of solution to the same underlying focal conflicts and the stimulation of group focal conflicts productive of insights into group dynamics.

Some Limitations of the T Group

The Lowest Common Denominator

It is one of the characteristics of a T Group that it can move along only as rapidly as the slowest member. In rare instances, a group can successfully "seal off" a deviant or laggard member and proceed as if he were not there. But even then, it is almost as if the group is keeping its eye cocked on this member and, whether by reason of guilt or real concern, it feels constrained repeatedly to return to the problem of this wayward member and try to include him.

In terms of focal conflict theory, the slow member of the group becomes a deviant who continually produces solutional conflicts in the group, since it must deal with him and his attitudes in order to move along. Typical focal conflicts engendered by this type of individual are—

Group Focal Conflict:

| Need to include everyone in the group in dealing with any problem | ←→ | Fear that the group will stagnate and its integrity be destroyed |

An interesting issue that is worthy of examination is the number of persons of this type (stubborn, dogmatic, opinionated, and so on) that a group can tolerate without falling apart. Our educational system has dealt with a similar problem in a variety of ways. They have classes for retarded children, handicapped children, or children with marked behavioral disturbances. But these children are segregated only when the disturbance is severe; when it is more subtle it is patently undemocratic to remove these children from the bulk of the class and they, therefore, remain as a yoke on group progress.

Severely Neurotic and Psychotic People

This is essentially a subdivision under the problem of the lowest common denominator. These people act as persistent deviants and interfere with the progress of the group by directing the discussion along idiosyncratic lines which are very difficult to generalize into learning experiences for the rest of the group. When the focal conflict of the group encroaches on the individual nuclear conflict of a group member (i.e., his core method of responding to problems), he becomes a deviant to defend his own habitual way of responding (Whitman and Stock, 1958). When a person has too many vulnerable spots or is too inflexible to consider other ways of dealing with interpersonal relations, he becomes a repetitive sore point in the group and must be dealt with. That this is no easy matter is shown in our larger society, where methods of dealing with psychological deviants are very poorly developed. One of the most anguished persons one may meet is the individual who has no dispositional channels available to deal with a severely neurotic or psychotic relative who has no insight into his psychological deficit.

The Tenacity of Habit Patterns

People do not change easily. Actually, what most of this chapter has discussed is the creation of optimal conditions for change. These are mild anxiety, group and trainer support and protection, interpretation of group and individual behavior, models of alternative solutions of problems, and heterogeneous composition. Nevertheless, the time limitation of the T Group, the successful defenses against involvement and commitment, and the energy-saving characteristics of automatic habit patterns, all oppose change.

Furthermore, when change does occur, it is often too minute to be pertinent for behavior. It is also a general psychological rule that the most recently acquired habit patterns are those most easily destroyed under the pressure of different external conditions. This leads us to the fourth item as a natural corollary to a field theory of personality.

Changes in the Field

From the supportive, questioning, experimental atmosphere of the usual T Group, the individual must return to his former habitat. There he meets all the internal and external forces which maintain the status quo. The National Training Laboratories, in its training programs, has tried to mitigate this effect by the use of the "buddy" system, which is a natural outgrowth of some of the experiments of Solomon E. Asch on the difficulty of standing alone, as well as of clinical experience. Two people standing together have a far greater chance of success in promoting change. It is an unfortunately common experience, reported by T-Group participants, that their initial enthusiasm often quails before the jaundiced eyes of their superiors and fellow workers in their attempts at innovation.

Inappropriate Use of the T-Group Experience

Often individuals return to their original settings with greatly increased knowledge of group dynamics. Sensitivity to interpersonal relations has increased markedly. Yet they make the mistake of applying this knowledge to situations where it is inappropriate. In highly task-oriented groups, where time is a decisive factor, discussing nuances of behavior is often superfluous. Of course, time is often emphasized as a factor in order to avoid looking at interpersonal relations, and this should be recognized. Also, as was shown in the study of one particular type of group, unless the staff leader is backing change in group procedures or attitudes, any effort at change is doomed to failure (Whitman, 1956). Disappointments through misapplication soon discourage further experimentation. Timing and tact in suggesting examination of process to groups are among the most difficult skills to acquire.

General References

Benne, K. D., and R. M. Whitman. "A Seminar on T-Group Aspects." National Training Laboratory in Group Development (now known as the National Training Laboratories' Annual Summer Laboratory in Human Relations Training), Bethel, Maine, summer 1953.

French, T. M. *The Integration of Behavior,* Vols. I, II, and III. Chicago: The University of Chicago Press, 1952, 1954, and 1958.

French, T. M. "The Problem of Consensus." Presented at the midwinter meeting of the American Psychoanalytic Association, New York, December 2, 1954.

Hamburg, D. "Studies on Anxiety." From a summary given at Chicago Institute for Psychoanalysis Seminar on Research, November 1955.

Lewin, K. *Field Theory in Social Science.* (Ed. by D. Cartwright.) New York: Harper & Bros., 1951, pp. 188–237.

Redl, F. "Group Emotion and Leadership." *Psychiatry,* 5:573–596, 1942.

Stock, D., and R. M. Whitman. "Patients' and Therapists' Apperceptions of an Episode in Group Therapy." *Human Relations,* 10:4:367–383, 1957.

Whitman, R. M. "The Rating and Group Dynamics of the Psychiatric Staff Conference." *Psychiatry,* 19:4:333–340, 1956.

Whitman, R. M. (with J. Frank, G. Bach, G. Watson, W. Bennis, and others). "The Contribution of Group Dynamics to Group Psychotherapy." Panel Meeting, American Psychological Association, Chicago, September 1956.

Whitman, R. M., and D. Stock. "The Group Focal Conflict." *Psychiatry,* 21:3: 269–276, August 1958.

Whitman, R. M., H. Trosman, and R. Koenig. "Clinical Assessment of Passive-Aggressive Personality." *Archives of Neurology and Psychiatry,* 72:540–549, 1954.

12

Studying Group Action

Robert R. Blake

Increasingly, decisions that deserve action are made in small, face-to-face groups. Therefore, if critical choices for action are being made in group situations, group leaders and members need to know much more about processes at the group level.

The T Group affords an excellent opportunity for studying group behavior. When a work task confronts a group, members may become so committed to the issues to be solved that they find it difficult to observe the underlying psychological problems blocking effective solution. The pressure of the situation or the urgency of the decision may not provide the time necessary for the detailed analysis required in order to understand the processes actually operating in the situation. Furthermore, a T Group provides opportunities for provisional tryouts (i.e., "experimentation") of a kind that would be impossible in real work groups. Finally, the T Group makes possible the development of participant-observer skills, a fundamental requirement for effective group leadership or membership.

This chapter attempts to describe the T Group in terms of certain processes and social-emotional events that are common both to a T Group and to a work group. The chapter also considers responsibilities and behavior of the trainer, which aid participants in acquiring the sensitivities and skills of group action.

SECTION I.   MEMBER REACTIONS TO THE TRAINER
AND TRAINER BEHAVIOR

Member Reactions to One Trainer

From the first meeting, a variety of important issues develop in connection with my role as a trainer,[1] "Is he our 'leader,' or is he not? Will he be critical and punitive, or will he be helpful? Does he know what he's supposed to be doing? What's going on in this group? Why do people in our group pay so much attention to what he has to say? Why do we react aggressively to members of other groups, with *each* member thinking his trainer is better?" By virtue of the role the problem of reactions to authority figures is contained in members' reactions to me as a trainer. Such reactions are appropriately regarded as examples of ways of relating to authority figures in outside work situations. Insights developed under training conditions may initiate significantly altered behavior in work situations involving groups with designated leaders or in superior-subordinate relationships more generally considered.

Learning How To Adjust and Relate to Me as the Trainer

At the beginning of the initial meeting, I usually do no more than provide a brief statement of purposes for the T Group. The next step often involves group members' introducing themselves or directly attacking the problem: "What *should* we talk about next?" With a competent person in charge of the T Group, a common expectancy is, "He will suggest what we should do now."

As I do not spontaneously suggest to members what to do, it is highly probable that some member will ask for guidance and help. He does this either to "please" me, or because he is fearful that my silence implies criticism. Forces that would restrain this action also

---

[1] Member attitudes, of course, develop toward every trainer. The specific pattern of attitudes is in part a function of the particular trainer and his style of relating to the training situation. In the interests of accuracy, therefore, it seems to be preferable to use the first person, thereby indicating that the actions and reactions to which reference is being made are my actions. By doing so it is possible to avoid overgeneralizations that might be associated with talking about the trainer role as though it were constant from one trainer to another.

are present, but generally are weaker. A typical one is, "Let's flounder a bit more and see if we can get going by ourselves."

If I were to respond to a request for help by giving procedural or content suggestions, I should be establishing the precedent of controlling the group by selecting its discussion material. However, my goal is to create conditions under which members will accept responsibility for developing their own material of discussion. Only in this way can problems of decision making, leadership, consensus, and so on become critical issues within the group, from which increased understanding of group action is possible. The situation I face, then, is whether or not to intrude into the content of discussion. Since this dilemma occurs again and again, it is appropriate to discuss my rationale in greater detail.

The basic assumption guiding the action of the group at this point is typified in the statement, "You have seen many groups start, and undoubtedly you can help us to begin." The common response of group members to me as a trainer is as though I am their *leader*. Therefore, the request for help is understandable. People who customarily turn to the leader for direction, support, or authorization are inclined to do so under T-Group conditions, particularly at the beginning. Likewise, those who find themselves frequently opposing leadership in work situations are likely either to remain quiet or actively to contest with the trainer what they may regard as already-present evidence of "poor leadership."

From the viewpoint of my trainer role, both kinds of reactions are inappropriate. They indicate personal needs of members to be directed or needs to resist accepting direction. In either case, I ask myself: "Into what role is the group (or are certain members) trying to maneuver me by these requests or remarks?" and "Why do they want me in that role at this time?" If, in line with training rationale, the role the group wants me to take is inappropriate, then I ask myself, "How can I avoid accepting the role and yet clarify the motivations working to place me in it?"

I am attempting to understand whether the group as a whole (or some member) is acting in terms of dependency or resistance or whether an objective request for information is being made. I usually interpret the underlying motivations directly. Suggesting a discussion topic might produce a dependent group. Reacting defensively might produce a counterdependent one. By dealing with the underlying motivations, I may be able to clarify them, and, through this means, to reduce the tensions within the group. Simultaneously, an example of the kind of psychological evaluation which members themselves can make through accepting the participant-observer role may be provided. Understanding of dependency, and resistance and hostile reactions to a trainer constitute critical learning possibilities within a T Group. Such types of behavior are of direct significance for appreciating and dealing with similar types of behavior in work groups. However, as a trainer, I personally try not to act in such a way as to accentuate these aspects of responding. Rather, I deal with them *only* if they appear as routine, spontaneous events within the interactions of the group.

During the first meeting the field of forces within the group is likely to emphasize dependent rather than aggressive types of behavior. Then I am faced with the problem of ways to avoid giving suggestions for discussion content. At the same time, I want to clarify the motivations that produce pleas for help. I may re-emphasize the trainer (as contrasting with director) nature of my role. Alternatively, I may interpret the plea directly, further indicating that when the boundaries of a situation are uncertain, one common reaction is to turn for help to authority figures. Then additional remarks can direct the attention of members to the psychological properties of the situation itself. These may be sufficient to clarify an alternative course of action. Members themselves can accept increasing responsibility for dealing with the problems of developing a work structure or of identifying content for discussion.

As the group moves through its early meetings, other difficulties in group action mount. Dependency needs in some members increase. Gradually, more subtle efforts may be made to manipulate me into the leader position. For example, I am asked, "How do other groups get started?" Some members may say, "We don't want you to lead us. As a resource person, just tell us what to do."

The situation in a T Group is comparable to work-group situations. When difficulties arise in outside groups, feelings of dependency on some person in a position of power may quickly appear. Depending upon his skill and resourcefulness, he may or may not perpetuate a pattern of "lean on me when the going gets tough." A critical time to evaluate the quality of a work group, or the learning in a T Group, is *not* when things are running smoothly. A far better time is when the problems are undoubtedly complex and an authoritative answer would provide a "solution." If, under these conditions, effective procedures are maintained, without evidence of leader-dependency or attempts to construct artificial "leaders," the prediction is that it is an effective problem-solving group.

Resistance Shown through Requesting or Insisting on Training Rationale

The expression of negative feelings toward me as a trainer, whether expressed indirectly or directly, may stem from several sources. Trainer-interventions that are either requested but not given, are poorly timed, or that fail to deal with underlying problems may create hostility or antagonism. Alternatively, even when interventions have been appropriate, the group may contain members who are "naturally" aggressive.

In any case, the motivation of exaggerated criticisms of me as a trainer is most probably in the resistant, aggressive area. They are intended to reduce my stature or to bring the rationale for training into a new, negative focus, making it unnecessary to "take the training" seriously. Refusing to deal with such issues constitutes an implicit admission that the criticisms are "correct." To respond in kind is to act in a counterdefensive manner. Two courses of action are possible. One is to interpret the motivation directly. A second is to accept the challenge, but to provide a direct interpretation (if necessary) only *after* group members have sought to analyze the psychological properties of the situation. The latter course is preferable, however, since members can diagnose and test their perceptions rather than being "led" to an answer.

Characteristics of Trainer Behavior

As a trainer, I need to be aware of members' attitudes, feelings, and behavior toward myself. I also need to be clear about the major dimensions of my role and the bases upon which I should order my behavior. In addition, I should be able to recognize the points at which my behavior is most crucial to the group. Some discussion of the characteristics of trainer behavior seems pertinent at this point.

Identification of Critical Process Events

My primary objective is to create conditions under which members learn about group behavior by taking part as participant-observers. I must ask: (1) When should I intervene? (2) At what level or

"depth" should I make remarks about some critical process event?
(3) How can I establish the participant-observer orientation, while
avoiding becoming an "expert" and creating more dependency reactions?

WHEN TO INTERVENE. Interventions may occur every few minutes or
may not be made for an entire meeting. It is difficult to specify the
appropriate frequency or time for intervention. A general rule I follow
is that my interventions decrease as member participant-observer contributions increase. If successful in introducing the participant-observer role, my interventions are less frequent in later rather than in
earlier group meetings. Yet, even this rule is limited by other considerations, as mentioned below.

LEVEL OR DEPTH OF INTERVENTIONS. One procedure is for me to
intervene in order to focus attention on events for which the motivations and assumptions are likely to be evident. Once attention has
been placed on them, these motivations should be clear not only to me
but also to members themselves. This means that early interventions
often are more superficial and restricted. Later ones can be deeper
and more fundamental. The direction, therefore, is from surface to
depth. The direction is dictated by the fact that as insights develop
into the dynamics of group functioning they can be used to produce
more fundamental insights. My level or depth of interventions is likely
to become the *standard* for participant-observer evaluation by members. Thus, it is important that I lead rather than follow members in
the pursuit of more fundamental explanations.

ESTABLISHING THE PARTICIPANT-OBSERVER ORIENTATION. The participant-observer orientation should not be introduced by "stunning" the
group with brilliant interpretations. Nor should interventions raise
the level of anxiety that members experience. They may serve to
clarify an important event which was being overlooked, or for which
the motivation was unclear, or which opens up subject matter for analysis. Members can be aided in accepting the participant-observer role
by an invitation to discuss, add, or correct my interpretations. I might
even suggest that an important event has occurred which would be
fruitful to examine in terms of motivation, assumptions, or procedural
implications. In any event, the training rationale is that members
learn about group functioning primarily by developing their own insights. They learn only incidentally by accepting my account of some
process event. The adoption by members of this rationale can go far
toward solving the dependency problems.

No Participation in Content

The topic discussed is not dictated by me as the trainer or by formal ground rules or any standard curriculum. It is created by members. I do not participate in topical discussions for at least three reasons. The first is that sooner or later such participation would determine the content. Members would come to know the kinds of topics of interest to me. Members might try to please me by moving discussions in those directions. Alternatively, they might try to prevent such topics from being discussed to punish or frustrate me.

Another reason for not participating at the content level is that it frequently is necessary to take a partisan point of view. If I do, I place myself in alliance with some members and in opposition to others. Partisan behavior of this character can seriously weaken my ability to facilitate learning of the process aspects of group functioning. A third reason is that when I discuss a topical issue it becomes more difficult to remain alert to process events and their causes. My responsibility to facilitate the examination of the process aspects of group functioning is discharged most effectively by my not getting lost in content matters.

Contacts with T-Group Members "Outside" Group Meetings

Members frequently will "hold" observations, with the idea of discussing them with me outside the group. Such discussions are likely either to increase dependency, through giving acceptance and security, or to reduce hostile reactions, through making me more acceptable to antagonistic or negative group members. Therefore, I avoid pairing with individuals or cliques. For the same reasons, I avoid initiating discussions with group members outside or inside meetings which would have similar kinds of effects.

When I am approached for a "private" discussion, I have options available other than accepting or rejecting the person who seeks to initiate a discussion. My question to myself is, "Would this discussion discharge tensions (i.e., give security) and thereby resolve a problem which more appropriately should be dealt with in the group itself?" If the answer seems to be, "Yes," I suggest that the matter might be brought up in the group. Most discussions initiated outside the T Group are of this type. However, there are some types of matters that members may wish to discuss or that are of such an objective character that dealing with them directly could be more appropriate. In general, then, my endeavor is to maintain objective rather than to develop affective relationships with members in contacts outside the group meetings. I try to create conditions under which feelings toward me can be explored publicly within the group situation rather than allowing them to be discharged, drained, or bound outside the group sessions.

Calling Attention to Feelings and Problems of Maintenance

Because of the properties of a T Group, involvement often runs high, with positive and negative feelings arising among members. Interventions which (1) recognize the significance of feelings by relating them to the situations that produce the feelings and (2) clarify the importance of constructively dealing with feelings as problems of group maintenance can lead to significant insights concerning social problem solving. Social-emotional aspects of group functioning are equal in importance to cognitive or procedural factors in decision making.

Protection of Individual Members

A critical aspect of my role as a trainer is concerned with ways to deal with a situation where a member, through high involvement, naïveté, or antagonism toward others, "overexposes" himself. Such a member creates a situation within which others are motivated to affiliate, criticize, psychoanalyze, stereotype, or attack. My questions are: "Is this behavior appropriate to a T Group?" and "If so, are the reactions that are being given constructive for the person whose behavior is under consideration and for the group as a whole?"

If, from the standpoint of training rationale, the behavior is regarded as inappropriate, and particularly if it is destructive, intervention is indicated. This usually takes the form of assessing the basis for the behavior and pointing to its wider mental health implications. Failure to deal with this problem in a T Group can result in a distortion of the aims of training. Members should engage in the analysis of individual behavior to the extent that such investigation will facilitate understanding of group problem solving.

Rewarding and Punishing Individuals or the Group as a Whole

Rewards and punishments, in even a subtle smile or frown, can indicate my pleasure or disturbance with the way individuals or the group as a whole is working. These can produce dependent and resistant kinds of reactions and a false sense of progress or failure. They also can change the course of group action without members' developing insight as to what altered their reactions.

My purpose is to react in as objective a fashion as possible. I try to avoid circumventing other more basic issues that my rewards or compliments might cover up. In addition, I want to avoid creating feelings of guilt and insecurity and eliciting retaliation by members because of inappropriate criticism. On the other hand, if real issues requiring direct, evaluative types of responses do arise, I do not avoid them by denial, by throwing the issue back to participants themselves for analysis, or through indirect procedures such as asking for clarification. The orientation which is maintained, therefore, is that phenomena being examined are a consequence of conditions as they exist. They are neither "good" nor "bad." If I clarify that my interactions are intended *not* to carry value connotations, members may correct me when they do. In any event, members come to recognize that what superficially may appear to be a reward or a punishment may, at a deeper level, have nothing to do with personal feelings.

Recapitulating Longitudinal Trends

Reactions from the point of view of a participant-observer are, characteristically, to immediate events rather than to long-term trends. If group members are to learn to evaluate longitudinal trends or changes in the group structure and behavior over time, it is likely that attention to them will originate through trainer-interventions. From my perspective, I may be able to see clear signs of changing organization within the group worthy of note. If such changes are positive in that they are due to learning, pointing them out can motivate further change. If changes are negative, the group frequently can be "unblocked" by finding the areas of malfunction.

Use of Mechanical or Formal Procedures for Achieving Coordination or Direction

A range of mechanical or formal procedures with which members have had experience in non-T Groups is likely to be suggested and tried. This usually occurs once it becomes evident that as a trainer I will not act as an ordinary leader. The training situation provides an excellent opportunity to investigate the reasons why these procedures are suggested and also their effects on the group. Some of them are discussed in this section.

Developing a Formal Role Structure by Appointing or Electing a Leader. When introductions have been completed and dependency pleas ("What should we do now?") have been interpreted rather than answered, the situation for the group still is unstructured and unclear. There are two common ways to go at this point. One is to develop a set of traditional roles. The other is to work directly toward developing an agenda. It will be assumed that the former course is taken.

At the beginning, the most reasonable way of solving the problem of having neither a leader nor rules to guide them is for members to accept traditional methods used in outside work situations. "Let's have a leader." "Joe, you be our leader." If Joe accepts, then by one criterion of agreement or another, he becomes the leader for a while. He—the appointed leader—behaves under the silent assumption that it is his job to do all the things that "leaders" do. Through silent communication, people place the responsibility on him for doing those things that are so difficult to define that they have not been specified. ("He's the leader, so he will know what to do.")

When I do not act like a leader, group members "save" themselves by creating one. On further examination, it turns out that this is not really a solution to the problem. Now the question is, "What is the leader going to do?" He usually does not have a content topic. If he does, the chances are that as soon as he proposes it for discussion the topic will be of little interest to the other members. Here, then, is a leader without followers. He is created by the followers, but when he tries to lead he is unsuccessful. Group members often were not foresighted enough to place degree of authority, length of service, or other limits on his position. Now the leader faces difficulties with members and members face difficulties with their leader. The group has the beginnings of a formal role-structure, but it turns out that the structure is not satisfactory. Soon the person granted leadership responsibility asks himself, "How can I abdicate gracefully?"

The significant decision point is that at which the suggestion of having a leader is discussed. For the members, the question is, "Would this step of designating a leader further our progress in learning about group functioning?" This question is rarely asked. Members are likely to be working toward the solution of short-term problems, and the situation usually is a rather tense one. Having a leader is an attractive suggestion.

The decision problem from my perspective is, "Would learning be helped or hindered if the group were to establish a leader?" One answer is that the learning possible is sufficiently great that an intervention is made after some exercise of the authority and responsibility of leadership has occurred. At that time, it is possible to examine the motivations, basic assumptions, and decision-point behavior. The degree of satisfaction with the results obtained from person-based leadership under T-Group conditions also can be evaluated.

The Social Stereotype for Assessing Consensus: Taking a poll. Particularly in early phases of development, a pseudo-pattern is likely to appear around the testing of consensus problems. Having heard that consensus is one "possible" criterion of agreement in a T Group, someone will say, "Okay, let's go around the table and find out what each of us thinks." This proposal may not receive support from even one other group member. Nevertheless, its proponent starts around and insists that each of the other participants acquiesce or provide clear and sufficient reasons for not doing so.

Polling is predicated on two kinds of assumptions. One is, "Agreement is present if only other members would speak up." The other is, "A member has no right to remain silent." The further implication is that agreement can be seen only by a forced question-answer operation. This kind of poll taking is likely to produce hostility and resentment. Its use under T-Group conditions may signal deeper-lying doubts about the topic under discussion which are felt but unexpressed. Because people are unable to agree fully they remain silent.

As a trainer I can focus attention on the way in which agreement was assessed and invite members to provide a critical evaluation of the effect of the poll on the group and of their reactions to it. Members usually have had enough experience with poll practices so that this procedure will release them to evaluate polling in a clear manner. Real learning about appropriate and less appropriate action in decision making can occur.

MECHANICAL CRITERIA FOR DECISIONS.   The group has the further problem of discovering when it has made a decision. If the discussion becomes heated and the group begins to divide into sides, the chances are that someone will say, "Let's take a vote." The suggestion will probably come when the group is weakest, when it is balanced about fifty-fifty with apparently a little more weight on one side than on the other. A decision is made on a split majority vote. Recalcitrant members who did not go along with the vote know they are supposed to abide by the majority decision. So they do—at one level. Psychologically, however, they may remain quite resentful because the decision fails to give adequate consideration to their minority position. The motivation underlying the "vote" is that of establishing a decision, possibly favorable to one's own position. The effect on the group is disregarded as well as the benefit which could come from arguments presented by the minority position.

The point being made is that a majority criterion is being used as the basis for determining agreement without considering other possible actions. The assumption is that the practices of outside work groups apply equally well in the present situation. Testing of this assumption, through participant-observer or trainer reactions, can give a richer meaning to the interpretation of majority rule. It can also serve to demonstrate the wisdom of using a variety of rules for decision making under certain conditions.

If members fail to evaluate spontaneously this critical process event, my training responsibility is to interrupt the flow of events. Both the motivation that led to the vote and the silent assumptions controlling the action of the group are discussed. It is the unconscious use of the majority criterion, rather than the majority criterion itself, which is considered at this point. Under certain conditions, there may be no better measure of agreement than a simple majority. It does not follow, however, that for T-Group conditions it is necessarily the best one to use.

Premature Goal or Agenda Setting.   During the early meetings of a group some member usually directs the group toward goal or agenda setting for the entire period. "Here is what we want to do," or "Here is where we want to be at the end." Because of inexperience in the group, lack of knowledge of the resources of members, and so on, goals set this early are likely to be quite unrealistic. However, once established, they are difficult to abandon and may place a burden on the further development of the group.

Underlying the formulation of rigid specifications is a sense of insecurity. The urgency for establishing certainty forces action which is inconsistent with the ability of the group members to perform. When such action is taken by the entire group, it is a fair assumption that the "fear that we aren't learning anything" is forcing them to set premature goals.

Greater learning for the group as a whole may be gained if this particular set of actions is forestalled. If the interpretations above are correct when they are made, group members gain insight into the unrealistic and "fear-provoked" nature of the endeavor. Furthermore, if the action is not interrupted, the group is likely to pursue probably unattainable goals for some time. If an interpretation is made after the group has achieved a sense of accomplishment from setting goals, it is likely to be seen by members as a rejection of their efforts and as a block to their further progress.

SECTION III.   FORMING AN AGENDA OR DEVELOPING TOPICAL MATERIAL

The core of group functioning is contained in formulating an agenda. A satisfactory procedure for developing an agenda similar to that used by any "outside" group in problem solving is one in which the resources of all members are pooled and a decision is reached by shared agreement. Many approaches to this problem can be observed in the efforts of group members to "get moving." Several are discussed below.

Developing an Agenda from "Outside" Problems. Group members may suggest an "outside" problem which is not a work problem. Integration, segregation, some political issue, or a whole variety of widespread outside problems may be mentioned. It is assumed that such problems are common to all. But some members have deep involvement in them, and others do not. The result is that, though discussed for a short time, the problems turn out not to have the interest that problems directly related to the group might produce.

Outside work problems also may be presented for discussion. Two kinds of considerations underlie these suggestions. The first is person-centered motivation. An individual assumes that a problem significant to him can be discussed in such a way as to increase his understanding of the issues involved. Alternatively, by revealing the magnitude of the problem he may expect to gain a more favorable evaluation by others. "I am the head of a corporation employing a large number of research physicists and chemists. As you know, such people don't want to concern themselves with problems of administration. My problem is to mold this group into a professional team. I need help." The individual has placed himself in a prominent position in an organization of highly trained people. Rather than actually wanting help, he may want to establish his importance in a work situation.

By formulating the question, "Why has the group been talking about this particular problem?" members can assess their own motivations for participating in the discussion and the reactions that such discussion has produced. Members usually are able to spot factors that produced the discussion. They also may see the connection between inadequate procedures for developing a *common* problem and readiness to discuss an outside problem. At one level, therefore, the solution is in the procedural area, since there are many issues which could produce worthwhile discussion if an adequate procedure for locating them were available.

Agenda Setting by Asking, "Does Anyone Know Where We Ended Yesterday?" After the group has been together for a few meetings, with some tradition and experience to guide future action, it is common for someone to ask, "Where did we end yesterday?" The assumption is that such a point will be an appropriate beginning place for today. Rarely is it so. When it is, usually it is because "yesterday's" important discussion was unfinished at the time of closing, leaving tensions that were unresolved. The group may even have designated a beginning point for today. In neither case, however, is it necessary to ask, "Where did we end yesterday?" and then deliberately to reconstruct the situation. Such a question implies mechanical continuity between yesterday and today. From a motivational standpoint, such a question shows features in common with other mechanical means for developing group action. The question, moreover, is "safe," in that continuity *logically* may be presumed to exist in the interactions of a continuing group. That it does not is because discussion frequently proceeds in *units* rather than as a continuous flow. When one unit is completed, it is likely to be followed by a topic of quite different content.

The training issue formulated by this question may be dealt with directly (particularly if discussions have taken *unit* form). Assumptions that are logical can be contrasted with those that are psychological. This emphasizes the importance of *discontinuity* at the content level as against the logical presumption of continuity.

Dividing into Smaller Groups. When a role-structure has failed, someone may propose, "Let's break up into small groups. We can express ourselves more freely if there are just two or three of us."

This idea is based partly on the assumption that the authority problem can be solved in this way. The suggestion often generates anxiety. Someone else will say, "If we start breaking apart now, we will never be able to get back together again." This kind of thought is not entirely different from a disturbance that may arise when a larger work group aspires to designate some smaller committee to take over a particular task. "What will go on in that committee that we will want to know about? What kinds of decisions will they make that will be committed to us for implementation?"

Brainstorming. Another method occasionally proposed as a basis for developing an agenda is brainstorming. All members agree to suspend a judicial, critical attitude and for a period to free-wheel on the kinds of problems that might serve as agenda material. The next step is to review the proposals from a more critical point of view and to distill them into a set of possibilities for discussion.

The motivation for brainstorming may be "just to experiment." It may be a genuine conviction that this method is a good procedure for developing agenda material. One interpretation of brainstorming is that it is symptomatic of faulty organization. An effective group *should* be able to produce ideas and, through sequential criticism of them, be able to produce better ideas. Brainstorming, at least within a training group, may constitute a way of going around problems or criticisms felt from authority figures or other group members. It is as if to say, "Since we feel personal rejection from criticism of our ideas, let's create conditions where we are not responsible for the ideas we produce. Then we can review them to see whether any ideas of value appeared." The feeling of personal attack, resulting from criticism of an idea, is avoided. The implication is that existing maintenance problems are not being dealt with in the group.

The "Handclasping" Method of "Getting a Topic." One aspect of the agenda problem is characterized by the "handclasping" phenomenon. This may occur when members of the T Group as yet do not have an adequate discussion structure for defining a common problem by joint agreement. One member, John, may propose an idea which Mary reacts to. Mary says, "I think that's a good idea. John, why don't you start it?". No member suggests that there should be a more open group discussion first to determine whether others also are interested. Rather, after receiving the support of only one member, John says, "Okay, here is the way I see it." Then, perhaps for twenty minutes or for an hour or longer, the group discusses the topic. Yet, the discussion stems neither from mutual consent, desire, nor majority agreement. It is initiated by bilateral agreement—by handclasping.

The motivation behind handclasping can be evaluated in the following way. Group members possibly have experienced and rejected other methods. They realize they cannot make effective use of an elected leader to solve problems for them. At present they are insufficiently skillful to employ a more mature developmental method. For example, they have little or no prior basis for knowing how their efforts can be coordinated when the responsibility for coordination is not placed on one person. Handclasp, to support one another in pairs or triplets, becomes a basis for authorizing a discussion. The support elicited may not be genuine. Because Mary and John are anxious, she would have supported any proposal and he would have accepted "authorization" from any member.

This pattern appears when the group has accepted responsibility for agenda setting, but has not yet accepted the assumption that discussion topics should represent group-wide and valid agreements that have been established deliberately. Certain assumptions underlying the actions can be inferred. First, the person who presents the topic acts without awareness that his problem may be of little interest to the other members. He makes no effort to evaluate whether silent members are in agreement or whether they are just "going along." Second, nonparticipating individuals fail to exercise member responsibility to clarify their positions concerning the proposal. No one in the group is acting in terms of the basic assumption of group-wide acceptance of a topic. Learning how group action may be controlled by handclasping is one of the rewards of T-Group experience, particularly because such learning has direct transfer value for use in work situations.

Trainer decisions with respect to interpreting handclasping are difficult since they relate to other kinds of phenomena. A decision made by handclasping may occur so quickly that it may be difficult for the group to appreciate either the action or its significance. Also, members are so accustomed to this action that sometimes it is difficult to recognize it at all. Furthermore, to interrupt in order to interpret the phenomenon may be seen as disturbing a natural flow of discussion. In addition, it may be that after the group starts to analyze the problem it becomes a rather genuine one and provokes widespread interest. It seems there is an effective discussion and members are happy. Everyone is involved and the interaction is fruitful. However, the procedure was technically defective in that an ineffective method was used to determine the topic.

At this point in development, groups frequently mistakenly interpret their own experience and say, "We really hit that problem from every side. We had good agreement. We worked effectively right down the line." A critical feature that has training implications is absent. The group did not determine, through deliberate mobilization of its joint resources, whether the problem it dealt with represented common agreement concerning the direction to move most profitably.

As a trainer, I might focus the problem by asking, "How did we get into this discussion?" If members are aware of the bilateral aspects of the decision, a discussion of it can occur immediately. If they are not, a decision has to be made whether to confront the issue at that time or withhold remarks until several examples may be used to identify the widespread use of this device and its consequences for group action.

The handclasping phenomenon may be prominent during the entire period of the meetings. Indeed, it even may be the basis by which efforts to use authority or outside procedures occur. However, it seems most appropriate to reserve consideration of it until efforts to use authority and other mechanical procedures have failed. The significance of the phenomenon can be appreciated most readily after members have had considerable experience as participant-observers. If introduced too early, the handclasping phenomenon may be regarded as a trivial detail.

Topic Jumping. Another pattern, related to handclasping but actually different from it, is topic jumping. After a topic has been presented and a discussion commenced, some member may emphasize a side aspect of the basic problem as initially formulated. Now some other person accepts the altered emphasis and, thereby, shifts the discussion. The second issue may be so unrelated to the original topic that the connection between the two becomes quite remote. Here again is evidence of how members may unwittingly "use" the group by swinging the discussion into line with their own needs and interests. Topic jumping would not occur if members were performing functions such as "clarifying the issue," "restating the problem," or "testing for direction." It shares with handclasping the feature that agreement between two members is sufficient to *shift* the entire item of discussion.

Topic jumping is less likely to occur when the problem under discussion has been decided upon by common agreement. Then members already have committed themselves to consideration of the central theme. Prior discussion usually clarified the topic sufficiently so that a clear distinction can be made between central and side issues. Topic jumping may occur because an individual emphasizes a side aspect without realizing that the entire course of the discussion is being diverted. This, too, signals faulty procedure in the inability of group members to recognize the need for and to supply direction.

Once I place significance on an understanding of the action, topic jumping is relatively easy for members to identify. A remark such as, "How did we come to discuss this topic when earlier the topic under discussion was _____?" focuses the group's attention on the differences between the two topics and may provoke a diagnostic review of the decision-making points.

The "Plop." There is another very important related situation. A member may say, "Let's talk about this topic." The remark falls on deaf ears. Someone else says, "Let's talk about this [different] topic," and that remark stimulates no response either. This phenomenon has been described as a "plop," "thud," or "dud." A proposal is placed on the table, but it provokes no response either. Now the T Group *really* is faced with technical difficulties. People stop listening on a bilateral basis, as in handclasping and topic jumping. Also, group members have entirely stopped listening to one another. No one hears what the other person is saying. Each member seems to be listening only to his own "inner noise." The period in which plops occur is a difficult one for a T Group. It almost always produces anxiety, feelings of personal rejection, and finally, rejection of others or the group as a whole. Now, members say, "We are a bad group. We don't have *esprit de corps*. We don't have anything. I wish I were not in this group." Long silences are likely to occur. Hostile feelings among members may be more evident than in other periods.

To solve the problem of the plop, a group member has to give up some of himself and become more attentive to and accepting of what others are saying. It is as though there were a moving equilibrium, a balance between "how much I'll let you talk" and "how much will you listen to me in return." During this period the equilibrium is upset. After the plop problem is resolved, one becomes more ready to listen closely to ideas carried in the other person's words. The result is that one's own contributions more readily are understood by others. People are learning the urgency of listening. They are "listening" *outside* their ears, rather than *inside* them. Because the quality of listening is subject to measurement, changes in listening ability may represent one of the more fruitful areas for research into the effects of training.

Recognition of Decision-Making Points. Discussions in which decision-making points pass unrecognized result in group action in unanticipated directions. After this type of event occurs repetitively, members are likely to begin to test for the feasibility of a proposal for action *before* the action actually occurs. Deliberate evaluation of the significant decision points and skill in considering feasibility of actions are likely to develop quickly. The basis for moving forward is the idea of concern for decision-making points.

Actual use of the concept of decision-making points is possible only after the participant-observer orientation has become standard within the group. Active use, with consequent advantages in increasing decision effectiveness, is possible only when members themselves spot decision-making points without trainer participation.

Assessing Procedural Possibilities. Another indication that a group is working in a sound fashion is found in the way procedures are placed in use. It is not assumed that one procedure is as good as another. Rather, deliberate consideration is given to identifying what procedure would be more suitable for the problem under discussion.

The procedure used to assess agreement may be quite different, for example, when a factual matter is being discussed from when opinions are being expressed. In the first case, consensus might be the appropriate procedure. In the second case, the procedure might be to summarize and to locate areas within which opinions are both common and different as an initial step. Next, members might deliberately agree to proceed farther, based either on the areas of communality or on the areas of divergency. In the two cases, the difference in *procedures* is dictated by the nature of the material under discussion.

Again, progress in assessing procedures is likely only after the participant-observer orientation is well established. For me as a trainer to "prod" means that members have not learned the importance of such an assessment and, therefore, are unable to use diagnostic cues themselves.

Agenda Setting Through a Problem Census, Followed by Elimination of Items and Revision in the Priority Order of Items That Remain. Contrasted with the above methods is agenda setting through a problem census. Members, by common agreement, first explore procedures to be employed. Then a problem census is conducted, possibly by using some flexible method of recording (e.g., a blackboard) to list suggestions. Items not directly related to the basic problem are eliminated. The remaining items are then shifted into a sequential order. Such a procedure is "fitted" to the psychological properties of a training group. It provides a deliberate procedure for discussion. The way is opened for the material to be discussed to be determined by the members themselves. The order of discussion is both systematic and functional. The list of topics is relevant to the basic problem and ordered in a progressive sequence. Difficulties in discussing the method of procedure are anticipated and are resolved *before* discussion occurs.

Agenda-Setting Problems

From my point of view as a trainer, these are among the important considerations that arise in a T Group around the agenda problem. They also characterize important types of problems that a work-group leader can expect to face when a shift is made from leader-determined agenda content to agenda items which are member composed.

SECTION IV.   PERSONAL AND INTERMEMBER PROBLEMS OF A SOCIAL-EMOTIONAL CHARACTER

Social-emotional reactions can either hinder or facilitate the problem-solving effectiveness of a work group. Therefore, it is important to examine them within the T Group in order to gain insights regarding basic dimensions involved. Typical social-emotional problems and their implications for training are discussed below.

Getting Acquainted. Because of the importance of the first meetings for later group development, the theme of "getting acquainted" will be discussed in some detail.

Soon after the start of the first meeting, it is most likely that someone will propose, "Let's introduce ourselves, so we will know who we are and so we can work better together." Assuming that as the trainer I do not intervene to prevent it, this suggestion in all likelihood will be accepted. Group members will then start a round of introductions.

Although several motivations are likely to underlie the suggestion of introductions and to drive toward its adoption, four are sufficiently general to merit examination. The first is that of *reducing anxiety*. Something active of this sort avoids the tension that might develop if group members are left with nothing concrete to discuss. A second set of motivations served by introductions is *identifying boundaries for future behavior*. For example, if the group contains a member identified with labor, then one must be more circumspect about attitudes and opinions expressed in that area. Alternatively, if some member is identified with management, medicine, religion, or the military services, such knowledge can serve to set limits for what appropriately can and cannot be said. (Indeed, in certain cases, introductions may serve to identify occupations or interests which others feel are subject to attack and thus to develop a basis for rejection.) A third set of motivations is in the *area of status*. Members have the opportunity of judging their own "outside" positions against those of others. Possible alliances and aversions also may become evident at this point. A fourth motivation is that of seeking to judge the probable *level of action* that can be attained from knowledge of the others. All in all, the power of the social stereotype that action is facilitated by self-presentations is strong.

Operating to prevent introductions are several other motivational factors which are likely to be relatively weaker. Included are the desires immediately to identify and to develop a content task, fear of revealing one's lack of back-home accomplishment, anxiety that the trainer may want the group to act other than in this manner, among others.

There are basic assumptions upon which a group acts when it solves its initial problems through introductions. One is that introductions will serve to acquaint members with one another; another is that verbal, autobiographical self-accounts, even though given without specifications, help members to get to know one another. Both assumptions need further examination. The first is, perhaps, correct within a very narrow range. Much of significance for understanding individual behavior, however, either is deliberately withheld or is not given because the speaker is unaware of its possible future importance for others. In either case, introductions rarely satisfy the purpose for which they are intended.

The second aspect of introductions, emphasizing their verbal, autobiographical character, suggests why they often are not too useful in aiding group action. Unless group action is prevented until criteria are established for the type of content to be presented, introductions are subject both to conscious and unconscious screening. The selective factors are dictated by a variety of personal needs. The likelihood is great that, without discussion of procedural standards for introductions, only positive content will be revealed. Each member listens either to improve his self-presentation or, if noncompetitive, to decide how much to leave out in order not to appear inadequate. Thus self-presentations frequently are mechanical and not too useful as the group gropes for some way to get started.

The assumption here is that a trainer-intervention does not interrupt the behavior already described. The sequence, however, is important. After the suggestion of introductions is made, there is a decision-making point both for the trainer and the group members. The options for either are to interrupt and to make suggestions as to the more useful dimensions to be included in the introductions. Since only rarely is such a suggestion likely to be made by a member, the present discussion is limited to my options as a trainer.

I can interrupt to suggest that introductions may be more useful if certain considerations are included. For example, indicating the kind of behavior in which a person seeks self-improvement often is of value. In so doing, however, I establish the precedent of *setting procedural standards*. A warm, friendly atmosphere may be created within which members are ready to accept dependency on me. In my view, the preferred solution is to permit the introduction phase to take its "natural" course and then to take advantage of the situation thus produced for introducing the *participant-observer orientation* through a suggestion that members may wish to evaluate the entire procedure.

If unsystematic self-presentations have not been forestalled, then it can also be asked how the decision to introduce was reached. Common is the situation where one person says, "Let's have introductions." A second person indicates, "Okay, why don't *you* start?" If two or three others nod in agreement the sequence is likely to begin. A decision has been reached which controls group action for a considerable period of time. Such support of two or three members, but without involvement or commitment by the group as a whole, is an excellent example of handclasping. After the sequence is completed, as the trainer I invite participant-observer consideration of the events leading up to and through the decision to introduce. Insight into handclasping as the basis for decision making is one of the most valuable sources of learning in a T Group. (See Section III of this chapter for a more detailed discussion of handclasping.)

Interpersonal Alliances from Handclasping and Topic Jumping. Both positive and negative interpersonal feelings will begin to be evident when the material under discussion has arisen from handclasping or topic-jumping behavior. Pairing and clique formation among those controlling the discussion and hostility and antagonism among them and others who feel negative or resistant, frequently appear. Lack of member commitment to the topic discussed can be seen in side remarks and conversations which indicate little involvement in the task. More explicitly, the need is to express views which will not become part of the "public record." At this time, alliances can be spotted within the group. These can serve as the basis for pairing and cliques both inside and outside the T Group. Such cliques frequently are invisible, with contacts among members occurring in living quarters and social-recreational settings. Cliques of this type may indicate that the group is not dealing with feelings and problems of maintenance.

Cliques have positive and negative aspects. On the positive side, two or three or a few members, talking informally, may be able to clarify the issues being faced by the group. They may then be able to act more constructively toward their resolution of difficulty within the group. On the negative side, such alliances are likely to produce areas of private agreement which limit members from participating freely within the group. As I see the problem, it involves dealing with cliques and interpersonal alliances in such a way as to increase understanding of how they form and their effects on the group. This may be done by introducing a discussion of the problem at the point where members indicate that alliances are forming on the outside. A remark such as, "What are the tensions in the group which have led to private discussions on the outside?" can release members to express feelings which ordinarily are withheld in work groups. Feelings toward the trainer, the group as a whole, and specific other members are likely to be verbalized. If they are dealt with in a procedurally adequate manner, both a cathartic and insight-producing value can result. One "rule" is that remarks, particularly negative ones, are expressed and supported by reference to specific, concrete actions that have occurred within the group. In this way the discussion moves in the direction of feelings related to the actions that produced them, rather than to some vague set of "personality" characteristics.

Gate Keeping To Increase Partisan Strength or To Weaken Opposition. To be contrasted with concern for the opinions of others is gate keeping for the purpose of increasing partisan strength rather than of providing a blocked member access to the group. The motivation is to force a member to express his views, either to gain his support or to bring his opposition into the open. Under such conditions, gate keeping has a quality of manipulation. As such it may cause resentment and division among group members.

Participant-observer evaluation which contrasts differences between maintenance gate keeping and gate keeping for partisan objectives can clarify the meaning of the term. Also diagnostic cues as to the motivations on which it is based can be provided. Members will then frequently intervene to prevent manipulatory gate-keeping actions and also to aid a blocked member to participate.

"Let's Talk Personalities." After the group has been meeting for some time, a rather strong emphasis may be placed on personality factors in group behavior. "Tell me what you think I've done wrong. I can take it." This apparently spontaneous remark can change the atmosphere of the group and produce significant effects on future meetings.

Several types of motivations drive toward positive reactions to this proposal. Without trainer interpretation, it is most likely to be accepted. Frustrations have arisen in the group, and people may have reacted strongly and in such a way as to disturb others. One way of expressing hostile feelings is through direct personality evaluation. There are also the following commonly stated convictions: "I can really improve if people will tell me what I've been doing that disturbs them." "Since I can't see myself too well, it might be helpful to see myself as I am seen by others." Because of a cultural stereotype regarding the acceptance of criticism, it is very difficult for members, who might genuinely be disturbed, to react negatively to it. Other motivations, including using this form of behavior as a way of defying group opinion, also may be evident from time to time.

If discussing individual personalities and motivations is accepted as a basis of group action, it is probably by handclasping. As a trainer I intervene to suggest (1) the importance of ensuring consensus for such action and (2) that if members' personal behavior is to be discussed the framework of discussion should be planned in advance. Valuable learning is likely to be the result. Personal evaluations carried out in an unsystematic way, however, are not indicated. Too frequently they provide a guise for direct, hostile attack. Unfortunately, members are not necessarily in a position to assess whether the defenses and personality organization of evaluated persons readily allow for acceptance of criticism.

Not infrequently, when groups analyze the issues involved, the conclusion is that the effort is worth more than the hazards contained. Furthermore, training groups primarily are concerned with group behavior and with personality only to the extent that personal feedback aids members to interact more effectively in accomplishing group objectives. Therefore, a *significant* shift into personality analysis is likely to emphasize psychodynamic problems and to take on some of the properties of a therapeutic group. The point made here is not that personality is unimportant in group behavior or that personality assessment may not be useful, but that training is not therapy, even though it may carry therapeutic overtones. Finally, the skills required for effectively dealing with personality problems are, in my view, quite different from those employed in conducting a training group centered on group-level events.

In my experience, the best setting for exploring personal factors in group effort is in the actual work team, that is, the so-called family work group. Under the team situation, participants have known one another over an extended period of time. They have available for examination a rich reservoir of relations with one another which is likely not to have been openly communicated and evaluated in any depth. The team T Group makes this kind of personal feedback possible.

My personal conclusion is that the kind of learning depicted in this chapter is very difficult to acquire in a team T Group. The kind of rich personal learning afforded by a team T Group is not easy to acquire in a T Group initially composed of strangers. Both are desirable. Experience to date suggests that the regular T Group, followed by the team T Group, constitutes the optimal sequence.

"Groupiness"—Trying To Develop Cohesion. Once a T Group experiences a sense of progress, a feeling of "groupiness" is likely to appear. Often certain members orient their remarks around the "We're-a-good-group" point of view.

Underlying the groupiness reaction are several motivations. The first is pride in accomplishment. The effort of members has produced a series of steps which appear to indicate progress. Members take satisfaction from participation in a group which seems able to solve problems. Equally important are the cohesion feelings produced when a threat to group integrity has been met successfully. The third is more complex and is unrelated to the quality of group per se. Rather it appears to arise from satisfaction in *belongingness* as an end in itself. It is related to the need for affiliation—a need which sometimes is not satisfied through membership in more formal types of work groups. When satisfaction with group action deriving from this source is verbalized, it also has a contagion effect. This occurs in part because of successful efforts by members to achieve training objectives and in part because it brings to the fore belongingness needs in others. In the extreme, the latter motivation constitutes a "social hunger" and functions as a "cause" for individuals pursuing membership opportunities.

The distinction between the two factors producing feelings of groupiness is a difficult one for group members to draw. Sensitivity to the dynamics of cohesion can be increased if I, as a trainer, initially point out that such a distinction is possible. Then members can diagnose which factor is the dominant source of feelings of cohesion at different times. Introducing the distinction is all that is needed for members to use it. Understanding of the sequence that relates work accomplishment (the successful solution of a threatening problem) to cohesion feelings is important for group members. This sequence is basic to an understanding of "team spirit" and *esprit de corps* in work groups as well as within the training situation.

Fear-Provoking Remarks. One of the most subtle, as well as effective, ways of "freezing" a group with indecision and creating anxiety is the fear-provoking remark. Such a remark often takes the form of an untested assumption about what others will think of some course of action. Presumed negative consequences usually are claimed to follow some decision. Sometimes the simple statement, "It won't work," is all that is said. Characteristically, such remarks are not documented with reasons or "evidence."

The motivation of a fear-provoking remark is the personal anxiety of the individual who initiates it regarding an action being considered by the group. By definition, it is not a reality-based observation. Therefore, while it may appear "real," it is, in fact, a false assessment. While from an objective point of view the fear is unfounded, it has psychological "reality" for the person expressing it and requires attention within the group.

Fear-provoking remarks frequently are not sensed by members. As the trainer, therefore, I may intervene by suggesting that the remark is an important one for group members to understand and deal with. Frequently, it becomes clear that the initiator failed to understand an intermediate step to be taken by the group in changing from its present activity to some new one. Oftentimes, by members' asking for documentation, the initiator realizes that psychodynamic rather than reality factors are motivating his concern. Equally important for analysis by group members is why it is possible for a fear-provoking remark to immobilize action through its contagion effects.

Silences. It is typical for silences of a few seconds to several minutes to occur occasionally in T Groups. Several factors can cause silences. One is that there seems nothing more to say. Yet, shifting the topic is not feasible because someone may want to add to the present discussion or there is no agreement on a new topic. Silence is the result. A second factor in producing silence stems from the group's being divided into two sides and, apparently, being completely blocked. Since no one seems to know how to resolve the impasse, silence results. Another is when a proposal is made which others wish neither to object to nor to support. Still another is when the group has failed, and members feel the situation is "hopeless."

Regardless of the cause, silences at the beginning of a group are tension producing. Frequently the silences are of only short duration, since in groups of this size there usually are members who will break them. However, as the group develops they may become longer. This usually indicates that members have been able to withstand a degree of tension; and the capacity to withstand silences indicates that they are not "just talking to avoid them."

From the training standpoint, silence represents a critical decision point in group action. It is common for the remark which breaks the silence to shift the topic into a new area. Equally significant is the fact that after the participant-observer orientation has been established, members are likely to regard a marked period of silence as denoting an appropriate time for process evaluation. Alternatively, and depending on my assessment of the reasons producing the silence, I may take advantage of a period of silence as an opportunity to introduce new process considerations.

The Silent Member. The discussion here will be limited to a consideration of the reactions of others to the silent person. Different reasons for members' being silent are not considered. Often, when the group seems unable to move smoothly, some member will say, "We are in difficulty. Since the silent ones have not participated they should be able to help us out." All too frequently the silent person is in "double trouble." He may have no effective basis for participation. Nonetheless, his participation is explicitly requested, as it has not been when the group was satisfying to its active members.

Intervening which invites participant-observer evaluation can serve to protect silent members from criticism or attack. At the same time, it clarifies the motivations that bring attention to them during such periods. Such a procedure also can have the result of releasing the silent person to express his feelings, providing a bridge for his more active participation.

The point of view expressed here, as throughout this section, is that care should be exercised to ensure that feelings are related to the concrete events that produce them, rather than to abstract statements about "personality."

Summary

A T Group may experience many significant agenda problems, process events, and social-emotional problems in the pursuit of its goal of learning how groups work. An early period is typified by joint efforts coordinated through mechanical or arbitrary methods. A later period may be identified through integrated and functionally sounder problem-solving procedures. Characteristics of T Groups that have been presented are apparent only in the kind of group situation described. They may or may not appear in an orderly progression. Ordinarily they do not. One characteristic may appear and then, because of some critical problem that the group faces, it may function in a more mature way as the result of the natural resources of people. However, group members are unaware of why the group happened to proceed in this fashion. Members, therefore, have not yet learned the fundamental aspects of integrated group functioning. At some later time the same mature behavior may occur through deliberate, conscious planning and action. Still later the group may revert to an earlier pattern with a continuous course of movement, backward and forward and forward and backward, depending on the total forces acting on the group. "Now we are happy; we had a group which was wonderful today." But later, "The group is terrible. Today it was just awful." "We didn't make any progress," or "We couldn't get started; we couldn't find our direction; we couldn't remember what we did yesterday. It took deliberate effort to get our group started." The point is that skill in dealing with process difficulties does not develop in an orderly direction. Yet, a general order can be abstracted in which later developments can occur only when earlier ones have been experienced. Each time a T Group goes back to an earlier pattern of behavior, the proposition is that it remains there for a shorter period of time. By this time it is able to solve its problems and move forward again by better methods than were used previously.

A major contribution of the trainer in making this development possible is to establish within the group a participant-observer orientation. He does this by establishing the precedent of giving examples of the *level* of phenomena that can be examined. He also suggests the legitimacy of evaluating motivations, by emphasizing the importance of analyzing procedures for their effectiveness, and by identifying decision-making points. The T Group is thus very different from many of the groups in which people are located and work. Does this mean that such training is irrelevant? In every work group there is a control system. We may not recognize it. It has leadership which either is imposed or created. The leader operates with varying degrees of freedom from control because the conditions of his operation and authority are unstated. It has rules that may be unsatisfactory for establishing what is fair and what is not. These may be suitable or not suitable for the requirements of problem solving under which the group is organized. Identifying the problem, or problems, of common significance to a group is important in both training and work groups. Formulating agenda topics so that they are accessible for discussion and problem solving is important in a T Group or a work group. The ability to make explicit the group's rules is important in a T Group or in any kind of work group. When a group is able to accept a leader who can function in the sense that his responsibility is that of *creating* rather than controlling the problem-solving procedures, it has passed one of the tests of being a mature group.

Leadership is important—very important—but leadership is not an "unknown." It is not simply a person-based position of undefined authority. As people become better and better acquainted with the properties of groups in problem-solving operations, more and more leaders come to reinterpret the authority and responsibility under which they operate. They see themselves, not as persons to control or to guide or to direct or to get right answers from others, but rather to discover how to create the conditions of work under which the right answer can be achieved. The evidence is plentiful that when effective discussion of a complex problem takes place and when only partial information is held by any person, the products or decision of best quality are ones achieved through joint discussion.

13

Training in Conflict Resolution

Murray Horwitz

The analysis of T-Group operation, which follows, will refer frequently to the distinction between individual needs and group goals. "Individual needs" are used to refer, somewhat roughly, to states of dissatisfaction, deprivation, discomfort, and the like, within the individual. "Goal" is used to refer to a particular activity or environmental outcome which may be need reducing.

The Goal of the T Group

Some critics allege that T Groups are designed to make people anxious in order "to see what happens." Although certainly there are unstructured features of a T Group, the T Group does generate a group goal which, however, will ordinarily differ from the individual goals with which trainees enter the group. Frustration arises from the goal's being difficult to define and exceedingly difficult to attain.

The trainee may be oriented toward reaching a more or less specific goal—X′, e.g., to deal more effectively with persons in authority. A second trainee may be oriented toward reaching a specific goal—X″, e.g., to work better with subordinates. By contrast, the trainer is oriented toward what might be called the meta-goal—X, namely, establishing the group conditions which are necessary for maximally meeting the needs of the various members who enter the group with discrepant individual goals. This goal is enforced upon members by the particular characteristics of T-Group interaction.

The underlying task of the T Group is to develop a social system which enables maximal satisfaction for each of its members. Working to develop a social system of this type is a relatively novel experience in our society. In the course of this effort, individuals are given the opportunity to test old, accustomed practices in groups. They may come to see and to try out new possibilities for behavior. They may come also to a fresh examination of their own emotional reactions to others, recognition of which was previously defended against or distorted, and thereby be led to more effective ways of dealing with these reactions. Thus, although all persons involved in T Groups may be found to verbalize a similar goal for the group, upon analysis it becomes evident that their actual goals must turn out to be quite dissimilar.

Early Conflicts in the T Group

Typically, trainees will expect the trainer to launch the T Group with some statement of the group's goal. This expectation is in line with experience in other groups, but would seem also to be based on the present necessity of developing coordinated effort on a new and undefined activity by a collection of individuals who may be relative strangers. The trainer may choose to say nothing about the goal of the T Group, in which case he places himself at the outset in conflict with the group's expectations. Characteristically, however, trainers will attempt a first statement of the group's goal, either within the T Group or in an orientation meeting preceding the session. Either by implication, or explicitly, the trainer tells the group that (1) *they* will do the curriculum planning, with his help if desired; (2) there is no optimal curriculum, but that this will have to be developed more or less *de. novo;* and (3) it does not matter too much what they decide to work on—that they will learn something from any experience that develops or is developed.

The trainer and trainees are likely to have different understandings of the meta-goal implications of the verbalized group goal. The trainer's introduction is therefore usually experienced by both trainer and trainees as unsatisfactory and as having poor value for guiding the group's first steps. Unless members are unusually sophisticated in group dynamics, they can have little appreciation of the complexities of social organization which are implied by the verbalized or manifest goal and are therefore unlikely to understand the notion of working on the meta-goal of developing a group that is capable of attaining the manifest goal. Under these conditions, they are apt to feel that there is something peculiar, either charlatanic or manipulatory, in the trainer's not having, or withholding, a curriculum. The notion that the trainees will learn something of value, no matter what they tackle, may be reassuring to the trainer, since what the trainees may experience as floundering can properly be seen by the trainer as exploration of the necessary background conditions for individual goal attainment. However, from the trainees' standpoint there should be specifiable knowledge or skill coming from the T-Group experience. And if specifiable, why does not the trainer attempt to make such a specification? The trainer, however, is faced with the problem that in attempting such a specification (which, incidentally, would probably require a very extended period of didactic presentation), he would not be able to gear his necessarily abstract presentation into the diverse interests, backgrounds, and frames of reference of the group—all of which he cannot know. Frequently, therefore, trainers feel that their introductory remarks are somewhat ritualistic, i.e., nonfunctional in relation to helping the group select its first or subsequent activities. However, the trainer performs the ritual since members expect it, and he thereby avoids both too early a disturbance of members' expectations and too great a focus on the "strangeness" of his own behavior, which is motivated by goals not shared by the members.

In line with the manifest goal of the T Group, the group's next apparent task, following the trainer's attempt at orientation, is to develop some activity which will be profitable for the members. Left to their own devices, members may drift into such activities as introducing themselves to one another, discussing some general topic of personal interest to one member, starting a problem census, and so on. If the trainer chooses to be active at this point, he can elaborate such activities into designs which enable rather detailed study by the group of the effects of their action; e.g., he might suggest that the group *plan* member introductions or even experiment with different methods for getting acquainted. Some trainers may go further, providing pre-planned exercises with content which would not ordinarily occur to trainees, but is judged to aid the group in getting started. It is probably true that any opening activity, whether mainly influenced by members or trainer, will generate conflict. Even so apparently innocuous an activity as members' taking turns around the table to introduce themselves entails divergent interests, hinging around such matters as back-home status and facility in impromptu speaking before a group of strangers. Ordinarily, these divergences are not too clearly recognized, but are readily identified in subsequent discussion about how members felt about the conduct of the introduction.

Let us follow first the course of the problem census. Frequently, the listing of problems proceeds to awesome dimensions, quite beyond the capability of any group to handle. To get the list into manageable shape, classifications are necessary. And these groupings of the problems make explicit the fact that some persons' problems are closer to some members than to other members.

The following are possible ways (among others) of reaching agreement about a problem for common work:

1. Discovering or inventing a goal for the group, which either incorporates each of the separate *goals* listed in the problem census or is a totally new goal which satisfies members' separate *needs* (as distinct from members' goals).

2. Developing a compromise solution whereby each member agrees to relinquish some of his own interests in order to proceed with work on some task which will have at least partial satisfaction-value for all.

3. Developing a goal on the basis of legitimation, according to which each member agrees to adopt a given goal accepted according to some criterion of legitimacy (e.g., tossing a coin, doing what the "expert" trainer "tells us to do," depending on majority vote, and others).

Option one is usually impossible for one of two reasons. In relation to inventing an inclusive goal—a formidable task even under ideal circumstances—there is the probably inevitable difficulty that the individual goals which have been listed are inadequate statements of the goals which members really had in mind. In relation to finding a goal which will satisfy members' needs (as distinct from the listed goals), the group is in an even worse position, for members have not at this point discussed their needs; and it is probably unlikely, in view of the restraints attendant on working with strangers, that they could carry out such a discussion effectively, if indeed at all.

A difficulty in pursuing the second option of compromise is that there are no clear criteria existing in the early stages of the group about how much each member should give up with respect to his own need satisfaction, as related to the need satisfaction of others. It would appear that the group must set up some form of legitimacy system in order to proceed with defining its goal. The group, in other words, now has a problem concerning its underlying mode of operation which is shared by each individual—namely, to find a way of establishing criteria for the legitimate resolution of disagreement. The task of finding something in common to study already has been accomplished, although perhaps not completely recognized, and during this period the main learning of the group will follow from the pursuit of this particular problem. It would appear that the initial setting out of poorly formulated goals is necessary—necessary in that it furnishes the opportunity for learning what must happen if group goal setting is to be geared into the individual desires of group members.

We have said that other modes of opening the group are possible. The preplanned experience set up by the trainer would be expected to have at least two immediate effects: (1) it supplies members with a common reservoir of experience for coordinated work; (2) the salient feature of the experience may be that it is trainer-imposed. In the latter event, the underlying problem of the group becomes the matter of dealing with authority relationships. While this may be a fruitful task, it has the disadvantage that the learning needed by the trainees may extend into other types of relationships, which may now become underemphasized. Where there is primary focus on authority problems, the problem of how to develop agreement among members is not avoided but is considerably complicated by the fact that agreement must be sought while members are doing battle with a relatively powerful authority figure. The group may coalesce around the task of dealing with the trainer, but the danger is that both for subjective and external reasons it may come to fixate upon the task at the expense of the more general problem of developing criteria for reaching agreement among all members of the group.

The Development of a Legitimacy Structure as a Background Condition for Group Work

We have suggested that a necessary condition for the resolution of conflict (or what is the same thing—for making a group decision) is that members must agree upon the criteria for legitimizing decisions. At least three alternatives may occur in something like a sequence of phases. On first coming together, members are likely to apply quite diversified criteria for the acceptance or rejection of alternative suggestions before the group. Members may variously feel that special weight should be given to the opinions of those who are "experts," or to the opinions of individuals who give evidence of having been successful in other situations generally, or to persons most like themselves in whom they have trust, or to persons who hold high status outside the group and are thereby accustomed to "command." Other members may feel that major weight should be given to considerations of "realism," i.e., how feasible or realizable the suggestion is or, on the other hand, to considerations of how psychologically appropriate a suggestion is, in the sense of "meeting needs."

Such diversity should create the perception within the group that members cannot predict how others will line up on a given issue. Persons using different criteria may sometimes agree with one another on a specific issue, but this gives no assurance that they will not disagree on another. The task of the group, at this point, becomes that of ascertaining the bases for decision of the various members. It is likely that members will feel they cannot understand one another, that they are unsure about what makes the other person "tick," and that, in the absence of mutual understanding, they cannot act together. One may expect to find that members, in their bewilderment, will give evidence of dependency on the trainer, on other authoritative persons, or even on authoritative documents.

Through working together—either as incidental learning or through more focused effort—group members should develop increasing knowledge of the various criteria for decision making that exist in the group. The group task then becomes one of arriving at some set of mutually agreed-upon criteria. Let us assume (as I believe to be true) that the requirements of the group situation force members into adopting criteria for evaluating suggestions along one or the other (or both) of two dimensions: adequacy with respect to enabling locomotion on a task; adequacy for satisfying the various individual needs of members. At this point, members can be located in one of two "dimensional" camps. On our assumption, members believe they know where others in the group stand, and the parties to any conflict should be mutually perceived as representing one or the other of the opposing positions. Thus, disagreement on an issue implies conflict for the control of the social system. It is likely that conflict at this point will be not between individuals but between subgroups representing given positions.

Let us assume now, as the third phase of developing a legitimacy system, that a working agreement has been reached, according to which members say, "We will give 50 per cent weight to considerations of 'needs' and 50 per cent to 'task locomotion or goals.'" The basis for arriving at legitimate decisions now exists. Conflicts which arise within this legitimacy system may be of two forms. One is based on variations in individual interpretations on how the legitimacy criteria are to be applied; these differences presumably could be resolved by some method of adjudication. However, the second form of conflict which may arise implies, in essence, that some member is rejecting the agreed-upon legitimacy system. That is, if A's proposal should be carried over B's proposal, but B refuses to go along, then he is "reneging" on the rules of the system. He should be perceived as acting only in relation to his own needs, as acting "arbitrarily." Simultaneously, he should be perceived as attacking the system to which others have agreed. Under these circumstances, the group members would be expected to feel resentment, since B, in effect, is attempting to increase the weight given his own desires at the group's expense. Rationally, the group should attempt to restore its expected weight to its initial level; emotionally, this attempted restoration should be experienced as a counterattack, since B's action has threatened the group's capacity to function. The case is even more marked where the legitimacy structure assigns so much weight to each person's desire per se (e.g., as chairman, A's desire has so much legitimate weight, whatever the basis of his desire). Then if B ignores A's weighted desire, this constitutes direct usurpation of A's expected weight and should create threat for him individually, producing rather clear-cut tendencies toward counterattack.

The General Course of T-Group Development

The previous account of various forms of legitimation procedures did not consider how the group might arrive at the third, and presumably most desirable, phase. Let us assume that in working toward an agreed-upon legitimacy system—as in work toward any other type of agreement—each member strives to influence the outcome to satisfy his own needs. Now, characteristically in public discussion, persons will be more inclined to talk about the goal they would like to pursue than about the needs they are trying to meet. For goals are more impersonal, less revealing of "weakness"; moreover, they give the impression that the person is offering a "constructive" suggestion to the group, rather than simply raising problems. Although the goal statement contains information about needs, this information is quite incomplete. Thus, the judgments which others make about the person's needs will tend to be relatively inaccurate. In the course of presenting possible goals (as in the problem census) the group has skipped a necessary phase in its problem solving, namely, giving adequate attention to defining the problem. In this sense, the group is attempting to get adequate definition of the problem by considering a "motion" for action. It might be noted that it is likely that such parliamentary procedure has taken this course for the reasons alluded to above. In many situations, it is difficult to expect (1) that persons will feel free to talk about needs as opposed to goals, (2) that persons will have the ability to define their own needs in a straightforward statement, and (3) that persons will be able to communicate the relevant aspects of the need, where relevance depends at least in part upon knowing something about the auditor's needs as well.

This situation leads to special difficulties. Given a need, it is clear that many goals can be potentially satisfying. But each person states a particular goal. The discrepancies among the various goals produce an impression of incompatibility—that there are too many goals to handle and that they are too divergent. On the other hand, if needs could be stated, it would appear that not a single goal, but a range of goals, would be potentially satisfying to a member. It is more likely, then, that members would be able to design activities to yield more widespread satisfaction and that the task of finding a common goal would be made easier.

Functionally, then, it would appear necessary that a group which is aiming at consensus talk about needs. But how is this to be done, given the restraints noted above? To talk about needs means that standards and opportunities must exist in the group which encourage the discussion of personal values and personal feelings—encouraging such discussion, moreover, on a necessarily vague level because the remarks about needs are in the nature of self-exploration. This implies that a high degree of tolerance and attentiveness must exist in the group in order to ascertain the meanings of inevitably poor communication by members.

If members realize the desirability of discussion on the level of needs—as they appear to when there is talk of being more candid, "of letting one's hair down a bit more"—they find they are unable to do so effectively. Even with the best intentions and great articulateness, it is probably impossible to make an adequate statement of one's own needs. Such a statement would require an account of the background of the individual and of the deficiency conditions in this background out of which the needs arise. And this background is not before the group. The group might listen to each member in turn, as does a therapist, to get the necessary background; but this is not feasible, given the time limits. Moreover, such a procedure would not be an efficient one, since for most group purposes it is scarcely necessary to go so thoroughly into the personal background of each individual.

But how far is it necessary to go? Neither the individual nor the group knows. Furthermore, the individual may reveal more than he intends, or he may be seduced into a position of therapeutic dependency, with which the group is not qualified to deal. This may prove threatening both to the individual and to the group, by immobilizing them with guilt or anxiety. The group, therefore, requires some basis for testing limits on what the group can handle at a particular phase of its development.

In talking about needs, the group will likely find that its discussion is either relatively abstract and meaningless or that it becomes embarrassingly and threateningly therapeutic. Complicating this, members find that the discussion does not lead to group locomotion, which is additionally frustrating. Conflict then tends to become polarized between the "feeling-minded" members, who are committed to further discussion concerning needs, and the "work-minded" members, whose commitments lie in promoting group locomotion.

At any given moment in the group's development, the ideal condition may be stated as one in which members have gone as far as possible in shaping the group goal to square with individual needs, while still maintaining a group goal upon which work can be accomplished. The normal course is to adopt some tentative decision which balances these two factors. As the group proceeds, the members can test the adequacy of the decision by assessing its potentialities for need satisfaction. Since we may assume that no resolution will be entirely or equally satisfying for all members, we may expect that dissatisfaction will build up during the course of the group's work and the members' testing. Thus, revolts occur in more or less overt form, new resolutions are developed, and the cycle is repeated.

Adding intensity to this dialectic, some trainees come to experience the release of productivity which comes from working under "own" as opposed to "induced" forces. Thus, as the group proceeds, there develops a strong, but differentially distributed, impetus toward maximizing the shaping of group activity in relation to individual needs, reinforcing the continuing dilemma of coordinating group work under conditions of heightened individual sensibility to own needs. The effect is to generate considerable frustration, since it is difficult to determine when planning for member satisfaction has gone as far as it can without the group's bogging down in "navel gazing." Thus, there develops a counterforce in the direction of avoiding too great investment of group energy in planning for need satisfaction in the interest of getting something done.

This intragroup conflict between work and emotionality—or, in the terminology used here, between need and goal orientations—is paralleled by intrapersonal conflict. Group members have learned, outside the T Group, to inhibit those claims which are generated by needs which they cannot readily satisfy. Such inhibition involves committing personal energy to various defensive operations. As it becomes apparent that it may be possible to satisfy previously inhibited needs, the previously erected defenses are apt to come under reappraisal. While forces exist toward the relaxation of these defenses, it nevertheless remains true that even in the T Group not all needs can be satisfied. The individual must be able to assess what he can realistically hope to satisfy and then to establish defensive systems at a new level, which permits a lesser commitment of energy to defensiveness. This process is likely to be accompanied by periodic rises in anxiety. Thus, the progress of the T Group may be seen as movement involving increasingly effective integration of member needs and group goals. On the individual level, it involves the successive breaking down and rebuilding of defensive structures to permit increasing need satisfaction of members. Groups tend to find levels, after excitedly working through conflict, at which the amount of need they must defend against is reduced, as more of the need is satisfied. But given the force toward maximizing need satisfaction, there arises an additional tendency to unfreeze the level, moving to a "deeper," i.e., more need-satisfying, level. This tendency involves members' seeking greater freedom for expression of own needs, re-examining and possibly altering systems of defense, freeing previously inhibited feelings—in order to explore possibilities for greater need satisfaction. Countering this are the forces toward realistic work in and on the environment, the uncomfortableness associated with altering defenses, the threat and guilt involved in attempting to move other members, whom one suspects of weakness or inflexibility, toward lower levels of inhibition.

In the light of the group task set by the continuing conflict between group goals and individual needs and between individual needs and defenses, the method which appears best suited for work on the task is an "experimental" one. This involves taking some action step representing the group's best, *tentative* guess about what would be satisfying. In the course of this activity, persons will accumulate information about their own feelings, values, personal deficiencies in relation to *that* task. If the group then evaluates the consequences of work on the task in relation to need satisfaction of members, this provides public data about members' feelings, i.e., about the nature of their needs. These new data are germane to, and exploration of them is objectively limited by, the job confronting the group. Discussion of feelings then can be focused in a way which can be used for further action planning and for modifications of the group goal. Such a procedure not only provides the group with information about what its members want, but in the course of having acted, the group can learn something about what the possibilities for need satisfaction realistically are, i.e., what activities it can engage in, what it cannot, what may be invented, and so on. We have described, in short, the functional necessity for the development of an action-research procedure. Action is used not only to satisfy needs but to provide data to the group which will enable better need definition (what is or is not satisfying, and why) and better goal definition (what is or is not possible, and why). This learning of how to build action-research procedures into group and individual problem solving becomes one of the key learnings of the T Group. And if used effectively, the group can reach successively deeper understanding of one another's needs, can find it increasingly possible to peel away layers of defensiveness, and for both reasons can become capable of developing greater resourcefulness in setting fruitful and satisfying tasks.

Implied in the preceding discussion are group tasks related to background conditions in the areas of communication, functional roles, standards, and individual dynamics. A further comment on each may be helpful.

Miscellany of Other Background Conditions

Communication Structure

One of the conditions for a group's effectively working on the previously described tasks is the existence of any adequate communication structure. Since the adequacy of any message depends on its being understood by the recipient, the communication structure should permit member A to test for the adequacy of his message by permitting—indeed encouraging—feedback from B concerning his comprehension of A's message. If A has missed the mark, the communication structure should permit A to reformulate the point he is trying to make. Indeed, if the group is to think together (or even to encourage creativity by A alone), it should encourage members to transmit vague messages in order that these can be tried out or reality-tested for improved formulation.

A communication pattern of this type, while it may produce a wide distribution of personal involvement in the discussion, will also be relatively inefficient since it creates difficult problems of coordination. Thus, we find represented in this area, too, the underlying conflict found earlier between considerations of group effectiveness and individual need satisfaction. The type of communication structure which develops—who speaks to whom, with what percentage of total group time, and so on—becomes implicated in the problem of developing an adequate legitimacy system, and may sometimes become implicated in power struggles associated with this problem.

Functional Roles

The needs-task conflict is represented in the double classification of functional roles, namely, task functions and maintenance functions. To what degree should the group attempt to provide for maintenance functions—for eliciting expression of, for aiding in the formulation of, and for dealing with individual discomforts? To what degree should the group devote the major part of its energy to getting the group's task accomplished? The task or maintenance roles which members are permitted or encouraged to play would thus appear to be influenced by the relative weight given to dealing with needs versus tasks.

The Development of Group Standards

The structure of the group depends in part on the development of commonly held beliefs or standards about group operation. Apart from the content of standards, how are standards to be arrived at? One pair of alternatives is between experiential and cognitive learning. Experiential learning is probably most effective, not with respect to setting up in the minimum time the minimal standards necessary for getting a job done, but with respect to getting mutual understanding among the various members of the group. Cognitive learning probably can be accomplished much more quickly, but probably with larger areas of "surplus" meaning not understood. The tendency to emphasize one or the other type of learning procedure would thus seem to parallel the relative weight given to individual needs versus the group task.

Individual Dynamics in the T Group

Given a collection of individuals, among whom the range of defenses differs in kind and in extent, one would expect conflicts to develop among members related to the emphasis on a "safe" task or goal orientation versus an "unsafe" need orientation. It is necessary that T Groups build conditions under which the individual will be relatively free to relax defenses and to explore new behavioral possibilities for need satisfaction. Probably the process will be aided if, in addition, members feel free to retreat to "defensive," albeit reality-based and task-oriented, activities. In any case, the release of energy attendant upon relaxation of defenses, as well as the corresponding possibility of increased need satisfaction, can be expected to be gratifying to members and to impel some of them at least toward moving deeper and deeper toward therapeutic change. In doing this, members will be acting without regard to the limits which are necessary for functioning effectively in a group which is attempting to combine both need and task considerations. Intermediate resolutions of the need-task conflict, which may be threatening to some, remain unsatisfying or overly limiting for others.

One finds that the group task of building an agreed-upon legitimacy system is never completed. Characteristic of achieving any one level of nondefensiveness is eventual dissatisfaction when the problem must be faced all over again.

Although the "ideal culture" is never achieved, the net learning effect of this cycle of activities is to leave members with some realization of the possible satisfactions available in social activity and the types of action which may lead to the improvement of given group structures in order to increase the chances of realizing these possible satisfactions.

Conclusion

Finally, I wish to state briefly how T-Group training, as described above, may be viewed in a somewhat larger context. While it is difficult to support so sweeping a statement, it is not unlikely that if one examined institutional arrangements in their natural state, institutions generally will be found to give greater weight to considerations of task effectiveness than to considerations of need satisfaction. That is, the various procedures which are developed will tend to be based upon the exigencies of coordinating members for work, and such individual unhappiness as arises within the institution will tend to be handled by developing pressures toward inhibition.

From this standpoint, the T Group is almost unique in that it explores the possibility of building a small-group culture which, while keeping an eye to the problems of effective work, gives special attention to the possibility of altering productivity-oriented arrangements for the sake of minimizing the frustration and inhibition of individual needs. The two types of considerations stressed here are not *necessarily* incompatible. It is possible that under some conditions increased need satisfaction may increase productivity. In the sixteen years of experimentation with T-Group training, trainers and trainees alike have noted the remarkable release of individual and group creativity which sometimes appears upon the reduction of socially induced defensiveness.

14

Explorations in

Observant Participation

Herbert A. Shepard

Value Premises and Training Goals

It has been said that the T Group is a social microcosm in which the potential exists for experiencing and learning along many dimensions of existence and relationship. But that which is everything fits all descriptions. It is better to say that the T Group is no single thing. Better still to refer to a norm which is characteristic of T Groups: a joint commitment among interdependent persons to "process analysis," i.e., to shared examination of their relationship in all aspects relevant to their interdependence. When this commitment exists and is highly valued, the interaction can be called T Grouping. The T-Group process usually consists of unlearning the norms and procedures which prevent shared examination and of learning fruitful ways to proceed with it. The term, "observant participation," is synonymous with these "fruitful ways" and refers not only to the actor's noticing what is going on between himself and others but also to the actor's and the others' jointly noticing—that is, communicatively noticing—what is going on among them and between their own group and its environment.

One value premise underlying this T-Group norm underlies all scientific work: namely, that it is a good thing to know what you are doing, whether you are an individual, a group, or a society. Joint commitment to the norm implies another value premise, also traditionally shared in scientific work: namely, that such learning is an undertaking shared by all mankind, rather than the private property of individuals or groups to be used for exploiting other individuals and groups. The requirement of shared human responsibility sometimes confronts T-Group members with such force, and in such contradiction to the norms of society at large, that even the trainers may back away from its implications. Cultural emphasis on interpersonal and intergroup competition leaves members without an adequate language, philosophy, reward structure, or set of behavioral skills for collaboration in work and in the resolution of conflict. In a culture that makes personal isolation synonymous with personal autonomy, T-Group training means the reawakening of painful processes which gave rise to present patterns of interpersonal adaptation.

The Trainer's Responsibility

The trainer's major responsibility is to help the group to overcome obstacles to observant participation. The major obstacles are the forces which prevent valid communication among members—forces which distort the member's perception of himself in relation to others, or inhibit the expression of his perceptions. The notion of valid communication is similar to Sullivan's [1] description of mental health for the person; namely, that the self becomes coextensive with the personality. The widespread use of such more or less synonymous terms as "leveling," [2] "authenticity," [3] and "openness" indicates a high degree of consensus among trainers about the importance of valid communication in T-Group work.

The term, "valid communication," can be further understood by identifying two organic properties common to individuals and groups. If a person is to "know what he is doing," the components of the person must come to be in nondistorting communicative relations with one another and with the environment. If a group is to know what it is doing, its components must come to be in nondistorting communicative relations with one another and with its environment. A person's communication with self and others is often characterized by what Sullivan called "selective inattention," whereby he consistently over-

[1] H. S. Sullivan. *Conceptions of Modern Psychiatry.* Washington, D.C.: William Alanson White Psychiatric Foundation, 1947.

[2] R. R. Blake, J. S. Mouton, and M. G. Blansfield. "How Executive Team Training Can Help You." *Journal of the American Society of Training Directors,* 16:3–11; January 1962.

[3] C. Argyris. "Explorations in Consulting-Client Relationships." *Human Organization,* 20, 3:121–133; fall 1961.

looks certain aspects of what happens. For example, in the T Group, member involvement in what is held to be a mutually enlightening discussion of leadership theory may be motivated by an unrecognized need to influence the trainer or a need for dominance by one or a few members. Groups or subgroups in interaction are as much a prey to forces distorting communication as are persons in interaction. For example, groups in conflict see only their differences.

T-Group Theory and Laboratory Design

During the early years of the National Training Laboratories, concern with the realization of such values as valid communication and observant participation, combined with personal and professional doubts about methodological and theoretical adequacy, operated to discourage experimentation with conditions and outcomes. The initial laboratories were themselves anxiety-arousing ventures into the unknown; that they were "successful" experiments led to a degree of rigidity and to focusing on particular issues within the rigid framework. Certain issues were intensely debated, but the issues were narrowly drawn and some questionable assumptions were widely accepted as valid. For example, hostility of group therapists and traditional social scientists toward what was regarded by the former as amateur and irresponsible attempts at therapy and by the latter as a do-good social movement, aroused anxiety among trainers and defined largely irrelevant issues as central. Beyond these, questions like the following were also viewed as central: whether trainer-interventions should be at the individual or group level; whether "hot" groups were good or bad training; and whether the trainer who aroused hostility was better than the trainer who smothered it. NTL was eight years old before any trainers formulated and exposed their training theories for open seminar discussion.

Relativism has replaced absolutism in recent discussions of the above issues, especially as widespread assumptions about other aspects of training and of therapy have become subject to question and experimentation. A very restricting set of conditions was formerly assumed to be necessary for successful T-Group training. Durations of three weeks were regarded as appropriate. Care was taken to ensure that each T Group was comprised of persons who were strangers to one another. Each T Group in a laboratory was considered to be a complete social system, and an effort was made to minimize interdependence and interaction with other segments of the laboratory. Many thought that T-Group learning would be adversely affected if the T Group undertook anything but T-Group work or if the trainer adopted any role but the one he considered to be his "T-Group trainer" role. It was assumed that the trainer was a necessary presence in the group for its safety and success. Heterogeneity as to group composition along many dimensions was considered desirable. Such assumptions acquired the character of doctrine.

In the past few years many dimensions of laboratory training have been explored and new dimensions discovered. There have been innovations in trainer style, group composition, laboratory purposes, length and continuity of laboratory, methods of group-process analysis and individual feedback, use of simulation experiments, case method, Gestalt therapy, existential analysis, and the instrumented laboratory. Laboratory design has become less mechanical, and theories of total program design are emerging. As a result the T Group has lost its mystique, but at the same time it has become more difficult to distinguish the T Group from the other parts of a program of individual, group, organizational, and community development.

Innovations

Of the many innovations which have emerged from combinations among the above variables, a number have a degree of wholeness which warrants description and analysis. As with other social inventions made by NTL associates, the ideas and procedures are not the product of any one person. It is a basic proposition underlying our concern with social process that social inventions are the emergent products of creative social interaction. Some of the inventions have their roots in experiments made years ago by persons relatively unassociated with more recent developments. Under these circumstances, acknowledging the contribution of particular individuals is a hazardous undertaking. In terms of my own interpersonal experience, profound contributions to the development of the instrumented laboratory, organizational family-group training, and intergroup training have been made by Robert R. Blake.[4] Michael Blansfield has also

[4] See, for example, R. R. Blake and J. S. Mouton. "The Instrumented Training Laboratory," an original paper based on work conducted originally at the Human Relations Laboratories of The University of Texas, and now utilized in a number of industrial, university, and hospital settings. In Irving Weschler and Edgar Schein (Eds.), *Issues in Human Relations Training*, Washington, D.C.: NTL Selected Readings Series, No. 5, 1962.

pioneered in family-group and intergroup training. Goodwin Watson shared in the methodology of the triangulation group, and Paul Buchanan, Murray Horwitz, and Warren Bennis have contributed a great deal to my understanding in all of these areas.

The Instrumented Laboratory

The instrumented laboratory takes its name from its extensive use of measuring instruments (questionnaires, scales, tape recorders) to facilitate learning. In an instrumented laboratory no trainer is present in the T Group.

The instrumented laboratory takes seriously the notions that a laboratory should be the locus of experiments, that the experiments should be as systematic and quantitative as is feasible, and that the participants in the laboratory should be the subjects, observers, analysts, and interpreters of the experiments. To some extent they may also be the designers of the experiments, though the design is primarily the responsibility of the trainer.

The trainer works with the total group in a number of roles or role functions: orientation to each phase of the laboratory, introduction and elaboration of concepts used in the instruments (e.g., content and process, work, play, and flight), instruction in methods of analyzing, displaying, and interpreting data. As the leader in discussion of experimental results, he uses them as the basis for theory presentation. Data processing may be done by technicians, by the use of simple computing machines, or by the participants themselves.

Special Features of the Instrumented Laboratory. In designing an instrumented laboratory, attention is focused in a number of issues which are less salient in other types of laboratories:

TRAINER CENTRALITY. While the trainer in an instrumented laboratory often feels himself to be in a more directive role than he would in a more traditional laboratory, members are less dependent psychologically on him. Groups and individuals quickly develop a good deal of autonomy. For example, in a laboratory composed of psychiatric patients, a morning was spent in intergroup visits. Visualizing the possibility that intergroup hostility might make the procedure ineffective, the training staff asked—as delicately as possible—whether the groups would like to have a staff member present. The patients replied: "Would you like to listen? Please feel free to come along if you like."

ADDITIVE KNOWLEDGE. The use of instruments facilitates comparison of T Groups from many laboratories along a number of dimensions. Their use confronts the designer with the problem of how to measure the many subtleties of T-Group development perceived by T-Group trainers. A well-designed experiment that throws light in measurable quanta on a number of aspects of interpersonal or organizational relations is replicable, and through replication, provides a basis for generalization. (It becomes possible to see whether generalizations based on college freshmen hold for business executives.)

DESIGN PRINCIPLES FOR TRAINING LABORATORY EXPERIMENTS. At least the following criteria should be applied in determining the suitability of an experiment for laboratory use:

1. *Relevance to the needs of members.* Experiments which demonstrate a point perceived as trivial or obvious are of course to be avoided. Labors that give birth to a mouse, especially when the needs are elephantine, are felt to be a waste of time. Similarly, the use of "games" as analogies to certain group experiences should be avoided if the experiences themselves can be dramatized and subjected to systematic analysis. If an experiment has to be "staged," it is usually not worth doing. For example, the learning impact of an experiment in intergroup competition appears to be greatest where the competition is between T Groups, and at a stage in laboratory life when feelings of intergroup competitiveness are greatest because of the projection of unresolved intragroup-process problems.

2. *Avoidance of deceit.* Dramatic experimental results can sometimes be achieved through the use of "stooges," unsuspected traps, misinformation, and the like. While impressed by the results, participants are usually even more impressed by the fact that they have been tricked by trainers who give lip service to openness, leveling, authenticity, and so on. On the other hand, where the participants have "trapped" themselves, they are impressed with the power of social forces determining their behavior. For example, when a member of one T Group is asked to visit another group to serve as a consultant to it, neither he nor the visited group feels tricked when the outcome is displayed and the classical conformity-deviation phenomena are recognized. But when a stooge is planted in a group (i.e., secretly asked by the staff) to take a deviant role, the group is likely to feel that it has been unfairly manipulated, and the stooge is likely to regret his collusion with the staff.

3. *Breadth of participation.* Experiments which involve only a few of the participants in active roles deserve their title of "demonstra-

tions." Here the learning value suffers as it does in demonstration role playing. Multiple and mass role playing appear to have more impact than demonstration role playing. Similarly, simultaneous replication of small-group experiments is more meaningful to participants and, in addition, provides an opportunity for comparison of results.

4. *Sharpness, clarity, and simplicity.* Designs which have only a few points to make and make them clearly, are hard to come by but worth the effort. Data which show statistically significant differences due to the presence or absence of certain variables are impressive only if the difference is socially or personally large. Intellectually the operation of the variable may be understood, but if it is only one of many variables producing an outcome, its relevance to action is small. For related reasons, in a complex and loose design of the type usually found in laboratory simulations of large organizations, the temptation to measure many aspects of the system should be resisted.

Training in T-Group Work Method in the Instrumented Laboratory. In a sense, everyone knows what "group process analysis" is. But in our culture, process observations are seldom shared, and hence, useful words for sharing them are not part of our society's common usage. Providing concepts and creating norms which legitimize communication of process observations are critical staff contributions. How are these contributions made in an instrumented laboratory?

One of the most powerful methods is the set of scaled questions to which T-Group members respond at the end of each meeting. When the responses are charted, similarities and differences of perception among members provide a useful basis for discussion of process issues. During the first few days of the laboratory new questions may be added to the original list. Each question relates to a concept that is useful in process analysis, and a short lecture on the concept assists the T Groups in using the data they collect for purposes of analysis.

The use of "T-Group vignettes" further clarifies the nature of T-Group work. Each T Group is observed at work by the other parts of the laboratory. Observers may be equipped with instruments for noting aspects of the functioning of the observed group, and may then feed back their observations to the group. Special exercises in tape listening and in the use of T-Group charts for diagnostic purposes provide additional aids to process analysis. And the use of T Groups as the social units in experiments provides environmental inputs to each T Group which raise new questions for its members about the group's internal structure and processes.

To aid the groups in working at the individual, as distinguished from the group, level, consultation teams and individual rating forms may be used. Typically, the consultation teams are subgroups of the T Groups, within which each member serves and by turn receives consultation from the other members concerning his role in the T Group. Descriptive rating forms may be filled out by every member about all other members. The data are compiled for each member and then reviewed by him and the group.

Applications of the Instrumented Laboratory. The instrumented laboratory has been used with "cousins" (members of an organization selected diagonally rather than vertically or horizontally), with strangers, in headquarters-field settings, in citizens' community relations laboratories, and with psychiatric patients. The following observations have been made. First, the instrumented laboratory offers certain economies—in the number of trainers required and hence in the cost of the training. Second, the instrumented laboratory provides an opportunity to collect systematic data for feedback to participants and also for purposes of action going beyond the laboratory. Third, if alumni of traditional laboratories are present in the T Groups, the T Groups are likely to have as much learning value for members as trainer-led T Groups. Fourth, members are unlikely to be "awed" by the laboratory experience—to feel that there is a special mystery about T Groups. Fifth, members gain a respect for data, a research orientation toward themselves and their own organization/s and an understanding of how relevant data could be collected in their own organization/s and used in planning. Sixth, there are certain drawbacks, certain pitfalls to which an instrumented laboratory is susceptible, and certain situations in which it is less likely to carry impact than traditional laboratories. The pace needs to be lively. The potential usefulness of the data needs to be clearly demonstrated, and members need to be trained in the analysis and interpretation of data. Finally, there is evidence that groups in instrumented laboratories may sometimes become arrested at a particular stage of development or be unable to face and resolve some relationship issues.

Although the instrumented laboratory has been used with considerable success in all the situations mentioned above, it appears to be ideally suited with psychiatric patients. Robert Morton has demonstrated the power of the instrumented laboratory for ameliorative work with patients at the Veterans Administration Hospital in Houston. In groups of about twenty-five in a self-governing ward, the patients participate in a month-long instrumented laboratory. Great improvements in their ability to cope with their problems of living are noted.

The appropriateness of the instrumented laboratory for patient groups is apparently due to the particular difficulties associated with "neurosis." Sullivan's insight that emotional disturbance is associated with difficulties in interpersonal communication and Rose's definition of neurosis as "inability to act reasonably effectively for the achievement of socially acceptable and personally accepted goals" [5] are relevant here. But it is the trainerless feature which is of greatest importance. The therapist inevitably confronts the patient with his own inadequacy, just as the traditional hospital setting emphasizes his helplessness and impotence. The instrumented group provides an opportunity and support to practice socially responsible behavior and to learn and practice the social and communication skills the patient needs in order to "act reasonably effectively."

The Triangulation Group

The triangulation group or, more accurately, triangulation procedure, arose as an attempt to improve the usefulness of personal feedback in the T Group. It takes its name from the notion that views from at least two positions are needed to locate a point in space. It often happens, for example, that a member is provided feedback as follows: "You often frown when you speak. At first, that made you somewhat forbidding. People think you are frowning at them." The action implication for the recipient of this message is that he should not frown when he speaks. He tries to remember not to frown—probably a hopeless undertaking. It is usually not in the least evident to the person providing feedback or to its recipient just what it is that produces the frown. Neither sees how it is related to anything else, and hence the matter of getting this bit of interpersonal communication—the frown—under control is an awkward undertaking. It involves conscious inhibition of an impulse that is unconsciously produced. A "valid" insight might make the impulse disappear. The frown would then look after itself.

This is an old problem in psychotherapy. What approaches to its solution are available to the members of a T Group? We begin by ruling out the traditional therapeutic approaches, contenting ourselves with something more like the simple behavioristic rule of the social anthropologist: People do these things because they do those other

[5] A. M. Rose. "A Social-Psychological Theory of Neurosis," in A. M. Rose (Ed.), *Human Behavior and Social Process*. Boston: Houghton Mifflin Company, 1962.

things. The important insight for the person receiving the feedback is that he see the connection between this thing that he does and other things that he does.

As the T Group goes through its normal phases of development, its members begin to emerge as persons for one another, and some of the behavioral patterns characteristic of each person become recognizable to others as patterns. But the group is confronted with a number of unknowns: To what extent is a member's behavior induced by forces in the group? To what extent is it induced by forces in the person—forces one may think of as induced by his memberships or anticipated memberships? To solve these unknowns, the T Group has two potential resources: the member's characteristic way of explaining his own behavior in the group and such data as he may provide about his membership in other groups. The group can use the former tool as a means to at least partial understanding of how the data he provides about his other memberships are connected to the behavioral patterns he exhibits in the here-and-now.

The triangulation group thus has three major phases. In an initial phase of normal T-Group development, members become familiar with one another's behavioral patterns and patterns of explanation. There is then a second phase during which each member discusses at some length his relations with and experience in past groups which are still felt by him as important, his present relations of importance, and his future relations (usually expressed as values and goals to be realized in life). Finally, there is a third phase of personal feedback in which the member and the group join in a search for connections between his membership behavior in the T Group and his reported experiences and anticipations with other groups. It is important that this latter search be the member's responsibility, with the others in "helping" rather than "interpretive" or "directive" roles.

The triangulation procedure has been used with useful results by a number of groups—both stranger groups and organizational family teams. In the latter case, the uncertainties and unknowns are somewhat reduced by the much greater range of firsthand experience each member has had with the others. The values of the procedure appear to be threefold: deeper and more realistic identification of members with one another ("If I had had your experiences I'd be more like you"); enhanced ability on the part of at least some members to "apply their learning" after the laboratory, presumably because they have a better understanding of, and control over, the forces determining their behavior; the discovery of more adequate conceptual schemes for understanding oneself and others.

Obviously this procedure requires a relatively high degree of trust, mutual identification, and intimacy to be effective. Without this, the third phase can degenerate into a game or some kind of pseudo-therapeutic procedure. However, the second phase, which should not be undertaken until a good level of cohesiveness has been reached, is itself conducive to the development of the trust, intimacy, and identification needed for the work of the third phase.

Organizational Family Groups

To the problem of "fade-out," organizational family-group training promises a solution. But for a long time family-group training seemed too risky. How could work-group members open their sometimes competitive and brittle relationships to examination and revision? They have to continue to work together after the laboratory is over. In a "stranger" laboratory, the authority of the trainer is a myth, so dependency and counterdependency needs can be freely expressed. But in a family laboratory the authority of the boss is a long-term social reality. Will members dare to open up? Would it be wise for them to do so?

These are good questions. They help explain "fade-out." No wonder participants in stranger laboratories experience difficulty in applying their learning back on the job. If relations among family members cannot be opened for examination and improvement in the supportive atmosphere of a laboratory, then it would indeed be miraculous if a lone member of the family could effect such changes as a result of his participation in a stranger laboratory.

Learning how to design a laboratory adequate for family training was a logical necessity, if hopes for organizational and community development were to be realized. Research and theory have long pointed to the significance of the face-to-face group as the basic building block of organization. NTL itself had begun with an interest in group dynamics rather than psychodynamics, yet the impact of training had been felt by individuals rather than groups. The stranger group had been a vehicle for individual learning; at the end of the laboratory, the group died and the individual survived. Implicit recognition that individual development was the lasting consequence of training had led to increased focus on individual dynamics. Group-level interventions by the trainer were replaced by more personally oriented interventions. It appeared that Western Training Laboratories was moving more rapidly in this direction than NTL. But NTL began to focus on the problem of "giving and receiving feedback," and in recent years personal feedback has seemed to be the most important feature of the T Group.

From time to time individual trainers had experimented with family training. More often enthusiastic alumni attempted to hold T-Group sessions in their organizations (usually on a meeting-a-week basis), and the results sometimes confirmed the worst fears of trainers.

A number of trainers early experimented with modifications of T Groups and laboratories for families, cousins, and especially for persons at the same status level in organizations. A variety of organizations—a government laboratory, a military establishment, a religious organization, two national voluntary organizations, some industrial organizations, and consulting firms—experimented with cousin, peer, and family enterprises during the middle fifties. Within the last two or three years a great many trainers have had experience with family-team training, and some of the methodological issues are beginning to take form.

A variety of designs have been used for family-team training. The following are illustrative:

THE SURVEY-BASED LABORATORY. Data relating to the family's operating effectiveness—its internal and external relations in the organization—are used as the initial input. The data help to focus needs for improvement and change in behavior, distribution of responsibilities, relationships with other groups.

THE ROLE-RELATIONS LABORATORY. Here the focus is directly on membership relations from the start. Members begin by sharing role perceptions, expectations, and desires. The focus is kept almost continuously on process issues.

THE CONTENT-AND-PROCESS LABORATORY. Here the group may develop an agenda of task problems, then use its work on each task as a consensual experience for examination, process analysis, and the invention of procedures for exploring special process issues if and when they become salient: e.g., personal feedback procedures, or sharing of values and goals.

THE INTERGROUP LABORATORY. Here two or more family teams train together, spending a part of their time as separate families examining internal process issues and planning for intergroup exchange on matters in which the families are interdependent. Periodically, the family teams meet together, discussing common problems, exchanging the perceptions held by each team of the other, examining the dynamics of their intergroup relations. Special adaptations of the intergroup laboratory include headquarters-field laboratories and merger laboratories. The intergroup laboratory foreshadows the laboratory for the organization or community as a whole. Intergroup training methodology has already progressed to the point of deserving separate treatment in a volume like the present one, and much of the story of future developments in training is likely to be the story of intergroup designs.

While there is unlikely to be general agreement on what the major methodological issues in family training are or on how they are most appropriately resolved, the following considerations are worth recording as a basis for future refinement or rebuttal.

The Composition of the Family Group. Behind the idea of family-group training lies the notion that the face-to-face group is the basic building block of organization. It is commonly assumed that the referent is the superior-and-his-immediate-subordinates, which may be called the hierarchical family group. In practice, it often seems appropriate to include certain "staff" personnel whose relation to the hierarchical group is more complex. For example, the staff person may be intimately related to several such family groups and should be included in all of them.

This imperfection in hierarchical symmetry is normally resolved on the basis of expediency. However, it does not follow that the original concept is the most useful one. In some organizations, the hierarchical family group is comprised of persons whose task-interdependence is great. In other organizations, the hierarchical group members may have little task-interdependence—the principle which binds them together is the authority structure of the organization rather than its structure of tasks. Frequently the former structure has been dictated by traditional concepts of functional organization—grouping persons of like skills together—a structure which emphasizes the forces of interpersonal competition, and hence, a structure in which solidarity is frequently accompanied by conflict with other groups.

Many organizations, particularly industrial firms, have been moving in recent years toward an increased use of project teams and task forces for the accomplishment of company objectives. The severe restrictions placed by bureaucratic forms on an organization's adaptation rate have led to experiments in decentralization and the use of project forms.

But whether the formal structure emphasizes project or functional forms, it is unusual to find an intra-organizational definition of "family" which cuts across many status lines, even where the requirements of task-interdependence would imply the need for more intimate working relationships across these lines.

The promise of intergroup laboratories for the future lies in the opportunities they provide for experimenting with new structures for work. Meantime, family-team training faces the problem of working within the presently existing formal structure. The discovery and implementation of new structures which might be more appropriate to the organization's needs are little facilitated by this method. However, the common belief that any organization structure can be made to work reflects the fact that, for effective functioning, all organizations require that their members be capable of maintaining effective membership in a number of subgroups. Hence, a possible procedure along family-group lines is to follow hierarchical family laboratories with laboratories comprised of persons who constitute families from the standpoint of some other dimension of interdependence.

The trainer's role in family T Groups is still in an exploratory phase. The following propositions are based on personal experience and do not represent a consensus among trainers:

First, the trainer should provide a model of openness. In a stranger group, it can be argued that the trainer serves projectively as an authority figure and can use this fact in helping the group to examine its power problems. In the family group, he is likely to be seen as a stranger, but he is not automatically seen as an authority figure. Indeed, if he behaves in such a way as to become an authority figure, he is likely to produce unresolvable confusion. The relevant authority issues are to be found in the relations between the family head and the members. The norm of openness is intended to reduce the stranger quality of the trainer and hence the extent to which group members are preoccupied by his role. In this sense, though dedicated to the task of maintaining the members' preoccupation with one another, he should be the least preoccupying member of the group.

The trainer performs a modeling or catalytic role in another sense. His presence personifies the goal of the laboratory, which almost always implies the replacement of old group norms by new ones. Often the trainer must be the person to break an old group norm by opening communication in areas which were formerly closed. In most groups, one of the old norms governs feedback to the group head. In general, openness between the group head and the group precedes openness among the group members. Trainer-interventions and the trainer's willingness to express his own reactions are usually crucial factors in accomplishing this first step.

A second feature of family-group training which sets it apart from stranger training is the culture of the group. In entering a T Group of strangers, the trainer can make reliable predictions about its development needs and about the kinds of problems it will confront. He usually wants to know in advance something about the background and character of each of its members, but even without such information he can approach the group with a good deal of confidence. The family group is less predictable. Relationships among members have already been formed; members have "adjusted" to one another. The group has a private language containing references to its past and future, to its task, and to its self-perception in relation to other groups —a private language which is often beyond the powers of an experienced trainer to decode in a short period. In this sense, the hidden agenda of the family group seem massive and complex—but only because the trainer is a stranger and has not participated in the past development of the group. While it is possible and, in some sense, legitimate for the trainer to prove his skill by working with the group in the absence of any prior understanding of its culture, he is likely to be able to serve more adequately as a resource if he invests the necessary time in advance of the laboratory to familiarize himself with the group culture. In addition, prior acquaintance can facilitate understanding of his role so that this preoccupation does not delay the progress of the laboratory.

A third important feature of family-group training stems from the group's persistence as a unit beyond the laboratory. Stranger groups, having no future, need do no planning for it. In the family group, however, planning is a necessary feature of the last hours of the laboratory. New understandings, the prospect of improved working relationships or decision-making procedures, the possibility of experimenting with new structures, needs for further development work—all these are likely to emerge in the course of the laboratory. Unless specific agreements on action, roles, responsibilities, and procedures are reached before the laboratory adjourns, it is likely to be followed by uncertainties, disappointment, confusion about initiative taking, and loss of the shared innovative spirit generated in the laboratory.

Summary

Valid communication, observant participation, process analysis, and experimentation with new behavior and new structures are core concepts of the laboratory method in all of its applications. During the years since 1947, these concepts have been enriched, principles of laboratory design and personal intervention have been developed, and new fields for experimentation and application have been opened. With these developments the T Group has lost its mystique, its centrality, and its identity as a unique process. Similarly, the laboratory in many applications must be seen simply as one element in a larger process of social change, though the present chapter has made no effort to examine the strategy of major change processes.

The potential scientific contribution and social utility of laboratory method are exciting prospects. The present time is one of transition, development, and learning. Much of what has been said in the foregoing pages will seem primitive in a few years if the laboratory method can retain its vital spark. More than any other factor, the secret of progress in laboratory method has been the creative opportunity provided by laboratories for social scientists to work closely together in an innovative process. The laboratory as catalyst, as the vital spark producing innovation not only in the client system but also in social science, is NTL's most important invention.

15

A Survey of Research

on T Groups

Dorothy Stock

Ever since its beginnings in 1947, the T Group has been recognized both as an important social invention deserving study for its own sake and as a special setting in which a variety of problems in group functioning and individual learning can be studied. The research that has been undertaken has perhaps always had a double goal: that of clarifying the character of the T Group itself and its impact on the learner, and that of adding to theoretical knowledge about the functioning of small groups.

As a special educational opportunity for adults, a host of questions arises as to the character of the T Group and its contribution to learning and change: What does the individual gain from his experience in the T Group? How lasting and transferable are these learnings? And what are the factors—in the personality of the individual, in the T Group itself, or in the individual's work situation—which facilitate learning for some persons and make it difficult for others? As a group which has no history and operates outside the usual institutional contexts, the T Group offers unique opportunities for studying various aspects of group formation and functioning: How does the group evolve? How do members develop commitments, find a structure, resolve mutual problems, and develop into an effective working group? What sorts of sociometric patterns arise? How quickly, and on what basis? How do groups establish appropriate boundaries on intimacy and the expression of positive and negative feelings, relate to authority figures, and integrate individual needs and preferences with work toward group goals? Further, how does the group generate goals? How do group standards develop, and how are they maintained and modified? What is the role of the trainer, what kinds of interventions does he make, and what are their effects on the group's movement?

In the seventeen years since the first human relations laboratory, a large number of research studies dealing with a wide variety of problems has been undertaken at Bethel, at other workshops, and at universities. Some have been brief and self-contained; others were elaborate and multifaceted. Some have been experimental studies utilizing T-Group members as subjects; others have involved naturalistic observation of T-Group processes.

During the early years, the researcher typically wanted to utilize the special opportunities offered by the laboratory, and especially by the T Group, in order to deal with some research question of interest to him. Usually this question would also be of at least tangential interest to NTL. Ordinarily if the proposed research was of general interest and the design did not make excessive demands on participant or staff time, permission to conduct it would be granted. As time has gone on there has been a gradual shift in emphasis. For example, in the last three or four years a proportionately greater interest in understanding aspects of the laboratory experience relevant to individual learning has replaced the earlier focus on aspects of group functioning. A related trend has encouraged research in which either the design, the underlying theory, or the findings can be made immediately available to the participants as part of their learning. Very recently, there has been more interest in projects generated by NTL itself, usually on some training issue requiring clarification.

In discussing this body of research, this chapter proceeds from a consideration of the character of the T Group, to attention to the individual member and his perceptions and behavior in the group, and finally to the impact of the T Group on learning and change.

The Course of Development in the T Group

It is generally recognized that, while each T Group is unique, there is a family resemblance among all T Groups which includes an initial period of exploration and floundering, the gradual emergence of some sort of functional structure, and a concomitant attention to problems of authority and power and of relationships among peers.

It is assumed that the development of a functioning group out of the initial vacuum and the associated examination of interpersonal and group issues constitute the medium in which learning can occur. Thus the question of how a T Group develops is of great practical and theoretical interest in understanding its character and potential as a setting for learning. In addition, the T Group offers a perhaps unique opportunity to study the general process of group development, since it begins without a prior history.

Kurt Back (Back, 1948) studied the development of two T Groups from the point of view of participation pattern (who spoke to whom) and type of interaction (work-oriented, positive meaning, or negative meaning). Back utilized a modification of a rating system devised by Robert F. Bales (Bales, 1950) and compared for each group the first half of the series of meetings with the second half.

Back found that in some respects the development of the two groups was similar. Both groups, during the last half of their existence, expressed about the same amount of work (68 per cent and 72 per cent) and about the same amount of affect (32 per cent and 28 per cent); both groups expressed relatively more negative feelings during the first half of the T Group and relatively more positive feelings during the second half. But the two groups were quite different in the ways in which they arrived at their common end-point. The first group began by being less work-centered; a good deal of both positive and negative feeling was expressed, with negative feeling predominating. Throughout this group, the same members tended to contribute most to the group discussion; as the group went on, it paid more and more attention to the trainer and less attention to the group as a whole. The second group was quite different: in this case, as time went on, the group decreased the expression of work and increased the expression of feeling. It is as if this group was rather rigidly work-oriented to begin with but later developed into a more relaxed group which could express feelings more readily. In this group, the participation pattern shifted and attention to the trainer decreased, while intermember interactions increased.

In a separate analysis of the contributions of the trainers, Back found that they consistently expressed more positive than negative feelings. He felt that their example might have influenced the shift in this direction among the members of both groups. Back concluded that the status struggles of the members and the influence of the trainer are important in the dynamics of group growth and development.

Also in 1947, Murray Horwitz and Dorwin P. Cartwright (Horwitz and Cartwright, 1953) studied five T Groups at the Bethel laboratory.

The main purpose of this study was the development of a new diagnostic instrument, a Group Thematic Apperception Test.[1] However, in the process of validating this instrument, data were collected relevant to the character of group development. It was found, for example, that after three weeks of daily meetings, a relationship could be observed between group productivity and group cohesiveness. The T Group which displayed the greatest cohesiveness was also the most productive. Also, groups in which the participants showed greater "membership orientation" (defined as moving away from a concern about liking and disliking and toward a concern with intermember influence) also showed less distractibility from the task. Groups with greater membership orientation also showed greater awareness of group structure. Groups displaying a good deal of interpersonal hostility were more defensive and more likely to respond to social inductions with positive or negative emotionality.

From the point of view of group development, an interesting finding was that these relationships could not be identified during the early stages of the group's development but could be seen clearly in the measurements taken after three weeks of daily sessions, apparently a product of the members' interaction.

In an observational study of a single T Group (Margaret E. Barron and Gilbert K. Krulee, 1948), group growth seemed to follow this definite pattern: ". . . initial resistance to accepting responsibility and to the mode of operation, gradual understanding and acceptance of the method of operation, and finally a period of well-organized and productive meetings. . . . The period of resistance helped to focus the attention of the members on their behavior as it contributed to or hindered the functioning of the group."

In 1951 a research team headed by Herbert A. Thelen studied the kind and degree of emotionality expressed in the group and the relationship between the emotionality expressed and cognitive work on the group's task. Basing its view of groups on the theoretical work of W. R. Bion (Bion, 1948–1951; and 1952), this team developed rating and summarizing procedures for characterizing each group session in work-emotionality terms.[2]

---

[1] In this procedure, group members tell a story to an "Ambiguous Group Structure Picture"—a picture in which a number of persons are grouped around a table in vague or contradictory attitudes. The general assumption is that the members' interaction while telling the story as well as the story itself will reflect certain characteristics of the group.

[2] In this rating system each statement made in the group was rated for the quality of the work expressed (four possible categories) and the character of

For one fourteen-session T Group (Dorothy Stock and Saul Ben-Zeev, 1958), it was found that while the over-all amount and kind of emotionality expressed remained constant, the average work level tended to increase over time. The development of this group could be divided into four phases, representing shifts in the type of work expressed and its relation to emotionality: (1) work consisted of exploratory attempts to establish procedures or identify a goal, with the emotional tone either quite *flat* or quite *excited;* (2) work involved the carrying through and elaboration of plans, but was sober and lacked accompanying affect; (3) the group could express intense feelings and at the same time maintain a high level of creative and coherent discussion; and (4) work continued to be high-level in character, but was accompanied by relatively little expression of affect.

No phases were pure, but included types of interaction which had appeared in earlier phases. What appeared to have happened was that the group had learned how to utilize affect in the service of work. Phase 3, which involved the integration of high-level work and the intense expression of affect, seemed to represent optimum conditions for effective work. It was assumed that Phase 4 reflected a need for members to withdraw affect from the group.

A second group (William F. Hill, 1955) showed quite a different pattern of development. In this case, the work level remained about the same throughout the fifteen meetings. The amount of emotionality expressed was somewhat higher than in the first group and fluctuated greatly from meeting to meeting. The most typical interaction involved essentially exploratory work, with sweeping alternations between excited outbursts of feeling and flatness. This behavior corresponds to the kind of interaction which occurred in Phase 2 of the first group which was studied. Further investigation suggested that differences between the two groups were related to differences in composition and internal structure. These factors will be discussed in the next section.

In a study conducted by Warren Bennis (Bennis, 1956) the hypothesis was tested that the group would move through two phases: a general concern with the authority problem and a general concern with the intimacy problem. A concern with authority would be evidenced, for example, by power struggles among the membership or by a preoccupation with relationships with the trainer. A concern with intimacy

the emotionality (four possible categories: fight, flight, pairing, and dependency). Summarizing procedures included computing the average amount of emotionality and work per statement for "natural units" of interaction within each meeting and for each session as a whole.

would be evidenced by concerns about how much self-revelation could occur in the group or how close members could get to one another. A questionnaire was filled out following each group session by the trainers and training associates of six groups. The questionnaire consisted of a series of multiple-choice items about the major concern of the group during that meeting. Bennis found that his two-phase hypothesis held true for only one of the six groups. In a second group, a brief authority phase was followed by an intimacy phase, which was in turn followed by a second authority phase and a final intimacy phase. The remaining groups showed a continuous dealing and re-dealing with these two problems.

Several studies which will be discussed in greater detail in later sections will be mentioned briefly here for their relevance to the issue of group development. In a study of sociometric choice, Roberta Norfleet (Norfleet, 1948) points out that in friendship choices reciprocal choices tend to increase as time goes on and that judgments about productivity tend to converge and become concentrated on a relatively small number of members. Bennis et al. (Bennis, Burke, Cutter, Harrington, and Hoffman, 1957) found that norms about member behavior were established early in the group's history and persisted throughout the life of the group. A study by Morton A. Lieberman (Lieberman, 1958), in which it was found that members consistently maintain a common image of the "good group" (work-oriented, friendly), also suggests that certain norms are established very quickly and persist in the group.

Summary. These studies strongly support the general assumption that as a T Group continues to meet, definite structure emerges out of an initially more undifferentiated state. Certain aspects may emerge more quickly than others. For example, very close to the beginning, members may display consensus about the character of a "good group." Perhaps such norms cannot be said to be a product of development but of pre-established standards inherent in our general culture. With reference to its ability to deal with problems, there is some evidence that the group moves toward an appropriate balance among various kinds of affect and toward an effective interaction of work and emotionality. There also appear to be lawful relationships among emerging total group characteristics such as cohesiveness and productivity.

In general, there appears to be greater resemblance among mature groups with regard to structural characteristics than with regard to the *processes* by which they arrive at this point. There is some agreement that affective characteristics and interpersonal issues such as a concern with problems of authority and intimacy are significant elements in understanding group growth. However, these are not so much experimental findings as assumptions about the relevance of emotional dimensions in group life.

Group Composition

In planning a human relations laboratory an effort is often made to compose T Groups heterogeneously. In a general laboratory this means as much variety as possible with respect to age, sex, occupation, and geographical location. In a specialized laboratory, where the members may come from the same organization, it means including in the same T Group individuals with varying job roles and from different levels of responsibility and status. This principle is based on the assumption that a varied composition multiplies learning opportunities in the T Group and that differences such as occupational choice are likely to reflect differences in personality and experience, and hence, behavior in a group. Another view sees value in homogeneous groupings based on similar back-home roles or similar personality orientations. Here, the assumption is that homogeneity may facilitate communication and the transfer of laboratory learnings to the back-home situation.

The basic questions for research are, "What is the influence of group composition on other characteristics, such as the course of development, the prevailing atmosphere and level of anxiety, the subgroup structure, and member satisfaction and learning?" and, "In what ways are the various principles of group composition relevant to specific training goals?" Among the studies in this area two methodological approaches are represented. In one type of research design some principle of group composition is predetermined and tests or ratings are administered to potential members to determine composition. In another design the composition of existing groups is specified by identifying relevant personality characteristics of members and their distribution in the group. Once the group composition is known, its effects on group characteristics and/or individual learning are examined.

In research conducted at the University of Colorado, Jack R. Gibb and Anthony W. Gorman (Gibb and Gorman, 1954) studied the effects of "induced polarization" on defensive behavior and perceptual accuracy. In this study, the authors composed ten experimental groups in which half the members had answered "yes" and half had answered "no" to the question: "Should sex criminals be permanently imprisoned?" The behavior of these experimental groups was compared with that of control groups composed entirely of people who answered "yes" or entirely of people who answered "no." Observers tabulated the amount of defensive behavior expressed in both experimental and control groups. "Defensive behavior" was defined rather broadly and included aggression, flight, counterdependence, and the like. It was found that the experimental groups expressed much more of this kind of behavior.

The authors also studied the effect of polarization on perceptual accuracy (determined by having each member rank all members on three variables: "Whom would you choose as a leader?" "Who did the best thinking?" and "Who was the most interested in the discussion?" and then asking each person to estimate his own rank in the group). Groups with induced polarization did less well than control groups. A similar procedure compared perceptual accuracy of members before and after their experience in the discussion group. It was found that perceptions having to do with feelings of group members and attitudes toward leadership were more influenced by polarization than those having to do with beliefs on socioeconomic problems.

A study referred to in the preceding section described two groups: the first moved toward effective work and the adequate control and utilization of affect; the second seemed to "stick" permanently at a stage of routine exploration, alternating between flat and explosive affect. Further investigation (Hill, 1955; Stock and Hill, 1958) suggested that these differences might be related to composition. Tests were administered through which each person described himself as a group member. Then within each group the members were grouped according to similarities in self-percepts. (Q-sort and factor analytic procedures were employed.) In the first group most of the members shared a certain way of looking at themselves as members. The suggestion is that in this group there was enough of a common approach to group interaction that the members could struggle through toward an effective way of dealing with one another. The second group was made up of incompatible, mutually opposed subtypes. Of two major subtypes, the first preferred an impersonal, structured atmosphere, while the second showed a strong desire for intimate relationships and direct, aggressive outlets. Both subtypes wished to gain control of the group. A third subtype was essentially withdrawn. The trainer, incidentally, belonged to the first subtype. It is possible that his own position relative to the group made it difficult for him to help the group to resolve its differences.

Ida Gradolph conducted a study (Gradolph, 1958) which compared the behavior of three kinds of groups (composed on the basis of responses to a sentence-completion test). The subjects were formed into four groups of six members each: one group was composed of "work-pairing" members (interested in maintaining friendly relationships and in working on the tasks); a second group was composed entirely of "flight" members (tending to want to withdraw); two other groups were composed half of work-pairing and half of flight members. All groups were presented with the same two tasks: making a group decision and telling a story to a TAT picture.

Observers agreed that members of the flight group were uncommitted to the task and uninvolved with one another. The members of the work-pairing group expressed more affect of all kinds, were more involved, and were interested in talking over the experience. Neither of the two mixed groups completed the second task and both expressed frustration and anger. This study suggests that groups which are homogeneously composed are likely to behave in ways that are direct expressions of the emotional orientations of the members. Groups composed of two quite different types find it more difficult to find a common way of approaching their tasks.

In research conducted at Bethel in 1954, Morton A. Lieberman (Lieberman, 1958) studied two differently composed T Groups. All the members of this laboratory filled out a sentence-completion test several months before the laboratory started. These tests were analyzed, and a number of persons were selected who revealed relatively clear-cut (or "primary") tendencies to express five kinds of affect: fight, flight, pairing, dependency, and counterdependency. "Pairing" and "flight" have already been defined. A "fight" person is one whose major way of interacting with others involves the expression of aggression and hostility; a "dependency" person characteristically presents himself as weak and appeals for help from others; a "counterdependency" person presents himself as strong and actively resists accepting help. The two groups were composed so that the first included about an equal number of persons with each of these five primary emotional tendencies. In the second group pairing persons were omitted. Observers tabulated the amount of pairing, fight, flight, dependency, and counterdependency behavior actually expressed in each group during each of the three weeks of the group's existence. Lierberman found that the groups differed most with respect to the expression of pairing and counterdependency. In the first group (which included pairing members) about one-fifth of all the affect expressed involved pairing for all three weeks. In the second group (with no pairing members) the percentage of pairing was much lower to begin with, but gradually increased until here, too, about one-fifth of all affectful comments involved pairing. The behavior of the trainers with respect to pairing also differed; the trainer of the first group expressed the same amount of pairing throughout, while the trainer of the second group expressed five times more pairing the third week than the first week. The inference is that this trainer was attempting to fill a need for warmth. With respect to counterdependency, the first group expressed about the same amount throughout its existence; the second group began by expressing more, then gradually reduced the expression to the same percentage as the first one. This study suggests that a variety of kinds of affect in certain proportions is essential to group functioning and that when certain expressions are missing an imbalance is created with which the group members or trainer deal by modifying their habitual behavior.

At the first session of the human relations laboratory at Bethel in the summer of 1960 the T-Group staff developed a research design in which the regular T Groups were interrupted and the delegates were regrouped into E (Experimental) Groups which met for six sessions. The original T Groups then resumed meeting (Stock and Luft, 1960). Of special interest were three of the E Groups: one, persons who preferred conditions of high structure (preference for specific goals and procedures); one, persons who preferred conditions of low structure (preference for the exploration of feelings and interpersonal issues); and one, which included equal numbers of high- and low-structure persons. The judgments were made by trainers and associates in the original T Groups.

The E-Group trainers (who were not informed of the basis for composition) were asked for their impressions. The trainers of the high-structure group reported that they felt they had a very fast-moving group whose members were sociable and quickly worked out problems of consensus and feedback. At the same time the discussion seemed to remain shallow. The trainers felt that they had to keep introducing process issues. The members themselves felt extremely pleased and tended to value the E Group over the original T Group. In contrast, the trainers of the low-structure group reported that their group was highly verbal and process-oriented—to the extent that they were disinclined to interrupt their self-analysis in order to have the kind of experiences which could then be analyzed. The trainers found themselves pushing to introduce content and structure. The members of this group were very much excited about it at first, but lost some of their enthusiasm as the group seemed to stagnate. The trainers of the mixed group reported that their group seemed to have little tolerance for conflict. No one took a stand that persisted for more than a few comments, and the group seemed unable to deal with their feelings. The group was process-centered, but there was much fight, and they had a hard time getting down to anything.

This study suggested that group composition based on the variable "preference for high or low structure" was directly expressed in the mode of interaction characteristic of each group. There was some feeling among the staff that the homogeneous low-structure group did not contribute greatly to the learning of its members but that the homogeneous high-structure group deserved further study as a potentially useful experience for this type of participant. It was recognized that the laboratory culture as a whole supports values associated with low structure—for example, personal feedback and the exploration of group process.

High-structure individuals may find themselves at odds with the laboratory as a whole as well as with their individual T Groups. In the E Group they seemed to feel both relieved and elated. They were more valued by their fellow members and found mutual support in avoiding (initially) close attention to process. Yet this group moved toward some examination of process and personal feelings. It is as if the demands of the group required such exploration and that in the congenial atmosphere of the E Group the members allowed themselves greater readiness to learn more about processes and feelings.

Summary. Taken together, these studies suggest that group composition (based on certain personality variables) is a potent factor which finds rather direct expression in the character of the group interaction. It is as if the characteristics of the members can become the standards of the group and find uncontested expression in the group interaction.

A question arises as to which personality variables are most relevant to group functioning. T-Group members—because of self-selection as well as the standards of the National Training Laboratories—are likely to be homogeneous to begin with in regard to intelligence, job competency, and emotional stability. The studies which have been conducted thus far have focused on what might be called "affective orientation" or preferences for expressing certain kinds of affect or functioning in certain cognitive-emotional interpersonal settings. A wide variety of other bases for composing groups is theoretically possible. Of particular interest to NTL is composition based on back-home job role or family groups versus heterogeneous groups. These are yet to be explored via research.

With reference to dichotomous groups, the available evidence suggests that such groups are likely to be less efficient at problem solving, to display more frustration and anger and a higher level of affect, and to display less perceptual accuracy. One possibility is that such "two-type" groups devote much futile effort to an attempt to resolve their interpersonal problems. The absence of "bridging" members makes it difficult to find common or compromise ways of approaching their problems. Most of these groups were especially composed and one might ask how likely it is to find such a group outside an experimental situation. Judging from Hill's study, groups *approximating* this dichotomous condition are sometimes found *au naturel*. For example, one might find two major subgroups locked in a struggle from which other group members have abdicated.

Homogeneous groups seem to reinforce and permit expression of the individual tendencies of the members, at least initially. In short-term experimental groups one seems to see only the translation of individual tendencies into the culture of the group. In longer-term groups this initial tendency may yield to development in other directions. Among the homogeneous groups represented in these studies, this occurred only for the high-structured E Group conducted at Bethel in 1960. It is possible that this shift is related to the prevailing culture of the human relations laboratory, which was in opposition to the tendencies of this group. The other homogeneous groups were seen as offering little challenge for experimentation or change, since the already stable tendencies of the members were reinforced by the culture generated in the group. While by no means conclusive, these findings suggest that whether or not one regards a homogeneous culture as advantageous depends on the goals of the group (e.g., problem solving or exploring group process). Further, whether or not a homogeneous group displays development may depend on its duration as well as the social context in which it operates.

Lieberman's study suggests that a group composed of a variety of affective "types" may constitute a group in which a wide range of issues is likely to be elicited and made available for exploration. (Lieberman's work is consistent with Back's, in that both found there seemed to be a balance among the expression of various kinds of affect toward which groups work. When the composition does not provide such a balance, effective interactions may become more difficult.)

The Character of the T Group as Described by Members

Each delegate experiences the T Group in his own special way, depending on his background, previous experience and needs, the reasons he came to the laboratory and his expectations of it, his current sensitivities and his blind spots, his position in the group and the personal meaning its composition has for him. Such individual differences are expressed in each person's perceptions of his own role in the group and of the group as a whole.

Robert R. Blake developed a set of eleven T-Group scales (after experimentation with a much larger number) designed to represent fundamental characteristics of group behavior. The specific items ask group members to describe a particular session in terms of their feelings and their assessments of various aspects of the group interaction. A large-scale factor analysis (Blake, Mouton, and Fruchter, in press) of responses to these scales showed that three basic dimensions were represented. The first, which Blake calls *cohesion*, deals with feeling joined up, being open and free, listening to others with respect, feeling that one's group is a good one, and interacting according to the merits of the issue. The second, called *group accomplishment*, deals with digging hard into the discussion; feeling that the goals of the group's activity are clear; having a topic which is concrete, specific, and down to earth; feeling that the group is a good one; and feeling that one's remarks are listened to and considered with respect. The third dimension, called *group development feedback*, includes using process feedback and discussing problems of working together as a group in contrast to talking about "outside" topics. These three areas of group perception and behavior can be regarded as dimensions capable of independent variation within the group.

Morton A. Lieberman (Lieberman, 1958) studied the way in which members of two T Groups described their groups and their own roles. After each session, each member filled out a questionnaire consisting of two parts—one describing the way he saw his own role during the session, and one describing the way he saw the group as a whole. The two parts of the questionnaire included parallel items, so that both the self and the group could be described in the following terms: warmth, politeness, aggressivity, irritation, irrelevance, need for help, need to dominate, interest in the task, and interest in process.

In spite of the considerable diversity, there was a tendency for everyone to describe himself as warm and work-oriented. Independent information from personality tests and behavioral ratings showed that this kind of behavior was certainly not universal. Similarly, although observers' ratings showed that the two groups behaved quite differently, both from day to day and compared with each other, there was a tendency for everyone to describe his group as warm and work-oriented and to deny that discussion was irrelevant. These findings strongly suggest that there was a stereotyped impression about the characteristics of a "good group member" and a "good group" and that these stereotypes influenced the way members saw themselves and the group.

Jeanne Watson (Watson, 1950) administered a questionnaire at three points (beginning, middle, and end) of a T-Group experience. Members of six groups at the 1950 Bethel laboratory were asked to indicate which of the following they felt were the principal functions of the T Group: principles and concepts, skills and techniques, diagnostic skills, putting Bethel ideas into action, how to help others (train others), sensitivity, and insight into self. Most members felt the main functions of the T Group were to communicate principles and concepts, develop skills and techniques, and develop sensitivity to others and insight into the self. Applications of learning, either to the back-home setting or in training others, were de-emphasized.

Irving R. Weschler and Jerome Reisel, in their monograph, "Inside a Sensitivity Training Group" (Weschler and Reisel, 1959), describe a T Group from the point of view of the subjective impressions of its members. Each member kept a session-by-session diary of his personal reactions, insights and learnings, and assessments of the group interaction. The authors were able to identify the unique character and meaning of the T-Group experiences for each person as these developed and shifted.

Martin Lakin studied the subjective reactions of twelve T-Group members to their group immediately following and six months after the close of the group (Lakin, 1960). Each member was asked to identify and describe his feelings and reactions to the session which stood out most in his memory, the best meeting, and the worst meeting, and to describe what he felt he had gained or lost. Like Weschler and Reisel, Lakin was tapping the unique phenomenological experiencing of the T Group. The reported themes had to do with concerns about symbolized authority, self-exposure, peer conflict, and self-insight. Members felt good when they felt accepted and able to influence the group process and when they felt in harmony with the trainer. Worst meetings were those in which there was authority conflict or inconsistency and disagreement. Absent were themes related to cognitive aspects of the group such as formulations of group processes or the learning of skills. Emotional disengagement seemed to occur after six months.

Summary. Our information about this area is rather scattered. The various studies focused on quite different aspects of group life and are not directly comparable. It is interesting that, according to Watson's study, participants emphasize a wish for cognitive, theoretical, and skill learnings as against emotional or personal learnings; yet Lakin reports that what seems to have the greatest impact are affect-laden, interpersonal episodes around such issues as intermember conflict, personal exposure, and problems with authority. (Of course, nine years elapsed between these two studies; and there may have been a general shift in the perceived function of the T Group among the participant body. Or, it is possible that what people say they want to learn does not jibe with what actually happens as a result of the T Group.)

These studies report subjective impressions. While not necessarily an accurate reflection of what actually occurs, they reveal important implicit agreements about the character and purposes of the T Group that can be regarded as a common core of assumptions within which individual learnings and diversified experiences occur. For each person, what is important in the final analysis is how he experiences and perceives the T Group as it moves along (Weschler and Reisel, 1959) and how he later organizes and structures his T-Group experience and infuses it with personal meaning (Lakin, 1960).

The Role of the Trainer in the T Group

It is generally recognized that different trainers may vary considerably in the extent to which they introduce cognitive content; focus on total group, interpersonal, or individual aspects of the interaction; and introduce special devices such as role playing, buzz groups, recorders, or feedback and evaluation periods. In recent years Robert R. Blake has developed an "instrumented" T Group in which there is no trainer, and the group steers and evaluates itself with the help of feedback from daily administered T-Group Scales.

A number of research questions come to mind: "Is the trainer necessary to the T Group?" "What is the range and character of trainer styles?" "Can trainer-interventions be classified, and what is their impact on the group?" "How does the trainer's personality influence his trainer style?"

Relatively little work has been done in this area. An early, essentially clinical study was conducted at Bethel in 1947 (Deutsch, Pepitone, and Zander, 1948) in which the personality of a single T-Group trainer was studied in depth and related to his training philosophy, his goals, and his behavior in the group. This team of researchers utilized intensive interviews and such clinical techniques as the Rorschach test and the Thematic Apperception Test.

Since then, no study has focused specifically on the role of the T-Group trainer, although several studies reported in this chapter touch on this issue incidentally. In a study on group development, Back (Back, 1948) suggests that the trainer's behavior may function as a model for the group members, particularly with reference to the kind of affect expressed in the group. In two related studies (Hill, 1955; Stock and Hill, 1958), it is suggested that the differential course of development of two groups could be understood, in part, in terms of the trainer's location within the subgroup structure of the group. In a group in which the trainer belonged to one of two mutually incompatible and warring subtypes, it was felt that he was hampered in his efforts to help the group to resolve their conflict. In a study of group composition (Lieberman, 1958) it was demonstrated that in a group deficient in pairing members the trainer was stimulated to introduce more pairing behavior than might have been a natural part of his style under other circumstances. A similar phenomenon seemed to occur in two especially composed high-structure and low-structure T Groups (Stock and Luft, 1960), where the trainer of the high-structure group reported himself pushing more than usual for process analysis and the trainer of the low-structure group found himself trying to generate interaction.

Summary. The Deutsch, Pepitone, and Zander case study demonstrates for one trainer the complex ways in which personality characteristics may find expression in training philosophy and behavior. Other work suggests that a trainer adapts his style to each particular group. A trainer may be sensitive to missing functions in the group and may either deliberately try or unconsciously tend to supply the missing element. The trainer may sometimes function as a protagonist for a particular point of view, perhaps not always to the advantage of his group. He may also provide a style of participation which members utilize as a model.

Individual Behavior in the T Group

It is commonly recognized that people behave in characteristic ways in groups. For example, members may come to realize that a particular person can be counted on to volunteer for committee work, or to oppose the trainer's suggestions, or to depreciate the value of the group. More complexly: A member avoids participation, and then expresses resentment and hurt when he is not drawn into the group. Or a member, not realizing that he has presented his ideas in a condescending way, is baffled when they are not accepted. Repetitive behavioral patterns are assumed to be rooted in fairly stable personality characteristics. It is assumed that in the T Group each member participates in ways which have been characteristic of him in other group situations. Under the special conditions of the T Group, each member has the opportunity to reflect on his behavior, to perceive (and be informed about) its impact on others, and to shift and experiment with new behaviors if he chooses to do so.

In this area of individual behavior, research has tended to concentrate on the problem of identifying personality characteristics which may be relevant to behavior in groups and then relating these to specific behavioral patterns.

Jeanne Watson (Watson, 1952, 1953) conducted a major study on the relationship of basic personality organization and social behavior, using as subjects 400 participants from the 1950 through 1954 summer laboratories at Bethel. Working within the framework of psychoanalytic theory, Watson developed a typology which differentiated among individuals along two major axes: "orientation to the world" (oral dependent, oral aggressive, anal compulsive, and none of these); and "orientation to the self" (narcissism, anxiety, narcissism with anxiety, and none of these). Out of 20 possible (5×4) categories of personality, 11 actually occurred frequently enough for behavioral relationships to be identified reliably.[3]

The "oral dependent" category illustrates the kinds of relationships found. This group was predicated from psychoanalytic theory to display a "need to receive emotional supplies from others and to relate

[3] Assessments of personality were made from two projective tests: the Blacky Pictures and the Krout Personal Preference Inventory. Assessments of behavior were made from trainers' ratings of behavior, ratings and sociometric choices from peers, member ratings of satisfaction with the T Group, member ratings of personal change, member ratings of personal behavior, member estimates of agreement with other members, and member responses to an ideology test.

to others in a dependent manner" (Watson, 1952, p. 85). The various ratings and responses to questionnaires indicated that members' behavior could be characterized by eager overtures to others and high willingness to be influenced. Their objective seemed to be to achieve a situation of cooperation and good will among equals. Values emphasize the "strong man" and a yearning for prestige and admiration, with a rejection of "society" and its unfortunates. All of these behavioral elements can be seen as part of a dependent orientation toward life.

In addition to describing personality types, Watson also summarized the behavioral correlates. In general, it was found possible to relate personality organization to behavior in a T Group, if certain "bridging" inferences were made about the general implications of these orientations for behavior.

Robert R. Blake and Jane S. Mouton (Blake and Mouton, 1956) also studied the relation between personality and behavior in a group situation. They selected two specific personality factors—language skill and ascendancy-submission—and studied their relation to a variety of behaviors and attitudes.[4] The subjects were the 24 members of three T Groups which met at the Human Relations Training Laboratory at Las Vegas, New Mexico, during the summer of 1956. Subjects were divided into those high in language skill and ascendant; those high in language skill and submissive; those low in language skill and ascendant; and those low in language skill and submissive.

The results showed that ascendant subjects (compared with submissive ones) are seen by their peers as clashing more frequently with other group members. Ascendant subjects who are also high in language skill are described as participating more, competing with others, keeping themselves "in the limelight," and being aggressive toward the trainer. Submissive subjects, on the other hand, are described as needing direction and support by the trainer, avoiding conflict, and placing group goals above personal goals. Language skill is also an important factor: Individuals high in language skill do better on the "Sensitivity to Group Functions Test." In general, they tend to be constructive and central members of the group.

---

[4] Language skill was measured by a 40-item test constructed from past issues of the *Reader's Digest*. Ascendancy-submission was measured by the Allport-Allport A-S Reaction Study. Various behaviors were measured by three devices: observers' counts of frequency of participation, sociometric questionnaires (in which members were asked, for example, to judge one another with respect to who was most influential, protective, aggressive, or withdrawn), and a specially constructed "Sensitivity to Group Functions Test."

Bennis and his colleagues (Bennis et al., 1957) studied a twelve-member T Group conducted at Boston University in an attempt to predict group behavior from a variety of personality measures.[5] The personality tests included the Cattell 16 P.F. test, the Edwards Personal Preference Schedule, Harrington's Self-sort test, and Schutz' FIRO. Sociometric measures (individuals as described by others) were used as the measures of behavior with which personality test results were compared. In utilizing standard tests not originally intended to predict group behavior (such as the Cattell and Edwards tests), the research team singled out test items which seemed particularly relevant to group behavior and made specific predictions about them. For example, from the Edwards Schedule they predicted that high need-abasement people would be among those who lead least in the group. In spite of the care taken to make specific and plausible predictions, none of the predictions made from the Cattell or Edwards tests was upheld. Of the self-sort modalities (pairing, counterpairing, dependence, and counterdependence), only pairing showed a significant relationship to behavior. That is, individuals who described themselves as high in pairing were seen as most friendly by other group members. With respect to the FIRO test, the only significant finding was the fact that those persons with high inclusion needs (those who want to join groups) were seen as low in participation. Evidently high inclusion as measured by the FIRO can represent a wish rather than a behavioral characteristic.

The authors discuss some of the methodological difficulties in research of this sort—for example, the problems involved in using members' perceptions of an individual's behavior as a measure of actual behavior. They also underline the importance of selecting measuring instruments specifically tuned to the social situation to which predictions are to be made.

Summary. With respect to the question, "Can behavior be predicted from an assessment of personality traits?" these three studies produce rather mixed results. In no case could all of the personality characteristics under study be shown to be related to all the behavioral measures. But in every case some predictions could be upheld. Part of the problem is methodological. When the measure of behavior involves the perception of the subject by other group members, one cannot be sure that the perceptions accurately reflect behavior. Prediction is more likely to be successful when the personality trait being measured is

[5] Other aspects of this study are relevant to individual change and to group development, and are discussed elsewhere in this chapter.

specifically relevant to the behavior. When personality is conceptualized at a "deeper" or more comprehensive level (as in the Watson, 1952, study), appropriate bridging concepts are necessary in specifying expected behaviors.

It is interesting to speculate about some of the specific findings as well as about some of the failures in these studies. Bennis makes the plausible prediction that need-abasement will be associated with low participation. When this does not occur, is it because the inference is incorrect or because such individuals have learned to compensate for or otherwise block behavioral expression of the trait? Some of the relationships shown in the Watson (1952) study are immediately plausible, but others are more puzzling. Why, for example, should an anal-compulsive personality be inclined to perceive himself as retiring?

All this suggests that a relationship does exist between personality characteristics and behavior, but intervening explanatory concepts may be required in order to understand the processes which may block, translate, *or* permit the behavioral expression of personality characteristics.

Members' Perceptions of One Another: Sociometric Choice

In any small group, members develop a variety of feelings and attitudes about one another. Taken in sum, such feelings and attitudes define the sociometric structure of the group—the complex pattern of subgroups, pairs, and isolates; the leaders and the followers; the valued and the unvalued. Such patterns may have an important influence on the course of group events. From the point of view of the individual, his location within the sociometric structure of the group may be a major factor in the way he experiences the T Group and in the learnings he can derive from it.

Two general interests are represented by the research in this area. One is the relationship among the various kinds of judgments members make about one another and between these judgments and their behavior in the group. Another is the relationship between personality factors and sociometric choice.

Roberta Norfleet (Norfleet, 1948) studied the sociometric choices of the members of five T Groups from the 1947 Bethel laboratory. Each member was asked (early, midway, and late in the group) to choose those persons who he felt contributed most to the productivity of the group and those with whom he would most like to spend his leisure time. It was found that choices in responses to the "productivity" question were widely and apparently randomly distributed at first. As the group went on, a relatively small number of persons were seen consistently as productive by most group members. Choices in response to the "leisure-time" question were widely distributed throughout the three-week period. Although choices became fixed and there was increased mutuality of choice, there never developed the concentration on a few members that was characteristic of the "productivity" judgment. Norfleet concluded that judgments of productivity and friendship are largely independent of each other. Group consensus develops with respect to ratings of productivity but not with respect to friendship.

In research conducted at the 1949 Bethel laboratory, Milton W. Horowitz, Joseph Lyons, and Howard V. Perlmutter (Horowitz, Lyons, and Perlmutter, 1951) studied the relationship between members' positive or negative feelings about one another and their judgments of one another's acts or suggestions. Their general assumptions involve the idea that persons are seen as sources of acts and as connected with acts and that there is a tendency to wish to maintain equilibrium by having the same attitude (either positive or negative) toward a person and toward his behavior. The authors hypothesize that when disequilibrium exists (for example, when a person who is liked performs some disapproved act) there is a tendency to resolve this conflict by reevaluating the person, reinterpreting his behavior, or dissociating the person and the act.

An ingenious research design was developed for testing these ideas: the members of a T Group were studied during a single three-hour session. Sociometric questionnaires were administered in order to determine initial positive and negative feelings. Then, after observing the group interaction for a two-hour period, the experimenters selected certain behaviors which they felt were important, conspicuous, and tied to specific members. Finally, they asked for attitudes about these behaviors and readministered the sociometric questionnaire.

The results supported the authors' general hypothesis, but the relationship between one's feeling about a person and one's judgment about his behavior was most marked when the feeling was an intense one. Interestingly, this relationship could not be demonstrated when the criterion for attitude about a particular act was actual behavior in the group rather than a response to a questionnaire. The authors suggest a number of explanations for this discrepancy: that likes and dislikes may shift subtly during the course of a meeting; that an individual may be influenced by many factors not present when he is responding to a questionnaire; that in an actual group situation a member may be influenced by many factors other than a general feeling of liking or disliking; or that the act judged might not be typical.

Saul Ben-Zeev (Ben-Zeev, 1958) related sociometric choice and patterns of participation in a sixteen-member T Group from the 1951 Bethel laboratory to determine whether or not members are likely to participate with those whom they like and fail to participate with those whom they dislike. Information about members' likes and dislikes was obtained by the usual questionnaire procedures. Patterns of coparticipation were identified by noting whether or not various pairs of members participated during the same periods. It was then possible to correlate positive or negative sociometric choice with extent of coparticipation. At first the results seemed unclear: some members tended to participate with those they liked while others did not. Ben-Zeev then examined personality data gathered from a sentence-completion instrument and found that members who participated with those they liked showed a tendency on the projective test to express warmth and friendliness and to inhibit expressions of hostility and anger. Conditions of mutual friendliness were seemingly perceived as conditions under which they could participate freely and actively. Those who did not participate with those they liked were found to have a tendency to express hostility and anger and to inhibit the expression of warmth and friendliness. Such persons seemed most stimulated to participate with those whom they disliked, i.e., under conditions of conflict and controversy.

Anthony J. Smith, Jack Jaffe, and Donald G. Livingston (Smith, Jaffe, and Livingston, 1955) studied the relationship between consonance and effectiveness in a nineteen-member T Group at the 1950 Bethel laboratory. The authors use the term "consonance" to refer to the extent to which a member is "in tune" with the way the group as a whole looks at its members. (Consonance was measured by comparing an individual's judgments with an averaged group judgment.) The general hypothesis was that members with high consonance would be seen as most effective by outside observers and most powerful and valuable by group members. In addition, it was predicted that a member will believe he can contribute most to, and be most benefited by, those persons whose perceptions correspond most closely with his own. Consonance was measured with reference to judgments about productivity, power, the extent to which the rater could benefit the person, and the extent to which the person could benefit the rater. Observers who were present at all the meetings rated each member for personal effectiveness.

The results showed that the most consonant members were seen as most effective by outside observers and most powerful by members, but were not necessarily seen as most valuable. A small but significant relationship was also found between consonance and feelings of mutual benefit.

The authors concluded that "the person whose perception of certain aspects of group process conforms closely to the group judgment concerning these matters will be seen both by the group and by observers as being highly productive. Furthermore, his colleagues will see him as a power figure, determining what occurs in the group. Finally, a person is inclined to believe that he can contribute to and aid significantly, and will in turn be benefited significantly by, the individuals with whom he agrees" (Smith, Jaffe, and Livingston, 1955, p. 393).

The second general interest of the research in this area is the influence of personality on sociometric choice.

Shirley A. Browne and Marilyn Crowe (Browne and Crowe, 1953) and Milton Rosenberg (Rosenberg, 1950) conducted studies related to the work of Jeanne Watson. In these studies, the eleven personality types which Watson related to behavior patterns were related to sociometric choice.

Browne and Crowe were interested in determining whether certain types were likely to choose or reject specific other types. Their subjects were the one hundred persons (divided into six T Groups) whom Watson also studied during the 1950 Bethel laboratory. Two sociometric questions were asked during the second week of the laboratory: "Who are the five members of your T Group with whom you would like to spend leisure time?" and "Who are the five people you consider most like yourself with respect to the philosophy of social change?" A general hypothesis was that there would be a close relationship between "leisure-time" and "similarity-of-change-philosophy" choices, inasmuch as friendship is often based on agreement about basic values. This relationship was demonstrated. A further interest was in determining the personality types chosen by each type. Watson's original eleven types were recombined into five types: (1) the dependents, (2) the self-sufficients, (3) the rigids, (4) the inhibited hostiles, and (5) the overt hostiles. The results showed that the rigid, tense members tended to choose one another; the self-sufficient members to choose one another and the rigid members; the overtly hostile members to choose one another and the inhibited hostiles; and the dependent members to choose the inhibited hostiles; while the inhibited hostiles chose the dependents.

Two choice patterns seem to exist. First, certain members tend to choose people like themselves. Second, members tend to choose people who have what they want. For example, the inhibited hostiles tended to choose dependency members (who displayed the control over hostile feelings for which the inhibited hostiles were striving). At the same time, the dependency members tended to choose the inhibited hostiles (who seemed relatively freer in expressing aggression).

Milton Rosenberg (Rosenberg, 1950) approached the same problem in a somewhat different way. First he identified, by means of sociometric questionnaires, members who received the most and least number of choices as leisure-time companions and as productive members. He then administered a number of personality tests (the Runner-Seaver, the Guildford-Zimmerman, and the Allport-Vernon Scales) to identify the personality characteristics which distinguished between "overchosen" and "underchosen" persons. Rosenberg found that the rejected members (on both questions) tended to be more compulsive, competitive, and energetic, and less friendly than the accepted members. They also showed less capacity for personal relations. The author used the term "anal" to define this combination of characteristics. He formulated the general hypothesis that members displaying this combination of traits would be likely to be rejected by others.

Rosenberg studied a second T Group, first administering personality tests and dividing the membership into two groups in such a way that the first group displayed anal traits while the second did not. His prediction that the first group would be more likely to be rejected was upheld when checked against actual sociometric choices. However, the prediction held true only for the final of three administrations of the sociometric questionnaire. The author concludes that the tendency for this relationship to become established only after a period of time "is consistent with our hypothesis that on the basis of an accumulation of interaction experiences, the members came to judge one another and evaluate one another at the personality or character level" (Rosenberg, 1950, pp. 6–7).

Warren Bennis and Dean Peabody (Bennis and Peabody, 1962) discuss the relationship between "dependency" and "personalness" in sociometric choice. It was assumed that these two orientations—toward authority and intimacy—exist as major issues in all groups and that the members' orientations toward these issues are a major influence on subgroup formation, loyalties, and communication. The basic hypothesis was that members with similar personality orientations would tend to select each other sociometrically. Personality classifications were made on the basis of trainers' ratings: to determine sociometric preferences each member was asked to list three members with whom he got along best, and three with whom he got along least. The basic hypothesis was clearly upheld for counterdependents and over-personals and was less clearly marked for dependents and counterpersonals. With regard to the personality dimensions themselves, the results suggested that the two ends of each continuum (e.g., overpersonalness and counterpersonalness) may occur together in a conflicted individual.

Dorothy Stock (Stock, 1952), studying a seven-member T Group conducted at The University of Chicago, used self-perceptual data to predict sociometric choice. Each member's perception of his own emotional role in a group situation was measured (by means of a self-perceptual Q-sort, and with reference to fight, flight, pairing, counter-pairing, dependency, and counterdependency). From this self-per-ceptual information, Stock estimated the "need system" of each indi-vidual, including his preferred mode of emotional expression, emo-tional areas in which conflict was present, and the kinds of defenses employed against conflict. Predictions of sociometric choice were made for each member on the basis of two different assumptions: first, that members accept or reject others on the basis of facilitation or interference with operation in the individual's preferred emotional mode; and second, that members accept or reject others on the basis of support for or threat to central defenses. These predictions were checked against actual choices of those "liked" and "disliked" made during the final meetings of the T Group. The results suggested that persons *unconflicted* with respect to their preferred emotional mode will prefer those members who facilitate operation in their preferred emotional mode. Members who are *conflicted* will prefer those who can reinforce their defensive structure.

Morton A. Lieberman's study on group composition (reported in a previous section) is relevant in part to relationships between person-ality and sociometric choice. Persons with primary tendencies to ex-press five kinds of feelings—fight, flight, pairing, dependency, and counterdependency—were formed into two T Groups. Following each session of the T Group, each member was asked to indicate the mem-ber or members he agreed with most, agreed with least, considered the major spokesman for the group, felt closest to, and felt furthest from. During the early stages, members of a particular type tended to make choices as a unit and the choice patterns were fairly complex. As time went on, the choices of a particular subtype became more diverse. Lieberman suggests that this change may reflect a general increase in security which made it more possible for members to choose behavior "rationally" in response to changing group events.

Summary. Studies of sociometric choice have addressed themselves to a rather wide variety of issues. Rosenberg found that compulsive, competitive, energetic, and unfriendly persons were most likely to be rejected. Smith, Jaffe, and Livingston found that the most consonant members were seen as most powerful, but not necessarily as most valuable. This study suggests that different kinds of judgments may be independent of one another. In contrast, the Horowitz, Lyons, and Perlmutter study indicates that there is some tendency for consistency among judgments, so that an individual who likes someone is also likely to value his acts or suggestions. Yet these consistent attitudes were not always expressed in actual behavior. Ben-Zeev also found that one cannot always assume the direct translation of sociometric choice into behavior: some people tended to coparticipate with those they liked and others did not. The differentiating factor seemed to be certain personality characteristics.

"Who chooses whom, and why?" The usual hypothesis was that persons similar in certain personality dimensions would be likely to choose one another. What tended to happen was that this could be demonstrated for some personality types but not for others. Several investigators suggest that choices may depend not entirely on similarities in personality but on such issues as "Who displays the kind of behavior I would like to be able to display?" or "Who supports my defenses and helps me to maintain my self-percept?"

The Impact of the T Group on Individual Learning and Change

The T Group is aimed toward facilitating learning of a special type: increased sensitivity toward group processes, increased awareness of the character of one's own group participation, and increased ability to deal with a variety of group situations. The learnings which an individual gains at a human relations laboratory are valuable to the extent that he is able to utilize them in the groups which are important to him in his back-home setting.

A multitude of questions can be asked: What kinds of learnings take place? To what extent are learnings transferred to back-home groups, and what factors influence the character and extent of transfer? Are some people better able to profit from the T Group than others? And if so, what makes the difference? What is it exactly about the laboratory or the T Group which contributes to change? Questions such as these are highly relevant to the basic issue of what constitutes and contributes to learning. They are of great practical interest to the National Training Laboratories as an organization, with its commitment to the further education and personal growth of individuals and, through this, to the more efficient functioning of organizations.

This section is misnamed: Much of the research described here focuses not on the T Group as the specific agent of change, but on the laboratory as a whole or some specific technique in the T-Group experience. It is difficult to separate out any single aspect of a laboratory and say *this* is what influenced learning. The laboratory is deliberately designed to include lectures on theory, and demonstration and practice sessions, on the assumption that these plus the T Group constitute an integrated whole. Participants often experience the T Group as having had the greatest impact, but while this subjective reaction underlines the involvement usually generated by the T-Group experience, it does not necessarily testify to its primary role in learning.

A large number of research studies have been conducted in this area. Some have attempted to deal with all or most of the questions listed above. Others have singled out some aspect of the learning process for investigation. In presenting this material, the most comprehensive studies are presented first.

A research team from the Research Center for Group Dynamics at The University of Michigan collected extensive data during the summers of 1951 and 1952 (Watson, Lippitt, Kallen, and Zipf, 1961). Their purpose was to identify the learnings which occurred at the laboratory, the kinds of learnings which could be transferred to the back-home job situation, and factors which might be related to differences in learning and in the application of learnings.

This study primarily utilized questionnaire and interview data. Data were collected at the beginning and end of the laboratory and again six months later. Some of this data collection involved direct questions about objective facts—for example, facts about age, sex, and organizational role. There was also a check list for techniques learned at Bethel and later utilized. Other questions asked for impressions or analyses of hypothetical situations, the responses being scored according to certain criteria or categories (e.g., sophistication about group dynamics and ability to analyze human relations problems).

One of the questions investigated by this study was: Do people from different kinds of situations, with different kinds of motivations and training, learn different things at Bethel? The authors report [6]

[6] This account should not be taken as a complete or balanced summary of findings, since the study is quite complex and writing is still in progress.

that a complex of feelings and attitudes which they call "response set" appeared to be an important factor. That is, certain attitudes about the laboratory seemed to go along with certain ways of describing back-home jobs and attempts to apply laboratory learnings. For example, individuals who gave favorable answers to a series of questions about Bethel also displayed a higher readiness to learn and tended to describe their jobs as high in change potential and to formulate clear change objectives. People who expected when they arrived that Bethel would not be relevant for them reported later that they had made little use of techniques after they returned home and felt that they had not increased in self-understanding or self-confidence.

Interesting relationships were found between participants' feelings about the laboratory and their reports about obstacles and blocks to the application of learnings which they expected or found in the back-home situation; for example, people who found their experience at Bethel frustrating expected obstacles back home. Once back on the job, a report of few blocks might reflect indifference on the part of the participants. Some participants who reported high gains in self-understanding and self-confidence, as well as success in the use of Bethel techniques, reported many blocks in the back-home situation. This suggests that individuals who tried out new ideas and techniques might encounter blocks, while those who did not might remain unaware of potential obstacles.

With regard to the influence of personality, one clear finding was that anxiety is associated with a low level of application: little success in using techniques, little use of Bethel ideas, and little acceptance of "group dynamics values." But on the whole, personality seemed more related to the ways in which people responded to questionnaires than to their behavior in the group or later application of learnings. For example, a desire to please leads individuals to give positive answers to questions, and a tendency to be critical leads individuals to give negative answers. Nor could behavior in the T Group be shown to determine what happens later. There was some suggestion that responsive, outgoing persons were more likely to find ways of applying what they had learned, but here, too, a response set might be operating.

Persons who had difficulties in the T Group showed a negative reaction to Bethel training. However, it is interesting that difficulties which involved alienation and frustration had a deleterious effect on benefit, but difficulties which took the form of fighting or clash did not.

The authors report "virtually no evidence" that differences in the type of institution from which the participants come, in their power or their point of view, affect the kind and amount of participation in the T Group.

Matthew B. Miles developed a general theory about laboratory learning (Miles, 1957) and applied it in a study of change conducted at a laboratory for school principals (Miles, 1960). He suggests that the learner can be described in terms of successive states which include a desire for change, the unfreezing of old behavior patterns, involvement in the T Group, and the clear reception of feedback. Three personality factors were thought to facilitate these steps: ego strength, flexibility, and need-affiliation. It was assumed that certain organizational factors (security, objective power, autonomy, own perceived power, and perceived adequacy of organizational functioning) would influence the individual's entry into the training situation and his initial desire for change. It was felt transfer of learnings would be facilitated if the individual perceived clear learnings in himself, regarded these as relevant to his job, and developed specific action-images and plans.

Thirty-four members of the 1958 Laboratory for Elementary School Principals were studied and compared with two control groups totaling 148 persons. A variety of instruments was administered before, during, and eight months following the laboratory.

It was found that the learner's explicit desire for change was not related to gain from the experience, nor were the organizational factors of security, objective power, and the like related to the participant's initial desire for change. However, the three factors of unfreezing, involvement, and feedback were all found to be significantly related to change during the laboratory. The most useful means of change at the laboratory and back on the job proved to be the T-Group trainer's judgment about change, related both to change on the job and to an index of self-perceived learnings. The three personality variables seemed to be only *indirectly* related (high flexibility, ego strength, and need-affiliation facilitated unfreezing, involvement, and the reception of feedback, and these in turn influenced learning). Three instruments were used to measure changes in job performance: a Leader Behavior Description Questionnaire (Stogdill and Coons, 1957); the Group Participation Scale (Pepinsky, Siegel, and Van Alta, 1952); and an open-ended perceived-change measure developed for the study. Of these, the first showed no change, and the second showed improvement for both experimental and control subjects. However, the third instrument showed that 73 per cent of the experimental subjects showed change, while only 17 per cent and 29 per cent of the two control groups showed change. Improvement occurred in sensitivity and behavioral skill, but not in diagnostic ability. The hypothesis that transfer would be facilitated by self-perceived learnings related to clarity, relevance, and action images was only indirectly supported.

A modification of Miles's open-ended perceived-change measure was used by Douglas Bunker (Bunker, in progress) to study the long-range effects of participation in the 1960 and 1961 summer laboratories at Bethel. This research was intended to replicate the Miles behavioral-change finding with a heterogeneous population of both participants and control subjects, to refine the perceived-change measure in order to explicate the dimensions of change, and to compare the differential consequences of three-week laboratories conducted at Bethel in 1960 with those of the two-week programs of 1961. Behavioral descriptions were obtained ten to twelve months following the laboratories and were coded into empirically derived categories by trained scorers.

The 1960 results reveal significant differences between participants and control subjects in both the magnitude of change scores and the kinds of changes described. Participants were seen by respondents to have changed particularly more than controls in communicating more clearly and effectively with co-workers; sharing and encouraging responsibility and participation among peers and subordinates; and in analytic understanding of human behavior, insight into group processes, sensitivity to the feelings and needs of others, and increased understanding of self and personal roles. Descriptions of controls' behavior changes tended to be more global, characterological, and vaguely evaluative than those of laboratory participants.

Since the follow-up data from the 1961 laboratories have not been analyzed completely, the relative effects of two-week laboratories compared with three-week programs have not been determined. Whatever the importance of the duration variable, however, there are apparent in the 1960 data some striking differences between laboratories. These, with some equally provocative differences between T Groups within laboratories, demonstrate the need for continuing research to examine the impact of each of the many variables in the group training process.

In the four studies to be described next, certain characteristics of the learner are measured at the time he enters the training experience and again at the end of training. These studies ask the question, "What learnings occur as the result of the laboratory experience?" and have focused on several different kinds of learnings.

The Evaluation Committee of the Second American National Red Cross School for Management Development conducted a study to determine whether changes occurred in the ways in which participants analyzed work problems (Glidewell, 1956). It was agreed that in this area the goals of laboratory training are to encourage participants (1) to see organizational problems in terms of multiple rather than single causation, (2) to develop awareness of their own involvement in the multiple causation of organizational problems, and (3) to define problems in terms of functions rather than of the adequacies or inadequacies of individuals. It was important to know where each individual stood with respect to these three variables at the time he entered the training program. Therefore, a questionnaire was administered at the start and near the end of training. Each participant was asked six open-ended questions about problems in his job situation and his analyses of causal factors. A coding system permitted assessments of each person's approach to work-problem analysis in terms of causation, personal involvement, and functional problem definition. It was found necessary to look at all three variables in relation to one another, rather than at each variable separately. Also, in order to understand change, it was necessary to look at the kinds of people who changed in specific directions. The data suggested that certain major *syndromes* of problem analysis exist—for example, the "stepchild" syndrome. This kind of person worried about the way he was treated by others and hoped that others could be induced to treat him differently. Two-thirds of this group moved toward seeing the outcome of their problems as determined by the development of skill and awareness in interpersonal relations in which both they and others were involved.

The "innocent bystander" syndrome was the name given to another pattern. These individuals were inclined to see problems as belonging to others. Seventy-one per cent of these persons changed in the direction of greater involvement and greater concern about developing skill and awareness in interpersonal relations. Two other syndromes were the "service" syndrome (the crucial factor in solving problems seen as their own ability to give service to others) and the "do-it-yourself" club (problems seen as human relations problems, with the outcome determined solely by oneself). Of these two groups, 67 per cent and 42 per cent, respectively, showed constructive change. A syndrome which showed little or no change was labeled "managers-of-the-year," to refer to participants who at the beginning of training already displayed maximum constructiveness in their views of problems. Over-all, 60 per cent of the participants could be said to change in a constructive direction.

R. L. Burke and Warren Bennis (Burke and Bennis, 1961) studied the impact of the human relations laboratory on changes in the perception of self and of other group members. A "Group Semantic Differential" test was devised and administered to each member of six T Groups twice—early and late in the three-week laboratory. Each person was asked to describe (1) the way I actually am in this T Group; (2) the way I would like to be in this T Group; and (3) what each other T-Group member is like. First of all, it was found (by means of factor analysis) that members tend to organize their perceptions of others around three major dimensions: the first includes elements of friendliness, acceptance, and positive evaluation; the second combines dominance and leadership with strength; and the third refers to extent of participation or activity in the group. It was found that perception of self and of ideal self tended to converge, mainly because of changes in the way the self was perceived rather than in the way the ideal self was conceptualized. It was also found that the way people see themselves and the way in which they are seen by others become more similar over time. Members also tended to agree more with one another about their perceptions of particular individuals, but only with regard to the extent of participation. Perceptions having to do with friendliness or domination showed just as much variation toward the end of the T Group as at the beginning.

Gibb and Miles developed a measuring instrument—the Group Behavior Task—designed to evaluate an individual's diagnostic ability and his sensitivity to feelings, to the behaviors of others, and to group decisions. This test was administered, early and late in training, at five human relations laboratories conducted by the Protestant Episcopal Church in 1959 (Miles, Cohen, and Whitam, 1959). Group members are asked to work as a group to rank-order ten statements about the behavior of a trainer of a working group. After fifteen minutes' interaction they are asked to fill out a questionnaire on the interaction. The sensitivity and diagnostic ability of each person is assessed by comparing his responses with certain criteria derived either from objectively measured characteristics of the discussion (e.g., number and character of decisions made) or the trainer's judgments (e.g., his diagnosis of the group's difficulties). The results of this study show considerable variation both among laboratories and among individual participants with reference both to initial sensitivity and diagnostic ability and to change. In sum, participants tended to do two-thirds to three-quarters as well as they theoretically *could* have done. Most consistent improvement was in the variable, "sensitivity to feelings." The remaining factors changed for some laboratories but not for others, or even showed a downward trend. The authors point out that median scores were utilized and may have obscured some of the individual change patterns, that in some instances a high median score to begin with meant little room for a positive change, and that familiarity with the test may have influenced performances on the post-test in inconsistent ways.

In a study previously reported (Bennis et al., 1957), subjects were asked to describe themselves in terms of 34 interpersonal roles at the beginning and end of the T Group. It was found that there was no change in the items persons saw as like or unlike their group behavior, but there was a shift toward seeing their behavior as more like that in the 34 items at the end of the group than at the beginning. The authors suggest that the individuals either have actually increased their behavior in these roles or have become more sensitive to their own role behavior.

A study by Roger Harrison (Harrison, in progress) is investigating laboratory learnings from the point of view of dissonance theory. Of special interest is the theoretical basis of the study, since it suggests a process by which learning may occur within the T Group. Harrison assumes that people experience dissonance when events do not follow predictably from one another. In the T Group, dissonances occur when the trainer does not behave as expected; when behavior which has been effective elsewhere does not seem to work in the group; and when the individual observes unexpected, confusing, or inconsistent behavior on the part of others or even himself. The learning potential of the T Group lies in its generation of dissonant situations (so long as they are not too overwhelming) and the individual's tendency to want to try to reduce dissonance. If he does so through expansion of his ways of perceiving individual and group behavior, useful learning may occur. He suggests that "the ideal training design, by exposing members to unexpected, difficult-to-understand events, creates dissonances for participants in an amount which can be reduced by changes in the participants' views of how people and groups behave. When too much dissonance is produced, or when appropriate new concepts are not available, trainees cannot use problem-solving ways of reducing dissonance."

The next group of three studies have focused on factors either in the learner's personality or in the character of the T Group which may influence the nature and extent of learning.

Andrew G. Mathis (Mathis, 1955) combined Bion's and Lewin's concepts of group operation to develop an index to predict an individual's potential for learning and change. From Lewin's concepts he reasoned that internal conflict would stimulate an individual to search for solutions to problems arising through group interaction. From Bion's concepts he reasoned that tendencies toward pairing and fight would provide the individual with supportiveness and aggressiveness to enable him to move "toward" problem situations and interact "personally" with the problem. The existence of intrapersonal conflict, plus tendencies toward free expression of fight and pairing, were thus selected as positive indicators for trainability ("adient" characteristics).

On the other hand, tendencies toward dependency and flight were considered to inhibit learning because they would deter the individual from becoming involved in the problem situation and from taking responsibility for actively experimenting with possible solutions. Tendencies toward becoming immobilized in stress situations would also block learning. Thus, dependency, flight, and immobilization were considered negative indicators for trainability ("abient" characteristics). The trainability index consisted of the ratio of adient to abient indicators, as determined for each participant from his responses to a sentence-completion test.

Fifty persons were studied from the 1952 Bethel and Chicago laboratories. The ten persons receiving the highest scores on the trainability index were compared with the ten persons receiving the lowest scores. A wide variety of types of change were assessed by means of interviews, sociometric procedures, and a sentence-completion test. The high-scoring persons showed greater increases in the integration of work and emotionality; they increased more in ability to predict how members will rate one another sociometrically; and their confidence in their acceptance by other group members increased. In addition, independent judges rating follow-up interviews and questionnaires ranked them higher on sensitivity, sophistication, and productivity.

Dorothy Stock (Stock, 1958) studied changes in the self-percepts of twenty-nine members of a training group conducted by Herbert A. Thelen at The University of Chicago during the winter of 1953. Pre- and post-self-percepts were collected by means of Q-sorts, in which members were asked to describe themselves in terms of feelings and behaviors involving aggression, withdrawal, warmth, dependency, and counterdependency.

The seven members who changed most were compared with the seven who changed least. It was found that as far as the *content* of self-perception was concerned, no generalizations could be made as to the kind of change which occurred or the kinds of people likely to change most. However, there were other definite differences between the initial self-descriptions of the "most change" and "least change" members. The "least change" members displayed more clearly defined self-concepts. They tended to subscribe to a sort of stereotype of the "good group member": the warm, work-oriented member who retains interest in the group and does not need to be led. The "most change" members were a more diverse lot and were a good deal less sure of the kinds of people they were. It seems reasonable to suppose that the "most change" members were motivated to use the T Group as an opportunity to resolve some of their inconsistencies and conflicts.

The Lieberman study (Lieberman, 1958), reported previously, dealt in part with the effects of different group cultures on individual change. Of the two groups studied, one displayed an atmosphere of warmth and easy relationships with the trainer; the other, an atmosphere of struggle for leadership. It was found that in an over-all sense neither group was superior to the other in leading to change in individuals. However, the groups differed in the kinds of persons who showed change. Both a sentence-completion test and behavioral ratings showed that counterdependency persons were the ones who changed most in the first group. In this same group, pairing and dependency members changed least. In the second group it was the dependency members who changed most and the counterdependency members who changed least. Lieberman explained these results by assuming that the generally warm relationships with the trainer in the first group made counterdependency an inappropriate way of behaving and forced the counterdependency members into another mode of behavior. Similarly, the prevailing atmosphere of counterdependency in the second group forced the dependency members to change.

The next rather large group of studies concentrated on two specific techniques and procedures—feedback and role playing—and their impact on various kinds of learning.

Gordon Lippitt (Lippitt, 1959) studied the effects of feedback on changes in individual behavior. First, data were collected about the ways each person was perceived by his fellow members and the ways in which they would like him to change (in terms of his frequency of participation, the degree to which he welcomed or resisted the ideas of others, and the extent to which he sought attention or avoided recognition). In the next step, seven matched pairs were selected from each T Group. Both members of a pair were alike in the *way* they were described by others and in the extent and direction others would like them to change. One member of each pair was told, in a personal counseling interview, about the ratings he had received and the way his fellow members would like him to change. The other member did not receive this feedback.

Nonparticipant observers rated the behavior of all subjects before and after the feedback period. Second, the members repeated their ratings of one another toward the end of the T Group. Thirteen out of the fourteen persons who received feedback changed in the direction the group wanted them to change, while only eight out of the fourteen who received no feedback showed change.

Jack R. Gibb and his associates conducted a series of related laboratory studies which investigated the effects of feedback on individual behavior and group process and the differential effects of particular kinds of feedback (Lott, Schopler, and Gibb, 1954, 1955; and Gibb, Smith, and Roberts, 1955).[7] This work demonstrated that groups which received feedback differed from those which did not in that members felt more favorable toward the group, displayed a higher level of aspiration for their group, and expressed more negative feelings. Since the feedback included negative evaluations of certain members, the group as a whole may have felt freer in expressing negative feelings. It is possible that this increased freedom made the group a less frustrating experience and led to increased positive feelings.

It was found that feeling-oriented, positive feedback resulted in the greatest efficiency, least defensiveness, and greatest spread in participation.

In these studies, members had no previous experience with one another. A further research interest was in determining whether feedback techniques would have a different effect on groups whose members had had considerable experience with one another in a T-Group situation. Presumably these members had had training and practice in examining and understanding their own and others' feelings as co-members of the T Group. The effects of feedback were compared for persons who had shared a T-Group experience and persons who had not (Roberts, Schopler, Smith, and Gibb, 1955).

Twelve trained groups were compared with fourteen untrained groups. Six trained groups and seven untrained groups received only feeling-oriented feedback. The remaining groups received only task-oriented feedback. The groups were compared for problem-solving efficiency, degree of defensive feeling, and feelings of task progress. The results showed that feeling-oriented feedback improved the task efficiency of untrained groups more than it improved trained groups. This was consistent with the authors' expectation that the trained groups had already achieved a high level of good communication and task efficiency. With regard to defensiveness, the trained groups

---

[7] These and related studies are now summarized in a monograph, "Defense Level and Influence Potential in Small Groups." (See Gibb, 1960.)

were less defensive to begin with. Although defensiveness decreased slightly in all groups, the greatest reduction occurred in untrained groups who received feeling-oriented feedback. With regard to "feelings of task progress," the trained groups rated themselves considerably higher than did the untrained groups.

The authors concluded that a T-Group experience is effective in reducing feelings of defensiveness and in increasing task efficiency. Moreover, problem-solving skills learned in a T Group can be applied in other kinds of problem-solving situations.

Pearl Pollock Rosenberg (Rosenberg, 1952) studied the influence of role playing on three groups of people: the role players, other members asked to identify with particular role players, and members who observed the role playing. A variety of devices were employed to measure diagnostic perception, emotional involvement, and behavior change.

Members actually participating tended to become very much involved in the situation and to have strong positive and negative feelings about it. They were biased in their observations—particularly with respect to their own roles—and found it difficult to suggest other ways that they might have behaved. They were most active during the post-role-playing analysis, and showed the greatest behavioral change. The observers seemed to fall into two types: the passive watcher and the active, objective observer. The former were uninvolved and could make few suggestions as to alternative ways of behaving. The more active observers were more critical and analytic and made many useful suggestions as to other ways the role players might behave. The third group of members did not role-play but were asked to identify with one of the role players. They seemed to be influenced partly by their objective role as observers and partly by their ego-involved role as "identifiers." Their judgments were highly critical, and they were best able to suggest alternative behavior. They stood midway between the observers and the participators with respect to bias and involvement.

Jack R. Gibb has conducted several laboratory studies designed to test the effects of role playing and feedback as combined techniques on such variables as self-insight, the capacity to conceptualize a new role, and role flexibility.

One of these studies conducted with Grace N. Platts (Gibb and Platts, 1950) focused on changes in self-insight. An experiment was designed to test whether self-insight (defined as awareness of the perceptions that others have of the self) can be improved through special training (including role playing) alone, or through special training plus feedback. It was found that groups receiving neither special training nor feedback showed no change. Groups receiving one or the other showed some change, but the group which received both showed the greatest changes. The most noticeable gains in self-insight were with respect to likeability, sociability, and adjustment. The authors concluded that self-insight, defined in this way, can be improved by special training. It can be increased further by knowledge of the results of tests of self-insight (feedback).

A second study (Gibb, 1952) investigated the specific effect of role playing with and without feedback on self-insight, the capacity to conceptualize a new role, and role flexibility. Gibb divided 140 college students into five groups. Subjects in all the groups were given pre- and post-tests designed to measure the three variables mentioned above. Members of Group A shared a T-Group experience, were given continual training in role playing, and were given individual knowledge of all pretraining test scores. Group B shared a T-Group experience and were told about pretraining test scores but received no training in role playing. Group C shared a T-Group experience but were given no role playing or feedback. Groups D and E did not participate in a T Group but differed in that Group D received knowledge of pretest results, and Group E did not.

With respect to the "self-insight" variable, Gibb found: "The significant difference between Group C and Group E indicated that the training, even without role playing and knowledge of results, improved self-insight. . . . The significant improvement of Group A (role-playing group) over Group B (all aspects of training but no role playing) suggests that role playing adds a significant increment to the training methods we are using" (Gibb, 1952, p. 3).

The second variable, "ability to conceptualize a new role," was measured in an ingenious way: the Guildford-Martin Scale was administered to all subjects, and two dominant roles were determined for each person. Each person then took the test a second time but now was instructed to reverse his two dominant roles. For example, if an individual originally scored as a tense and inferior person, he was asked to respond the second time as a relaxed and superior person. The individual's ability to fake a test score was thus a measure of his ability to conceptualize a new role. The results showed that the groups displayed this ability in the predicted order: A was better than B, B was better than C, and so on. However, Gibb reports that the differences were rather small and that a more sensitive instrument than the Guildford-Martin seems required.

The third variable, "role flexibility," was measured by having each subject role-play in front of a group of naïve observers who then described his behavior by means of an adjective check list. In a second role-playing situation, the subject was asked to reverse his role. Again, observers described his behavior and also rated him for "sincerity." The results showed that the differences between groups were in the predicted direction. The assessment of "sincerity" proved to be particularly important in differentiating among groups.

Miles conducted a study (Miles, 1958) to identify factors which influence the effectiveness of feedback. It was hypothesized that negative feedback would be more effective in inducing change than positive or neutral feedback. Second, it was assumed that the greater the gap between performance and standard, the more change would occur. Third, it was predicted that feedback content which is congruent with an individual's motivational state would be more effective than feedback whose content is not congruent. For example, feedback referring to warm, friendly behavior would be congruent for an individual with high need-affiliation but incongruent for an individual with low need-affiliation. Finally, it was hypothesized that an individual who is oriented toward achieving goals would be more responsive to feedback than an individual who is primarily oriented toward protecting himself from threat.

The subjects were twenty-four persons who participated in a series of three short-term human relations workshops. It was found that strong negative feedback was most effective in inducing change. Behavior involving warm interpersonal relationships was more responsive to feedback than behavior related to task definition and accomplishment. When the content of the feedback had to do with warm interpersonal relations, the factor of congruity with the individual's motivational state was important: congruity facilitated change. But when the feedback had to do with task accomplishment, congruity was not a factor. A related finding was that whether an individual was oriented toward goal achievement or toward threat influenced responsiveness to feedback about warmth and friendliness but not to responsiveness to feedback about task accomplishment. Miles suggests that a next question for research is whether there exists a critical range of feedback which interacts with subject motivation to produce optimal change.

Summary. Perhaps the basic question in this area is "How many people gain from a human relations training laboratory, and what do they learn?" The studies reported here demonstrate how difficult it is to answer this apparently simple, but actually complicated, question. A few studies have come up with figures (usually 60 per cent to 75 per cent of the participants were shown to have gained), but their authors are the first to point out the problems in interpreting such figures. An individual who is already quite effective when he arrives at the laboratory may show no change. Is he to be counted as a failure? Some of the most important changes may not show in behavior and therefore may not be visible to others. Yet when self-report is relied upon, the results are contaminated by factors of attitude and response set which may have little to do with what actually has been learned.

All of the following have been shown to be influenced by laboratory training: various perceptions of the self, affective behavior, congruity between self-percept and ideal self, self-insight, sensitivity to the feelings or behavior of others, role flexibility, sensitivity to group decisions, diagnostic ability, behavioral skill, utilization of laboratory techniques, self-confidence, and approach to diagnosing organization problems. And this is only a partial list. But these factors have also been shown to change *for some people, under certain conditions.* Much research has addressed itself to the question, "What accounts for the fact that some participants learn certain things and others do not?"

What the individual is like when he comes to the laboratory seems to have a great deal to do with the learnings he takes away with him. In separate studies, Stock and Mathis suggest that conflict or some internal awareness of lack of fit or consistency have something to do with readiness for learning. But Watson et al. suggest that there is some ceiling on this: highly anxious persons learn little. Consistent with this, Harrison has hypothesized that individuals so threatened by confrontation with dissonance that they must defend against it with rejection of the laboratory, distortion, and so on, are likely to close themselves off from opportunities to learn. Miles, too, found that threat-oriented individuals were less receptive to feedback of certain kinds. Mathis suggests that tendencies toward pairing and fight make for readiness to learn, while tendencies toward dependency and flight work against learning. This seems consistent with some of the findings of Watson et al. that responsive, outgoing persons are more likely to apply laboratory learnings. Miles found that the personality characteristics of ego strength, flexibility, and need-affiliation are relevant in that they facilitated unfreezing, involvement, and the reception of feedback, and these in turn influenced learning. On quite another level, Glidewell found that certain approaches to problem solving are more likely to be influenced by laboratory training than others. These findings converge on the idea that personality factors having to do with receptivity, involvement, lack of defensiveness, and a certain kind of energy or openness may be important facilitators of learning.

Although little is known about this factor, Lieberman's study suggests that the particular emotional culture which develops in the group may facilitate learning for certain personality types and make it more difficult for others.

The evidence thus far suggests that characteristics of the back-home job situation or the individual's role in his organization is a less potent factor than might be supposed. Neither the Miles nor Watson studies could show that the individual's power, role in the organization, and so on, were significant factors in learning or application. Watson suggests that an individual's report of obstacles to application in the job situation are more a product of response set and personality than an accurate assessment of the actual situation.

The question of what it is about the T Group that promotes change is one of the most difficult to get at methodologically. Two approaches have been adopted. A large number of studies have focused on the specific techniques of role playing and feedback and their influence on learning and change. That these techniques are effective is amply demonstrated. These studies have also clarified the differential impact of various types of feedback and the interaction between personality factors and types of feedback. A second approach has been to develop theory about the phases of learning and the processes involved in learning. Miles hypothesized that initial desire for change, unfreezing, involvement, and feedback are successive steps (cyclically repeated) in the process of learning. He was able to demonstrate that the last three factors are related to change during the laboratory. Harrison is in the process of testing the hypothesis that dissonance is a necessary condition for change but that actual learning outcome is dependent on the means the individual utilizes for the reduction of dissonance.

Conclusion and Comment

Research about T Groups suggests a large checkerboard, incompletely and unevenly filled in. Some areas show a considerable concentration of work; others are nearly empty. In some areas, the questions have been asked and answered. In others, the questions are clear, but methodology or relevant theory is not yet fully developed. In still other areas, even the questions are not yet well defined. To complicate the analogy, the checkerboard is expanding, and issues which previously did not exist are constantly emerging in response to new applications and modifications of the T Group.

Among these are the utilization of the T Group with "families" of persons who work together in the same organization; the rapid expansion of laboratory training in non-American and even non-Western cultures; and the development of the "instrumented" T Group. It has always been assumed that the heterogeneous composition of the T Group and the "cultural island" quality of a setting like Bethel have played a considerable role in the effectiveness of the T Group. Yet work within organizations where neither of these conditions prevails has already demonstrated the versatility and broader usefulness of laboratory training and of the T Group in particular. Placing the T Group in an organizational setting suggests new principles of group composition, raises questions about the influence of previous contact among members on the functioning of the group, and suggests new approaches to bridging the gap between the T Group and the work setting.

The T Group is an invention of Western, specifically American, culture. Those who have conducted T Groups in other cultural settings (Thelen in Western Europe and the Near East, Nylen in Nigeria and Scandinavia, and Coffey in Japan) have commented on the commonalities they have found as well as on some special characteristics and problems not so typical of American groups. Interesting theoretical questions emerge about aspects of T-Group functioning and development which may be culturally influenced, as well as practical questions about modifications in design and approach.

The development of the "instrumented" (trainerless) T Group raises obvious questions about the comparability of the two types of groups. Do the same experiences and the same range of learnings occur?

In the more traditional T Group, the issue of the trainer's role is one of the relatively unexplored areas. On a descriptive level, we do not know how much variation there is in the styles of different trainers or the type and range of trainer-interventions likely to be made in a T Group. With reference to process, we do not know how different trainer styles influence the functioning of the group and its usefulness to the individual participant. More microscopically, we have yet to understand the impact of specific interventions on the flow of the group interaction. The important issue of the timing of interventions is still unexplored. Another area which needs further exploration is the meaning of the T-Group experience for the individual member.

The list of needed research can be extended almost indefinitely.

We know something about how personality influences sociometric choice, but little about the differential impact of the training experience depending on one's sociometric position in the group. We know something about group composition based on certain affective characteristics of members, but nothing about composition based on problem-solving approaches. And so on. Each reader is invited to provide his own ending to the incomplete sentence, "Why doesn't someone study_____?"

It is difficult to identify trends in research over the past sixteen years and still more difficult to predict the future. But, in general, there appears to be a shift toward emphasizing research which is rather specifically relevant to training and has simultaneous implications for application and theory. At the same time, there appears to be a more consistent interest in developing and testing theory which may be relevant to the functioning and impact of the T Group.

In considering past accomplishments and omissions, current trends, and future needs, two important influencing factors seem to be operating: the available research methodology and the role of research in NTL as an organization.

As with other fields of study having to do with interpersonal interaction, curiosity about issues outstrips methodological resources. Often the researcher is confronted with a choice between a well-established, tested instrument which has doubtful or tangential relevance to the laboratory situation, or a tailor-made but untested new instrument. There has been a natural tendency to utilize established, validated measures rather than to rely on homemade devices whose deficiencies may become apparent only after all the data have been collected. Yet, as Bennis points out, "If research instruments are to be used as a basis of prediction, they must be acutely tuned to the purposes and methods of the group. . . . Instruments must be developed specifically for the social context under study" (Bennis et al., 1957, p. 340). One of the very significant products of the research of the last sixteen years has been a number of especially constructed research instruments—most of them well seasoned and tested by now—which actually do the job for which they were designed.

Some of the questions in need of further study—such as the specific examination of events within the T Group which make for learning or the impact of the trainer on the interaction—require the analysis of group processes. In order to do this effectively it is necessary to find some way of studying an inevitably complicated *sequence* of events, of doing justice to multifaceted phenomena, and of summarizing events which do not lend themselves well to categorization. So far, researchers have utilized either a "successive snapshot" approach (which loses many data) or a clinical, case-study approach (which makes categorization and comparison difficult).

Some of the studies reported in this chapter have been conducted under carefully controlled laboratory conditions; others have involved the naturalistic observation of group process; still others have studied the T Group *in situ* but have introduced control through the manipulation of certain variables such as composition and/or through experimental design and statistical treatment. Further development of the third kind of research may well contribute a great deal to our eventual understanding of the T Group. There is some indication that progress is being made in preserving the complexity of the real situation while some control over the data is retained.

The role of research in an organization which is primarily dedicated to training has been a topic of interest and some controversy within NTL for many years. In a general way, there has been a consistent, clear commitment to research. This commitment is inherent in the very idea of laboratory training, with its dedication to experimentation and continual testing and revision. Commitment also derives from the strong personal interest of many staff members in research activity and their inescapable recognition of the T Group as a rich field for investigation. At the same time, NTL is primarily a training organization, and it has sometimes happened that the formal demands of a particular research project have intruded on the training design of the laboratory.

Official policy about research has been evolving over a long period of time. At present it can be stated as follows: As a matter of principle, NTL is interested in supporting research; in keeping with its primary mission as a training organization, it is most interested in research which is relevant to training and supports and is integrated into the training design. There are indications that this is a feasible goal. In Harrison's research, several theory sessions were presented, based on the concepts being tested in the research design. In Miles's study of factors affecting feedback, the feedback sessions with the participants were an integral part of both the training design and the research design. There have been several attempts to encourage the training staff of a laboratory to design and conduct research on the spot, blending together their curiosities as trainers with their skill as researchers. What seems to be happening is that a new image is developing of the trainer-researcher: the trainer who is alert to opportunities for building research into his training activities, and the researcher who is finding new ways of working within the laboratory setting. Hopefully, it will be possible to approximate more and more closely the goal of a training-research design in which both aspects are so well integrated and dovetailed that each contributes to the other, at the cost of the quality of neither.

General References

Back, K. "Interpersonal Relations in a Discussion Group." *The Journal of Social Issues,* 4:61–65, 1948.

Bales, R. F. *Interaction Process Analysis: A Method for the Study of Small Groups.* Cambridge, Mass.: Addison-Wesley Publishing Company, 1950.

Barron, M. E., and G. K. Krulee. "Case Study of a Basic Skill Training Group." *The Journal of Social Issues,* 4:10–30, 1948.

Bennis, W. "The Relationship Between Some Personality Dimensions and Group Development." Unpublished material, Boston University Human Relations Center, 1956.

Bennis, W., R. Burke, H. Cutter, H. Harrington, and J. Hoffman. "A Note on Some Problems of Measurement and Prediction in a Training Group." *Group Psychotherapy,* 10:328–341, 1957.

Bennis, W., and D. Peabody. "The Conceptualization of Two Personality Orientations and Sociometric Choice." *Journal of Social Psychology,* 57:203–215, 1962.

Ben-Zeev, S. "Sociometric Choice and Patterns of Member Participation," in Dorothy Stock, and H. A. Thelen. *Emotional Dynamics and Group Culture.* New York: New York University Press, 1958.

Bion, W. R. "Experiences in Groups." I-VII, *Human Relations,* 1948–1951.

Bion, W. R. "Group Dynamics: A Re-view." *International Journal of Psychoanalysis,* 33:235–247, 1952.

Blake, R. R., and Jane S. Mouton. "Personality Factors Associated with Individual Conduct in a Training Group Situation." Human Relations Training Laboratory, Research Monograph No. 1, Printing Division, The University of Texas Press, 1956.

Blake, R. R., Jane S. Mouton, and B. Fruchter. "A Factor Analysis of Training Group Behavior." *Journal of Social Psychology,* in press.

Browne, S. A., and M. Crowe. "Personality Structure as a Determinant of Sociometric Choice." Dittoed material, Research Center for Group Dynamics, The University of Michigan, 1953.

Burke, R. L., and W. G. Bennis. "Changes in Perception of Self and Others during Human Relations Training." *Human Relations,* 2:165–182, 1961.

Deutsch, M., A. Pepitone, and A. Zander. "Leadership in a Small Group." *The Journal of Social Issues,* 4:31–40, 1948.

Gibb, J. R. "Effects of Role Playing upon (*a*) Role Flexibility and upon (*b*) Ability to Conceptualize a New Role." *American Psychologist,* 7:310 (Abstract), 1952.

Gibb, J. R. "Defense Level and Influence Potential in Small Groups." *Research Reprint Series,* No. 3, National Training Laboratories, Washington, D.C., 1960.

Gibb, J. R., and A. W. Gorman. "The Effects of Induced Polarization in Small Groups upon Accuracy of Perception." Paper read at the American Psychological Association Meetings, September 1954.

Gibb, J. R., and Grace N. Platts. "Role Flexibility in Group Interaction." *American Psychologist*, 5:491 (Abstract), 1950.

Gibb, J. R., E. E. Smith, and A. H. Roberts. "Effects of Positive and Negative Feedback upon Defensive Behavior in Small Problem-Solving Groups." Paper read at the American Psychological Association Meetings, 1955.

Glidewell, J. C. "Changes in Approaches to Work Problem Analysis During Management Training." Washington, D.C.: Second American National Red Cross School for Management Development, 1956. Unpublished mimeographed manuscript, 22 pp.

Gradolph, Ida. "The Task-Approach of Groups of Single-Type and Mixed-Type Valency Compositions," in Dorothy Stock, and H. A. Thelen. *Emotional Dynamics and Group Culture*. New York: New York University Press, 1958.

Harrison, Roger. "A Study of Dissonance Theory Applied to Laboratory Learning." Dittoed research proposal, Yale University, in progress.

Hill, W. F. "The Influence of Subgroups on Participation in Human Relations Training Groups." Unpublished doctoral dissertation, The University of Chicago, 1955.

Horowitz, Milton W., J. Lyons, and H. V. Perlmutter. "Induction of Forces in Discussion Groups." *Human Relations*, 4:57–76, 1951.

Horwitz, Murray, and D. P. Cartwright. "A Projective Method for the Diagnosis of Group Properties." *Human Relations*, 6:397–410, 1953.

Lakin, Martin. "Participants' Interpretations of a Group Sensitivity Training Experience: A Case Study." Typewritten manuscript, Duke University, 1960.

Lieberman, M. A. "The Relationship of Group Climate to Individual Change." Unpublished doctoral dissertation, The University of Chicago, 1958.

Lippitt, G. "Effects of Information about Group Desire for Change on Members of a Group." Unpublished doctoral dissertation, American University, 1959. *Dissertation Abstracts*, Vol. XX, 10, 1960.

Lott, A. J., J. H. Schopler, and J. R. Gibb. "The Effects of Feedback on Group Processes." Paper read at the Rocky Mountain Psychological Association Meetings, 1954.

Lott, A. J., J. H. Schopler, and J. R. Gibb. "Effects of Feeling-Oriented and Task-Oriented Feedback upon Defensive Behavior in Small Problem-Solving Groups." Paper read at the American Psychological Association Meetings, 1955.

Mathis, A. G. "Development and Validation of a Trainability Index for Laboratory Training Groups." Unpublished doctoral dissertation, The University of Chicago, 1955.

Miles, M. B. "Personal Change Through Human Relations Training: A Working Paper." New York: Horace Mann-Lincoln Institute of School Experimentation, Teachers College, Columbia University, 1957. Mimeographed manuscript, 50 pp.

Miles, M. B. "Factors Influencing Response to Feedback in Human Relations Training." New York: Horace Mann-Lincoln Institute of School Experimentation, Teachers College, Columbia University, 1958.

Miles, M. B. "Human Relations Training: Processes and Outcomes." *Journal of Counseling Psychology*, 7:301–306, 1960.

Miles, M. B., Sanci K. Cohen, and F. L. Whitam. "Changes in Performance Test Scores after Human Relations Training." New York: Horace Mann-Lincoln Institute of School Experimentation, Teachers College, Columbia University, 1959. Mimeographed manuscript, 35 pp.

Norfleet, Roberta. "Interpersonal Relations and Group Productivity." *The Journal of Social Issues*, 4:66–69, 1948.

Pepinsky, H. B., L. Siegel, and E. L. Van Alta. "Criterion in Counseling; Group Participation Scale." *Journal of Abnormal and Social Psychology*, 47 Supplement: 415–419, 1952.

Roberts, A. H., J. H. Schopler, E. E. Smith, and J. R. Gibb. "Effects of Feeling-Oriented Classroom Teaching upon Reactions to Feedback." Paper read at American Psychological Association Meetings, September 1955.

Rosenberg, M. "A Preliminary Report on the Relation of Personality Factors to Sociometric Position in Bethel Groups 5 and 6." Dittoed material, Research Center for Group Dynamics, The University of Michigan, 1950.

Rosenberg, Pearl P. "Experimental Analysis of Psychodrama." Unpublished doctoral dissertation, Harvard University, 1952.

Smith, A. J., J. Jaffe, and D. G. Livingston. "Consonance of Interpersonal Perception and Individual Effectiveness." *Human Relations*, 8:385–397, 1955.

Stock, D. "The Relation between the Sociometric Structure of the Group and Certain Personality Characteristics." Unpublished doctoral dissertation, The University of Chicago, 1952.

Stock, D. "Factors Associated with Change in Self-Percept," in Dorothy Stock, and H. A. Thelen. *Emotional Dynamics and Group Culture.* New York: New York University Press, 1958.

Stock, D., and S. Ben-Zeev. "Changes in Work and Emotionality during Group Growth," in Dorothy Stock, and H. A. Thelen. *Emotional Dynamics and Group Culture.* New York: New York University Press, 1958.

Stock, D., and W. F. Hill. "Inter-Subgroup Dynamics as a Factor in Group Growth," in Dorothy Stock, and H. A. Thelen. *Emotional Dynamics and Group Culture.* New York: New York University Press, 1958.

Stock, D., and J. Luft. "The T-E-T Design." Typewritten manuscript, National Training Laboratories, 1960.

Stogdill, R. M., and A. E. Coons. "Leader Behavior: Its Description and Measurement." Research Monograph No. 88, Bureau of Business Research. Columbus: Ohio State University, 1957.

Watson, J. "Members' Perceptions of the Functions of a Training Group." Unpublished material, Research Center for Group Dynamics, The University of Michigan, 1950.

Watson, J. "Some Social-Psychological Correlates of Personality: A Study of the Usefulness of Psychoanalytic Theory in Predicting Behavior." Unpublished doctoral dissertation, The University of Michigan, 1952.

Watson, J. "The Application of Psychoanalytic Measures of Personality to the Study of Social Behavior." Paper read at the American Psychological Association Meetings, 1953.

Watson, J., R. Lippitt, D. Kallen, and S. Zipf. "Evaluation of a Human Relations Laboratory Program." Typewritten manuscript, Research Center for Group Dynamics, The University of Michigan, 1961.

Weschler, I. R., and J. Reisel. "Inside a Sensitivity Training Group." Industrial Relations Monograph No. 4. Los Angeles: Institute of Industrial Relations, University of California, 1959.

16

Training and Therapy

Jerome D. Frank

Both human relations T Groups and psychotherapy groups are quite heterogeneous with respect to methods of procedure and underlying theory, so that the task of comparison is a difficult one. Perusal of various chapters in this book indicates the range of thinking and method of procedure among T-Group trainers. The range in group psychotherapy is even wider, partly because it is applied in a much greater variety of settings with corresponding variation in membership. Settings include institutions, outpatient clinics, and the private practitioner's office. Patients include children, adolescents, and adults, with all possible diagnoses: psychoses, psychoneuroses, personality disorders, alcoholism, psychosomatic ailments, and so on. Each setting and type of patient influences to some extent how the therapy is conceptualized and conducted.

It is well to make explicit that the generalizations offered in this chapter are drawn chiefly from my personal experience. The type of therapy group with which I am most familiar is probably characteristic of the usual procedure with nonhospitalized psychiatric patients. The T Group I had the pleasure of attending was conducted by Robert Blake along the lines described by him in the present volume. It is each reader's task to evaluate conclusions drawn from this rather narrow experience, in the light of his own experience.

The therapy groups on which these observations are based consist of adults who come to a psychiatric clinic of a general hospital to get relief from distress. This distress is related to chronic difficulties in getting along with other people. Diagnostically, most of the members would be labeled neurotic. Their major complaints are disturbances of various bodily systems, anxiety, and depression. All are able to function in the community, though often with distress and diminished efficiency. Each group is composed of five to eight patients who meet once a week for an hour and a half and is conducted by a psychiatrist. The duration of any particular group is not limited in advance. Characteristically, there is a rapid turnover of members during the first few weeks, after which a relatively stable group forms, with one or two members being added or leaving every few months. There is no agenda, and the doctor exerts leadership indirectly through the kind of behavior he encourages or discourages and the nature of his interpretative comments.

Early meetings are apt to be uneasy affairs. The patients are strangers, and many feel self-conscious about revealing their need for psychotherapy. All are uncertain as to how to proceed and expect to be called upon to reveal intimate, personal problems. They see the group leader as the sole source of help and, therefore, compete with one another for his attention. This situation rapidly elicits patients' habitual ways of coping with stress. They resort to the usual social techniques of getting to know one another, search for superficial similarities in symptoms or experiences, and offer carefully selected and edited items of personal history. The doctor, while maintaining a generally accepting attitude, tries to reinforce those trends which make for a therapeutic group atmosphere—that is, one in which everyone's contributions are taken seriously and free emotional expression is encouraged, provided the patient assumes responsibility for trying to understand why he feels as he does. The doctor encourages interaction among the members, which gradually results in a decrease in efforts to seek his individual attention.

In an established therapy group, patients have come to see themselves as being helped by the group and the doctor, rather than by the doctor in spite of the group. As they develop confidence that their underlying feelings will be accepted, patients are better able to tolerate tension, which appears higher than at early meetings because feelings are expressed more bluntly. During this phase, the chief function of the doctor is to help patients examine the attitudes revealed by their interactions.

The theory of neurosis here utilized assumes that psychoneuroses are maladaptive processes resulting from disturbance in the normal processes of maturation. These disturbances arise from conditions, especially in the formative years, which do not afford suitable opportunities for growth or produce chronically anxiety-producing situations with which the inadequately equipped child must deal. As a result of these unfortunate early experiences, the patient experiences conflicting urges and feelings which he cannot resolve effectively, such as feeling utterly dependent on a parent whom he at the same time fears. These conflicts, and his futile efforts to deal with them, lead to habitually distorted ways of perceiving himself and others, resulting in inappropriate responses to current interpersonal situations. That is, he carries over his childhood conflicts into his adult life. The sources of the patient's conflicts, as well as the distortions to which they give rise, are more or less concealed from him. He is mainly aware of his distress, which he often does not relate directly to personal problems.

The crux of the psychotherapeutic problem is that the neurotic seems to be unable to learn from experience. His self-respect is damaged to the point that he lacks the courage to try new responses, but instead, clings to habitual ones which, however self-defeating, are comfortably familiar and often yield pseudo-solutions to his difficulties. The reasons for this loss of self-respect include the patient's awareness that he is not living up to his capacities, the fact that his illness tends to keep him dependent on others, his awareness of unacceptable feelings, the stigma which our society attaches to this type of illness, and—above all —the repeated experiences of failure resulting from the maladaptive nature of his behavior patterns.

From this viewpoint, the goal of all psychotherapy is to supply new interpersonal influences which help the patient find more satisfying ways of handling his chronic interpersonal and internal conflicts. As the patient begins to experience some successes in his dealings with others, this reinforces the new way of behaving; and so, if all goes well, the maladaptive patterns are progressively weakened and the more successful ones strengthened. Thus his potentialities for further emotional growth are progressively mobilized. Psychotherapy can be thought of as a learning situation which attempts to help patients to unlearn faulty responses and learn more appropriate ones. As such, it has many features in common with other learning situations, as the reader will see by comparing the following analysis with that offered by Leland Bradford in the present volume. (See Chapter 7.)

The therapeutic efficacy of a therapeutic group depends largely on aspects of its functioning which can be grouped under the headings of evocation, support, and implicit direction. Treatment must evoke neurotic responses, because only a response which is operating can be changed. This evocation must be accompanied by emotion, which supplies the energy needed to disrupt old patterns and motivates the search for better ones. The evoked response usually must be verbalized. The patient's subjective experience must be filtered through his discriminatory verbal apparatus if he is to profit from it. The therapy group fosters evocation of the patient's pathogenic attitudes in many ways. It is implicit in the group code, in that patients expect to discuss feelings and problems. The absence of a formal structure forces members to engage with one another in ways which are characteristic for them, many of which are neurotic. The group standard of free, direct expression of feeling further operates to evoke underlying attitudes. Therapeutic groups encourage the development of conflicts between equals, something which is not possible in individual therapy. These conflicts may be based on real-life differences in values and attitudes or on neurotic distortions, such as transference and mirror reactions. The presence of a leader is a guarantee that feelings evoked in these and other ways will not get beyond the patient's control, so that he feels free to express himself.

If emotional tension becomes too great, learning is hampered rather than facilitated. In order to keep tension within bounds, and for other reasons, the therapeutic situation must supply emotional support. The patient must trust the therapist—must believe that he wants to help him and is able to do so. Therapeutically more important may be the ability of the therapeutic situation to strengthen the patient's self-esteem. Without protection and, if possible, enhancement of self-esteem, patients lack the courage to face themselves, much less to relinquish neurotic ways of feeling and behaving. Although neurotics are characteristically contemptuous of themselves and therefore of one another, a successful therapy group does strengthen the self-esteem of its members. It does this partly by combating the devastating sense of isolation which most mental patients experience. In a therapy group they feel, often for the first time, that they are being understood, because they find other people who suffer similarly. Moreover, they are taken seriously. A patient may experience the anger of another patient toward him as supportive, because it indicates that his antagonist cares enough about him to be angry with him. A particularly important source of strengthened self-esteem is the discovery of patients that they can be helpful to one another. In individual therapy, all the help flows from the therapist to the patient; in group therapy, a patient learns that his own advice or insight may help someone else. Finally, members develop a feeling of group belongingness, largely on the basis of a history of shared experience. Even though the original reason for joining a therapy group is usually felt as derogatory, patients come to feel that there is a certain virtue in having had the good sense to come into psychotherapy, in contrast to other people who are equally miserable but have not taken this step.

The third ingredient can be summed up as "implicit direction," which means that the patient is helped to become clear about his feelings and behavior and to perceive alternative ways of reacting. Merely evoking an attitude is of little help, unless conditions are such as to help the patient to develop a better one. Some ways in which a therapy group offers implicit direction to each member are supplying feedback from the other members and the leader as to the impression his behavior makes on them; exposing him to values and standards better than those under which he is currently operating; and offering him models of different ways of behaving which he can identify with, imitate, or reject. This occurs in a setting where there is a chance to experiment with and practice new behavior, without serious penalty for failures. In therapy groups implicit direction derives largely from certain ground rules. One is emphasis on maintaining communication, no matter how angry or otherwise disturbed one gets, until the situation becomes clarified. Another is that insofar as possible patients should express their reactions honestly. A third is that merely expressing an emotion is not enough; it is equally important to examine its meaning. The group provides multiple models with different values, attitudes, and behaviors. Finally, it has a real-life quality, so that the patient can readily transfer what he learns to his outside life.

We may now turn to a comparison of one type of therapy group with one type of T Group. It is obvious that they have many features in common and are perhaps to be viewed as points on a continuum. Both are learning situations which have the aim of bringing about changes in their members. Both stress learning to communicate accurately with others as an important means. Both value mature, group-centered, altruistic, responsible functioning of members—therapy groups because it is a sign of improvement in individual patients; T Groups because it improves group functioning.

In neither is there a sharp distinction between task and maintenance functions. Neither group has an adaptive, instrumental function with respect to the outside world. The goals are those of individual members—in therapy groups, to obtain relief from distress; in T Groups, to deepen knowledge of group functioning. In T Groups, goals of individual members automatically coincide. In therapy groups, they have enough in common to make group formation possible. This derives partly from the fact that improvement in one member encourages the others. The absence of a clearly defined instrumental function is a source of considerable perceptual unclarity and emotional tension in both groups. The question "What are we doing here, anyway?" looms large, especially in early meetings. In both groups the agenda for each meeting grows out of the group's own functioning. In both, finally, the most useful meetings seem to be those in which there is an issue or "focal conflict," which is of interest to most or all of the members, and arouses their emotions. (See Chapters 11 and 15.) Moreover, some of these issues are the same in both groups—such as conflict over dependence on versus rebellion against authority and between desire for and fear of closeness to peers.

These similarities, however, should not obscure certain fundamental differences which arise basically from the differences in composition of the two types of groups.

Members of therapy groups are seen by themselves and others as patients; they are sick people seeking treatment to relieve suffering. This suffering is assumed to arise, at least in part, from their failure to solve certain interpersonal problems in their real-life situations because of emotional blocks.

Members come to T Groups, not because they are suffering, but to learn new interpersonal skills which previously they have lacked the knowledge or opportunity to master. They wish particularly to learn to function more effectively as members and leaders of groups.

This distinction is not without exceptions. Individuals may join T Groups in the secret hope of obtaining relief from distress due to interpersonal difficulties. The trainers, therefore, must have enough diagnostic knowledge to know when to refer a member to psychotherapy or to recognize that the T-Group experience may be more than he can stand. The main clue that a member is really a patient in disguise is probably a display of emotion which is more intense than the situation warrants.

Difference in membership implies a difference in goals. The purpose of a therapy group is to relieve the distress of the members through helping them to modify attitudes and behaviors which seem to be contributing to the distress. The ultimate goal is change in the individual patient, and change in the functioning of the groups to which he belongs is subsidiary to this.

The ultimate goal of T Groups is to improve the functioning of the groups to which the members will return. The goal for these groups —whether in industry, community, or the church—is to function more productively with less internal friction.

Though both groups share the aim of improving the accuracy and sensitivity of members' perceptions of reactions of themselves and one another, this is an end in itself for the T Group. For a therapy group, it is a step toward the end of improved mental health. The T Group has served its purpose when the group has learned how to select a task and develop a social structure which enables it to work effectively. The usefulness of a therapy group increases as it approaches this, but it can never completely achieve it because the members' dependence on the therapist cannot be fully resolved. Thus, to overstate the point somewhat, the therapy group reaches maximal usefulness at the point where the T Group ceases to be useful.

The attitudes which the therapy group attempts to change concern persons close to the patients and important to them, usually family members. They are central to the patients' personalities. The attitudes which T Groups hope to modify are more peripheral, involving accurate perception of and communication with relative strangers. This distinction is not absolute but is nevertheless important.

The attitudes of patients are relatively difficult to change. They have a vested interest in them. In therapy groups, therefore, much attention must be paid to loosening up old patterns of behavior, to unblocking the patients' emotions. Therapy groups are as much or more concerned with helping patients to unlearn old patterns as they are with helping them to learn new ones. T Groups can concentrate more fully on the learning of new patterns.

These differences imply certain differences in the role and functioning of the leader. In therapy groups, there is an irreducible gap between the leader and the members, because the leader is in the role of a practitioner of a healing art from which the patients hope to benefit. The therapist may himself benefit from participation in a therapy group, and one of his aims is to become a member of the group; but he can never completely become a group member because he is not a patient. Nor do patients expect to become therapists after treatment.

The position of the therapist gives him high prestige automatically and great power to reassure or disturb. It also causes the members to depend heavily on him at first. In all their activities, they are concerned with the effect of what they are doing on his opinion of them. Thus, it may be said that a therapy group can develop self-reliance only through initial reliance on the therapist as a kind of temporary scaffolding, and this self-reliance is never complete.

The trainer of a T Group differs from the members only in the possession of superior knowledge and skill in a certain area. To the extent that he successfully imparts this knowledge, the gap between him and the group members progressively diminishes until, at the end of a successful T-Group experience, there is no difference between trainer and members. Such prestige as the trainer has he must earn, and members' dependency on him is limited to looking to him for guidance as to how to proceed and for clarification of what is happening in the group. It is relatively easy for such a group to become genuinely self-reliant and eventually to absorb him as another member.

Growing out of these differences are certain differences in functioning. Because the goal of a T Group is more limited, it can be achieved in a relatively short time. A T-Group experience of even two or three days can be of value, and three weeks is the usual maximum. Thus, very frequent meetings and closed membership are both more necessary and easier to achieve.

In general, the therapy group more actively protects its members and is also more threatening to them. The greater support which the leader can supply is necessary because of the greater vulnerability of patients as compared with members of T Groups. The threat has several sources. In therapy groups, there is no limit to the task, which is personal modification in its broadest sense. In T Groups, the task is limited to the elucidation of group-relevant attitudes. Underlying motivations are explored, if at all, only enough to clarify the meaning of overt behavior. In therapy groups, the process is reversed; overt behavior is used as a means of elucidating underlying motivations, which is the real aim. Depending on the therapist's theory of psychotherapy, this may involve more or less extensive investigation of historical roots of the patient's current feelings.

It follows that in therapy groups there is no limit to the content which is legitimate grist for the group's mill. It includes feelings or actions about which members may be deeply ashamed, such as hostility toward those one is supposed to love, lustful preoccupations and sexual activities, and feelings of personal inadequacy. All such material, with its anxiety-provoking potentialities, is out of bounds for a T Group.

A further source of greater tension in therapy groups is that they focus on individual members. Group process is studied for the light it can throw on the motivations of those involved. In T Groups the focus is on the group. Contributions to the group process are considered from the standpoint of the group, not for the light they may throw on the members who make them. Thus the trainer in a T Group I attended at one point reviewed different attitudes toward the trainer, but he carefully refrained from identifying the members involved. In treatment groups, this identification would occur as a matter of course. This, of course, adds to the threat of the situation. There is more anxiety in therapy groups also because of the fact that the members are emotionally ill and therefore have their feelings under less firm control. It is probable that to produce a shift in central attitudes more emotion is required than to produce a shift in peripheral ones. Therapy groups, therefore, not only tolerate but may try to elicit emotional tension—something which they can do with relative safety because of the strong potentialities for support offered initially by the therapist.

Just as T Groups try not to stir up too much anxiety, so—usually—do they make less effort to offer explicit support. They do not hesitate at times to expose the distorted perceptions of a member, on the assumption that he can tolerate this without undue anxiety and can learn from the experience. In therapy groups, this exposure is frequently made also; but the therapist always has in mind how much the patient can stand and is prepared to intervene, if necessary.

The difference is epitomized by the attitudes of each group toward conflicts among members. In T Groups the aim is to bring about a resolution of the conflict. In the course of so doing, light is cast on the contributions of various members to the development of the struggle and its solution. In therapy groups the occasion of conflict is seen as a means of evoking and clarifying the distortions and neurotic attitudes which are highlighted by the struggle, whether it is resolved or not.

In summary, both human relations T Groups and therapy groups are concerned with increasing the sensitivity of the members to their own functioning and to that of the other members and with correcting blind spots and distortions. For therapy groups, this is a means to the end of relieving neurotically caused distress of the members. For T Groups, it is a means to the end of improving the functioning of the groups to which the members will return.

In both types of groups the situation is left largely unstructured, and the agenda of each meeting grows out of the members' own functioning. In both types of groups, task and maintenance functions are not clearly distinguishable.

Although group therapy and T Groups thus fall on a continuum in many respects, there are clear differences between them. Therapy groups are composed of patients seeking relief from distress. T Groups are composed of individuals trying to learn new skills. Therapy groups attempt to modify more pervasive and more central attitudes, and so they put relatively more emphasis on unlearning old modes of behavior as compared with learning new ones, and take longer to achieve their aims.

The initial dependence on the therapist is marked, and his capacity to disturb or reassure members is correspondingly great. Moreover, the therapist never can become fully a member of the group, though he may approximate this. A therapy group cannot wean itself completely from dependence on the therapist. The nature of the material brought to the group and the personal characteristics of the members result in a higher tension level in therapy; at the same time, the leader is prepared to support members more actively, and his power position enables him to do this. Finally, in therapy groups, the ultimate focus is always on the attitudes of the individual members; in T Groups, it is on the group's functioning, with the attitudes of individual members being brought in only insofar as necessary in order to elucidate the group's ultimate focus.

17

The T Group and the Classroom

Matthew B. Miles

Social trends are shadowy phenomena at best. Yet, in today's America, two general trends relevant to the present book seem reasonably visible. The first might be named "the growth of the tough human relations approach," and is exemplified in T-Group training. The technology and, possibly, some of the basic goals of laboratory human relations training are diffusing steadily through various strata of American occupational life. Gouldner (1959) has pointed out that the skills of the social scientist are becoming more and more crucial to the operation of bureaucratic organizations. Human relations training comprises only a fraction of the applied social science wares available today, but it is a vigorous and growing fraction.

The second trend underlies phrases like "the crisis in education." Perhaps we are entering a neoclassical period; in any event, there seems to be a striking increase in public concern about the schools as instruments of intellectual excellence. Most of this concern is genuine, and thus pleasing (if often upsetting) to educators. But a good bit of it centers around a conception of "achievement" which involves the mastery of "subject matter" (defined as almost anything that is external to the day-to-day life of the child in school).

We note here an interesting paradox. American adults are beginning to spend large amounts of money to understand "human relations" in their work; American children are to be forbidden such learning,[1] because it is not "subject matter," because it is the province of the family, the church, or the social agency, or because it is somehow irrelevant to "national survival."

The paradox is more apparent than real.[2] Even so, much bridging needs to be done. The trainer and the teacher have much more to say to each other than either has been willing to admit—at a time when both are making realistic demands that we improve the quality of teaching and learning in the American classroom.

Organization and Approach

The first section below discusses outstanding differences in emphasis between the T Group and the classroom. The second section reviews the similarities. The final section, to complete the dialectic, reviews some contributions which trainers and teachers can make to each other, and identifies some significant problems which need vigorous joint effort.

"T Group" is here taken to mean a face-to-face group, set up to aid its members to learn about social phenomena by analyzing what is taking place in the group. "Classroom" signifies a collective formal learning situation, set up for children in the American public schools.[3,4]

Neither T Group nor classroom is thought of as being inherently superior to the other (although, clearly, each is a better instrument than the other to accomplish certain specific goals). The attempt in this chapter is to examine two types of learning situations on their merits. Differences will be articulated in some detail on the theory

[1] One well-known critic, though he rightly emphasizes the learning of disciplines rather than subject-matter memorization, still stoutly asserts that the school has no business with "social conditioning," personality development, or the teaching of "acceptable conduct within a group and between groups" (Bestor, 1959).

[2] It is a genuine commentary on today's "climate" that one feels impelled to remind the reader that the school is, after all, a social situation. (See, for example, Wright's finding (1951) that 70 per cent of one small boy's time in a Midwestern rural school was spent in interaction with others.) Thus, it is more than slightly plausible to assert that paying some explicit attention to classroom group processes may free more energy for content learning.

[3] For thoughtful comments on the group-relevant aspects of adult education, see Lerner and Kelman (1952).

[4] Although the focus in the present chapter is on formal learning situations, the reader should remember that a great deal of learning (not all of it "legitimate") goes on in extracurricular and informal friendship relationships outside the classroom. Gordon (1957), for example, found that a decidedly minor portion of adolescents' energy goes into classroom learning.

that unless we can make clear distinctions, attempts to locate continuities and make mutually beneficial syntheses are bound to be superficial and unfruitful. The differences will be presented mainly through an analysis of the classroom.

Differences between Classroom and T Group

Purposes

Subject-Matter Focus. The purpose of the classroom tends to be internalization by the learner of a wide range of publicly dictated subject matter. The emphasis, more often than not, is on there-and-then matters—events and relationships removed in time and space from the classroom.

Cognitive Change. In spite of much discussion of attitude change and value change in schools, it is probably fair to say that knowledge, understanding, and the ability to manipulate symbolic materials are the main business of the schools. "Knowledge" may include skills of a certain sort, but the basic type of change envisioned in the learner is cognitive.

This view of the classroom as a transmitter of the cognitive "cultural heritage" can be quarreled with as being excessively narrow.[5] The fact remains that the teacher is faced with an externally given body of content on the one hand and a batch of more or less interested and capable learners on the other. The teacher's job, as Thelen (1954) has pointed out, is to bring together, via the processes going on in the classroom group, the externally given subject matter and the unique needs of each learner.

Group processes, rather than being of direct interest, as in the T Group, are seen in the classroom as non-self-conscious vehicles for the induction of changes in children—changes that are mostly cognitive, occasionally attitudinal, and almost never behavioral.

Preparatory Set. Learning in the classroom tends to be seen as a process of making the child into a man who can cope with the demands

[5] Especially so, if the "cultural heritage" is seen to involve norms and values; the school thus becomes a secondary socializing agent of no mean power (cf. Brookover, 1955; Parsons, 1959). Yet, most often the school is involved with teaching *about* values and attitudes, rather than with direct induction of value change.

which will be placed on him—*later*. Like the T Group, the classroom is a protected setting where learning can take place; but the learners are thought of as being immature and as merely *preparing* for adequate functioning. Thus, the distinction usually made in training laboratories between the training process and the demands of back-home job situations is not present.

What, precisely, is the "job" of the schoolchild? It is not at all clear in the typical classroom whether school is meant to improve the student's functioning in here-and-now roles—what he actually is *doing*, just at this very moment, with other people. The student's here-and-now task, as classroom learning goes forward, is, in effect, to please— or at least not to displease—the teacher. The teacher is pleased mainly when the student manages to invest himself with some intensity in the there-and-then of subject matter. Neither teacher nor student spends much time, *officially*, discussing the interpersonal here-and-now.

Purpose Clarity. Since classroom purposes are externally given and, in most cases, are explicitly written down, they usually have less ambiguity than T-Group purposes. Conflicts and ambiguities do exist, but they stem mainly from organizational malfunctions and from the demands made on the school by its environment.

Ambiguity in T-Group purposes, on the other hand, probably comes mostly from other sources: the necessity for stating goals very abstractly (e.g., "increased ability to diagnose group phenomena"); the deliberate use of ambiguity as a device to force attention to the here-and-now; goal conflicts between members and subgroups (see Chapter 13); and the ego-defensive "misunderstandings" of group members about "what we are supposed to be doing here."

Context and Design Factors

Every social system exists in an environment and develops a "shape" in time and space. Such general structural features may or may not serve the official goals of the system, but they function as important limiting conditions within which specific processes go forward.

Accountability. An important contextual difference between the T Group and the classroom is the American school's public accountability. Parents, the secondary clients of the school, can enter the system at any level and influence any occupant, from a Board of Education member to the student himself. This vulnerability, coupled with the fact that all adults have had some classroom experience, generates fairly explicit role definitions. Thus, role occupants have relatively little autonomy; the teacher has fewer opportunities open to him for creative, new role behaviors than does the trainer.

The T Group, on the other hand, takes place in a temporary "shipboard culture"—the training laboratory.[6] In this "irreal" situation, status occupants have more freedom than usual to experiment with their behavior. It is no accident that the T Group is described by participants as being "like nothing I ever saw before." And in spite of the growing body of mythology about the trainer role, the trainer can be fairly bizarre or mysterious without negative consequences, if only because his accountability is primarily to the flexible here-and-now of the immediate situation.

Time. Most T Groups last 8 to 40 hours. In a typical sixth-grade classroom, a substantial minority of the children will have worked with one another for six or seven thousand hours. A high-school class is far briefer, but may meet 150 hours or more. Even allowing for the intensity of T-Group experience (which certainly could not be maintained for an entire school year), it seems clear that many more events can take place in the classroom than in the T Group.

Note, too, that the segments of the classroom experience are spread over a period of six months to a year, rather than being concentrated in a few days or weeks. Thus, the characteristic effects of "predated group death," described in Benne's chapter (see Chapter 8) of the present book, are unlikely to appear. Too, children tend to build up reputations as they move through the school from year to year, and this is an added restriction on autonomy and personal experimentation.

Group Composition. The classroom group differs from the T Group in at least two compositional respects. First, the "clients'" ages usually fall in a two-to-three year range (even though ability in any given subject area usually ranges far more widely). Second, the guiding agent in the classroom occupies a different age status from that of the clients.

Conversely, in the typical T Group the age range may be as great as 30 to 40 years. The guiding agent (trainer) is seen by group members as an age peer; his authority, therefore, is derived mainly from procedural and substantive knowledge rather than from his occupancy

[6] An exception occurs when a laboratory forms part of the training program of a single organization. Even then, however, laboratory directors, to maintain autonomy, place great emphasis on isolation from the physical location of the organization, keep control over training procedure, and the like.

of an age status defined *a priori* as more powerful than that of the clients.

The presence of a wide age range and perception of the trainer as falling within it are probably major forces in defining the T-Group task as a cooperative struggle to construct a workable social system which will aid learning. In the classroom, on the other hand, age-range restriction and child-adult differentiation serve to narrow role definitions, increase teacher authority, and facilitate the publicly demanded focus on external subject matter.

Group Size. Finally, the typical classroom contains 20 to 40 children; the typical T Group, 8 to 20 adults. It is probable (for example) that the classroom, just because of its size, requires a more stable control system, cannot be so responsive to individual need, and can exist with many inconspicuous, uninvolved members.

Client Population

Both the classroom and the T Group exist to cause change in their members, but the member characteristics of the two groups differ most notably in the learning set implied and in the kinds and extent of heterogeneity present.

Learning Set. In the classroom, the learning set may be said to be primarily educative in intent, not re-educative. It is true that remedial, corrective work goes on in the classroom, and no responsible educator takes the *tabula rasa* concept seriously. But the schoolchild has far less unlearning to do than the adult T-Group member, who often must give up, not without pain, existing cognitive map regions and behavior patterns, before he can learn new ones.[7] In the first few days of kindergarten, the young child is asked to extend his social skills, to *add* to what he already can do. In the first few days of a T Group, however, the member is confronted with the dire fact that his existing social skills do not seem to work any more.

Heterogeneity. Membership in the classroom group is involuntary, at least up through late adolescence. Thus, much heterogeneity is likely

---

[7] It is interesting to note, here, the regressive character of early T-Group experience. It is as if members must come to feel partly helpless and childlike before re-education can proceed (the phrase, "We're acting like babies," is not infrequent), although Whitman has pointed out in the present book (Chapter 11) that the regression resembles adolescent behavior more than child behavior.

to be present in ability level, socio-economic background, and interest in learning. Such heterogeneity sometimes is used, of course, as a rationalization for arbitrary control methods and standardized approaches to content; it has led also to very strong concern in American education with individual differences, individualization of instruction, and the guidance and counseling movement.

T-Group members, on the other hand, are usually self-selected from a rather narrow range of social class membership, ability, background, and interest, or are drawn from a single organization which has undertaken T-Group experience for its employees. Most T Groups are not genuine microcosms of society at all; lower-class persons, dull persons, and uninterested persons are underrepresented or missing.

Guiding Agent Role

Given the differences in purposes, context, and clientele described above, the teacher and the trainer must inevitably behave somewhat differently.[8]

Role Clarity. For one thing, the teacher must be considerably more explicit than the trainer. Ordinarily, it is quite dysfunctional for the teacher to be vague, indeterminate, or noncommittal. The children are *not* in school simply to project their anxieties on the blank screen of a neutral "leader's" behavior; nor are they there to understand more deeply their own feelings about authority figures. The teacher's job is to help the children as persons in the process of confronting some externally given subject matter. The child must *understand* the teacher's authority, even (or especially) when the teacher chooses to share it.

Role Differentiation. Frank has pointed out (Chapter 16) that the trainer's role tends to become indistinguishable from that of the member. In the classroom, though children are expected to become somewhat more like the teacher (more knowledgeable, more critical in their thinking, more "grown-up"), there remains at the end of any classroom experience a very considerable gap between child and adult. Also, children are *not* usually expected to teach other children (and this is perhaps unfortunate); while T-Group members usually do begin to perform training functions for one another.

Role differentiation is related to the effectiveness of both the class-

---

[8] Trainer and teacher ordinarily differ in extent of academic background; this undoubtedly affects performance quality in some ways. But the point is that the role prescriptions differ somewhat to begin with.

room and the T Group. Judging from what is known about the anchorage of beliefs and attitudes in group memberships, the teacher or trainer who is seen as an external agent, unrelated to the immediate system of the classroom or the T Group, cannot expect to induce much durable change. It is probably true, however, that the teacher can get away with less group membership than can the trainer. He may, in fact, be able to substitute a kind of multiple dyadic relationship with students, to the end that each individual student identifies with him sufficiently to sustain learning. The traditional classroom, where interaction is largely channeled through a central teacher-figure, encourages precisely this sort of relationship. Under these circumstances, the teacher is minimally bound by group norms, and may consider them as falling clearly outside the formal teaching function. ("My students really confide in me as a friend, but when the time comes for work they know who's boss.")

Role Centrality. The clear, differentiated role of the teacher is also *central* in the classroom social system. The trainer's role may be central early in the T Group's life, when his behavior frustrates member expectations (generated from past experience with leaders and teachers). But this prominence disappears as the group's role structure develops.

Teacher centrality has two aspects. First, the teacher is less likely to act as if the control function should be interdependently shared among the group. As an agent of the school, he maintains nearly full control over subject matter. In addition, he need not be concerned with group validation of his methodological proposals, but can proceed to install methods which his diagnosis leads him to feel are appropriate.[9]

Much trainer behavior, on the other hand, consists of attempts to vest more and more power in the group: remaining silent, encouraging independent decision making, and turning questions back to the group, among other methods. The trainer's intent is to work himself out of a job, as the social system of the T Group becomes more viable, more capable of coping with the stress of inquiry.

The teacher usually spends little conscious effort in developing the power of the classroom group as a group, although he certainly is

[9] This power is highly legitimized (partly because teacher-pupil role relationships are subsumed under adult-child role relationships); thus teacher behavior is an extremely vigorous determinant of classroom group processes. The striking results in Lewin's Iowa studies (see Lippitt and White, 1958) can be accounted for partly by adult-child role differentiation and its consequences for power distribution.

deeply committed to the notion that individual pupils should be growing more self-controlling, more capable of independent inquiry. Where group-shared control is sought deliberately, it tends to be valued in the service of content-achievement goals (as when the kindergarten teacher stimulates self-policing activities so that each child can be heard). This is, of course, consistent with the notion that the school does not exist to understand interpersonal phenomena—but does use such phenomena instrumentally in the accomplishment of subject-matter goals dictated by the "culture."

The second major consequence of role centrality, coupled with the demands of subject matter, is that much *stimulative* teacher behavior ensues. The work of Ryans (1958) is instructive in this respect. His factor analyses of teacher behavior disclosed that most of the variance was accounted for by three factors: a warmth factor (friendly versus aloof); a task-operation factor (responsible, businesslike versus slipshod); and a stimulative factor (imaginative, surgent versus dull, routine).[10] Classically, the T-Group trainer does not stimulate directly, but tends rather to rely on the objective and potent demands of the situation itself as it unfolds.[11]

[10] Compare Carter's summary (1954) of five different factor analyses of group-member behavior, which identifies three factors: sociability, aiding attainment by the group, and individual prominence.

[11] No clear argument can be made for the idea that classroom learning involves less tension, anxiety, disruptive emotion, and so on, or is somehow less "potent" than T-Group learning. The feelings of the child who fails an examination or is ridiculed by peers or receives sanctions for deviant behavior are probably no less potent than the feelings experienced by adult T-Group members under analogous circumstances. School is the child's work, and success and failure at it carry genuine affect.

It is correct, of course, that the child's role behaviors—once he accepts school norms—are perhaps less likely to be questioned than are those of T-Group members; in this sense the T-Group member may feel more vulnerable, exposed, and anxious, especially if his defenses and anxieties are being discussed.

The ambiguity of early T-Group experience is another special source of disruptive feeling. But one cannot overlook the fact that emotions can be discussed explicitly and worked through, in the T Group; the upset child often must cope with his feelings covertly, either on the fringes of the classroom experience, or outside it (counseling, friends).

In addition, since teacher competence ordinarily falls in a wider range than trainer competence, classroom malpractice and increased child anxiety are probably statistically more likely.

The fact that adults often report a T Group as the most significant learning experience of their lives may mean only that they have forgotten what the third grade was *really* like. The reader who would like to be transported back to the guilts, joys, and terrors of that time is referred to Ozick's astoundingly potent reminiscences of life in Public School 71 (1959).

Group Processes

Thus far T-Group-classroom differences in purpose, design, clientele, and guiding agent [12] may have been etched more sharply than is justified. The reader is asked to withhold his rejoinders about commonalities for the moment and to consider a few essential process differences which follow from the structural differences already presented.

Interaction. Given the prepotency of subject matter and role differentiation, we might predict classroom interaction patterns in which teacher behaviors play a central part. Child-teacher interaction does appear to be more frequent than child-child interaction, at least if we focus on formal, "official" behaviors. Thus interaction chains like teacher-child$_1$, child$_1$-teacher, teacher-child$_2$, child$_2$-teacher, teacher-group, child$_3$-teacher, and so on, are more likely than chains like child$_1$-child$_2$, child$_2$-child$_1$, child$_1$-group, child$_3$-child$_{1 and 2}$, and so on. Traditional classroom seating arrangements both symbolize and reinforce interaction patterns like the former. Considerable informal interaction with nearby children goes on steadily, of course, but this is not used ordinarily by the teacher to aid the child in reaching learning goals, and may even be forbidden.

T-Group physical arrangements, role prescriptions, and emergent norms all tend to favor full, vigorous interaction among members (and trainer) on an egalitarian basis. Such interaction is aided materially by the fact that group events themselves are the focus of discussion.

Interaction patterns have their counterparts in control patterns. The trend—especially in the elementary school—over the past few decades has been away from teacher control and toward more cooperative planning and joint determination of classroom events. Yet, although generalizing from adult personalities backward to teaching methods is hazardous, it is interesting to note the resistance, anxiety, and plain clumsiness attested to in accounts of adult reaction to student-centered teaching (Cantor, 1946), to self-structured workshops (Kelley, 1951), and to T-Group training itself. Such phenomena are mute testimony

[12] These comments do not exhaust the distinctive properties of the teacher's role. Parsons has pointed out, for example (1959), that the teacher engages in a great deal of explicitly *evaluative* behavior, so that a clear ranking develops on the basis of achievement. A child's rank exerts drastic influence on his progress through school, and on his occupational destiny. Achievement ranking is simply not of concern in the T Group; more than one laboratory staff meeting has been thrown into a quasi-panic over the question of how to "grade" participants who desired university credit.

to a widespread lack of childhood practice in cooperative planning of learning experiences.

Content Norms. Persons in interaction come to share norms. Some of these norms concern what shall be talked about, or dealt with, in the group.[13] As already suggested, classroom content tends to have a there-and-then nature. Classroom norms, in effect, taboo the use of here-and-now events as legitimate content.

Under these circumstances, it is quite likely that recurrent questions of T-Group life—How shall we control our destiny? What are the badges of membership in this group? How close can we be with one another as persons?—will appear in the classroom in a far more covert form. Latent struggles over authority, for example, exist in most classrooms; but the important thing is that (except in passing, or if crisis impends) the brute fact of the struggle does not become a proper and legitimate topic for classroom discussion. This is as it should be; given the existence of prior bodies of subject matter, the teacher cannot afford to encourage, as content, a steady group diet of *process* events.

Using Bennis' outline of levels of intervention (see Chapter 9), it can be said that classroom discussion focuses mainly on Level 1 (content) and, occasionally, on Level 2 (behavior). Analysis of defenses (Level 3) and anxieties (Level 4) occurs only rarely in the classroom. It is true that characteristic personal defenses and anxieties are constantly at work, but the relevant norms tend to inhibit direct verbal attention to material other than formal content.

Thus the dominant coin of public exchange in most classrooms is cognitive. Explicit expressions of rage, pleasure, fear, depression, and love tend to appear at the periphery of discourse. They remain *private.* The sensitive teacher takes such expressions as cues for steering classroom planning and inquiry (cf. Thelen, 1954), but discussion of feelings as phenomena of significance in themselves rarely becomes central. Both the teacher—and the students—may privately assert, with e. e. cummings, that "feeling is first"; but it is a rare classroom where the primacy of affect is publicly acknowledged and acted upon.

The corollary here would seem to be that in the classroom the range of acceptable behaviors and feelings is probably narrower than in the T Group, and the norms implied by statements like, "It's safe to try things out here," tend to be feebler or absent. It may be indicative of this hypothesis that Wright's detailed study of one boy's classroom day (1951) found his classroom behaviors to be more restricted, less

---

[13] The reader may wish to refer to Gibb's discussion of T-Group norms in the present book (Chapter 10), and to Miles (1959), pp. 207–209.

creative or constructive, and less satisfying than his behaviors in adult-free environments.

Inquiry Norms. Classrooms and T Groups also must develop norms controlling *procedure*—the processes of inquiry—as well as content.

In most classrooms, dispassionate, rational attempts to make sense of the world are valued, "critical thinking" is sought, and the teacher tries not to impose his own values in relation to the subject matter. Objectivity in relation to specific events in the classroom, however, is probably less frequent, and may depend largely upon whether the teacher sees classroom group processes as necessary but distressing accompaniments to his teaching behavior or as the central vehicle of learning itself.

In the T Group, objectivity norms usually develop quickly. Events in the immediate social system are taken to be a complex resultant of the interaction which is taking place. Anger, "scapegoating," and desperate struggles for power can be studied fairly dispassionately—as real events in the real world, not as willfully caused projections of malevolent or benevolent personalities. Things, that is to say, are not "taken personally," although they are recognized as being a function of what persons, including the self, are doing. Above all, process events (in a fully functioning T Group) are not seen as "interruptions," but as raw materials for learning.

A second class of inquiry-regulating norms determines the broad approach taken to evidence collecting and inference making. In the classroom at its best, many such norms are at work, usually drawn from subject-matter disciplines: the logic of historical inference; modes of aesthetic explication; mathematical proof; the taxonomic, nonexperimental methods of sciences like astronomy, geology, biology, and botany; and the rational modes of inquiry common to the various branches of philosophy. When learning moves beyond textbook assignments and laborious parroting and uses the norms of investigation which are historically appropriate to the immediate discipline involved, the classroom can become the scene for genuine inquiry (cf. Bruner, 1960; Thelen, 1960).

In the T Group, on the other hand, the predominant mode of inquiry might be called "clinical-experimental." The preferred approach comes to be the experimental production of behavior, followed by analysis of it in some depth. *Ex cathedra* pronouncements, descriptions of outside situations, referral to the printed word or to external authorities—all tend to be devalued, sometimes unrealistically so. The usual emphasis is strongly inductive and empirical, even though few

T Groups manage to set up actual *experiments* in a scientifically respectable sense.

Thus, in the T Group all is "grist to the mill" of process analysis. At its worst, this inductive emphasis reminds one of the boy who shoots an arrow at a barn door and then draws a bull's-eye around the hole to demonstrate his accuracy. At its best, T-Group inquiry is extraordinarily flexible, highly sophisticated, and powerfully heuristic.

In the classroom, however, the teacher is not free to ignore the existence of a body of subject matter with internal structure of its own or to discard all modes of inquiry save the inductive. Indeed, exclusively inductive learning would make culture building ultimately impossible.

Hence, inductive inquiry often proves to be limited to the early stages of a project, to inquiry with young children,[14] or to problems where the existing structure of a subject-matter field is too restrictive and should be temporarily bypassed.

Finally, there are large areas of school content to which the here-and-now experience of the learner in the classroom group bears no more than a generally facilitative or hindering relationship. It is relatively easy to teach the social sciences by using events in the classroom group as a vehicle; but as content becomes less and less associated with the direct experience of the learner, direct examination of group processes becomes less and less justified. The need for *clarity* is not the least reason for maintaining a clear distinction between classroom content and process. The blurring of content and process in the T Group often makes for confusion and anxiety: *vide* one member's despairing, "We have to build a house and try to live in it at the same time!"

Similarities between Classroom and T Group

All these differences are real and visible, though they would have to be qualified in talking of specific teachers and trainers. The essential thing is that differences be neither exaggerated nor minimized, but seen clearly, as a precondition for discerning the genuine congruences and continuities we need as a base for collaborative inquiry.

[14] See, for example, the exciting and moving film, *Learning Is Searching* (Vassar College, 1955), which depicts the strongly inductive inquiry of a group of third-grade children into the meaning of tools in man's culture.

Learning-Focused Group

Classrooms and T Groups are settings for learning. Classrooms are more like T Groups in this respect than either is like an aircrew or a social club. The purpose is not to change the environment or to gratify but to cause learning to take place in members.

This broad similarity ensures that the teacher and the trainer must confront similar phenomena: resistance to learning in all its forms; the development of group norms which support learning, rather than induce superficial conformity; problems of clarity, consistency, and scope of individual learnings; the question of relative permanence of learnings.

Concern with Nonintellective Outcomes

No amount of official classroom concern with cognitive changes can obscure the fact that the child, like the adult T-Group member, is always learning as a whole person. Attitudinal, value-related, and behavioral changes are proceeding simultaneously with the cognitive changes. From a broader standpoint, as Foshay (1958) has pointed out, the schools must be as concerned with man feeling, doing, and acting—alone or with others—as they are with man thinking.

It was suggested above that teachers tend to stress cognitive outcomes, and trainers, behavioral ones. But certain facts imply more than a little convergence between these positions: (1) A good deal of cognitive teaching does go on in T Groups. (2) The child's experiences in the classroom actually do train him in what Parsons (1959) has called "role-responsibility"—the capacity to respond appropriately to others in present and future role relationships. (3) Recent decades have seen an increasing emphasis on the needs of the whole child, and on the importance of specifying, *in behavioral terms,* the outcomes of education (see French, 1957). (4) The characteristic T-Group concern with the integration of work and feeling has been a persistent concern in education since (for example) Prescott's work (1938). (5) Most American educators of recent years have been quite comfortable with the concept of man as a social being who must function adequately with his fellows, both while he is learning and after his formal learning has been "completed" (if we can take anguished outcries about "life adjustment" as presumptive evidence).

Group Development

The developmental growth central in each T Group's vicissitudes is paralleled in the classroom. Teachers acknowledge this when they make elaborate plans for the first day at school, when they characterize particular class groups as not having "settled down," and complain or boast of characteristics of 9B or 3A or "this year's sophomores" *as a group*. Classroom developmental processes are likely to be latent and less dramatic than those in the T Group, but even so, much implicit attention is given by teacher and students to the gradual development of a working social system.

Experimental Inquiry

Finally, many teachers focus, far more directly than has been implied in this chapter, on reflectively examined experience as the basis of classroom inquiry, even where a variety of subject-matter areas is involved. If some hardy residue of John Dewey's thought can be rescued from the ravages of his abusers, misinterpreters, and well-intentioned supporters, it almost certainly will be his emphasis on the experimental method of learning. The idea of inductively guided problem solving is very central to much of modern educational thought as well as to T-Group theory and practice. In fact, the problem-solving models appearing in several chapters of the present book owe much to Dewey's conception outlined in *How We Think* (1910).

Some Possible Mutual Aid

A decade ago there was much optimism about the mutual contributions possible between the T-Group brand of applied social science and contemporary educational practice.[15] It must be acknowledged immediately that this optimism has not led to extensive, solid work. Except for an early article by Trow and others (1950), the continued work of Thelen (1950, 1954, 1960) and its extensions (Flanders, 1954, 1960), and earlier work at Teachers College, Columbia University (Miel, 1952; Cunningham, 1951), there has been a striking lack of sustained inquiry which attempts to bridge between the demands of

[15] See, for example, "Group Dynamics and Education," a series of nine articles appearing in the *NEA Journal* during 1948–1949 (L. P. Bradford, Ed.).

the classroom and the insights of the training group (or even of the field of small-group study as a whole). Strang's recent text, *Group Work in Education* (1958), reveals no coherent conception of the class as a group with which to organize the welter of assorted reports of "sociometric cleavages in junior highschool English classes," and the like.[16]

To take a Lewinian point of view for a moment, one would infer the existence of barriers or restraining forces which prevent the making of common cause between human relations trainers and persons concerned with the improvement of classroom functioning. The following discussion presents, in turn: some possible contributions from classroom experience to T-Group practice; the converse; and some possible areas of joint concern. Where possible, forces which may restrain interpenetration of knowledge and practice have been identified. This procedure follows the Lewinian dictum that it is usually easier and more productive to remove barriers than to pile on pressures and exhortations.

Contributions of the Classroom to the T Group

Philosophical Clarity. Since school systems are characterized by a fairly strict degree of accountability, it is not surprising that much energy has gone into the development of systematic educational philosophies. Much T-Group practice, on the other hand, lacks a coherent sense of *why*. What conception of man is implied in T-Group procedures? Need theological questions be so often bypassed? What theory of knowledge is implied in the operations of T-Group inquiry? What ethical dilemmas are raised by the way trainers operate? In what senses may T-Group phenomena be said to be essentially aesthetic? Such questions are *not* psychological, but philosophical in nature. Confrontation cannot be postponed indefinitely (and indeed has begun to occur at some laboratories, notably those sponsored by religious organizations).

[16] Beginnings have been made. See Smith's (1959) contribution on group processes in the NEA "What Research Says to the Teacher" series, and the review of classroom-relevant studies by Jensen and Parsons (1959). See also the collection of articles (Henry, 1960) to which many T-Group trainers contributed, and the book of readings assembled by Charters and Gage (1963). The growing number of classroom group behavior studies stimulated by the Cooperative Research Branch (see Office of Education, 1962) is impressive. But no one would assert that we have an adequate model of the class as a group. Much steady work remains to be done.

A possible barrier to philosophical contributions from education to T-Group practice is the stereotyped assumption of many trainers that educational philosophies are rationalizations, prepared defenses, or justifications for withdrawal from conflict. In fact, for many school people, "philosophy" does tend to represent a series of preferred prescriptions, as in "My philosophy is, always be democratic." Yet, answers to fundamental questions about man's origin and destiny, conceptions of good and evil, responsibility and guilt, truth and beauty, must be assembled into a more-than-implicit world view by any trainer worth his salt.[17] The failure to do this must be related, one feels, to the sense of hollowness and emptiness sometimes encountered among hard-pressed trainers in today's seller's market for human relations training.

Curriculum Development. Since the schools must be concerned with subject matter, and since they have access to the child for years, it is natural that much concern should have centered around the sequence of learning experiences, their scope, and their appropriateness to the learner's needs and the demands of society.

The curriculum in most training laboratories tends to be assembled on a casual evolutionary basis; the curriculum of the T Group evolves mostly on an ad hoc basis. Yet a host of "curriculum" decisions are made steadily by the T-Group trainer. What types of situations will he respond to or "ignore"? What type of content is in or out of bounds? What problems can most profitably be tackled early (versus late) in the life of the T Group?

It would be difficult to defend the assertion that the curriculum field has an explicitly formulated set of principles to guide such decision making, as curriculum workers would be the first to admit. However, enough experience exists in this area for it to be of help to trainers.[18]

A major restraining force here, delightfully enough, is probably that of educational trade jargon ("meaningful," "integrate," "persistent life situations," "scope"). The trainer who dismisses attacks on the language of social science as constituting "resistance" may well find it painfully illuminating when the shoe is on the other foot.

Cognitive Clarity. Many teachers (in spite of a widespread occupational tendency toward sentimentalism) can tackle intellectual prob-

---

[17] A very useful source, Henry (1955), examines several philosophical stances (e.g., realism, logical empiricism, experimentalism, existentialism) and explores their relevance to education.

[18] A good treatment is found in Smith, Stanley, and Shores (1950).

lems systematically in the framework of subject disciplines. More important, they are clear on how to provoke critical thinking in students; the approaches being used in materials from the current major curriculum revision groups such as the Physical Science Study Committee, the School Mathematics Study Group, and Project English, are clear testimony. The cognitive aspect of T-Group learning is deeply important and frequently slighted; trainers sometimes allow the obvious potency of the T-Group experience to delude them into believing that good learning is only emotional in nature—that only "gut" learning experiences in the T Group warrant attention.

Contributions of the T Group to the Classroom

Now—to reverse the emphasis—what does the trainer have to suggest to the teacher?

The Class as a Social System. Perhaps the fundamental contribution of T-Group practice is a clear sense that the classroom is a miniature social system with regularities and predictable features which both aid and hinder learning. The hindrances are obvious enough,[19] but how to harness the forces for learning is far less clear. Thelen and Getzels (1957) and Baumgartel [20] have pointed out that classroom social system features such as laws, culture, and division of labor need not be treated as latent and unimportant concurrents of "real" learning but can profitably be noted and analyzed explicitly with children. Social scientists and educational practitioners need to confront together, and directly, the task of building a general model of classroom learning which will take into account the best of educational practice and available knowledge of the functioning of small groups. Such a model could generate suggestions for practice, as well as guide research. For example, the accountability of the American public school means that the classroom is a focus of conflicting value systems (cf. Williams, 1951; and Dahlke, 1958). Several of the T-Group theories in the present book (notably those of Benne (Chapter 8), Bennis (Chapter 9), and Whitman (Chapter 11)) discuss the dialectic that

[19] See Gordon (1957) for some vivid anecdotal material on such matters as the effects of prestige ranking, authority conflicts, and the influence of semi-formal (extracurricular) groups. Coleman's (1961) classic study extends this work.

[20] Howard Baumgartel's unpublished manuscript, "Some Rough Notes on the Class as a Miniature Society" (Department of Human Relations, University of Kansas, July 1958), is a thoughtful treatment of this theme.

seems to take place between the polarities of apparently irreconcilable alternatives as the social system develops over time.

A major restraining force which prevents such joint model building is status differentiation. Social scientists are inclined to believe that "thinking like an educator gets you nowhere"; and many educators accept (while denying) the social scientist's implied judgment of educator incompetence. This leads to dependency; it is not a coincidence that "laboratories" for educational leaders have too often proved to be situations in which social scientists supply training for educational practitioners rather than situations in which genuine joint inquiry is in progress.

Diagnostic, Experimental Intervention. Teaching, like T-Group training, is a complex business. Thus, the teacher must make a tentative intervention, study its effect, diagnose, and intervene again. Careful, concrete articulations of a diagnostic, experimental approach to teaching are much needed. Much of the present book is relevant here, as are the treatments by Thelen (1954) and Sheviakov and Redl (1956).

Restraining forces which prevent the spread of an adequately diagnostic classroom approach are many: anticipated loss of the gratifications that reside in the central, highly differentiated teacher role; fears of fallibility and loss of status; social science jargon; and the fact that, until the present book, almost no coherent descriptions of T-Group practice existed anywhere.

Learner-Centered Teaching. At its best, a good T Group can manage a flexible and creative coordination of highly diverse individual needs with the demands of a group-wide learning task. Arrangements exist which provide the learner with immediate knowledge of the results of his behavior. Too, most T-Group trainers are quite willing to experiment with methodological innovations which maximize attention to diverse individual needs. As a result of all this, many T-Group members find that never before have they been in such a supportive and personally compelling learning environment. Whether or not this potency can be generalized to subject-matter learning deserves rigorous joint investigation.[21]

[21] Durrell's work on "team learning" (as reported in the *New York Times* for June 15, 1959, p. 56) is very suggestive in this respect. He found that independent pupil-subgroups, working with self-pacing materials, developed high involvement and substantial increments of learning over pupils taught by traditional methods. The results may be explainable in terms of immediate feedback and correction, responsiveness to individual need, and the existence of learning-supportive norms—all features found in the usual T Group.

Many restraining forces can be identified here. For some teachers (let us call them the victims of the Mark Hopkins Syndrome), the teacher-pupil relationship is the only avenue to meeting learner needs. For others, "group" automatically summons up visions of sameness and homogeneity (note the widespread use of the label "grouping" to refer to the placement of pupils in noninteracting batches, as in the case of reading "groups"). Beyond these conceptual barriers, it is important to identify mutterings about "life adjustment" and mindless demands for "achievement" as forces away from learner-centered teaching.

It is also true that promising methodological ideas from T-Group practice may either be perceived as nothing new—"You mean progressive education, don't you?"—or be recategorized as "Bethel paraphernalia." Even when these restraining forces are absent, teachers lack skill in managing procedures with learner-centered features, if only because such procedures (e.g., the problem census) lay bare the awesome complexity of the classroom group.

Human Relations as Content. There is, finally, an often-ignored and demeaned contribution of T-Group theory and practice to education— the idea that the knowledges, skills, and attitudes centering about group participation are, in Benne's words (1952), "valuable subject matter in its own right—subject matter which deserves an important place in the general education of our people."

Most simply, what is involved here is a kind of practical ability, which is increasingly essential in a world where the problems (as Bertrand Russell has remarked) are less and less like those of driving in the desert, and more and more like those of driving in midtown Manhattan. Without the collaborative skills required for working with other people—the gigantic problems of "cultural lag" aside— things are bound to get even worse.[22]

At a deeper level, something like the internalization of social-scientific models of thought is involved. We usually hope that the child can come to think, in some degree, as a scientist, a historian, or an artist thinks, as he meets the demands of life. Perhaps, also, it is a good idea for him to be able to think in the way a social scientist

[22] This point is not so new to educators as trainers may think. For example, Foshay has remarked (1952): "Civic competence is skillful behavior with reference to social phenomena . . . that kind of behavior which is economical of effort and emotion, and in which the predicted consequences of the behavior are actually achieved . . . information [as such] is not competence." He identifies skills, such as locating functional leadership in a system, diagnosing situations, and developing organizations appropriate to the situation and the task, and proposes that they be learned by inductive generalization from firsthand experience.

thinks—to examine the functioning of immediate social systems in the frame of mind of "observant participation," eschewing easy stereotypes, blind rationalism, or *ad hominem* explanations of social phenomena.

Most fundamentally, perhaps, the insights that have developed gradually through T-Group experience over the last decade may conceivably be of help in the construction of a new social ethic, an ideology responsive to fundamentally new notions of man's relationship to his fellow man. The dimensions of such an ideology are by no means clear. As already suggested, much explicit effort must be given to coping with fundamental philosophical questions inherent in the laboratory method of training. One guesses that the new ideology will almost certainly involve a re-evaluation of "democratic" shibboleths and the rejection of cant phrases like "other-directedness" and "the organization man" in favor of explicit commitments to the value of human *relationships*, rather than solely to the separate, atomized "individuals" partaking in the relationships.[23] One can only be inarticulate about an as-yet-to-be-constructed social ethic; but it seems very clear that one is desperately needed, and that reflected-upon T-Group experience can play an important role in articulating this ethic.

Some Common Concerns

In one sense, all the "contributions" described above can serve as a focus of interaction between teachers and trainers. Beyond these, however, there are some additional problems, good solutions for which will clearly require joint inquiry—inquiry which can make a genuine difference in our thinking about teaching and learning.

Meta-Learning. As the "explosion of knowledge" continues in Western culture, it becomes more and more clear that the acquisition of any particular set, or sets, of subject matter is an insufficient definition of education. Rather, the major residue of anyone's formal education may well be taken to be the habits of inquiry, learning, and growth he has internalized. We need to know, much more clearly than we now do, just how it is that people "learn how to learn," and how learn-

---

[23] This comment draws upon the theological ideas of Buber (1956). His concepts of the "I-Thou" relationship and the "life of dialogue" are extremely relevant here.

ing experiences exert their effect on subsequent growth and development.[24]

Adaptation of Process Analysis to Subject-Matter Teaching. The experimental method of inquiry into the operations of a small group is an exceedingly powerful method for learning; this much seems clear. What many trainers (all too eager to condemn classroom teachers as "inflexible") fail to see is that analysis of the here-and-now is relatively easy and straightforward when the learning content at hand is social structure and functioning in the small group. But we need to know much more than we do now about fitting the analysis of here-and-now events to the learning of mathematics (see Fawcett, 1938), literature, philosophy, foreign languages. Most trainers simply do not understand what might be involved in such transformations, and most teachers have a sharply limited understanding of what "analysis of the here-and-now" is likely to mean.

Methods Research. Human relations training and formal education are alike in that a wide variety of teaching methods and agent behaviors are asserted to be efficacious, usually on the basis of extremely slim evidence. Most studies of "teacher-centered" versus "student-centered" teaching styles have been inconclusive, as have studies of "lecture" versus "discussion" methods.[25] As far as that goes, we do not have any clear idea of whether different styles of trainer behavior lead to different learner outcomes or, in fact, whether trainers are a necessary appurtenance of T Groups at all.

It seems likely, then, that joint inquiry in the general area now called "methods research" is highly important. A large fraction of existing research has dealt with phenotypical, superficial variables (lecture versus discussion); much wishful, ideologically labeled cognitive mapping has gone on (democratic versus authoritarian); and very little account has been taken of the small-group literature or the body of T-Group practice. This implies that a program of research on change induction via group membership [26] would be of inestimable value both to human relations training and to the broader field of education.

[24] See Miles (1957) for comments on the meta-learning problem in the case of human relations training.
[25] Relevant studies bearing on these questions have been reviewed by Riecken and Homans (1954, pp. 807–808), Jensen and Parsons (1959), and McKeachie (1962).
[26] For contributions to this area from the training side, see, for example, Bowers and Soar (1961); Gibb (1961); and Miles (1960). The acceleration of research in education in the three years since this manuscript was drafted has been very

Quality Control. Even more fundamentally, as Cronbach has pointed out (1959), we in education are doing a bad job of measuring educational output. Methods research, indeed, depends very centrally on the existence of adequate, validated criterion measures. We must know, far more clearly than we do now, what the effects are of a college education, a geometry class, or a T Group. Until we know with clarity what it is we are accomplishing, our faith in the perfectibility of man in society may turn out to be nothing more than naïve hope.

General References

Benne, K. D. "Theory of Cooperative Planning." *Teachers College Record,* Columbia University, 53:429–435, 1952.

Bestor, A. "Education and Its Proper Relationship to the Forces of American Society." *Daedalus,* 88:1:75–90, 1959.

Bowers, N. D., and R. S. Soar. Evaluation of laboratory human relations training for classroom teachers. Studies of human relations in the teaching-learning process: V. Final report. U.S. Office of Education Contract No. 8143. Columbia: University of South Carolina, 1961. Mimeographed.

Bradford, L. P. (Ed.). "Group Dynamics and Education." Collection of articles appearing in *NEA Journal,* 1948–1949.

Brookover, W. B. *A Sociology of Education.* New York: American Book Company, 1955.

Bruner, J. S. *The Process of Education.* New York: Harper & Bros., 1960.

Buber, M. *Writings.* W. Herberg (Ed.). New York: Meridian Books, 1956.

Cantor, N. *The Dynamics of Learning.* Buffalo: Foster & Stewart Publishing Corporation, 1946.

Carter, L. F. "Recording and Evaluating the Performance of Individuals as Members of Small Groups." *Personnel Psychology,* 7:477–484, 1954.

Charters, W. W., Jr., and N. L. Gage. *Readings in the Social Psychology of Education.* Boston: Allyn and Brown, 1963.

Coleman, J. S. *The Adolescent Society.* New York: Free Press of Glencoe, 1961.

Cronbach, L. J. "Education Approaches Period of Constructive Change." *Nation's Schools,* 63:72–75, 1959.

Cunningham, Ruth. *Understanding Group Behavior of Boys and Girls.* New York: Teachers College Bureau of Publications, Columbia University, 1951.

Dahlke, H. O. *Values in Culture and Classroom: A Study in the Sociology of the School.* New York: Harper & Bros., 1958.

Dewey, J. *How We Think.* Boston: D. C. Heath & Company, 1910.

Fawcett, H. P. *The Nature of Proof.* Thirteenth Yearbook, National Council of Teachers of Mathematics. New York: Teachers College Bureau of Publications, Columbia University, 1938.

Flanders, N. A. *Teaching with Groups.* Minneapolis: Burgess Publishing Company, 1954.

great (see Office of Education, 1962; Gage, 1963), and may be expected to continue.

Flanders, N. A.   Teacher influence, pupil attitudes and achievement.   Studies in interaction analysis.   Final Report, Cooperative Research Project No. 397. Minneapolis: University of Minnesota, 1960.

Foshay, A. W.   "Getting Civic Competence into the Curriculum."   In R. W. Crary (Ed.), *Education for Democratic Citizenship.*   Twenty-Second Yearbook, National Council for the Social Studies.   Washington: The Council, 1952.

Foshay, A. W.   "The Aims of Education."   Paper read at National Association of Educational Broadcasters' Seminar on Instructional Uses of Television and Radio, Purdue University, Lafayette, Indiana, July 21–25, 1958.

French, W.   *Behavioral Goals of General Education in High School.*   New York: Russell Sage Foundation, 1957.

Gage, N. L. (Ed.).   *Handbook of Research on Teaching.*   Chicago: Rand McNally & Company, 1963.

Gibb, J. R.   "A Framework for Examining Change."   Technical Report No. 9, Factors Determining Defensive Behavior Within Groups.   Group Psychology Branch, Office of Naval Research.   Washington: National Training Laboratories, 1961.   Mimeographed.

Gordon, C. W.   *The Social System of the High School: A Study in the Sociology of Adolescence.*   Chicago: Free Press of Glencoe, 1957.

Gouldner, A.   "Organizational Analysis."   In R. K. Merton, L. Broom, and L. S. Cottrell, Jr. (Eds.).   *Sociology Today: Problems and Prospects.*   New York: Basic Books, 1959, pp. 400–428.

Henry, N. B. (Ed.).   *Modern Philosophies and Education.*   Fifty-Fourth Yearbook, National Society for the Study of Education.   Chicago: The Society, 1955.

Henry, N. B. (Ed.).   *The Dynamics of Instructional Groups.*   Fifty-Ninth Yearbook, Part II, National Society for the Study of Education.   Chicago: University of Chicago Press, 1960.

Jensen, G., and T. Parsons.   "The Structure and Dynamics of Classroom Groups and Educational Systems."   *Review of Educational Research,* 29:4:344–356, 1959.

Kelley, E.   *The Workshop Way of Learning.*   New York: Harper & Bros., 1951.

Lerner, H., and H. C. Kelman (Eds.).   "Group Methods in Psychotherapy, Social Work, and Adult Education."   *The Journal of Social Issues,* 8:2:1952.

Lippitt, R., and R. K. White.   "An Experimental Study of Leadership and Group Life," in E. E. Maccoby, T. M. Newcomb, and E. E. Hartley (Eds.), *Readings in Social Psychology.*   New York: Henry Holt and Company, 1958, pp. 496–511.

Miel, A.   *Cooperative Procedures in Learning.*   New York: Teachers College Bureau of Publications, Columbia University, 1952.

Miles, M. B.   "Personal Change Through Human Relations Training: A Working Paper."   *HMLI Interim Reports,* December 1957.   New York: Horace Mann-Lincoln Institute of School Experimentation, Teachers College, Columbia University.   Mimeographed.

Miles, M. B.   *Learning to Work in Groups: A Program Guide for Educational Leaders.*   New York: Teachers College Bureau of Publications, Columbia University, 1959.

Miles, M. B.   "Human Relations Training: Processes and Outcomes."   *Journal of Counseling Psychology,* 7:4:301–306, 1960.

McKeachie, W. J.   *Procedures and Techniques of Teaching.*   In N. Sanford (Ed.), *The American College.*   New York: John Wiley & Sons, 1962, pp. 312–364.

Office of Education (U.S. Department of Health, Education, and Welfare).   *Cooperative Research Projects, Fiscal 1961.*   Bulletin 1962, No. 18.   OE-12004-61.   Washington: U.S. Government Printing Office, 1962.

Ozick, C.   "We Ignoble Savages."   *Evergreen Review,* 10:48–52, 141–163, 1959.

Parsons, T.   "The School Class as a Social System: Some of Its Functions in American Society."   *Harvard Educational Review,* 29:4:297–318, 1959.

Prescott, D. A.   *Emotion and the Educative Process.*   Washington: American Council on Education, 1938.

Riecken, H. W., and G. C. Homans.   "Psychological Aspects of Social Structure." G. Lindzey (Ed.), *Handbook of Social Psychology.*   Reading, Mass.: Addison-Wesley Publishing Company, 1954.   2 vols.

Ryans, D. G.   "Some Validity Extension Data from Empirically Derived Predictors of Teacher Behavior."   *Educational and Psychological Measurement,* 18:355–370, 1958.

Sheviakov, G. V., and F. Redl.   *Discipline for Today's Children and Youth* (revised edition by S. K. Richardson).   Washington: Association for Supervision and Curriculum Development, National Education Association, 1956.

Smith, B. O., W. O. Stanley, and J. Harlan Shores.   *Fundamentals of Curriculum Development.*   Yonkers-on-Hudson, New York: World Book Company, 1950.

Thelen, H. A. (Ed.).   "Educational Dynamics: Theory and Research."   *The Journal of Social Issues,* 6:2: entire issue; 1950.

Thelen, H. A.   *The Dynamics of Groups at Work.*   Chicago: The University of Chicago Press, 1954.

Thelen, H. A., and J. W. Getzels.   "The Social Sciences: A Framework for Education."   *School Review,* 65:3:339–355, 1957.

Thelen, H. A.   *Education and the Human Quest.*   New York: Harper & Bros., 1960.

Trow, W. C., A. Zander, W. C. Morse, and D. H. Jenkins.   "Psychology of Group Behavior: The Class as a Group."   *Journal of Educational Psychology,* 41: 322–338, 1950.

Vassar College.   *Learning Is Searching.*   Poughkeepsie: Vassar College, Department of Child Study, 1955.   16mm., sound, b/w, 2 reels.

Williams, R. M., Jr.   *American Society: A Sociological Interpretation.*   New York: Alfred A. Knopf, Inc., 1951.

Wright, H. F., R. G. Barker, J. Nall, and P. Schoggen.   "Toward a Psychological Ecology of the Classroom."   *Journal of Educational Research,* 45:187–200, 1951.

18

A Look to the Future

Leland P. Bradford
Jack R. Gibb
Kenneth D. Benne

The seventeen-year career of the T Group and of the training laboratory has been marked by continued internal experimentation and
change and by relatively rapid spread into various segments of society,
both in America and in other nations. It would have been impossible
to predict this evolution with any certainty fifteen or even five years
ago. It is quite as hazardous to predict future developments in any
detail.

It is, however, possible to locate four areas of unsolved problems,
the solution of which will determine the future growth of laboratory
education. The difficulties which underlie these problems have already been experienced, and experimental efforts to meet them have
been ventured. But the problems, practically speaking, are still unsolved. In this chapter, the authors identify some trends toward solutions—trends which to them seem desirable.

Professionalization of T-Group Training

As interest in T-Group and laboratory training has spread, in several
forms and under various labels, the demand for persons competent to
conduct such educational activities has steadily increased. This condition presents a clear, twofold danger that persons with inadequate
professional training or unfitted in terms of personality structure and

motivation will respond to this demand. T-Group experiences may be harmful to participants when they are not supervised by competent and ethical trainers. And T-Group methodologies will be discredited if users do not measure up to adequate standards of skill and ethics.

The problem is compounded by the fact that no well-tested program for the training of professional trainers exists and no academic institution has undertaken wholeheartedly to develop such a program. The situation is further complicated by the cross-disciplinary demands of effective T-Group training. Just what combinations of theory, knowledge, and skill are most important for professional trainers to develop is not fully clear. Nor could the most experienced trainers today agree readily as to the detailed character of an ideal program of professional training.

What does seem clear is that persons entering a course of professional development as trainers should have a well-developed background of training (academic and professional) in one of the behavioral sciences, preferably perhaps in social or clinical psychology. But understanding and appreciation of sociological, anthropological, and philosophical approaches to human behavior are also important. In addition, the prospective trainer should have a concern for developing his skills in processes of application of knowledge to human affairs. He should be committed to the growth of people and to improving himself in the helping role. He should be further committed to the continuing development of laboratory methodologies of education through theory building, research, and/or scholarship.

Responsible leaders in a number of academic institutions are now beginning to recognize the application of the behavioral sciences to processes of change and action as a *general* field of research and study that is at once intellectually challenging and socially important. *Special* efforts in universities to study processes of application have been developing over a number of years. But these studies are typically shaped by the assumptions and limited objectives of particular helping professions. Theory and research on general problems of application will require the combined efforts of academic departments and applied schools. It is upon such efforts that justifiable programs of professional education for laboratory trainers must depend.

The National Training Laboratories, as the organization in which methodologies of laboratory education have largely developed, has been concerned almost from the beginning with professional standards for laboratory trainers. Yet NTL has been able systematically to approach the problem of professional preparation only recently. Its intern program, developed with assistance from the National Institute of Mental Health and some cooperating industries, is promising but still in its infancy.

Probably the best guarantee of adequate professional training programs will lie in a pattern of closer collaboration between NTL and various university centers. Those beginning their study will need opportunities for supervised observation and practice in a *variety* of preprofessional and professional experiences. These opportunities NTL can best provide, though some university centers are also, in a more limited way, developing laboratories for learning. Participants in trainer development programs will require opportunities for research on problems of training, consultation, and knowledge-application. These opportunities NTL will continue to provide in some measure. But research facilities of university centers probably should be oriented to the study of such problems for optimum progress. University centers are also needed to furnish necessary cross-disciplinary challenges and learnings.

Obviously, not all significant human relations education occurs in academic settings. Programs of in-service staff development and of planned organizational improvement are already widely established in various agencies in the fields of health, industry, welfare, religion, community organization, and education itself. Such programs, under the mounting pressures of wider social changes, are almost certain to increase. University and NTL resources will continue to play an important part in these programs through consultation and pilot experimentation, but they cannot do the whole job. Organizational trainers will be required in increasing numbers. Somehow these trainers, as well as trainers based in academic settings, need to be drawn into continuing and deepening professional association. Just how programs for organizational change agents, as distinguished from programs for academically based trainers and consultants, will develop is still highly problematic. But it is certain that such programs will require extensive collaboration between the organizations in which such change agents function, existing professional associations, and practitioners in professional schools of universities.

A professional association for laboratory trainers will undoubtedly emerge to support processes of professionalization—a function thus far served, in part at least, by the network of Associates of NTL. However constituted, the association will need to bring into collaborative relationships those individuals, institutions, and agencies that have concern for the development of the new profession of laboratory education. A major task will be to relate the needs of members realistically to the requirements and policies of various employing institutions, including NTL and university centers, but not confined to them.

One characteristic of the needed professional association of laboratory educators arises from the fact that laboratory trainers today are also psychologists, psychiatrists, sociologists, educators, social workers, philosophers, and ministers. They do not lose their primary professional identifications when they become laboratory trainers. Nor should they. Indeed, out of the dialectical conflict among various previously segregated orientations and resources have come many of the innovations in educational rationale and practice which have characterized laboratory training in the past. Trainers have in turn carried leavening influences back into their primary professional and academic groupings. This suggests that any association should continue to be interprofessional. It suggests further that the association should define and maintain standards of professional competence and of inclusion which are premised upon multiple professional loyalties rather than upon some new, single loyalty. The development and maintenance of such an association will itself require social innovation of a high order.

Expansion of Research and Theory Development

In any area of professional activity empirical research is a requirement both to test existing theories and to generate new ones. The social-educational diagnosis underlying the innovation of the training laboratory emphasized the need to link processes of action, education, and behavioral research. Laboratory training was designed to provide both conceptual and associational bridges between these partly and unhappily segregated human enterprises. Part of the aim was to leaven social practice and action with the orientations, findings, and methods of behavioral research. It was designed equally to reorient behavioral research toward study of the processes of such leavening. In effect, this required the leavening of behavioral research with a sense of important human problems to be clarified and solved partially through research efforts.

Training laboratories have widely included research programs, within the limits of available means and resources, as a more or less integral part of their designs. Within the general purpose outlined above, research programs have sought to serve three more specific purposes. One has been to encourage studies of intensive training and change processes which are provided by every laboratory under at least semicontrollable conditions. A second aim has been to provide evaluation data concerning the effectiveness of various training formats and methodologies. Such evaluation research has been useful both to laboratory clients in estimating the usefulness of laboratory training and to laboratory practitioners in refinement of methodology and in the generation and testing of ideas and "theories" about training. A third objective has been to utilize research findings and processes in a given laboratory in enriching the data available to participants for their own learning.

Gibb's analysis, in Chapter 6, makes clear that gains have been made in theory development over the years. But it makes equally clear the need for further development and especially for a better gearing of theory development with processes of empirical research. In Chapter 15, Stock's summary of researches facilitated by laboratories, under NTL auspices, shows a significant research contribution, but it reveals also the inadequacy of past research efforts when measured by standards either of opportunity or of need.

Each laboratory provides a concentrated array of processes of behavioral change, of attempted application of behavioral science, and of re-education through group participation for firsthand study and, within limits, for controlled experimentation. Taken as a whole, laboratories provide an unusual range of adult and, increasingly, youth populations who are more than ordinarily willing to contribute data for behavioral research. The number and variety of laboratories offer an opportunity for replication of researches and, again within limits, for more or less systematic variation of independent variables within a larger research design.

One of the inherent limitations to fuller actualization of the research potential of a training laboratory lies in the necessity for reconciling research interests with training needs. Participants in laboratory training are collaborators with the staff in defining their own needs for learning and in devising and testing ways of meeting these needs. Variations in training processes designed to help a research staff test preformed hypotheses may interfere with the collaboration which is central to the training process. Frequently, training staffs and research staffs find themselves at odds over this issue. The requirements of each are legitimate. There are valid limits to the degree to which "participants" can be made into "subjects" for research. But, actually, experience has revealed wide areas of laboratory life in which research interests and training interests can be combined without jeopardy to learning and indeed with actual enhancement of it. The means for reconciling research and training interests lie in greater involvement of researchers and trainers in the goals of both and in their joint diagnosis and resolution of any conflicts generated. Indeed, research into this very area of conflict resolution, if well conceptualized and handled, will yield validated insights concerning the application of behavioral research in practice and action settings.

Another barrier to full realization of the research potential of training laboratories is their brief duration. Preparation for significant research cannot be made at the laboratory. Nor can the data collected there be fully processed within the time span of the laboratory session. Some of the data about participants and their learnings must be gathered before and after the laboratory session. Thus a considerable time investment is required by researchers. When research staffs are drawn from university-based social scientists, the difficulties of research in laboratory settings become acute. One solution is for an organization like NTL, which conducts many training laboratories, to augment its research staff and facilities, but the future of significant research relevant to training and application also requires involvement of universities and university-based personnel. This suggests fuller collaboration between an organization like NTL with university centers, with allocation of time of university personnel to research in training laboratories recognized as a part of regular university assignments. Both of these ways of meeting the time problem have been tried. The future will probably include some combination of the two.

The collection of data about behavioral changes following laboratory training is expensive, especially if observational and interview data are utilized. Beyond this difficulty lies the problem of cooperation by the organizations in which the participant has membership, particularly where data are to be collected both from the participant and his associates. Researches into laboratory learnings and the conditions which support and thwart transfer and application will be facilitated by extension of "family" group training designed for established working units. This is true not only because data can be collected more readily and economically but also because the use of family groups usually signifies a considerable degree of support of laboratory training purposes by the parent organization. Hopefully, this support can be extended to the furtherance of research purposes.

This suggests the need for NTL to develop continuing relationships with two types of organizations: first, university centers with resources for behavioral research and with interest in basic studies of the application of such research in practice settings; and second, organizations and agencies concerned both with planned changes in their institutional patterns and in researches designed to assess the strengths and limitations of laboratory training within a larger program of organizational change. Obviously, collaboration should be sought with a variety of organizations to facilitate the generalization of theories and hypotheses researched as well as to prevent the confinement of laboratory training to any one segment of society.

Perhaps a word needs to be said about the importance of keeping a balance between empirical researches and theory development in "knowledge building" relevant to laboratory education. As Gibb has made clear in Chapter 6, theory development serves a number of purposes. Theory facilitates the learning of participants. It also guides the practices of trainers and the processes of continuing professionalization of training. Seminar programs on theory development for trainers and other students of laboratory education will continue to be required—the more so as variations in the practices and rationales of T-Group and laboratory training become wider and consequent issues more sharply articulated. Theory development will need to focus both on the clearer differentiation of "normative" and "cognitive" assumptions and on the adequate integration of these in continuing experimentation with laboratory methodology.

Extensions and Modifications of T-Group Methodology

This entire book, especially Chapter 4, has emphasized the continued experimentation with T-Group methodology and with training laboratory design which has marked the brief history of these educational innovations. While there have been continuities in their undergirding value orientations, their internal evolution has been a drama of invention and more or less planned and evaluated variations in technologies and methodologies.

The problem faced now by laboratory education is how to maintain this experimental temper and way of life. Some of the forces working to standardize laboratory education have already been suggested. One is the effort toward professionalization. While the intention here is to set minimum levels of competence for trainers and to safeguard the welfare of participants and the good reputation of the profession, the effect may be to limit originality, to overemphasize the danger and underemphasize the promise in unfamiliar practices of training. Another effect of professionalization, unless it is planned otherwise, may be to narrow the interdisciplinary range of influences by narrowing the variety of people admitted to the regular associations and colleague relationships of laboratory trainers. These effects need not come to pass with increasing professionalization, but they may if the norm of experimentation does not function along with other partly inconsistent norms in defining the conditions of professional membership and in the actual composition of laboratory staffs. Some of the conditions of experimentation were adventitiously supplied in the early development of laboratory education, though some were planned. More will need to be supplied planfully if the practice and the spirit of experimentation are to be maintained.

Actually, the long-range hope for continuing innovation lies, in some large part, in strengthening programs of empirical research and theory development. But even these efforts may exert a standardizing influence in practice. The interest in replication for research purposes may, for example, call for an undue standardization of laboratory designs. Or, if research studies are planned primarily to meet the requirements of existing research methodologies, problems for research may tend to be chosen on the basis of available, tested means for study rather than on the basis of other criteria as well. Too much pressure for respectability may defeat the experimental temper in research as well as in training. And, on the "theory" side, theories always serve, in some measure, the purpose of justification of existing practice as well as the purpose of challenging it. In Mannheim's terminology, theory may be "ideological" as well as "utopian." And the "ideological" uses may, if not checked, tend to predominate.

The best guarantee of continued experimentation is probably to keep the community of laboratory trainers wide enough so that conflicting "ideologies" and "utopias" among them may be kept in dialectical interplay. The genius of NTL as an organization, at its best, has lain in its incorporation of conflict into its associational life, its policy making, and its planning, and in its serious efforts to use this conflict creatively. It is in the maintenance of this respect for dissent and difference that the best hope of continuing innovation and experimentation probably lies.

The Extended Use of T Groups and Laboratory Methods in "Nonlaboratory" Settings

The focus in this book has been almost completely upon educational methodology within the training laboratory. Miles has dealt, in Chapter 17, with the adaptation of laboratory methods for use in the classroom. This suggests as a fourth area of growth potential the adapting of this educational innovation for use in various nonlaboratory settings.

Promising beginnings have been made in exporting T-Group education into both academic and nonacademic settings. Academic use has been limited largely to learning enterprises where the content learnings sought are in the area of personal, group, or organizational behavior. Probably most experimentation with T Groups has been in professional schools—in schools of business administration as part of management training, in nursing, social work, theology, and public health schools, and in schools of education where change-agent skills and understandings are seen as part of the professional role into which students are developing. In general education settings, T-Group education has tended to take on a therapeutic cast and to become assimilated to group guidance and counseling in which self-insight is the main aim. In some colleges, T Groups have been used in nonclassroom settings—in campus leadership training and in the educational programs of residence halls.

Most academic experimentation with T Groups so far has been at the college and graduate levels. This may be due in part to the lack of emphasis on behavioral science learnings in elementary and secondary schools. Social studies tend typically to be focused on historical and political science content rather than on content from psychology, sociology, or cultural anthropology. Perhaps the use of laboratory methods in elementary and secondary schools will increase as emphasis on behavioral learnings is increased.

One frontier that is relatively unexplored is the use of T-Group methods in building group media for more effective learning of nonbehavioral content, whether in mathematics, languages, or natural science. Enough has already been done in finding ways of facilitating learning from peers as well as from teachers to lend much promise to this area of experimentation.

The principal differences between T-Group operation in academic settings and in laboratory settings arise from two circumstances. One is that T Groups on campuses typically meet a few hours weekly without the support of the round-the-clock community life which a training laboratory provides. The tempo, the intensity, and perhaps the quality of T-Group learning are affected by this fact. A second circumstance is that students in a T Group are simultaneously taking the student role in classrooms where the assumptions about learning, about teaching method, and about student-student and student-teacher relationships are quite different. The problems generated for students by these multiple roles and the question of whether these problems can be well used for student learning are questions which deserve full exploration. Academic settings also provide opportunity for researches that will help to illuminate the virtues and limitations both of T-Group learning and of more traditional classroom learning. Perhaps new syntheses and mergers of the two approaches to education will be effected in the future.

The other nonlaboratory setting in which T-Group education has been mainly utilized to date is in organizations and agencies engaged in programs of organizational change. Both working units (family groups) and vertical or horizontal slices across the levels of the organization have been used in composing T Groups. Normally, T Groups are combined with other change efforts within the change design. Among them are preinterviewing and postinterviewing, on-the-job coaching by trainers, consultation, and the feedback and discussion of research results. Reducing the distance between the "reality" of the training session and the "reality" of the work situation obviates problems of transferring learnings from training to action. Whether resistance to deep self-examination and self-re-education is also increased has still to be determined. In any event, experience to date does indicate that T-Group processes can be used constructively in effecting behavioral changes in an organization or agency and that training methodology can be adapted and used effectively in a nonlaboratory context. Comparative researches upon laboratory T Groups and in-company T Groups should increase our knowledge both of laboratory education and of the processes of organizational change.

What is the future of T-Group and laboratory education? The answers are not now available. Answers will be found in responsible efforts to solve the problems on which continuing development depends—the further professionalization of training, the fuller realization of its research potential, the continuation of practical experimentation, and the extension of laboratory methodologies of education beyond the confines of the training laboratory.

Index